MIKE MEYERS' CERTIFICATION

Passport ★

CompTIA

Security+ ®

Exam SY0-501

Fifth Edition

DR. DAWN DUNKERLEY

New York   Chicago   San Francisco
Athens   London   Madrid   Mexico City
Milan   New Delhi   Singapore   Sydney   Toronto

Cataloging-in-Publication Data is on file with the Library of Congress

McGraw-Hill Education books are available at special quantity discounts to use as premiums and sales promotions, or for use in corporate training programs. To contact a representative, please visit the Contact Us pages at www.mhprofessional.com.

Mike Meyers' CompTIA Security+® Certification Passport, Fifth Edition (Exam SY0-501)

1 2 3 4 5 6 7 8 9 LCR 21 20 19 18 17

ISBN: Book p/n 978-1-260-02653-5 and CD p/n 978-1-260-02654-2
of set 978-1-260-02656-6

MHID: Book p/n 1-260-02653-1 and CD p/n 1-260-02654-X
of set 1-260-02656-6

Sponsoring Editor Amy Stonebraker	**Technical Editor** Bobby E. Rogers	**Composition** Cenveo Publisher Services
Editorial Supervisor Janet Walden	**Copy Editor** Bart Reed	**Illustration** Cenveo Publisher Services
Project Manager Neha Bhargava, Cenveo® Publisher Services	**Proofreader** Rick Camp	**Art Director, Cover** Jeff Weeks
Acquisitions Coordinator Claire Yee	**Indexer** Ted Laux	**Cover Series Design** Ted Holladay
	Production Supervisor James Kussow	

I dedicate this book to my incredible husband, Thomas. You have made my life happier than I could ever have imagined possible. I love you and thank you.

—*Dawn Dunkerley*

Becoming a CompTIA Certified IT Professional Is Easy

It's also the best way to reach greater professional opportunities and rewards.

Why Get CompTIA Certified?

Growing Demand

Labor estimates predict some technology fields will experience growth of more than 20% by the year 2020. (Source: CompTIA 9th Annual Information Security Trends study: 500 U.S. IT and Business Executives Responsible for Security.) CompTIA certification qualifies the skills required to join this workforce.

Higher Salaries

IT professionals with certifications on their resume command better jobs, earn higher salaries, and have more doors open to new multi-industry opportunities.

Verified Strengths

91% of hiring managers indicate CompTIA certifications are valuable in validating IT expertise, making certification the best way to demonstrate your competency and knowledge to employers. (Source: CompTIA Employer Perceptions of IT Training and Certification.)

Universal Skills

CompTIA certifications are vendor neutral—which means that certified professionals can proficiently work with an extensive variety of hardware and software found in most organizations.

Learn	Certify	Work
Learn more about what the exam covers by reviewing the following:	Purchase a voucher at a Pearson VUE testing center or at CompTIAstore.com.	Congratulations on your CompTIA certification!

Learn

Learn more about what the exam covers by reviewing the following:

- Exam objectives for key study points.

- Sample questions for a general overview of what to expect on the exam and examples of question format.

- Visit online forums, like LinkedIn, to see what other IT professionals say about CompTIA exams.

Certify

Purchase a voucher at a Pearson VUE testing center or at CompTIAstore.com.

- Register for your exam at a Pearson VUE testing center.

- Visit pearsonvue.com/CompTIA to find the closest testing center to you.

- Schedule the exam online. You will be required to enter your voucher number or provide payment information at registration.

- Take your certification exam.

Work

Congratulations on your CompTIA certification!

- Make sure to add your certification to your resume.

- Check out the CompTIA Certification Roadmap to plan your next career move.

Learn More: Certification.CompTIA.org/securityplus

CompTIA Disclaimer

Contents at a Glance

Contents

ix

Acknowledgments

Many thanks to McGraw-Hill Professional, especially Amy Stonebraker and Claire Yee. They are consistently on point and make me look good, even when I don't deserve it.

Finally, no words can describe my gratitude to my technical editor, Bobby Rogers, who is the best partner in this process you could ask for. All the good things in this book actually came from him.

—*Dawn Dunkerley*

Check-In

May I See Your Passport?

What do you mean you don't have a passport? Why, it's sitting right in your hands, even as you read! This book is your passport to a very special place. You're about to begin a journey, my friend, a journey toward that magical place called *certification!* You don't need a ticket, you don't need a suitcase—just settle in and read this Certification Passport, because it's all you need to get there. Are you ready? Let's go!

Your Travel Agent: Mike Meyers

Hello! I'm Mike Meyers, president of Total Seminars and author of a number of popular certification books. On any given day, you'll find me replacing a hard drive, setting up a website, or writing code. I love every aspect of this book you hold in your hands. It's part of a powerful book series called *Mike Meyers' Certification Passports.* Every book in this series combines easy readability with a condensed format—in other words, it's the kind of book I always wanted when I went for my certifications. Putting a huge amount of information in an accessible format is an enormous challenge, but I think we have achieved our goal, and I am confident you'll agree.

I designed this series to do one thing and only one thing—to get you the information you need to achieve your certification. You won't find any fluff in here. Dawn and I packed every page with nothing but the real nitty-gritty of the CompTIA Security+ certification exam. Every page has 100 percent pure concentrate of certification knowledge!

Your Destination: CompTIA Security+ Certification

This book is your passport to CompTIA's Security+ certification, the vendor-neutral, industry-standard certification developed for foundation-level security professionals. Based on a worldwide job task analysis, the structure of the exam focuses on core competencies in network security; threats, attacks, and vulnerabilities; technologies and tools; architecture and design; identity and access management; risk management; and cryptography and PKI.

Whether the CompTIA Security+ certification is your first step toward a career focus in security or an additional skill credential, this book is your passport to success on the CompTIA Security+ certification exam.

Your Guides: Mike Meyers and Dawn Dunkerley

You get two tour guides for this book: me and Dawn Dunkerley. I've written numerous computer certification books—including the best-selling *CompTIA A+ Certification All-in-One Exam Guide* and the *CompTIA Network+ Certification All-in-One Exam Guide*. More to the point, I've been working on PCs and teaching others how to make and fix them for a *very* long time, and I love it! When I'm not lecturing or writing about PCs, I'm working on PCs, naturally!

Dawn Dunkerley received a Ph.D. in Information Systems from Nova Southeastern University in 2011 with a doctoral focus on information security success within organizations. Her research interests include cyberwarfare, cybersecurity, and the success and measurement of organizational cybersecurity initiatives. Dr. Dunkerley holds a number of professional certifications, including the Certified Information Systems Security Professional (CISSP), Information Systems Security Architecture Professional (ISSAP), Information Systems Security Engineering Professional (ISSEP), Information Systems Security Management Professional (ISSMP), the Certified Secure Software Lifecycle Professional (CSSLP), and the Certified in Risk and Information System Control (CRISC).

About the Technical Editor

Bobby E. Rogers is an information security engineer working as a contractor for Department of Defense agencies, helping to secure, certify, and accredit their information systems. His duties include information system security engineering, risk management, and certification and accreditation efforts. He retired after 21 years in the U.S. Air Force, serving as a network security engineer and instructor, and has secured networks all over the world. Bobby has a master's degree in information assurance (IA) and is pursuing a doctoral degree in cybersecurity from Capitol Technology University in Maryland. His many certifications include CISSP-ISSEP, CEH, and MCSE: Security, as well as the CompTIA A+, Network+, Security+, CSA+, and Mobility+ certifications.

Why the Travel Theme?

The steps to gaining a certification parallel closely the steps to planning and taking a trip. All of the elements are the same: preparation, an itinerary, a route, and even mishaps along the way. Let me show you how it all works.

This book is divided into 14 chapters. Each chapter begins with an *Itinerary* that lists the objectives covered in that chapter and an *ETA* to give you an idea of the time involved in learning the skills in that chapter. Each chapter is broken down by the objectives, which are either those officially stated by the certifying body or our expert take on the best way to approach the topics.

Each chapter contains a number of helpful items to call out points of interest:

Exam Tip

Points out critical topics you're likely to see on the actual exam.

Local Lingo

Describes special terms, in detail and in a way you can easily understand.

Travel Advisory

Warns you of common pitfalls, misconceptions, and downright physical peril!

Travel Assistance

Directs you to additional sources, such as books and websites, to give you more information.

The end of the chapter gives you two handy tools. The *Checkpoint* reviews each objective covered in the chapter with a handy synopsis—a great way to review quickly. The end-of-chapter *Review Questions* test your newly acquired skills.

But the fun doesn't stop there! After you've read the book, take advantage of the free practice exams! Use the full practice exams to hone your skills, and keep the book handy to check answers. Appendix B explains how to access the electronic content.

When you reach the point that you're acing the practice questions, you're ready to take the exam. Go get certified!

The End of the Trail

The IT industry changes and grows constantly, *and so should you.* Finishing one certification is just a step in an ongoing process of gaining more and more certifications to match your constantly changing and growing skills. Read Appendix A, "Career Flight Path," to determine where this certification fits into your personal certification goals. Remember, in the IT business, if you're not moving forward, you're way behind!

Good luck on your certification! Stay in touch.

Mike Meyers
Series Editor
Mike Meyers' Certification Passport

Mission Assurance

Organizational Security and Compliance

CHAPTER 1

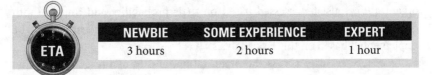

	NEWBIE	SOME EXPERIENCE	EXPERT
ETA	3 hours	2 hours	1 hour

As part of an overall company strategy, security should be officially recognized as a critical business objective just like any other important business objective. In the past, the IT department had to define security and access controls for the company network and data. In today's Internet world, corporate management adapts the legalities of the business world to computer networks by ensuring that electronic transfer of information is secure to protect both the company and its customers.

Organizations attempt to classify risk for various reasons. In order to provide a point of reference to base decisions on, risk is classified by the effect it has on the organization. The organization may classify risk, and its contributing factors, using qualitative or quantitative means, and then determine how much risk it is willing to accept.

Risk can be classified as *internal* or *external* risk. Internal risk comes from elements within the organization's control, such as organization structure, resources (personnel, time, money, equipment, and so on), and business goals and strategy. These elements are shifted by the organization at its own discretion, often in reaction to external factors. External risk, on the other hand, is usually the type of risk that the organization has limited control over. Examples of external risk factors include the stock market, government regulation, currency valuation, international and world events, and natural disasters. Although the organization can't control these factors, it must plan for them and develop strategies to mitigate risk.

To protect their assets, employees, and customers from security risks, organizations must analyze their security practices to identify the threats to their operations and protect themselves in the most cost-efficient way. Risks to your organization must be assessed based on their probability and impact (both quantitative and qualitative), and then security measures or metrics should be implemented based on this risk analysis.

To ensure security across the organization, and to assure customers that the company can be trusted, overall security policies must be implemented to include several component policies and procedures that govern how the organization uses computer networks, protects and distributes data, and offers services to customers. Each component of the security policy defines specific security best practices for a topic, such as a password policy. These policies and procedures include rules on company Internet use, customer data privacy, company structure, and human resources hiring and termination practices. Many companies, such as those in the financial and healthcare sector, are now required to comply with government regulations for the protection and privacy of customer data respective to their industry. Organizations must be diligent in crafting their policies to adhere to these regulations, and they must employ risk mitigation techniques to avoid violating these strict standards.

For a company's security policies to be effective, they must be communicated properly to the employees to ensure company-wide knowledge and compliance. Rules won't be followed if nobody knows they exist. Many companies make use of consultants to create and draft security policies and procedures, but these policies often aren't communicated to the user community and aren't used. Employees need to be aware of security issues and procedures to protect not only themselves, but also the company's services and data.

This chapter describes general risk assessment and mitigation strategies, as well as organizational policies that should be in place to protect an organization, its networks and data, its employees, and its customers.

Objective 1.01
CompTIA Security+
Objective 5.3

Explain Risk Management Processes and Concepts

Risk management is the act of identifying, assessing, and reducing the risk of security issues that can impact your organization's operations and assets. The following sections describe these risk-related concepts:

- **Risk control types** Risk control types can be separated into three logical divisions: administrative, technical, and physical. Each risk control type is a separate but cooperative layer in your overall risk management strategy.

- **Risk assessment** Use risk assessments to understand your current risks, their probability and impact, and the solutions to prevent them.

- **Risk management options** You have several options based on the nature and probability of the risk and the cost of the solution: avoidance, transference, acceptance, and mitigation.

- **Using organizational policies to reduce risk** Your organizational security is critical for ensuring that your company's risk management plan is properly detailed, communicated, and adhered to by your employees in all its activities through policies.

- **Risk register** A living document used to track different types of data elements, most commonly risk factors and risk scenarios.

- **False positives and negatives** Legitimate actions that are perceived as a risk or threat, or security issues that have passed your security controls as a legitimate action.

Risk Control Types

Risk control types can be separated into three basic groupings: administrative, technical, and physical. These three groupings generally serve six control functions: compensating, corrective, detective, deterrent, directive, and preventative. It is critical when you're choosing the combination of controls that will serve to protect your organization that they best support the security goals of the organization. Is the organization more concerned with data confidentiality? Perhaps constant availability is central to mission success. These considerations will both ensure that your choices are focused on your specific organizational needs and increase the likelihood of management support.

Administrative

Risk management is an ongoing high-level function within your organization. It begins with risk assessment and analysis to identify the risk of security breaches against company assets, assess the probability of a risk and estimate its impact, and define the steps to reduce the level of that risk. The solutions to these risks must be properly analyzed and budgeted to ensure that the probability and impact of the risks are properly factored into a cost-effective solution. Many risk management best practices include controls encompassing administrative, technical, and physical aspects of the organization, including implementation of an overall risk management framework and efforts to improve documentation.

Technical

Technical risk control describes the actual technical measures used to prevent security risks in your organization, which include deep-level network and system security (firewalls, antivirus scanning, content filters, and other network security devices) and improvements in secure coding practices. These controls perform the bulk of the risk mitigation and deterrence defined in your organizational risk analysis.

Physical

Finally, physical risk controls must be created and implemented throughout your company. Best practices include physical access controls (perimeter fencing, security passes, and surveillance), environmental controls (fire suppression and temperature controls), as well as operational considerations. Physical controls often include operational controls, which are concerned with how you conduct your daily organizational business to minimize the security risk to your organization and its business activities. This could include company-wide policies, which are created, distributed, and used to educate your employees on how to conduct their day-to-day activities while being vigilant about organization security, and improvement initiatives to make organizational processes more efficient and effective. Managing risk operationally means that you are concerned with how you conduct your daily organizational business to minimize the security risk to your organization and its business activities, and this also includes user education and vigilant monitoring and testing to make sure your plans are being adhered to by your organization and that its activities are constantly analyzed to protect against new threats.

As noted previously, controls serve different functions in an organization and are generally either compensating, corrective, detective, deterrent, directive, or preventative in nature. Compensating controls compensate for weaknesses or inherent flaws within other controls or a lack of controls, such as regularly scheduled third-party review of logs based on an inability to enable proper separation of duties across system administrators. Corrective controls correct back to a trusted or "known-good" state; an example is regularly tested backups limiting the time a critical database is offline. Detective controls detect and characterize events or irregularities as or after they occur, such as internal or external audits conducted on a no-notice basis. Deterrent controls deter and discourage an event from taking place (for example, roaming security guards and cameras placed around the facilities that are continuously monitored by personnel). Directive controls give official direction for how security measures will be conducted within the organization; an example is an organizational policy requiring two people to unlock and open sensitive facilities, such as those containing classified materials. Finally, preventative controls are implemented to prevent negative events from ever occurring, such as locks that prevent portable systems from being removed from their desktops.

Exam Tip

Administrative risk controls are the high-level risk management, assessment, and mitigations plans that define your overall organization security. Technical risk controls are those technical measures deployed to mitigate security risks. Physical risk controls deal with your day-to-day physical security and the security of your organizational business activities. Understand that the controls are not applied for one group at a time only; in fact, most of the time, a combination of controls is used. For example, an administrative control might be a password policy, the technical control might be the enforcement of the use of complex passwords on the system through technical means, and the physical part might be guards walking through your building making sure written passwords are not left on desks unsupervised.

Risk Assessment

Risk assessment and mitigation deal with identifying, assessing, and reducing the risk of security breaches against company assets. By assessing the probability of a risk and estimating the amount of damage that could be caused as a result, you can take steps to reduce the level of that risk.

Suppose, for example, that your company file server contains confidential company data. The file server asset is considered extremely valuable to the company, its clients, and its competitors. In this case, a considerable amount of financial damage may be incurred by the company in the event of server loss, damage, or intrusion. The risks and threats posed to the server could be physical (such as damage caused by a natural disaster or a hardware malfunction) or nonphysical (such as viruses, network hacker attacks, and data theft if the server is easily accessible through a network). The costs associated with reducing these risks are mitigated by the potential costs of losing data on the file server.

To help reduce these risks, you can take several actions:

- Use multiple hard drives and power supplies for fault tolerance.
- Implement a good backup scheme.
- Protect the server through physical security, such as door access controls.
- Install antivirus software.
- Disable unused network services and ports to prevent network attacks.

To identify the risks that pose a security threat to your company, you can perform a risk analysis on all parts of the company's resources and activities. By identifying risks and the amount of damage that could be caused by exploiting a system vulnerability, you can choose the most efficient methods for securing the system from those risks. Risk analysis and assessment can identify where too little or even too much security exists and where the cost of security is more than the cost of the loss due to compromise. Ultimately, risk analysis and assessment are both a cost/benefit analysis of your security infrastructure.

Risk analysis and assessment involve four main phases:

- **Asset identification**   Identify and quantify the company's assets.
- **Risk analysis**   Identify and assess the possible security vulnerabilities and threats.
- **Risk likelihood and impact**   Rate your various risks according to how likely they are to occur and their impact.
- **Cost of solutions**   Identify a cost-effective solution to protect assets.

Asset Identification

Company assets can include physical items, such as computer and networking equipment, and nonphysical items, such as valuable data. *Asset identification* involves identifying both types of assets and evaluating their worth. Asset values must be established beyond the mere capital costs; a true asset valuation should consider a number of factors. For example, a consideration should be the cost to repair the asset versus simply replacing the asset outright. Often, repairing the asset may be less expensive in the short run, but the cost of the different components required to conduct a repair should be considered. Also, it's important to remember that this might only be a temporary solution—one that could come back to haunt you (and your pockets) in the long run.

Another consideration is the depreciation value of the asset over time. This might reduce the amount of capital available to make a repair-or-replace decision. It is important to consider the amount of revenue that is generated by the asset, which might also shape your decision. Think about it this way: if it costs $10,000 to replace an asset, and that asset generates $2000 worth of revenue daily based on its function, the loss of that asset ($10,000) has to be considered along with the loss of its revenue ($2000 daily), and that contributes to the total asset valuation and quite quickly begins adding up.

A harder-to-quantify aspect is the value that the asset might be to a competitor. For example, a list of a company's clients can be easily re-created from backup if the original is lost or destroyed, but if the list finds its way into the hands of a competitor, the resulting financial damage could be devastating.

Finally, you should consider the exposure factor, or the percentage of the asset that could be lost during an event. In many cases, negative events do not render the asset completely unusable. For example, a server could experience degradation in its ability to effectively host a web application, but not be completely offline and unavailable. This is important to understand, because calculating the exposure factor allows you to better determine how much loss your organization can bear during an event, which in turn allows for you to better understand how much money, time, or other supporting resources should be devoted to repairing or replacing an asset. Generally, exposure factors are expressed in decimal format and relate to the percentage loss associated with the exposure. For example, a 50 percent loss would be 0.5, with a total loss being expressed as 1. As you can see, understanding the asset value is much more complicated than the list price of the asset itself, and ultimately the value and the criticality of the assets you're trying to protect drive the costs involved in securing that asset.

Exam Tip

The single loss expectancy (SLE) is calculated by multiplying the asset value (AV) and the exposure factor (EF).

Risk Analysis

Risk analysis deals with identifying, assessing, and reducing the risk of security breaches against company assets. By assessing the probability of a risk and estimating the amount of damage that could be caused as a result, you can take steps to reduce the level of that risk. To identify the risks that pose a security threat to your company, you can perform a risk analysis on all parts of the company's resources and activities. There are two generally accepted ways to perform a risk analysis: qualitative and quantitative.

Quantitative risk analysis is a strict dollar-amount calculation of the exact cost of the loss or a specific company asset because of a disaster. This is a straightforward method that can be applied for simple situations. For example, if a hard drive in a RAID (redundant array of inexpensive disks) system fails, it is simply replaced with a new hard drive. There is no loss of data because the information is rebuilt from the rest of the array.

Qualitative risk analysis must consider tangible and several other intangible factors in determining costs. Consider a denial-of-service network attack on your company's web store server that causes four hours of downtime and corrupted data on a back-end transactional database. You are not only faced with the monetary loss from your website being down and customers not being able to order products for many hours, but also the time it takes to perform countermeasures against the attack, get your web server back into operation, recover any lost data from your database, and consider data that cannot be recovered. The costs in this scenario include the manpower hours in recovering from the attack, the loss of orders from the web store during the downtime, monetary loss from corrupted data that cannot be restored, and even potential loss of future business from disgruntled customers.

Exam Tip

Quantitative risk analysis is a dollar-amount calculation of the exact cost of a loss due to disaster. Qualitative risk analysis includes intangible factors, such as loss of potential business, in determining costs.

Additional risks are often ignored in a risk analysis regarding virtualization technology and cloud computing. Using virtualization technology, a computer can host multiple instances of an operating system environment, all running from the same computer on the same hardware. The consolidation of many different types of services on the same hardware creates a security risk because if that system is hacked or fails, it will take down every virtualized server that runs on the system.

Travel Assistance

Considering risk and incorporating risk analysis are covered in more depth in Chapter 3.

The risk of a single point of failure for cloud computing is very similar. Cloud computing aggregates services in a virtual environment where all aspects of the cloud—from the platform, to the software, to the entire infrastructure—are based on a distributed web service. If the cloud service fails, you may lose all access to your services and data until the cloud service is restored.

Travel Assistance

See Chapter 8 for more detailed information on virtualization and cloud computing.

Overall, your risk assessment must be wide in scope to use both quantitative and qualitative analysis to determine your risk factors from all aspects of your company's operations.

Risk Likelihood and Impact

As part of your risk assessment and mitigation strategy, you will need to rate your various risks according to how likely they are to occur and their potential impact. The risks more likely to occur and their calculated impact are ranked toward the top of the list to indicate where solution efforts should be most concentrated. For example, for a company that already practices strict physical security and access control methods, the priority of risk scenarios could be geared toward nonphysical threats, such as viruses and network hackers, because this would have a greater impact on the company's ability to operate.

The likelihood and impact of a risk has a strong measure on your cost analysis for budgeting funds for risk countermeasures and mitigation. A calculation used to determine this factor is *annual loss expectancy (ALE)*. You must calculate the chance of a risk occurring, sometimes called the *annual rate of occurrence (ARO)*, and the potential loss of revenue based on a specific period of downtime, which is called the *single loss expectancy (SLE)*. By multiplying these factors together, you arrive at the ALE. This is how much money you expect to lose on an annual basis because of the impact from an occurrence of a specific risk. Using the ALE, you can properly budget the security measures to help protect against that risk if it occurs.

For example, if a file server is at 25 percent risk of being infected by a virus, its ARO is 0.25. During the time the file server is down and data is being recovered, none of your employees can work. For a downtime of two hours, you calculate $8000 of lost time and productivity. By multiplying these two factors (0.25 and $8000), you get an ALE value of $2000. You can use this amount to budget for additional antivirus software protection to help lower this risk and save money in your next annual budget.

Exam Tip

The annual loss expectancy (ALE) is calculated by multiplying the annual rate of occurrence (ARO) and the single loss expectancy (SLE).

Solutions and Countermeasures

After you've assessed and defined risk and management procedures, you'll have collected the following information:

- **Asset identification** A list of your assets (and their criticality to the organization), including physical assets (such as server hardware and hard disks) and nonphysical assets (such as the valuable customer data stored on the hard drives).
- **Threat profiles** A list of every possible threat against your assets.
- **Risks** An evaluation of the potential risk of each threat—such as the risk of a malicious hacker being able to compromise a database server. If the server itself is compromised but the valuable and confidential data on the database server is leaked by the hacker, and the impact to the business is substantial, the risk is far greater for this asset.
- **Impact** The potential loss in the event your assets are attacked or compromised by threats, including the assets' capital value (such as

hardware cost), plus how much it will cost to replace those assets, especially lost customer data. A failed hard drive can be a relatively low cost to recoup, but if you have no backup of the customer data stored on that hard drive, you might have lost tens of thousands of dollars' worth of data.

- **Probability** The risks that are more likely to occur are ranked toward the top of the list to indicate where solution efforts should be most concentrated. For example, within a company that already practices strict physical security and access control methods, the priority of risk scenarios could be geared toward nonphysical threats, such as viruses and network hackers.

Once this process is complete, a list of solutions and countermeasures to protect against each threat should be reviewed and documented. Examine your solutions with respect to what current security measures are in place and what needs to be done to make them more effective. Ensure that the functionality and effectiveness of the solution are sufficient to reduce the risk of compromise. Purchasing a fire extinguisher for the server room could seem like a fire-prevention solution, for example, but only automatic fire detection and suppression system can fully protect a room full of servers from a large, out-of-control fire that occurs in the middle of the night. Similarly, buying a firewall to protect your servers from outside Internet traffic is a great idea for network security, but if the network administrator hasn't been trained to configure it properly, the firewall might not be effective at all.

Any solutions must be cost-effective to ensure that the benefits are in line with the actual value of the assets. For example, there's no point in spending $100,000 on a security solution to protect data that's worth only $40,000 to the company if it's lost or damaged. Ongoing maintenance also needs to be factored into the final calculations. Although a large initial cost is incurred for a tape backup solution, the costs of purchasing new tapes as they're needed will be ongoing, and you'll have to pay for offsite storage of used tapes. Again, it is important to consider the security goals of the organization (confidentiality vs. availability, for example) before expending unnecessary resources.

Exam Tip

The cost of the risk management solution shouldn't exceed the value of the asset if it's lost. For example, if a file server and its data are valued at $35,000 and the proposed security solution to protect it costs $150,000, then it doesn't make sense to implement the proposed solution.

Risk Register

A risk register is a living document used to track different types of data elements, most commonly risk factors and risk scenarios. It might also include data that describes different technical or management findings contributing to the risk. Additionally, threats, vulnerabilities, assets, likelihood, and impact data can be included in the risk register. For example, a risk register might include the following items:

- Risk factors
- Threat agents, threats, and vulnerabilities
- Risk scenarios
- Criticality, severity, or priority of risk
- Asset information
- Impact of the risk on an asset
- Likelihood of the threat exercising the vulnerability
- Status of risk response actions
- Resources that may be committed to respond to risk
- Risk ownership information
- Planned milestones toward the risk response

Risk Management Options

When you have completed your risk analysis, and depending on your operations and budgets, you have several options for dealing with each risk:

- **Avoidance**   Depending on the type of risk, you can opt to avoid the risk altogether. This option is typically used when the cost to mitigate a threat, especially if it is unlikely or has little impact, means it is not worth implementing. This can also mean you take certain steps to avoid a risk altogether, such as disabling a rarely used feature in a web application because the benefits aren't worth the great security risk it causes.
- **Transference**   The organization can also transfer, or "pass on," the risk to a third party—for example, an insurance company that will pay out your damages in the event a certain risk occurs, or a trusting a third-party provider that can store your offsite backup media.
- **Acceptance**   In most cases in information security, a level of risk must be accepted with any type of information system network.

For example, your organization may want to sell its products directly from its website, and the potential revenues greatly outweigh the potential network security risks involved. On the other hand, if the risk is deemed too great in comparison to the benefit, the service might not be offered, or additional mitigation techniques might be required.

- **Mitigation** Based on your risk analysis, specific risks must be mitigated using countermeasures—for example, implementing a network firewall for network security, installing desktop and server antivirus protection, and implementing fault-tolerant systems to mitigate the impact of failed hardware.

False Positives and Negatives

A *false positive* is a legitimate action that is perceived as a risk or threat. It is a term often used in e-mail security scanning to indicate a legitimate message that was classified as a security issue, such as spam, content violation, or poor reputation check. False positives can be applied to almost any type of security scenario where security controls block what is essentially a legitimate action. For example, an intrusion detection system may send out constant alarms even though the traffic it's detecting is legitimate. The administrator becomes lax in responding to alarms because he knows they are more likely than not false positives. This can allow real intrusions to be ignored.

Occasional false positives are a fact of life when it comes to strict security controls, but too many can become difficult to manage and put a lot of burden on both the administrators and the end users to manage. Excessive false positives in your environment means that your security controls are too aggressive and need to be reconfigured. False positives are a consideration within many controls, such as biometrics.

Most security systems can be fine-tuned to allow future attempts from legitimate actions, if you can verify those actions are being performed by an authorized user or process in a secure way. In the example of legitimate e-mail messages being blocked, end users can create lists of trusted known senders so that future messages from the same sender can bypass certain types of scanning, such as content filtering. Intrusion detection systems can have their thresholds redefined to a lower value to prevent an increase in false positives.

Security controls that are not aggressive enough can result in false negatives. A *false negative* is a security issue that has passed your security controls as legitimate. For example, an e-mail message that is spam or contains illegal content may pass through your e-mail security controls and content filters as if it were legitimate mail. An intrusion detection system may let through a denial-of-service attack because it detects the event as a normal operation.

Security controls require continuous baselining and adjustments to properly set their thresholds to detect the difference between normal behavior and serious security issues. The baseline provides you with a report of what is considered normal activity, and then you set your thresholds on your security controls to detect anomalies to that normal activity. This period of recording baselines and making configuration adjustments can take several weeks to result in ideal security thresholds, but this ensures that you will have fewer issues with false positives and negatives in the future.

> **Exam Tip**
>
> A *false positive* is a legitimate action that is perceived as a risk or threat. A *false negative* is a security issue that has passed your security controls as a legitimate action. Although neither is particularly desirable, the false negative is a much worse scenario because it could allow unauthorized access to systems or data.

Using Organizational Policies to Reduce Risk

To provide effective security, security policy and procedure creation must begin at the top of an organization with senior management. These policies and procedures must then flow throughout the company to ensure that security is useful and functional at every level of the organization. Understanding company security must begin with an understanding of the basic laws, regulations, and legal liability issues to which the company must adhere to protect the company and its assets, as well as the employees and customers.

Security policies and procedures are official company communications created to ensure that a standard level of security guidelines exists across the entire organization. These policies define how the employees interact with company computer systems to perform their job functions, how to protect the computer systems and their data, and how to service the company's clients properly. The upcoming sections outline policies and procedures in the following areas:

- Security policies
- Network security policies
- Human resources policies

Security Policies

The following policies concern general organizational security, including physical access, access control to data, and security through proper organizational structures and data security principles.

Physical Access Security Policy   As part of your organization's overall access control policy, you must have a strong physical access policy and ensure that all employees are educated on its use.

Depending on the security level of the company, physical security may include guarded or unguarded entrances. Even on guarded premises, the use of security access cards makes sure that only identified and authenticated employees can enter a facility. Security access cards are coded with the authorization level of the user, who will be able to access only areas of the facility that are required by his job function. For example, only network and systems administrators would be able to access a server and networks communications room with their access card.

Employees must be trained to always close automatically locking doors behind them and not allow other unidentified people to follow them through. Most security access cards have photographs on them to further identify users in the event they are challenged for their identity. Employees must be encouraged to report suspicious individuals within the premises who are unfamiliar and do not have proper identification.

A published organizational security policy for physical access allows your employees to have proper knowledge of security procedures and be equally active in the responsibility for physical security.

Access Control Policies   The following access control policies help provide a consistent organizational structure and procedures to prevent internal fraud and corruption in your organization:

- **Least privilege**   The *least privilege* principle grants users only the access rights they need to perform their job functions. This requires giving users the least amount of access possible to prevent them from abusing more powerful access rights.

- **Separation of duties**   The *separation of duties* ensures that one single individual isn't tasked with high-security and high-risk responsibilities. Certain critical responsibilities are separated between several users to prevent corruption.

- **Job rotation**   *Job rotation* provides improved security because no employee retains the same amount of access control for a position indefinitely. This prevents internal corruption from employees who take advantage of their long-term position and security access.

- **Mandatory vacations**   *Mandatory vacation* policies require employees to use their vacations at specific times of the year or use all their vacation days allotted for a single year. This policy helps detect security issues with employees, such as fraud or other internal hacking activities, because the anomalies might surface while the user is away.

Travel Assistance

These access control concepts and best practices are discussed in more detail in Chapter 6.

Network Security Policies

Several policies provide standard guidelines for network security within a company and encompass areas such as the Internet and internal network use, data privacy, security incident response, human resources issues, and document security. These are often enforced by technical controls such as data loss prevention tools that monitor and report in the event of a breach of policy. Other tools may alert an administrator to machines joining the network that don't meet security requirements (having out-of-date antivirus signatures, for example) or report to an administrator when an unauthorized machine has been added to the network or inappropriate websites have been visited.

Travel Assistance

Data loss prevention will be covered more in depth within Chapter 12.

Acceptable Use Policy　An *acceptable use policy* is a set of established guidelines for the appropriate use of computer networks within an organization. The policy is a written agreement, read and signed by employees, that outlines the terms, conditions, and rules of Internet and internal network use for the company.

An acceptable use policy helps educate employees about the kinds of tools they will use on the network and what they can expect from those tools. The policy also helps to define boundaries of behavior and, more critically, specifies the consequences of violating those boundaries. The policy also lays out the actions that management and the system administrators may take to maintain and monitor the network for unacceptable use, and it includes the general worst-case consequences or responses to specific policy violations.

Exam Tip

An *acceptable use policy* is a set of established guidelines for the appropriate use of computer networks within an organization.

Developing an acceptable use policy for your company's computer network is extremely important for organizational security and to limit legal liability in the event of a security issue. Acceptable use policies should cover the following issues:

- **Legality**   The company's legal department needs to approve the policy before it's distributed for signing. The policy will be used as a legal document to ensure that the company isn't legally liable for any type of Internet-related incident and any other transgressions, such as cracking, vandalism, and sabotage.

- **Uniqueness to your environment**   The policy should be written to cover the organization's specific network and the data it contains. Each organization has different security concerns—for example, a medical facility needs to protect data that differs significantly from that of a product sales company.

- **Completeness**   Beyond rules of behavior, your policy should also include a statement concerning the company's position on Internet use.

- **Adaptability**   Because the Internet is constantly evolving, your policy will need to be updated as new issues arise. You can't anticipate every situation, so the acceptable use policy should address the possibility of something happening that isn't outlined.

- **Protection for employees**   If your employees follow the rules of the acceptable use policy, their exposure to questionable materials should be minimized. In addition, it can protect them from dangerous Internet behavior, such as giving out their names and e-mail addresses to crackers using social engineering techniques.

The focus of an acceptable use policy should be on the responsible use of computer networks. Such networks include the Internet—including web, e-mail (both personal and business), social media, and instant messaging access—and the company intranet. Acceptable use policies should, at a minimum, contain the following components:

- A description of the strategies and goals to be supported by Internet access in the company

- A statement explaining the availability of computer networks to employees

- A statement explaining the responsibilities of employees when they use the Internet

- A code of conduct governing behavior on the Internet
- A description of the consequences of violating the policy
- A description of what constitutes acceptable and unacceptable use of the Internet
- A description of the rights of individuals using the networks in your company, such as user privacy
- A disclaimer absolving the company from responsibility under specific circumstances
- A form for employees to sign indicating their agreement to abide by the policy

---

Travel Advisory

Many company websites contain an acceptable use policy or terms of use statement that protects the company from any liability from users of the site.

Social Media Policy   Websites such as Facebook, Twitter, and Snapchat are more popular than ever—and not just with teenagers. Employees often use these sites, sometime during the workday, to keep up with friends, family, and activities. While keeping your employees' morale high is a plus, it's important to limit social media usage at work, as it can be a hit to overall productivity. Perhaps even more importantly, employees who are posting negative comments about your organization, or even posting potentially private intellectual property, can be a competitor's dream. For example, consider a disgruntled employee who begins tweeting about your company's secret spaghetti sauce recipe, which is then copied by a competitor. Not good!

However, some pleasant scenarios for an organization can be directly attributed to employee social media usage. That's why it's important to determine what level of social media use your company is comfortable with while employees are on the clock. Many organizations have a policy that social media use during work is only allowed on breaks and lunch hours, and that employees may not discuss or disclose any information regarding their workplace or intellectual property.

Personal E-mail Policy   As with social media, many employees will have personal e-mail accounts that they may want to keep an eye on throughout the day; this lets them know that bills are being paid and their kids are being dropped off at sports activities. Maybe they even use e-mail to keep up with friends. Although this can be positive for employee morale, it is important that a company understand how personal e-mail is being used throughout the workday. An important consideration is the potential threat associated with sophisticated adversaries in cyberspace who know a great deal about the company's employees and may use their personal e-mail account for spearfishing and other nefarious activities. If malware is introduced through this personal e-mail usage during the workday, it then becomes your problem—assuming they're using one of your company systems. That malware could potentially leak trade or other secrets about your company. Again, as with social media, it is important for a company to dictate the terms of how personal e-mail will be used throughout the workday, and whether personal e-mail is allowed to be used on the company's more sensitive systems. For example, it is generally considered a bad practice to allow personal e-mail to be used on production servers, where malware could have a catastrophic effect if introduced into the environment.

Due Care, Due Diligence, and Due Process *Due care, due diligence,* and *due process* are terms that apply to the implementation and enforcement of company-wide security policies. A company practices *due care* by taking responsibility for all activities that take place in corporate facilities. A company practices *due diligence* by implementing and maintaining these security procedures consistently to protect the company's facilities, assets, and employees. Although many companies outline plans for security policies and standards, they often never officially implement them, or the information isn't properly shared with employees. Without direction from management in the form of training, guidelines, and manuals, and without employee input and feedback, security policies will not be successful.

By practicing due care, the company shows it has taken the necessary steps to protect itself and its employees. By practicing due diligence, the company ensures that these security policies are properly maintained, communicated, and implemented. If the company doesn't follow proper due care and due diligence initiatives, it might be considered legally negligent if company security and customer data are compromised.

Due process guarantees that in the event of a security issue by an employee, the employee receives an impartial and fair inquiry into the incident to ensure the employee's rights are not being violated. If, during an investigation or inquiry, the employee's rights are violated, the company may face legal ramifications via lawsuits or governmental employment tribunals.

Exam Tip

Due care involves taking the necessary responsibility and steps to protect the company and the employees. *Due diligence* ensures these security policies are properly implemented. *Due process* ensures an impartial and fair inquiry into violations of company policies.

Privacy Policy *Privacy policies* are agreements that protect individually identifiable information in an online or electronic commerce environment. A company engaged in online activities or e-commerce has a responsibility to adopt and implement a policy to protect the privacy of personally identifiable information (PII). Organizations should also take steps to ensure online privacy when interacting with other companies, such as business partners.

The following recommendations pertain to implementing privacy policies:

- A company's privacy policy must be easy to find, read, and understand, and it must be available prior to or at the time that individually identifiable information is collected or requested.
- The policy needs to state clearly what information is being collected; the use of that information; possible third-party distribution of that information; the choices available to an individual regarding collection, use, and distribution of the collected information; a statement of the organization's commitment to data security; and what steps the organization takes to ensure data quality and access.
- The policy should disclose the consequences, if any, of an individual's refusal to provide information.
- The policy should include a clear statement of what accountability mechanism the organization uses, such as procedures for dealing with privacy breaches, including how to contact the organization and register complaints.
- Individuals must be given the opportunity to exercise choice regarding how personally identifiable information collected from them online can be used when such use is unrelated to the purpose for which the information was collected. At a minimum, individuals should be given the opportunity to opt out of such use.
- When an individual's information collected online is to be shared with a third party, especially when such distribution is unrelated to the purpose for which the information was initially collected, the individual should be given the opportunity to opt out.

- Organizations creating, maintaining, using, or disseminating personally identifiable information should take appropriate measures to ensure its reliability and should take reasonable precautions to protect the information from loss, misuse, or alteration.

Each company must evaluate its use of the Internet to determine the type of privacy policy it needs in order to protect all involved parties. The privacy policy will protect the company from legal issues, raising customers' comfort levels regarding the protection of their information. A privacy policy should include the following elements:

- **Information collection**   Collect, use, and exchange only data pertinent to the exact purpose, in an open and ethical manner. The information collected for one purpose shouldn't be used for another. Notify consumers of information you have on them, its proposed use and handling, as well as the enforcement policies.

- **Direct marketing**   The company can use only non-personally identifiable information for marketing purposes and must certify that the customers' personal information won't be resold to third-party marketing firms.

- **Information accuracy**   Ensure the data is accurate, timely, and complete, and that it has been collected in a legal and fair manner. Allow customers the right to access, verify, and change their information in a timely, straightforward manner. Inform customers of the data sources and allow them the option of removing their names from the marketing lists.

- **Information security**   Apply security measures to safeguard the data on databases. Establish employee training programs and policies on the proper handling of customer data. Limit the access to a need-to-know basis on personal information, and divide the information so no one employee or unit has the whole picture. Follow all government regulations concerning data handling and privacy.

Exam Tip

Privacy policies must be easy to find and provide information on how to opt out of any use of personal information.

Human Resources Policies

A company's human resources (HR) department is an important link regarding company and employee security. The HR department is responsible for hiring employees, ensuring employees conform to company codes and policies during their term of employment, and maintaining company security in case of an employee termination. The following sections outline the responsibility of human resources during the three phases of the employment cycle.

Hiring Policy When hiring employees for a position within the company, the HR department is responsible for the initial employee screening. This usually takes place during the first interview: An HR representative meets with the potential employee to discuss the company and to get a first impression, gauging whether this person would fit into the company's environment. This interview generally is nontechnical and personality based. Further interviews are usually more oriented toward the applicant's skillset and are conducted by the department advertising the position. Both interviews are important because the applicant could possess excellent technical skills for the position, but his personality and communications skills might not be conducive to integration with the work environment.

During the interview process, HR also conducts background checks of the applicant and examines and confirms her educational and employment history. Reference checks are also performed, where HR can obtain information on the applicant from a third party to help confirm facts about the person's past. Depending on the type of company or institution, such as the government or the military, the applicant might have to go through security clearance checks or even health and drug testing.

To protect the confidentiality of company information, the applicant is usually required to sign a nondisclosure agreement, which legally prevents the applicant from disclosing sensitive company data to other companies, even after termination of employment. These agreements are particularly important with high-turnover positions, such as contract or temporary employment.

When an employee is hired, the company also inherits that person's personality quirks or traits. A solid hiring process can prevent future problems with new employees.

Codes of Conduct and Ethics Policy The HR department is also responsible for outlining a company's policy regarding codes of conduct and ethics. The codes are a general list of what the company expects from its employees in terms of everyday conduct—dealing with fellow employees, managers, and subordinates, including people from outside the company, such as customers and clients.

This code of conduct could include restrictions and policies concerning drug and alcohol use, theft and vandalism, sexual harassment, and violence in the workplace. If an employee violates any of these policies, that employee could be disciplined, suspended, or even terminated, depending on the severity of the infraction.

Termination Policy   The dismissal of employees can be a stressful and chaotic time, especially because terminations can happen quickly and without notice. An employee can be terminated for a variety of reasons, such as performance issues; personal and attitude problems; or legal issues such as sabotage, espionage, or theft. Alternatively, the employee could be leaving to work for another company. The HR department needs to have a specific set of procedures ready to follow in case an employee resigns or is terminated. Without a step-by-step method of termination, some areas might be ignored during the process that compromise company security.

A termination policy should exist for each type of situation. For example, you might follow slightly different procedures for terminating an employee who's leaving to take a job in an unrelated industry than an employee who's going to work for a direct competitor. In the latter case, the employee might be considered a security risk if he remains on the premises for his two-week notice period, where he could transmit company secrets to the competition.

A termination policy should include the following procedures for the immediate termination of an employee:

- **Securing work area**   When the termination time has been set, the employee in question should be escorted from his workstation area to the HR department. This prevents him from using his computer or other company resources once notice of termination is given. His computer should be turned off and disconnected from the network. When the employee returns to his desk to collect personal items, someone should be with him to ensure that no private company information is taken. Finally, the employee should be escorted out of the building.

- **Return of identification**   As part of the termination procedure, the employee's company identification should be returned. This includes identity badges, pass cards, keys for doors, and any other security device used for access to company facilities. This prevents the person from accessing the building after being escorted from the premises.

- **Return of company equipment**   All company-owned equipment must be returned immediately, such as desktops, laptops, cell phones, personal digital assistants (PDAs), organizers, or any other type of electronic equipment that could contain confidential company information.

- **Suspension of accounts** An important part of the termination procedure is the notification to the network administrators of the situation. They should be notified shortly before the termination takes place to give them time to disable any network accounts and phone access for that employee. The network password of the account should be changed, and any other network access the employee might have, such as remote access, should be disabled. The employee's file server data and e-mail should be preserved and archived to protect any work or communications the company might need for operational or legal reasons.

Exam Tip

All user access, including physical and network access controls, needs to be disabled for an employee once she has been terminated. This prevents the employee from accessing the facility or network.

Objective 1.02
CompTIA Security+
Objective 5.3

Implement Appropriate Risk Mitigation Strategies

Your risk analysis will inevitably uncover risks, and many of those risks will require security controls to lower risk to an acceptable level. The policies and procedures described previously help you implement security controls at the managerial, operational, and technical levels of your organization.

Security policies and procedures provide the template and framework for employees to follow and implement risk mitigation controls across your organization. Ensuring these policies are being followed, however, requires continued monitoring and auditing.

The following sections describe additional aspects of risk mitigation that require security policies and continued monitoring to ensure the policies are being followed and do not result in additional risks for the organization. These risk mitigation strategies and policies include change management, standard operating procedures, incident response, auditing, user permission reviews, and data loss prevention.

Change Management Policy

Change management policies are official company procedures used to identify and communicate current or forthcoming changes to some aspect of the company's networks and communications services. For example, the IT department might issue a change control document to all employees to notify them of a network outage because of an upgrade to networking equipment, or that an application will be down for several hours for a software upgrade. More detailed change control communications describe longer-term outages for specific technical changes to the company's systems or network infrastructure, such as taking down part of the network for a weekend for router and switch upgrades.

Tracking, controlling, and communicating outages and changes to your network infrastructure, systems, and applications are important to keep all departments in your organization up to date with IT maintenance activities to prevent accidental loss of data and services. For security reasons, this activity also ensures any unplanned changes or outages are quickly detected and investigated. System and network changes without prior knowledge or approval of management and the IT department could indicate a hacker or an intruder has compromised the network.

Incident Management and Response Policy

Incident management and response should be part of a company's overall security policy. In the event of some form of security incident—be it physical intrusion, network attack, or equipment theft and vandalism—some form of procedure should be in place to deal with these events as they happen. Without any clear directives, the aftermath of a security breach can cause even more damage if employees don't know how to handle an incident properly. A clearly defined incident response policy can help contain a problem and provide quick recovery to normal operations.

The policy should cover each type of compromised security scenario and list the procedures to follow when they happen. For example, in the case of a hacked server, procedures might be in place to deal with removing the server from the network, shutting down related network servers and services, and preserving evidence, such as audit trails and logs. The incident response policy should cover the following areas:

- Contact information for emergency services and other outside resources
- Methods of securing and preserving evidence of a security breach

- Scenario-based procedures of what to do with computer and network equipment, depending on the security problem
- How to document the problem and the evidence properly

Travel Assistance
Incident response is described in greater detail in Chapter 2.

Perform Routine Audits

Routine audits of your security procedures and policies are an integral part of continuous security awareness. Until serious incidents occur, you will not know if your policies are being followed and adhered to, which leaves your organization and its activities at risk. Recording and collecting logs of security activity aren't helpful unless you are able to review and analyze the data and compare it to your current policies and the level of incidents that occur.

Security and access logs should be carefully preserved and analyzed in case of a security compromise or policy violation. For example, there may be evidence of attempts at network intrusion that go completely unnoticed because of notifications and alerts in the security logs that went unnoticed or unheeded. In this case, you must review your IT incident response policies and procedures to understand why these activities went unnoticed and the risk continued. By auditing and reevaluating your policies, you can identify additional monitoring and mitigation measures that need to be put into place.

Audits of policies and procedures need to be performed at all levels of your organization, including deep-level network and account management policies, physical access policies, and human resource procedures. You may find that your current policies are correctly defined but are not implemented properly or communicated efficiently to all users. Employees can become lax, and often republication and retraining for specific types of policies may be required.

Develop Standard Operating Procedures

Standard operating procedures (SOPs) can be developed for a variety of contexts. An example of a common SOP would be how an organization plans to move source code from a development environment into a test environment, and then finally into the final production environment. The SOP would detail the step-by-step procedures to do this securely and perhaps how to roll back in the event of an error or failure. SOPs are often developed as more detailed documentation to execute on an overarching policy. Remember that SOP documents should be very detailed, kept as living documents, and updated regularly. The worst SOP is the one that is gathering dust on a shelf, never used by those who should consult it on a regular basis.

> **Exam Tip**
>
> Remember that standard operating procedures are more detailed documents used to implement higher-level guidance such as policy.

User Rights and Permissions Reviews

While auditing and reviewing overall organizational policies and procedures are critical for security maintenance, you must also regularly review and audit the rights and permissions granted to your users. While at a specific moment in time, the rights and privileges you have assigned for users may be accurate and secure, over longer periods of time, employees leave the company, move to different positions and responsibilities, and may possess higher or lower security clearances than what they had previously.

Regularly auditing user security rights and permissions is extremely important in ensuring that existing security lapses in user rights policies can be resolved before a user accesses or damages data to which that user should not be allowed access. Group-, location-, and department-based policies are very important to audit because users change groups, locations, and departments frequently. For example, a user who recently switched from the sales department to the marketing department needs her permissions reviewed to remove her from any access to shared sales department data.

User rights and permission reviews need close cooperation with human resources and department heads to be proactively notified when employees' positions and responsibilities change.

Data Loss Prevention and Regulatory Compliance

Data loss prevention (DLP) is a major growing trend for organizational security. While most security is concerned with inbound risks and threats, such as malware, network attacks, and hacker intrusions, internal data security and outbound data loss have also now become primary security targets.

DLP is a security concept focused on preventing the loss of data and protecting its confidentiality and privacy. This includes a company's own data and any customer data that it stores and communicates. Data must be protected from theft, loss, and interception in storage and in transit. Mitigation techniques for data loss require the use of both inbound security, using standard network security techniques such as firewalls and anti-malware appliances to prevent inbound threats, and security for outbound traffic, using content filtering and encryption technology.

Travel Assistance

Data loss prevention techniques are discussed in more detail in Chapter 12.

There are now several government- and industry-directed regulations, policies, and frameworks designed to protect data for companies in specific industries. For example, companies in the medical industry must prevent confidential patient information from being compromised. Financial organizations such as banks and insurance companies must provide several layers of security for protecting financial transactions and the confidential financial information of customers such as credit card and bank account data.

The most common data protection regulations include the following:

- **Health Insurance Portability and Accountability Act (HIPAA)**   HIPAA is a set of compliance regulations for the protection of confidential patient data in the medical, healthcare, and health insurance industry.
- **Sarbanes-Oxley (SOX) Act**   In the financial services industry, the Sarbanes-Oxley Act defines standards for publicly held companies and accounting firms for storage, access, communications, and auditing of financial data.
- **Payment Card Industry (PCI)**   This set of standards is defined for companies that process credit card financial transactions to help prevent fraud and identity theft. PCI defines several concepts that should be complied with when storing and communicating financial data.
- **EU Data Protection Directive (EUDPD)**   This European Union regulation requires organizations, including multinational companies, to provide privacy protection for stored and transmitted user data.

Generally, most compliance regulations and standards include these key factors for data security:

- Proper protection of data through network security principles and technology, such as firewalls and anti-malware devices
- Strong user account and password management for access control
- Use of encryption when storing and transmitting confidential data
- Extensive logging and auditing to be able to monitor and analyze reports and have audit trails for forensic evidence

| Objective 1.03 |
| CompTIA Security+ |
| Objective 5.1 |

Integrate with Third Parties

When you're considering the overall security posture of the organization and the data stored, processed, and shared, it is important to also consider how partners might use that data. It has become more common for one organization to host another's data or for organizations to share computing resources, so strong agreements detailing the framework for handling data acceptably, performing security functions appropriately, and reporting incidents in a timely manner are more critical than ever. Often, these terms have accompanying metrics, such as mean time between failures (MTBF), discussed more in depth in later chapters. These metrics help the customer determine whether the host is playing its defined part in ensuring mission success.

The following sections detail several types of agreements, along with common considerations.

Exam Tip

Agreements should consider the business context of the organizations. Government organizations might be more interested in the confidentiality of the information shared between the entities, whereas the commercial sector could prefer high availability. It is important that the appropriate documentation be developed and approved by a high-ranking member of management.

Interoperability Agreements

Interoperability agreements differ in content and context, but they have one tie that binds: they are designed to lay out the terms of agreement between two different entities—be they two internal or external entities—who are working toward a mutual goal. These are typically legally enforceable agreements that cover responsibilities both parties have toward each other in terms of service, data protection, and use, and may even allow access to each other's confidential or proprietary information. In some cases, these agreements may even allow access to customer or privacy data, so it's important to ensure adequate security protections are included in these agreements. Other areas to consider include on-boarding and off-boarding business partners (that is, how do you deal with creating and removing business partner accounts from your systems) and how your organizations will choose to approach social networks and applications. Putting these terms in writing might seem painful at the time, but delineating expectations at the beginning can save serious time and money if an incident is prevented.

Service Level Agreements

A *service level agreement (SLA)* is an understanding among a supplier of services and the users of those services that the service in question will be available for a certain percentage of time. For example, a web-hosting company could have an SLA that states the web servers that host the customer's web pages will be available 99.8 percent of the time. If the service level drops below this percentage, the customer might be reimbursed for business lost during the downtime.

The SLA policy describes the policies and procedures that a company performs to support the service level agreement, including the services performed to preserve the SLA uptime and the contingency plans and communications that must be performed if the availability of the organization's services exceeds the thresholds agreed to in the SLA.

Business Partnership Agreements

A *business partnership agreement (BPA)* describes how a new business will be established among partners. In general, there are three types of BPA arrangements: general partnerships, limited partnerships, and joint ventures.

General Partnerships   *General partnerships* are devised under the assumption that all profits and liabilities will be divided equally among the business partners. To this end, all management decisions, large or small, are generally divided among those same partners equally. If this is not the case, it should be noted within the BPA.

Limited Partnerships A *limited partnership* is similar but more complex than a general partnership, in that it allows partners to have limited liability and corresponding input based on the investment percentage.

Joint Ventures *Joint ventures* begin in the same way as a general partnership but have a shorter time frame, often for a single project. If the partnership is to continue past that defined point, a general or limited partnership must be filed.

Memorandums of Agreement/Understanding

Memorandums of agreement and understanding (MOA/MOU) are common within the government sector, and relate terms of cooperation between two organizations seeking a common goal, such as a joint continuity of operations site. These documents detail the distinct roles and responsibilities of both parties, and are generally signed by a high-ranking staff member. These documents are often high level in nature and are often accompanied by more technical documentation, such as an interconnection security agreement.

Interconnection Security Agreement

Whereas the other agreements described generally detail how organizations will conduct business in a manner that benefits both mutually as prescribed within the terms, an *interconnection security agreement (ISA)* details a technical framework in which two information systems—even those owned by a single organization—will directly connect and share data securely. National Institutes of Standards and Technology (NIST) Guide 800-47, "Security Guide for Interconnecting Information Technology Systems," details a life cycle of interconnecting information systems that includes planning, establishing, maintaining, and disconnecting the interconnection. These agreements will have an accompanying diagram depicting the connection, and they should be signed by authorities designated to approve interconnections, as appropriate.

Privacy Considerations

When you're considering data sharing between organizations, it is important to understand how each organization—even segments of the same overarching organization—approaches the concept of data privacy. For example, within a healthcare organization, the department that stores and processes patient data might view the privacy of their information assets in a fundamentally different light than the department charged with building the public-facing website. Understanding this, it is key to have open communications regarding privacy requirements and what are the laws, regulations, policies, and customer expectations.

Risk Awareness

Small and medium-sized businesses often consider managed security services or other third-party integration options as a solution or supplement to better secure their organizational assets. While these partnerships can enhance the overall security posture above and beyond the levels that the organization could afford to do alone, the risks inherent to the arrangement must also be considered. Not only are costs being shared among the partners, but also the responsibility for the health and well-being of the shared resources, including compliance obligations. The concept of acceptable risk is important when such an arrangement is being considered; the level of risk borne by both parties must be acceptable to continue the partnership. If not, an assessment of the sensitivity of data, the controls in place to protect that data, and the legal framework to protect the organizations must be considered.

Unauthorized Data Sharing

Any agreement must detail the data that should be shared between two entities, be it internal or external. Let's consider the previous example of a healthcare organization with sensitive patient data. If data is spilled from the department charged with its care, there should be provisions to deal with that situation. In this case, policies and procedures for spillage situations may suffice. In other cases, a full-blown client notification may result. These are not small ramifications for an organization, especially if it is charged with answering to the public and/or shareholders.

To this end, it is important to deal with the possibility of unauthorized data sharing through measures such as risk mitigation (additional controls between particularly sensitive data stores) and risk transference (often in the form of insurance).

Data Ownerships

Within partnerships where data is "owned" by one organization and stored and processed by another, it is important to detail within any agreement the requirements for legal and regulatory authority over the data. Particularly within the U.S. government, the "data steward" has succeeded the concept of a "data owner," because the true owner is the American public. Within this construct, a steward is appointed the responsibility for establishing the policies and procedures for the handling and dissemination of that data. Further, that steward will have the regulatory approval for any interconnections.

Data Backup

Anyone who has dealt with a system loss can understand how key backups are to the overall security posture of an organization. Backups allow a system to recover, if not in full, at least from a known baseline. However, relying on backups is only as good as the last successful, tested backup. When one organization is ceding some measure of responsibility for its security setup, and data backups are part of the security solution, it is important to have a framework in place for maintaining regular backups and verifying their utility.

At a minimum, organizations should consider how often data will be backed up, verify through testing that the backups are valid and useful, and use offsite storage locations (as described further in this text), labeling and storage processes, and restoration processes.

Verification of Adherence

In the end, a strong partnership must be built on the concept of trust. This trust is established through regular verification of adherence to the agreement. This is often accomplished through mutual vulnerability or risk assessments that evaluate the exposure to threats. The agreement between the entities, then, should detail how key steps will be taken in minimizing risk: how patches will be applied, how scans will be conducted, and how incident notifications will be made. If these are not properly adhered to, there is cause for concern and potential nullification of the partnership.

CHECKPOINT

✔**Objective 1.01: Explain Risk Management Processes and Concepts**   An acceptable use policy is a set of established guidelines for the appropriate use of computer networks. The company practices due care by taking responsibility for all activities that take place in corporate facilities. The company practices due diligence by implementing and maintaining these security procedures consistently and effectively to protect the company's facilities, assets, and employees. A specific separation of duties ensures that a single individual isn't tasked with high-security and high-risk responsibilities. Users should have only the access rights they need to perform their job functions. The employee termination process includes securing the work area, returning identification and company equipment, and suspending computer accounts. It is important to consider a few best practices encompassing technical, administrative, and operational controls that compensate, correct, direct, deter, detect, or prevent in order to best protect organizational assets.

✔**Objective 1.02: Implement Appropriate Risk Mitigation Strategies** Security policies provide the template and procedures for risk mitigation, but these policies need to be implemented and adhered to. Use change management policies for communication of network changes and outages. Unplanned changes in your network could indicate security breaches. Use an incident response policy so that procedures are in place to deal with security incidents. Perform routine audits of your policies and procedures to make sure they are being adhered to. Constantly review user rights and permissions to deal with security issues deriving from changing roles and responsibilities for end users. Use DLP techniques to protect the integrity and privacy of data, and adhere to government-regulated compliance policies for data protection.

✔**Objective 1.03: Integrate with Third Parties**   Agreements between two or more parties detail the roles and responsibilities between different types of partnerships. An SLA is an understanding between a supplier of services and the users of those services that the service in question will be available for a certain percentage of time. A BPA describes how a new business will be established among partners. An ISA details a technical framework in which two information systems will connect securely.

REVIEW QUESTIONS

1. After a few incidents where customer data was transmitted to a third party, your organization is required to create and adhere to a policy that describes the distribution, protection, and confidentiality of customer data. Which of the following policies do you create?

    A. Privacy

    B. Due care

    C. Acceptable use

    D. Service level agreement

2. You are performing a risk analysis for a complex web-based application. Based on your conclusions regarding the probability, impact, and mitigation cost of an attack based on domain name service (DNS) manipulation or poisoning against your web domain, you decide to place the responsibility of the risk on your Internet service provider (ISP), who handles your DNS services. Which risk management option is this an example of?

   A. Acceptance

   B. Deterrence

   C. Avoidance

   D. Transference

3. As the centralized management location from which you provide Internet-based application services to several external clients, which of the following policies do you provide to your clients as an agreement for service uptime?

   A. Code of ethics

   B. Privacy

   C. SLA

   D. Due care

4. There is a suspicion that a specific employee is performing illegal activities on your company's networks. To gather evidence about his activities, which of the following principles and techniques could you employ?

   A. Password rotation

   B. Mandatory vacation

   C. Need-to-know

   D. Separation of duties

5. As part of a risk analysis of a very large and extensive back-end database, you need to calculate the probability and impact of data corruption. Which of the following impact factors allows you to calculate your annualized losses due to data corruption?

   A. SLE

   B. SLA

   C. ARO

   D. ALE

6. You need to create an overall policy for your organization that describes how your users can properly make use of company communications services, such as web browsing, e-mail, and File Transfer Protocol (FTP) services. Which of the following policies do you implement?

   A. Acceptable use policy

   B. Due care

   C. Privacy policy

   D. Service level agreement

7. After the initial configuration of an anti-spam e-mail-filtering appliance on your network, users are complaining that too many legitimate messages are being flagged as spam in their mailboxes. Which of the following concepts is this an example of?

   A. Baseline threshold

   B. False negative

   C. False positive

   D. Legitimate positive

8. Your organization deals with sensitive health insurance information for patients that is covered by the HIPAA compliance policies. Which of the following DLP security techniques would you implement to help protect the confidentiality and privacy of your patient's health insurance data when communicating the information between healthcare facilities?

   A. Encryption of outbound data containing health insurance information

   B. A firewall to protect against inbound network attacks

   C. Antivirus scanning of patient data

   D. Strong physical access control of your facility

9. It has been discovered that a former member of the IT department who switched to the development team still has administrative access to many major network infrastructure devices and servers. Which of the following mitigation techniques should be implemented to help reduce the risk of this event recurring?

   A. DLP

   B. Incident management and response policy

   C. Change management notifications

   D. Regular user permission and rights reviews

10. Two friends have decided to go into business together to create a new gadget. They do not have existing businesses and wish to share the decisions and profits equally between them. Which type of agreement is most appropriate to begin the business?

    A. ISA

    B. MOA

    C. SLA

    D. BPA

REVIEW ANSWERS

1. **A** A privacy policy concerns the protection and distribution of private customer data. Any company, especially one engaged in online activities or e-commerce, has a responsibility to adopt and implement a policy for protecting the privacy of individually identifiable information.

2. **D** The risk of DNS attacks occurring against your web domain is something that can only be assumed by your ISP, who takes care of your DNS services. In this part of your risk analysis, you are transferring the responsibility of the risk to your ISP to protect your web services from DNS-based attacks.

3. **C** A service level agreement (SLA) is an understanding between a supplier of services and the clients of those services that the service in question will be available for a specific percentage of time. In this case, you might guarantee your clients a 99.5 percent uptime of communications services.

4. **B** When a user is forced to take a vacation, his activities can be audited, and any suspicious behavior will be more likely to be noticed and detected because the user is not there to prevent its discovery. You may also discover that the illegal activities completely cease while the user is away and then resume when he returns.

5. **D** ALE (annual loss expectancy) describes how much money you expect to lose on an annual basis because of the impact from an occurrence of a specific risk. ALE is calculated by multiplying the annual rate of occurrence (ARO) by the single loss expectancy (SLE).

6. **A** An acceptable use policy establishes rules for the appropriate use of computer networks within your organization. The policy describes the terms, conditions, and rules of using the Internet and its various services within the company's networks.

7. **C** A false positive is a legitimate action that is perceived as a risk or threat. The term *false positive* is often used in e-mail security scanning to indicate legitimate mail that was classified as spam.

8. **A** To comply with the HIPAA regulations, you must protect the confidentiality of your patients' health insurance information. When communicating this data, you must encrypt it to ensure that it cannot be read if intercepted or stolen.

9. **D** User rights and permissions must be constantly reviewed to make sure that users have only the rights they require for their current responsibilities. When users change roles and responsibilities in the organization, you must review their permissions and modify their access accordingly.

10. **D** A BPA is most appropriate type of agreement because the potential owners do not have existing businesses to interconnect and need to establish the ground rules and responsibilities for ownership, including how they will resolve differences and split any profits.

Security Training
and Incident Response

	NEWBIE	SOME EXPERIENCE	EXPERT
ETA	4 hours	3 hours	2 hours

Security is not just about technological security controls. Although network devices such as firewalls, antivirus and anti-spam appliances, and intrusion detection systems can help protect against most types of security issues, they cannot completely protect your users from social engineering attacks.

Social engineering uses behavioral manipulation to trick users into bypassing security controls and providing elevated access or confidential data to the attacker. Hackers using social engineering techniques can cause victims to unknowingly provide their login credentials or confidential information such as personal credit card numbers or bank account information. Social engineering techniques cover a variety of mediums, including networking, websites, e-mail, instant messaging, telephone calls, and even personal contact.

Social engineering is effective when it takes advantage of trust in the message being delivered—in any form—to the victim; for example, when an attacker takes the time to gather information regarding the organization or a specific user, he can use that information to build a sense of familiarity between himself and the recipient. Consider the wealth of information most people now share on social networks and how that can be used to tailor e-mails or telephone calls. Because of this, user education is key in preventing security issues arising from social engineering attacks. Awareness training helps users to understand the dangers of various social engineering hacking techniques and to be wary of intrusions when working through their day-to-day activities. Users communicate with other external users every day when using e-mail, phones, social media, instant messaging, and file sharing applications, and each application has its share of security issues, including the risk of malware and phishing. Although technological security controls help, user education and awareness are the most effective security measures against the risks of social engineering attacks.

In preparing for security incidents, organizations must also create policies and procedures regarding incident response. By considering the legalities of prosecuting computer crimes, most companies have trained their employees in collecting and preserving forensic evidence of such crimes. Because the evidence is usually electronic in nature, it can easily be tampered with, causing it to be legally invalid in a court of law. Therefore, the art of computer forensics is a critical part of preventing and prosecuting computer crimes.

This chapter describes user security training and policies, provides an overview of the most common social engineering attacks, and covers best practices for incident response and data forensics.

Objective 2.01
CompTIA Security+
Objective 5.1

Explain the Importance of Security-Related Awareness and Training

Security awareness and training are critical business objectives that must be directed from senior management and filtered throughout the company to every single employee. Different departments and divisions within a company need different forms of security education, depending on their job tasks and area of influence. The security procedures used by the financial department may be different from those used by sales or engineering, for example. Finance might need special procedures to protect confidential company and employee financial data from being exposed to other employees or companies. Engineering's security efforts will revolve around the protection and integrity of the source code or research data. Company reception personnel could be specially trained on security practices with incoming calls or the physical security of the main entrance. Each department must interpret the company's high-level goals into the functional procedures specific to a job function or information area.

To propagate security policies and procedures effectively to the user community, the company must make a diligent effort to communicate these policies. If no one knows about the security policies, there's no point creating them. The best methods for overall user-security awareness are through proper documentation and training.

Effective Security Training and Awareness

The first step in user security awareness is creating and maintaining proper documentation of all your security policies and procedures. Policies that apply to the company should be distributed to each employee, and each employee should sign and acknowledge that he or she has received them. These policies might include such areas as acceptable Internet use during work hours, employee codes of ethics and conduct, and safety and emergency contact information. More department-specific policies could be distributed only to employees in that department. The HR department wouldn't publish policies for the protection of employee salary information to other departments of the company, for example, so it wouldn't reveal or undermine any security procedures. The IT department would have different security policies because one of its main job functions is to be responsible for the security and protection of the company's network infrastructure and data.

Because security policies tend to change over time, manual distribution isn't always the most efficient and timely way to communicate security information. Employees should have a way to access the most current versions of these documents in a conspicuous place, such as in a binder located outside the HR area. Another more efficient method is to publish these documents on a company intranet so that employees can easily access the most current versions. Printed versions should still be available, but because this documentation frequently changes, only a few central copies should be created to prevent excessive paper waste. The advantages of online documents are that they're instantly available through employees' computers and they're always the most recent versions.

> **Exam Tip**
>
> The best place to store company documentation for easy access by employees is the corporate intranet.

Providing access to documentation is only one part of user awareness. Although printed documentation might be handed out to all employees or electronic versions made available online, no guarantee exists that they'll be read, understood, or implemented. To supplement the documentation and to ensure employee awareness, the company should provide education and training sessions.

Onboarding

Training sessions should be mandatory for all employees and are especially critical for new employees during their onboarding process. The training courses ensure that employees know the company's security policies and procedures and, most important, that they understand these policies and know how to enact them within their specific positions. Having formal classes also makes it more likely that any questions new employees may have will be raised and can be discussed. Classes can be based on overall security procedures, such as virus awareness and dealing with outside clients and inquiries. These should be attended by all employees to ensure they know how to handle security problems properly with communications media used company-wide, such as e-mail or the telephone.

You should also start a training record for each new employee as part of the onboarding process, both for compliance and HR purposes. IT professionals and security personnel will need additional training related to their duties, so that they are fully aware of the threats and vulnerabilities they may face and thoroughly understand their roles in dealing with these threats. Employees who are leaving the company should be offboarded through an exit interview that supplies them with their responsibilities to safeguard sensitive data. In the event there is a security clearance or nondisclosure agreement involved, this can be a lifetime responsibility with severe penalty. It is also helpful to gather feedback from the departing employee regarding their time at the company and their thoughts on how processes could be improved.

Onboarding training should include a basic overview of the company's security policies and procedures (for example, general threat awareness, acceptable use policies regarding company e-mail and telephones, virus awareness). Onboarding training also can include job-/role-specific training, as well as training targeted to the particular needs of a specific department (for example, policies for salespeople in dealing with sensitive customer data such as credit card information). All new hires should leave these onboarding sessions with a robust understanding not only of the various types of security threats they are likely to encounter, but also of what is expected from them, and what will happen to them if they don't practice due diligence.

Nondisclosure Agreements

Nondisclosure agreements (NDAs) are often utilized when an employee, or even a third-party vendor or supplier, requires access to sensitive or proprietary information, information that could provide an advantage to a competitor or, in the case of federal agencies or contractors, harm national security. NDAs enjoin the signee from disclosing such information under threat of serious penalty. Some people are frightened away by NDAs, so it is important to be sure that one is in fact required for any particular role, lest you put off incoming personnel unnecessarily.

Awareness Training

As mentioned earlier, role-based training can be particularly important. Various roles throughout the organization play a significant part in the protection of systems and data, and it is important that organizations identify those specific roles that require a more detailed level of knowledge and spend the resources to facilitate their learning and engagement.

Optimally, training should be developed to consider the role and organization, and the threats associated with both. Some different roles that should have specific training developed include data owners, systems administrators, system owners, users, privileged users, and executive users.

- **Users**   All users within your organization need training to better understand the current security threats as well as what their responsibility is to protect against them. This training can take the form of courses, briefings, online programs, or any combination of the different available solutions. What is important is to make your personnel aware of current security threats and vulnerabilities, as well as the best practices used to counter them. Users should understand what is expected of them, as well as the repercussions for not following organizational policy. This is a great opportunity to use any powerful, real-world anecdotes you might have (sanitized, without names, of course) to make your training more effective by showing situations that employees could be confronted with. For example, if you have had a large number of phishing e-mails targeting your organization, this would be timely and relevant information to include in your training and awareness program to let people know about it and what they should do. General security items, such as facility access control, can include training on identifying and authenticating users in the facility so that they can spot employees or strangers who are somewhere they shouldn't be. Network authentication standards, such as proper login and password management, are also applicable to all employees. Specialized training can be presented to laptop and mobile device users who'll be traveling to ensure they protect company equipment and data when they're not on the premises. Other education initiatives can be more specific to an individual user or department, depending on their job function. For example, the HR department can be given training on the security practices involved with hiring and terminating employees.

- **Privileged users**   Privileged users, or those users who have increased access to systems or data, should have a level of training commensurate to their level of access. These users must understand that with their privileged access comes increased responsibility for the safety and security of their area of expertise. It is important that privileged users in particular have regular access to current threat information so that they can spot anomalies that could be attributed to malicious actors, either internal or external.

- **Executive users**   Although executive users' time is often very valuable, there's no denying that they are subject to targeted threats and should have appropriate training developed for their unique context. For example, since phishing attacks are often targeted at executive users, they should be made aware of how these attacks could be used to gain the most sensitive organizational information. Although they may not be able to give you hours of their time, focused training courses of no more than 30 minutes will put you well on your way to keeping your executive users safe.

- **Systems administrators**   Systems administrators play such a huge role in protecting an enterprise that they require in-depth training programs based on current events. The informed systems administrator is a responsive, savvy systems administrator who understands the threats and recognizes anomalies and trends. Keeping these people aware and engaged is your first line of defense.

- **System owners** Although they may leave much of the day-to-day care and feeding of the system to the system administrator, system owners should be properly trained and/or certified to accept the residual risks related to the system.

- **Data owners** Data owners, similar to system owners, should receive training on the data they are responsible for, the controls put into place to protect it, and their responsibilities associated with those controls and the security and safety of their data. They should understand the sensitivity requirements specific to their organization and their department. For example, a data owner within the finance department should be aware of how and to whom financial data can and cannot be released.

Remember that the security department should be consulted when any type of security-related training is being developed for any population of users, because they are in the best position to know where the training deficiencies are within the organization.

Travel Advisory

If you are working within the U.S. federal government, there are now regulations detailing the continuous certification and training of employees fulfilling certain security roles. If you are working within—or are planning to support—such an organization, you should consult the most current regulatory documents to be sure you are meeting the mandates.

Users need to understand, no matter their privilege level, how policy violations are handled, as well as what adverse actions will be associated with those policy violations. For example, if pornography is found on a business system, there may be a policy to immediately terminate the guilty employee. These implications should be communicated to the employees to give them an understanding of what is *not* okay within the work environment—this is often presented to employees through the company's acceptable use policy (AUP), as discussed in detail in Chapter 1.

Finally, users should be cognizant of the sensitive data their organization processes—for example, personally identifiable information (PII), protected health information (PHI), classified data, or financial data—and how to treat that information. Certain organizations, particularly those within government or healthcare, will likely have strict policies on the handling, dissemination, and storage of this type of information. Each of these types of data may require special controls, such as data-at-rest or in-transit encryption, special networks that are not connected to the greater Internet, and data segmentation. It is important that training and awareness campaigns include these details should any of these types of data be an issue.

Continual Education

Just as it is important for your employees to be well trained as you bring them onboard, it is also important that they have access to continual education opportunities. This will expand their usefulness in your workplace, as well as their proficiency, and make them more valuable employees (and it may increase morale, too). In regard to continual employee education, consider the following anecdote: An HR person once asked an HR manager, "What if we train them and they leave?" The manager replied, "What if we *don't* train them and they *stay*?"

Education is often given as a "perk" or a benefit to employees, with options such as college degrees, specialized training, certifications, and certificate programs in the field, generally in exchange for a contractual commitment to the company. Investing in your employees is a smart choice toward a happier, more knowledgeable and productive workforce.

Threat Awareness

Threat actors are often seen as the "Jason Bourne" of cyberspace—individuals representing nation states (or not) who are the most stealthy, most capable, and most damaging. Although that might certainly prove to be the case, a threat actor could also be a kid down the street or any person using "cyber" as a means to an end—generally a negative end. You should be familiar with a number of different types of threat actors in order to fully protect against such threats. (Note that it is beyond the scope of this book to provide *comprehensive* coverage of the most sophisticated threat tactics, techniques, and procedures [TTPs].) The six major threat actor types are described next, and are generally categorized according to the following attributes: level of sophistication, resources/funding, intent/motivation, and whether they are internal or external in nature.

- **Script kiddies**   Script kiddies are the lowest-common-denominator threat actor; these are your teenagers sitting in their parents' basement, as the ugly stereotype goes. However, don't underestimate a so-called script kiddie! These adversaries excel in creating chaos based on sheer intent and numbers. Further, they can be utilized by more sophisticated organizations to provide larger numbers to operations. Often their tools are "point and click" in nature and have little sophistication.
- **Hacktivists**   Hacktivists utilize cyber means to effect an end (typically of a social or political nature). Consider, for example, Anonymous,

which may be the most famous hacktivist group around. Whether you agree with its motives and approaches, Anonymous has been effective at utilizing cyberspace to draw attention to various causes, such as its campaigns against Scientology, the Westboro Baptist Church, and others. Hacktivists can utilize script kiddies or other, more sophisticated personnel, but they have a more nuanced reason behind their attacks. It is not improbable that some nation-state actors use hacktivist groups to spread their messaging, so don't discount hacktivists.

- **Organized crime**   Organized crime is exactly what it sounds like: the extension of classic crime techniques into cyberspace to extort, harass, or otherwise pursue illegal ends. As with hacktivists, do not discount organized crime, and don't assume that nation-state actors don't utilize organized crime's personnel and infrastructure. Money tends to be their predominant end priority.

- **Nation-states/advanced persistent threats**   Nation-state actors are the top-tier cyber threat actors, and they bring a level of sophistication that, when executed well, allows them to be an advanced persistent threat (APT). Nation-states that have risen to the APT level are highly skilled, well funded, and are generally motivated to use cyber tools, techniques, and procedures to gain a certain end state—whether it be the exfiltration of another country's sensitive data, the disruption of an adversary's electrical grid, or even a denial-of-service (DoS) attack targeting a multinational banking system. Stuxnet, the malicious computer worm that in 2010 targeted and caused significant damage to Iran's nuclear program, is a good example of what can occur when nations that have invested heavily in cyber capabilities flex their muscles.

- **Insiders**   Insiders may be the most dangerous type of threat actor of them all due to skilled employees having the access inherent to their position. Think, for example, about a privileged user who becomes disgruntled and decides to turn over sensitive or classified information to a competitor or even another nation-state. The access and trust given to that insider means that he or she has a much easier time gaining access to the information—and given that many security controls focus on monitoring and stopping external threats, it is harder to spot a malicious insider. However, you not only have to be vigilant against malicious insiders but also mindful of the friendly insider who does not follow policy or user best practices. A user who can't seem to stop clicking on links in suspicious e-mails is a phisher's dream.

- **Competitors**   Although competitors are generally not linked to nation-states, for a non-government entity, they are of tremendous concern. Organizations need to protect their intellectual property

(IP), and their competitive advantage is at risk if their competitors gain access to it. Be aware that competitors could use hacking and social engineering techniques to reduce your company's competitive advantage. Competitors, especially those that are well funded, can be as capable as nation-states.

> **Local Lingo**
>
> The terms *capability* and *sophistication* are often used interchangeably to discuss a threat actor's level of skill.

It is amazing how much information can be gained through the use of *open-source intelligence*, or *OSINT*. In fact, your organization should have someone regularly combing through search engines looking for any sensitive information that is hanging out, easily accessible on the Internet. Also be mindful that information can be aggregated from press releases, newspaper, radio, and television. This information can be used to facilitate social engineering attempts, gain insight into policy decisions before they are announced, and even reproduce emerging product designs. OSINT is a low-cost/high-reward approach for a threat actor. Therefore, employees should be instructed to only post information about the organization and its activities on approved sites, such as the company intranet, and avoid discussing anything related to the organization on social media.

Recurring Training

After employees have completed their initial training, they should receive recurring training on a periodic basis—annually at the minimum, but ideally whenever the computing environment changes or new and significant threats emerge. As mentioned previously, you can utilize classes, online documentation, and briefings. Also, information can be sent to the workforce via e-mail or even as pop-up messages that appear when their computer is loading. This is vital to ensuring that your employees are aware of the most current threats and are equipped to play their part in dealing with them.

Security Metrics

Although training can prepare users to work in an environment where spam, viruses, and network breaches are common, it is key that management follow up and measure whether the training and awareness programs are having an impact on the number of security incidents occurring within the organization.

It is also important that management consider exactly what should be measured and tracked for the organization, such as the risk management considerations discussed in Chapter 1. Is constant availability critical, or is the confidentiality of data the more important factor? These considerations need to be codified by the organization's leadership.

Although metrics can focus on anything from network uptime to the time it takes for the IT helpdesk to deal with customer issues, the discussion here will focus on those security metrics that validate compliance and the organization's overall security posture. For example, a department (perhaps working with the chief information security officer) that has oversight over the organization's security posture might measure the number of unauthorized information systems plugged into the network within a month. It might also monitor the number of systems that are not properly patched, or the number of viruses contracted within a given time. Gathering this type of data allows management to spot trends and frequent offenders and to take corrective actions.

Data and Documentation Policies

Your company produces a wide variety of documentation—from publications for internal use, to confidential papers for senior management, to publicly available documents. Without proper controls, that documentation could be used to compromise company security. The company's document control standards and guidelines must ensure that all documents produced by the company are classified, organized, and stored securely to prevent their loss, damage, or theft.

As part of its governance and risk management programs, an organization should develop data sensitivity and classification programs. This process also contributes to the business continuity plan as well. The organization takes a good look at all its data, categorizes it in terms of sensitivity and type (PII, proprietary, government classified, and so on), and assigns classification values to it. To ensure control over the protection and distribution of data, it needs to be classified with a certain designation. This data classification indicates what type of document it is, whether the information it contains is confidential or can be made public, and to whom it can be distributed. The classification also defines what levels of data retention and storage are needed for that document. Finally, policies must exist concerning the legal status of data and what can be destroyed and what needs to be retained.

Standards and Guidelines

To ensure the continuity of documentation across the company, a set of documentation standards and guidelines should be introduced. These standards and guidelines can serve as templates for all documentation to guarantee they have the same look and feel and to ensure they'll all be distributed and stored securely, according to their scope or sensitivity.

The standards and guidelines should address the following topics:

- Data classification
- Document retention and storage
- Disposal

Data Classification   A company's documentation can be voluminous, comprising a variety of documents of varying value and importance. Depending on the type of document, the amount of security and types of procedures used in storing and distributing that document can greatly vary. Some documents might be considered public, so they can be posted in a public forum or distributed freely to anyone. Other documents can be highly confidential and contain information that only certain individuals should be allowed to see.

To aid in this effort, documents need to be assigned security classifications to indicate their level of confidentiality and then labeled appropriately. Each classification requires different standards and procedures of access, distribution, and storage. The classification also sets a minimum standard of privileges required by a user to access that data. If you don't have the necessary access privileges for that classification of data, you won't be able to access it. Typically, access is delineated using subjective levels such as high, medium, and low. These should be agreed upon by management, based on its sensitivity and the damage to the organization if the data is subjected to unauthorized access.

Several levels of classification can be assigned, depending on the type of company or organization and its activities. A typical company might have only two classifications: private and public. *Private classified documents* are only for the internal user of the company and can't be distributed to anyone outside the company. *Public documents,* however, would be available to anyone. Government and military institutions might have several levels of confidentiality, such as Unclassified, Confidential, Secret, Top Secret, and so on. Each level of classification represents the level of severity if that information is leaked. For example, the lowest level (Unclassified) means that the document is not considered confidential or damaging to security and can be freely distributed. At the highest level (Top Secret), documents are highly restricted and would be severely damaging to national security if they fell into the wrong hands. Each document needs to be assigned a classification depending on the sensitivity of its data, its value to the company, its value to other companies in terms of business competition, the importance of its integrity, and the legal aspects of storing and distributing that data.

> **Exam Tip**
>
> The type of security protections, access controls, data retention, and storage and disposal policies to be used all depend on a document's security classification.

Document Handling, Retention, and Storage   Depending on the classification of a document, the procedures and policies for handling and storing that document can be quite different. For example, a document might incur certain legal liabilities if it isn't properly stored, distributed, or destroyed. To ensure proper document management, companies have implemented data retention policies to help reduce the possibility of legal issues.

Certain documents are required to be archived, stored, and protected, while others should be disposed of after a certain period. These policies must be created by senior management and the legal department, which can define what retention policies apply to different classifications of documents. The data retention policy needs to be specific to your company's data. It also needs to consider items that could be legally damaging and information that can be damaging to the business if it's lost or falls into the wrong hands.

To protect documentation properly, it should be kept offsite at a special document storage facility. In case of a disaster, such as a fire at the company facility, this will ensure that all important documentation is secure and can be recovered. (Chapter 3 covers business continuity and disaster recovery.)

Document Disposal   Document disposal can often be a tricky issue. In some cases, a document needs to be destroyed to avoid future legal or confidentiality ramifications. In other cases, it's illegal to destroy certain documents that are required by law as evidence for court proceedings. Only your company's legal department can decide on retention and disposal policies for documents. Once decided on, these policies need to be communicated to the employees to ensure that sensitive documents are either destroyed or retained as per their classification.

When data is to be disposed of, the job must be done completely. When destroying paper documentation, most companies use a shredder to cut the document into pieces small enough that they can't easily be put back together. Simply putting documents in the trash or recycle bin isn't acceptable, because anyone can sift through the garbage or recycle containers for these documents, a practice called *dumpster diving*. As part of corporate espionage, some companies hire private investigators to examine garbage dumpsters of a target company, and these investigators try to discover any proprietary and confidential information.

Travel Advisory

To combat the problems of dumpster diving for confidential company documents, the physical security of your facility should include your garbage disposal and recycling operations.

Data Retention Policy

Many companies have been affected legally by archived e-mail or data that offers evidence against them during court proceedings. To prevent legal liabilities, companies have implemented *data retention* policies to help reduce the possibility of legal problems arising from past messaging communications and data.

Data retention policies should apply to electronic information, such as files, e-mails, and instant messages, and traditional paper documentation. Some clashes might occur between data retention policies and backup policies, where certain files are required to be archived, while others should be disposed of after a certain period. Only management and the legal department can define which data is covered under either policy. The data retention policy needs to be specific to your information and consider items that could be damaging legally, as well as information that can be damaging to business if lost. In the case of e-mail, the concept of data retention becomes complicated because e-mail can contain file attachments. Part of your policy might require that e-mail be retained for a certain amount of time before deletion, while the policy for actual electronic files could be different.

Hardware Disposal and Data Destruction Policy

Any policies must also include the disposal of old hardware. As the lifetime of computers is very low (three to five years), older equipment is constantly swapped out for newer, faster machines with more capabilities and resources. However, a critical security issue is apparent regarding the proper disposal of these systems. Servers and personal computers are typically returned with their original hard drives, which could contain sensitive and classified data. System administrators must follow a specific policy for the removal and disposal of hardware to ensure that any media containing data is completely erased or overwritten.

For electronic files, this process is more complicated. Merely deleting a file or e-mail from a hard drive doesn't necessarily delete the data. Many operating systems (OSs) use a special recovery method that enables you to recover deleted files easily. When a file is deleted, only the locator for the file in the hard drive directory has been removed; the data itself usually still exists in its original location. To ensure complete destruction of data on magnetic media such as hard drives, the media should be overwritten or the drive physically destroyed. Many "shredder" utilities are available that can overwrite the contents of a hard drive with random data to ensure that any information on the drive is unrecoverable. Also, many high-security organizations, such as the military and national security, opt to destroy the drives physically instead of using a shredding application.

IT Documentation

Beyond standard company documents, such as policies, procedures, guidelines, and training manuals, some specialized document sets require added attention regarding security and storage. Network architecture diagrams, change logs, and system logs and inventories are all documents created and managed specifically by the company's IT department. Because these documents can contain specific information on system and network devices such as logs, audit trails, network addresses, and configuration data, they are usually accessible only by authorized persons within the IT department and aren't accessible by other employees in the company.

Systems Architecture   The IT department should always have current diagrams of your overall company network architecture on hand. When troubleshooting network problems or security issues, engineers who have network diagrams are ready to identify devices and overall data flow within the company's network.

A variety of diagrams is needed to show different aspects of the architecture. Overall diagrams should be general and show the company network. These diagrams should indicate offices only by name—with wide area network (WAN) links in between them—for companies that have geographically distant offices. More detailed diagrams can be made of the internal network structure, showing all the routers, switches, firewalls, hubs, printers, and servers.

Each device should be clearly labeled with identifying information, such as the system name and the network address. Including end-user workstations on systems architecture diagrams is rare because in many organizations the number of workstations is so large that it would be difficult to include all of them on a single diagram. The general network used by the end users should be indicated, however.

As a security precaution, network diagrams generally shouldn't be published because the information can be used maliciously by a hacker to give him a roadmap of the company's network, including the Internet Protocol (IP) addresses of the most critical network devices and servers. Network architecture diagrams should be accessed only by authorized individuals from the IT department. Printouts of diagrams should never be posted in public places, such as on a notice board or even in the office of the network administrator. The diagram could be easily stolen, or a person could use a digital camera to quickly take a picture of it for later use.

Exam Tip

System architecture diagrams should never be displayed or stored in a public area, especially if they contain system IP addresses and other information hackers can use to compromise a network.

Logs and Inventories   General application logs, audit logs, maintenance logs, and equipment inventory documentation are also important documents within an IT department. Most of this documentation is related to the maintenance and operation of the company's computer equipment, but certain logs, such as system activity logs, should be carefully archived and preserved as evidence in case of a security compromise.

System and audit logs provide snapshots of what's happening on a system at a specific point in time. These logs need to be retained for auditing in case of some security compromise. For example, the hacking of a certain server could have gone unnoticed for a long period of time. But if the logs of that system are retained and archived, they can be audited to reveal when the compromise began and how it happened. To ensure the company's backup procedures and policies are being followed, the IT department might have to retain and store copies of backup application logs, which indicate when certain data was backed up and where it's now stored. Inventories of computer equipment enable the company to keep track of its assets and know where they're located. Maintenance logs also provide important evidence for service and warranty claims.

Best Practices for User Habits

Beyond security awareness training, you must enact several policies and best practices that users should adhere to during their day-to-day activities within the office. Security is an ongoing practice, and concepts learned in awareness training must be enacted within the office to make them effective. The following sections describe several interoffice security practices that should be followed by your users.

Password Policy

A strong password policy should be implemented and followed by all employees in an organization. Password policies ensure that all network administrators and users are aware of the rules and procedures in place for managing the user accounts and passwords that allow access to company resources. Password policies should be part of the company's overall security policy.

Typically, users create passwords that are easy to remember—such as the names of family or pets, phone numbers, and birth dates, all of which can be easily discovered by someone who knows the user, or even by a stranger who, through simple social engineering, asks the user only a few questions about her personal life. Other types of passwords that aren't secure are those based on any word found in the dictionary. Many password-cracking programs based on dictionary attacks are available that can find out any password in a short amount of time if it's based on a common dictionary word.

A minimum length password policy should be enforced for all employees. This prevents users from using short easy-to-guess passwords of only a few characters in length. The recommended minimum password length is 8 characters, with 14 characters being ideal. Password complexity must be part of your password policies to ensure that beyond a minimum length, the password is not easy to guess (such as a dictionary word) and does not contain information specific to the user (such as a birth date). Passwords should contain a mix of uppercase and lowercase characters, numbers, and symbols, and they should not be based on any word that can be found in a dictionary.

Most login and password authentication systems can remember a user's last five to ten passwords and can prevent the user from using the same one repeatedly. If this option is available, it should be enabled so a user's password will always be different. Also, the longer a password has been in existence, the easier it is to discover eventually, simply by narrowing the options over time. Forcing users to change their passwords regularly (password aging) prevents the discovery of a password through brute-force attacks.

Clean Desk Policy

Users should be aware of the risk of leaving confidential papers, sticky notes with sensitive information, cell phones, portable devices, and removable media on their desks unattended. These items can be quickly stolen or copied while a user is away from his desk. A clean desk policy maintains that any such items should be always kept in locked drawers. Users also should never write down login credentials and leave them on their desk or stuck on the front of their monitor, where they can be easily found by other unauthorized users. Whiteboards or drawings should be wiped clean or removed after they are used to prevent leaving confidential information on the board for passersby to view.

Personally Owned Devices

Users might bring a variety of personally owned devices, such as laptops, universal serial bus (USB) keys and drives, cameras, and other peripherals, into the workplace. To protect organizational security, your company must have a defined security policy in place that spells out the types of personally owned devices that are allowed in the workplace and the conditions under which they may be used. For example, you may have a policy in place (and enforced through technological controls) that allows personal laptops but prevents them from connecting to a corporate wired or wireless network unless a full virus scan is performed. Smartphones that can access corporate messaging servers should be protected with a password so that if a user ever loses her personal phone, an unauthorized user cannot access her company e-mail account. These security controls ensure that all devices have a minimum standard of security before they can connect to company resources and access data.

In very high-security environments, personal devices, especially cameras and smartphones with cameras, are banned and must be turned in to security before entrance into the facility.

Workstation Locking and Access Tailgating

Users must ensure that they lock and password-protect their workstation sessions whenever they are away from their desk. If a user leaves his current computer session still logged into the network, any passerby can "tailgate" onto his privileges and access confidential data, e-mail messages, and shared network resources. Network-wide policies implemented by the network administrator should automatically make sure workstations lock after a specified period of inactivity, such as ten minutes, but even that is enough time for a malicious user to find what she needs on an unprotected workstation.

Data Handling

Users should be aware of the classification of the data they are working with and should be properly trained on how to handle that data. Data that is highly sensitive will likely require special procedures for dissemination and destruction, and it is the responsibility of the users to follow organizational policies. If this is not done properly, an incident could occur. Data-handling policies and procedures should cover items such as access, use, transmission, storage, and disposal of data, based on its sensitivity and classification. Examples of data handling might include who has permissions to be able to print a sensitive document or even transport one from one company location to another.

Instant Messaging

One of the most popular Internet services is *instant messaging (IM)*, which allows users to send real-time messages to each other via their PCs. Web links, files, and other types of multimedia can also be exchanged between IM users.

Whereas e-mail messages can be protected by authentication and encryption tools, IM applications reside on a user's hard drive and are usually not protected by a firewall by default. This is even more critical in corporate environments, where IM programs used by employees make the corporate network vulnerable to attack because these programs are often not part of a company's traditional network security plan. To prevent users from using IM in the workplace, the administrator can configure the firewall to block specific IM ports. In certain cases, it may be necessary to allow IM within the company network but not allow it to connect to clients outside of the network.

IM can be used to send files to another user, and the same risks associated with attachments exist, such as receiving virus-infected files. When receiving a message with an option to download a file, the user must always establish the identity of the sender before replying or downloading the file. The best practice is simply to ignore the message unless the user has no doubt about its origin. Some IM programs enable the user to create a list of users whose messages will be automatically rejected. This is helpful if the unknown user continues to send a user messages even after being ignored the first time. Of course, an antivirus scanner should always be running on the system to protect against any type of virus, spyware, or other malware in downloaded files.

P2P Applications

Peer-to-peer (P2P) networking allows two computers to connect to each other directly and share files rather than connecting through an intermediary server or service.

The most popular application using P2P Internet file sharing is the trading (usually illegally) of music, movies, and videos. Unfortunately, many of these P2P programs contain security vulnerabilities that can give unauthorized users access to your system. The P2P application enables you to configure a specific directory on your hard drive that can be accessed by other users. The P2P servers can scan the contents of this directory to create a centralized master database that can be searched by users of the service. Once the user finds the file he is looking for, he connects directly to your computer to download the file. Insecure P2P software may put your system at risk by opening it up to network attacks and the possibility that other remote users can gain access to your unshared files.

The biggest issue with P2P sharing is that the files you download may be disguised viruses or Trojan horse programs. The open nature of this type of networking and file sharing means little trust and control exist regarding what files are offered for download. When using these types of file-sharing programs, you must ensure your computer is fully protected with a current antivirus program and a personal firewall to protect against network attacks.

> **Exam Tip**
>
> P2P applications have no place on a corporate network, and any P2P protocols and ports should be closed off at the firewall to prevent these applications from operating on the network.

Social Networking/Media

With the massive increase in social media use, such as Facebook, Twitter, and LinkedIn, security administrators are beset with many new avenues of risk within their organization. The same security risks that affect other communications media, such as e-mail, Web, IM, and P2P, are also inherent in social media applications; however, phishing and the spread of malware can be more prevalent in social media because most malicious links are spread by trusted users on the social network. When one person's social media application is infected with malware, it can quickly spread to other users as automatic messages are sent from the victim's computer to all her social media contacts. These types of social engineering attacks are very effective.

To provide a strong layer of security, many organizations have included social media with other restricted applications such as instant messaging and P2P apps and block their use on the network. If users do have access to social media sites, they require social engineering awareness training to educate them on the types of behavior to look out for when using social media.

Compliance with Laws, Regulations, Best Practices, and Standards

In the end, how an organization performs regarding compliance with applicable laws, regulations, best practices, and standards must often be tracked and reported to appropriate governing bodies. In some sectors, this is simply the security staff. In others, detailed reports must be released to government bodies charged with oversight. Noncompliance can mean fines, legal action, censure, or, in the worst case, dissolution of the department or entire organization.

To prevent this, it is important to have a very comprehensive understanding of what laws, regulations, best practices, and standards your organization is mandated to adhere to. Metrics should be developed to track the compliance with those requirements, and swift action must be taken to remediate any issues that seem probable. Consistent enforcement of those actions, from training to personnel dismissal, will facilitate a more positive security culture and improve compliance.

Objective 2.02
CompTIA Security+
Objective 1.2

Analyze and Differentiate Among Types of Social Engineering Attacks

The easiest way to discover someone's password often is simply to ask for it. *Social engineering* is defined as using and manipulating human behavior to obtain a required result. It typically involves nontechnical methods of attempting to gain unauthorized access to a system or network. This typically means the hacker tricks a person into bypassing normal security measures to reveal information that can help the attacker access the network. The hacker, in effect, acts much like a con man, who tries to uncover sensitive information through manipulating someone's basic human nature.

A user might be easily led to reveal her password or to provide personal information that might reveal her password. For example, someone might call a user on the phone, pretending to be from another department, asking for the user's password to retrieve a file. The user, thinking she knows who she is talking to, might give the unauthorized user the password without officially authenticating who the caller is or why he needs the information. The caller might make small talk with the user and trick her into revealing names of family members or her birth date so the attacker can try out this information as a password to the user's account.

Another typical example of this type of security breach is impersonation, which often occurs when an unauthorized user calls a helpdesk operator, impersonates a high-level user, and asks to reset his password. The user insists he is a high-level manager who needs access into his account immediately. The helpdesk operator, if not trained properly, could instantly give this user a new password without properly identifying the user. Now the hacker can log in using the account of a high-level person who could have access to sensitive information.

Protecting against social engineering security abuses requires user education and emphasis on the need to always follow security procedures, even when dealing with someone an employee knows within the company. In short, users should be taught to recognize that social engineering attacks prey on misplaced trust and to have strategies to deal with those attacks.

Other principles in the social engineering toolbox are important to understand. Social engineers often claim positions of authority to intimidate the victim into giving them access rights (the *authority* principle), or they act belligerent if denied (the *intimidation* principle). Conversely, they may be very personable or seek common interests to create a bond between the social engineer and the victim (the *familiarity* principle). They may cite professional credentials, known organizational information, or organizational status to create a feeling of confidence (the *trust* principle). They might also try and make a social connection, claiming that another trusted individual can vouch for their authenticity (the *social proof* principle, otherwise known as the *consensus* principle). Finally, a social engineer might claim that a situation is urgent (the *urgency* principle) or that she has very little time to verify her identity (the *scarcity* principle).

> **Exam Tip**
>
> Be able to differentiate between the different types of social engineering attacks and the reasons why they are effective.

Phishing

A *phishing* scam is a type of e-mail or web security threat that tries to trick an unsuspecting user into visiting a website and entering confidential personal information or replying to an e-mail with such information, often a username and password, or banking or credit card details.

Like other forms of social engineering, phishing relies on creating a false sense of trust, and therefore phishing e-mails often contain familiar logos, official-looking messages, and links to well-known trusted sites, such as a real bank or credit card company. However, any links in the message will redirect to the website of the phishing scam operator, rather than the trusted site. These websites are often made to look just like a real bank or credit card site. The user then unknowingly enters his login and password information and personal details into the website, when in truth, it is being added to the database of the phishing website operator.

This activity is most commonly related with identify theft, where the unauthorized user can collect enough personal information about his target victim that he can perform forged credit card and banking transactions using the victim's financial and personal details.

A variant attack called *spear phishing* is a targeted type of phishing attack that includes information familiar to the user and could appear to be from a trusted source such as a company from which the user has purchased a product in the past, a financial service that the victim has used previously, or even a specific trusted user. A spear phishing attack is much more sophisticated than regular phishing; in this kind of attack, the information targeted at the victim offers a greater inducement to click the links in the message and serves to gain the user's trust to enter confidential information. For example, the user's personal information, such as full name and postal address, could have been stolen from a mailing list, or the name of the user's bank manager could appear as the sender of the e-mail.

To help protect end users, many web browsers, e-mail clients, and antivirus software applications can detect behavior that may indicate the presence of a phishing e-mail or website. This is typically accomplished by parsing the universal resource locator (URL) links in a message and comparing them to lists of known phishing websites.

User education and awareness are important tools to protect against phishing attacks. Users must be aware that financial institutions will never ask for personal details, especially bank account numbers and credit card details, in an e-mail to a user. When a suspicious e-mail is received, it is also helpful to check the destination of any clickable links—simply hovering over the link will often do the trick—within the message to determine the location to which it is redirecting. If the destination site is not recognized, it is likely a phishing attempt. Many browsers can automatically check links for suspicious or obfuscated URL redirect links and warn the user before connecting to the site.

Travel Assistance

For detailed information and resources on phishing and best practices for reducing the risk of phishing attacks, see the Anti-Phishing Working Group website at www.antiphishing.org.

Whaling

Whaling is a type of phishing attack that is targeted at a specific high-level user. Most phishing attempts are general in nature and are sent to thousands of users, hoping that some of those users will fall prey to the attack. In a whaling attack, the victim is usually a high-profile member of the organization, such as an executive who has much more critical information to lose than the average user.

Many executives have their profile information posted on the organization's public website. Hackers can use this information to craft a unique message so specific to that user that it may seem legitimate enough for the victim to act and click a link containing malware, which is then installed on her computer, or else the link may redirect to a website under the hacker's control where the executive might enter sensitive credentials or banking information.

Whaling requires the same sort of protections as other phishing attacks, such as proper malware and antivirus protection on the computer, as well as user education on social engineering techniques.

Shoulder Surfing

End users must always be aware of their environment and the people in their surroundings when entering login names and passwords or accessing sensitive data. It is very easy for an unauthorized person to casually glance over the shoulder of an employee who is concentrating on the work at hand and watch the user as she enters usernames and passwords into the computer. The person who is shoulder surfing can easily see which keys the employee is typing on the keyboard and will use the username and password when attempting to access that account later.

The issue of viewing sensitive and confidential data, such as human resource records, while other employees are present is also important. An unauthorized person can watch from behind an unsuspecting employee and view the data the authorized person is accessing on the monitor, especially on today's monitors with large and wide screens.

Users must examine their surroundings before entering or viewing confidential data. If a user has her own office, she should ensure that her monitor is not easily read from a distance in the hallway and that it is situated in such a way that a casual passerby cannot see the monitor screen. In many environments, the desk can be oriented to face away from the doorway to ensure that the monitor screen is always facing the back of the office. Blinds can be installed on windows to prevent outsiders from looking in to the office. Screen filters can also be placed on monitors to prevent passersby, both innocent and malicious, from being able to view the content displayed on screens. In open-concept office spaces, this is more difficult, and it is up to the user to ensure that no one is standing behind her or viewing over her shoulder while she is entering and working with sensitive data.

Tailgating

Tailgating is one of the simpler forms of social engineering and describes gaining physical access to a facility by following an authorized user through the security checkpoint. For example, when a user swipes her access card to open a door to enter the facility, the unauthorized user will follow the authorized person while the door is still open. The unauthorized user might try to use conversation to gain trust and then entry by saying he has lost or forgotten his access card.

Organizations must have strict access control rules that prevent tailgating incidents and allowing unauthorized users into a facility without proper authentication or identification. All employees should be encouraged to report unknown individuals within the facility and never let an unknown user within the premises without proper authentication, including photo ID if possible. Many security access cards also include a photo as additional identification in case the card is lost or stolen. Visitors must always be accompanied by an employee and be properly signed in and given a temporary access card. The visitor must be signed out and the access card returned when leaving the facility.

As mentioned earlier in the chapter, *tailgating* can also refer to using another user's access rights on a computer. For example, a user might leave on her lunch break and forget to lock her office or log out of her session on her computer. An unauthorized user could get access to her computer and be able to read her e-mail messages, access her files, and gain access to other company network resources. Users must always log out of sessions or lock their workstations before they leave the work area.

Pharming

Pharming is a type of social engineering attack where a user is misdirected to an attacker's website without his knowledge. While much like phishing, where a user may click a link in a seemingly legitimate e-mail message that takes him to an attacker's site, pharming occurs when code is installed on the computer that modifies the destination URL to that of the attacker, even if the URL is entered correctly or chosen from a web browser bookmark. In some cases, the malicious code can change the hosts file on the victim's computer to point legitimate web domains to alternative IP addresses of the hacker. Through these methods, the user is tricked into browsing to the attacker's website even though he thinks he has gone to a legitimate destination. Just as in phishing, pharming can result in loss of confidential data such as login credentials and credit card and banking details; it can lead to identity theft as well.

Spim

Spim is instant messaging spam, and much like the more common e-mail spam, it occurs when a user receives an unsolicited instant message from another user, including users who are known and in the client's contact list. Instant messaging services provide a lot of information about users, including demographic, sex, and age information, that can be used for targeted spam advertising. These messages can contain ads or links to viruses, malware, and phishing sites.

Users can protect themselves from spim and other IM-related security issues by making sure that only people on their contact list can send them messages. In many cases, organizations have completely blocked access to external IM chat services.

Vishing

Vishing is a type of phishing attack that takes place over phone systems, but most commonly over VoIP (Voice over IP) lines. Using tools specific to VoIP systems, hackers can program their autodialers to send a recorded message from spoofed VoIP addresses. The recorded message can claim to be from a bank call center asking the customer to call back and verify her financial information. Because the VoIP source is difficult to trace, unsuspecting users might trust the call as legitimate and provide their private financial details to the hacker by inputting that information via the phone keypad.

Like other social engineering attacks, vishing requires user education to recognize the warning signs of scams, including any attempt to get financial information such as credit cards and bank account numbers over the phone.

Spam

Spam is a deliberate attempt to mass e-mail large numbers of users with unsolicited advertisements. Any time you enter your e-mail address on a public website or a newsgroup, you open yourself up to the possibility of having your e-mail address added to spam mailing lists. These mailing lists are shared among Internet spam advertisers, and sometimes you can receive multiple junk e-mails every day. This annoys not only users, but also networking administrators because of the amount of space and bandwidth these mass mailings can consume. Many Internet service providers (ISPs) and corporate networks use anti-spam mail filters that block incoming spam e-mail from reaching users' inboxes.

Travel Assistance
For details on anti-spam and e-mail content filtering devices, see Chapter 8.

E-mail spam continues to be one of the prime nuisances and security issues affecting organizations. Spam has evolved from the early years of simple text adverts to full Hypertext Markup Language (HTML) messages with clickable links, images, and even spam messages hidden in attached images and document files. The links in spam messages are often redirected to malicious sites containing spyware, malware, and phishing activities.

Hoaxes

One of the most annoying problems, a hoax is typically some kind of urban legend users pass on to others via e-mail because they feel it is of interest. The most common type tells the user to forward the e-mail to ten friends to bring him good luck. Another claims to be collecting e-mails for a sick person. Of course, this activity merely consumes network and computer resources because the number of e-mails grows exponentially as users send them to all their friends, and so on.

Travel Assistance

See www.hoax-slayer.com for an exhaustive list of known e-mail hoaxes.

Hoaxes are generally harmless and are caused more by social engineering than maliciousness; however, some hoax e-mail messages can be phishing attempts that try to get the user to visit a link in the e-mail message that redirects to a malicious website. The only cure for the spreading of hoax e-mails is user education to make sure that users know the typical characteristics of a hoax message and know not to forward it to other users. Organizational policies might also call for a notification to the security team.

Exam Tip

Know how to spot an e-mail hoax and how to handle it properly. The best solution is to delete it immediately and follow organizational policy for notification, if appropriate.

Objective 2.03
CompTIA Security+
Objective 5.4

Execute Appropriate Incident Response Procedures

When a security incident (or disaster scenario) occurs, the initial incident response can make all the difference—either it quickly mitigates a threat, preventing it from spreading and causing further issues, or the incident spins out of control, causing irreparable damage to your organization's ability to function.

Preparation

Incident response must be planned to ensure that your front-line employees are prepared in the event of a security incident to quickly contain the incident, preserve any evidence in the event of a security breach, and escalate issues as appropriate to company management or third-party authorities. Without a plan (in writing, not memory), those who discover an incident are likely to take incorrect steps, or no steps at all. Spend the time to put a plan in writing, signed by a member of management, and you will save time and money in the event of an incident. A comprehensive plan should include the roles and responsibilities for all the stakeholders who will execute the plan. This should include the incident response team and first responders, the reporting and incident escalation requirements and associated timeframes, and the specific steps that will be taken to handle different incident types and categories of crisis effectively and efficiently, while appropriately preserving precious evidence. For example, the reporting for a personally identifiable information (PII) breach sent by e-mail will have different reporting and escalation thresholds than finding child pornography on a company system, and there should be no guessing about what to do in the heat of the moment. The plan must be clear, simple, and understood by all stakeholders.

Further, any plans should be exercised to ensure that the parties involved feel comfortable executing the steps. Remember that in a time of crisis, people can "freeze up" and feel unsure of what to do. Having a written, exercised set of plans takes the burden of memory off your staff and allows them to have confidence that they are doing the right thing at the right time.

Incident Identification

After the discovery of the incident, company personnel must report it to the appropriate person, and this person should be identified ahead of time. The incident could have been discovered by a security guard, an employee working late, or, in many cases, the network or security administrator himself. The company's incident response plan should have defined the first responders from the incident response team who can be deployed to respond to the incident.

First Responders

A *first responder* is the first person (or persons) who is notified and responds to a security incident. For example, the network administrator may receive notifications from an intrusion detection system that a security breach has taken place; therefore, the network administrator is typically the first person to respond to the incident. A first responder must follow several responsibilities and procedures when she is the first person on the scene of a security incident.

The company's incident response policy should describe the exact tasks and responsibilities of the first responder. If a computer crime occurs, an effort must be made by the first responders to the incident to contain any damage and prevent further asset or data loss. The first responders must also try to leave the original environment and evidence intact and unaltered as best they can until the authorities have been contacted. If people begin to pick apart the crime scene after a physical crime, or if the network administrator begins poking around the file system or reboots the system, the evidence could be disturbed and considered inadmissible in court. Finally, first responders need to follow an escalation policy to notify other company officials or the authorities.

Incident Containment

The containment process stops the damage from escalating further and helps preserve the evidence for any possible future action. The number-one priority will be to stop the progress of any malicious activity, be it malware or a hacking action. Often, this will entail a quarantine of affected systems from unaffected systems to prevent the spread of the incident, or removal of affected devices from the network. At this point, the system(s) may undergo forensic analysis or be wiped clean, depending on policy and type of incident.

Damage and Loss Control

A major initial aspect of incident response is being able to contain an incident and the damage it is causing and prevent it from spreading or causing further damage. A company must create an incident response policy that indicates what can and cannot be touched if a security compromise occurs. For example, a worker at a company undergoing a denial-of-service (DoS) attack might panic and pull the plug on its Internet connection. This, of course, stops the attacks, but it also brings down the entire network so that no communication exists with the outside world, effectively stopping all e-mail and Internet business communications. If the business runs its operations through a web page, this can be devastating.

In other cases, such as a virus-infected server, immediately disconnecting the server from the network so that it does not infect other systems might be the best response. The incident-handling and response procedures provide information on what to do in certain scenarios. In the example of the DoS attack, to prevent the entire network from going down and to preserve any evidence of the attacks, the company might let the attack continue so that the network administrator can save logs and audit trails to help trace the source of the attack. Decisions must be made on how critical specific services are, such as e-mail, file and print services, and web services. If a file server is specifically attacked, it may be less critical to take that system offline than to disconnect an e-mail service that must be running to provide communications to the organization, even though it might be under a DoS or spam attack.

Data Breaches

Although damage can be quantified in several ways, such as manpower expended, system downtime, and availability loss, perhaps the most damaging outcome of an incident is a data breach. A *data breach* occurs when data is exfiltrated from an organization. This could occur from corporate espionage, nation-state activities, or malicious insiders. A data loss could also be caused by loss of backup media containing sensitive information, or theft of a portable device, such as a laptop that contains sensitive data. The loss of critical data should be considered ahead of a breach when risk management best practices are implemented.

Travel Assistance

For details on risk management, see Chapter 1.

Escalation Policy

An escalation policy must be enacted and followed to provide a specific list of managers or other authorities who must be contacted in the event of a security incident, as well as additional actions that must be taken. Depending on the department or area of the incident, one or more direct managers should be notified, along with any central security for the organization. Also, the incident should be escalated to various executives such as directors, vice presidents, and so on, as required for the type of incident and the downtime it has caused. For example, if a web server has been attacked overnight and the attack was discovered by the network administrator in the morning, she should notify her direct manager and the security administrator.

In the event the attacking suspect is an employee, the human resources department should be contacted immediately as part of the incident response policy. From there, it can be decided whether to keep the organization's investigation internal or to contact the authorities and any other outside agencies to aid in the investigation.

If the security threat is external, outside authorities may need to be contacted if the organization holds that the security breach or the damage it caused is serious enough to warrant notification of the police.

Reporting and Notification

When a security incident is being investigated, every single detail should be meticulously documented to ensure that every aspect of the incident, from the specific details of the security breach to every step taken during the incident response process, is recorded. This should include, at a minimum, the date and time of the action or event, a list of personnel involved, the event itself, and any data or equipment involved. This is especially important in an incident that may eventually go to court.

Keep careful track of the number of man-hours and expense required to respond to, investigate, and provide mitigation for the security incident. These statistics are very useful for future risk analysis and security budgeting, and they help assign a real dollar value as a cost for the incident beyond the costs incurred for loss of data and system downtime. Other departments, such as accounting and human resources, may have to provide the data (such as labor rates of personnel involved) to help substantiate this portion of the incident report.

During the post-incident response phase, your organization must determine whether to keep the investigation and response internal or to issue a public announcement to notify customers or users of the security issues. Companies are often reluctant to release information about hacking attacks, as this can affect intangibles such as public image, consumer confidence, and competitiveness in the marketplace. In some cases, there may be good reasons for keeping details of an attack from becoming immediately public, such as to prevent further attacks while the incident is under investigation or until more stringent defenses can be put in place. By keeping the information of a security breach from the public, the organization can ensure that details of its internal security (or lack thereof) are not published. For example, if an organization sends out a press release that one of its web servers had been hacked using a known exploit, other hackers who hear this information might try the same exploit on the organization's other web servers if they know the servers are vulnerable.

The decision to internalize or release public information on a security incident becomes very sensitive when dealing with security breaches that occur in financial institutions, such as a bank or stock trading firm, and especially for medical institutions that have strict guidelines for protecting clients' data. In these cases, the decision is often regulated by the government, and any security breaches that affect the privacy of clients must be published. For example, if a hospital computer is hacked and confidential patient records are stolen or damaged, or an Internet banking system is hacked and leaks tens of thousands of its customers' bank account and credit card numbers, it is necessary or even mandatory that the company release details of the incident to ensure customers know that data has been leaked. In the case of the bank, customers should be told to contact the bank to help secure their current accounts and lock them down before they can be abused. Privacy officers are responsible for maintaining the integrity of information considered to be privacy data, and for ensuring proper reporting when data is lost or stolen.

Reporting and disclosure are also critical issues for companies that manufacture software or hardware systems that are found to contain security vulnerabilities. Many companies are embarrassed by such security breaches in their products, and they quietly release patches to the product to fix the security breach to ensure the vulnerability does not become well known. In other cases, companies try to protect the customers by not disclosing or discussing any known security issues until they have researched the issue and released a patch to deal with it. Many companies take a very proactive approach and welcome information from third parties that tests their software for vulnerabilities, which helps the company solve the issue and prevent it from being exploited before news of the vulnerability reaches the public.

Mitigation and Recovery Steps

Mitigation will consider the eradication of any lingering negative elements, the effect of isolation, the damage that has occurred, and then set organizational policies. Perhaps the affected machines will be reimaged and put back on the network, or more advanced forensic analysis will occur. These decisions should take into consideration the nature and scope of the incident and the organizational policies and resources available to implement potential mitigations, including the time, cost, and scope of the proposed countermeasures. Ideally, the affected segments are recovered and reconstituted, the steps are appropriately documented, and there is a good sense of how many resources—time, money, and lost data—have been expended on the effort.

Lessons Learned

Even in the worst scenarios, it is important to take stock of the lessons learned. It is rare to have an incident and accompanying response take place with no hiccups; these should be documented. Were organizational policies not followed? Were the policies not sufficient to cover the scope of the incident?

Conversely, good can often be found in a negative situation. For example, did the team operate smoothly because the procedures were practiced ahead of time? This should be noted also.

Implement Basic Forensic Procedures

In adjusting to the legalities of prosecuting computer crimes, most companies have trained their employees from the incident and response team in the proper collection and preservation of forensic evidence of computer crimes. Because the evidence is usually electronic in nature, it can easily be tampered with by an uneducated investigator, which would cause the evidence to be legally invalid in a court of law. Therefore, the art of computer forensics is a critical part of evidence collection necessary for prosecuting computer crimes.

Forensics is the act of acquiring and preserving evidence to use in court as part of a legal proceeding. Typical forensics of crimes such as theft and murder includes gathering evidence such as fingerprints, weapons, and even DNA samples to help prosecute a suspect. In the computer world, evidence of a cybercrime can be difficult to properly obtain and preserve so that it will be allowed as evidence in a court of law. Because of its nature, most computer crime evidence is electronic, which can easily be erased, modified, and tampered with. After a computer crime—such as a server attack—is committed, an initial investigation by the network administrator can quickly ruin evidence the attacker left behind.

In the event that your legal counsel determines that evidence should be collected for any reason, be it a pending investigation, litigation, or other situation where evidence would be required, a *legal hold* is formally initiated. Legal holds halt the usual backup and disposition processes, and immediately put your personnel into data protection mode. Without these procedures being followed, your organization is at risk of losing required data to protect itself in a legal situation, and it is the company's responsibility to make reasonable efforts to act as soon as possible to protect data that might become evidence. Therefore, working with your legal counsel to better understand legal holds and how to act appropriately could save your company from fines or sanctions.

Travel Advisory

If a system is rebooted after a security compromise, certain evidence could be destroyed in the process, such as memory contents and system logs.

The following section outlines some of the special procedures required when acquiring and preserving evidence of a computer crime, which includes preserving the incident environment, collecting evidence, data volatility, and retaining a chain of custody of the evidence.

Data Acquisition and Preservation

Collecting evidence is a crucial aspect of incident response. Depending on the type of incident, there could be physical evidence, logs, system images, screen captures, and camera video, each of which needs to be carefully collected and preserved and protected from tampering.

Order of Volatility

When collecting forensic data evidence, it is important to realize that any type of digital data has a specific volatility, meaning that over time, the veracity or ability to recall the data declines. Some data is more persistent and less volatile; for example, a printout of a log file or a copy of the file on backup tape is less volatile than a live data log file on hard disk that is constantly being modified and overwritten. The RAM (random access memory) of a computer system is extremely volatile because the data is not persistent and can change at any time within a matter of seconds.

When capturing data for forensics, especially in the initial stages directly after an incident, you must consider the levels of volatility and focus your efforts on preserving the most volatile types of data before moving on to less volatile data. Your early focus should be on system memory or crash dump files, error messages on the screen, and log files before moving on to less volatile data.

Capture a System Image

In many cases, the entire contents of your hard drive, or an entire server with an array of hard drives, needs to be saved as evidence of your security incident. It is a best practice to create a system image, which is a snapshot of your entire data system at a specific time. The system image allows you to preserve the state of your data after the incident so that you can resume operations with your server, while the image of your hard drive is stored elsewhere.

If you do not make a system image, you could lose important log files, network traces, and crash dump files that get overwritten over time. You must also adhere to legal requirements to ensure that the digital evidence is not tampered with after the incident.

System images are typically saved to an external hard drive with MD5 hashing to preserve their integrity and then stored in a secure place. Your disk-imaging software and image drive need to provide bit-for-bit accuracy to create an exact image of your original drive and prevent alteration after the image is created for legal reliability.

Network and System Logs

Collecting and preserving evidence from a computer crime primarily concerns keeping and storing any logs or audit trails that detail step by step what the attacker was doing. Log files will contain specific date and time stamps corresponding to each aspect of an intruder's activity, including login credentials, commands used, and files accessed.

When an incident occurs, avoid panicking. If you suddenly reboot a network device or server to ward off the attacker, you not only disrupt access to that server for legitimate users, but you could also destroy valuable evidence in the form of audit trails and time stamps on files that might have been changed by the intruder.

Make sure you preserve copies of your log files before letting too much time elapse from the incident. Log files, especially network logs from firewalls and routers, can roll over very quickly; older log files may be deleted to make resources available for new ones. By immediately making copies of the log files, you ensure they are not accidentally deleted or lost.

Time Offsets

When collecting data evidence from your systems, be aware that not all network devices or servers may have their clocks synchronized, and the time stamp that one device puts on an action that appears in the logs may be different from that of another device. There is also the issue of time zones and how different types of devices stamp times. One device may use UTC (Coordinated Universal Time) without time zone offsets, while other systems may insert their own time zone offsets, depending on their configuration. When collecting and organizing your evidence, be aware of the issue of time offsets between different devices and time zone issues. Legally, you need to account for any time discrepancies in your evidence.

Use Hashing to Protect Evidence Integrity

For legal reliability, you need to be able to prove the logs haven't been altered in any way from the time of the original data capture. To help preserve data integrity, you can create an MD5 hash of the file immediately after the incident.

A *message digest* hash is used in encryption systems to create a "fingerprint" for a message. Hashing preserves message integrity by ensuring that the original data has not been tampered with. MD5 is a complex message digest algorithm that is widely used for data integrity checking.

The resulting checksum can be matched to the MD5 hash later. If the MD5 hash does not match, the file has been altered since the original capture.

Travel Assistance	
For more details on hashing and MD5, see Chapter 4.	

Take Screenshots

In certain cases, evidence of an attack may only occur as an error or diagnostic image that appears on the screen. You may even have a full transcript of the command-line instructions entered by an intruder during his attack. In this case, you will have to use a screen capture image program to take a snapshot of your current screen. This must be performed before any other action. If you clear the message, you may lose your evidence if it does not also appear in the log files. Screen capture files should be accurately labeled and time-stamped, and you should also use hashing to preserve the integrity of the file to prove that it was not altered or tampered with.

Capture Video

If the crime was physical in nature, such as the theft of equipment, the evidence required would be surveillance videos. If the theft took place in a secured area, it might be possible to analyze the access logs of employees who logged into the secured area at the time. If the company uses magnetic access cards for doors, a log can be created showing who went in and out at a certain time. In this case, only the video surveillance could show who was in possession of the access card, as the card might have been lost or stolen from the original user.

Make multiple copies of the video evidence to make sure you have additional copies if the original is damaged or lost. Surveillance video on tape should be transferred to a computer as a digital video file for backup purposes and more efficient retrieval.

Chain of Custody

When collecting evidence of a computer crime, maintaining a proper chain of custody is extremely critical. A *chain of custody* requires that all evidence be properly labeled with information on who secured and validated it. This process must also occur for everyone who encounters the evidence. Unfortunately, electronic evidence can be volatile, and in a court of law it can be easily dismissed because of possible tampering. Computer media can be easily destroyed, erased, or modified, so handling this evidence requires strict procedures. All media must be stored in a secure room or container that has restricted access that is logged fastidiously. In addition to the chain-of-custody process, you must also consider preservation challenges such as humidity, temperature, electrostatic discharge, and other environmental issues that can affect electronic devices and digital storage media.

If additional copies of data need to be made, reliability and integrity must be ensured so the copies can be considered tamperproof. Perform an MD5 hash of the data so that a checksum can be created for comparison later to prove the data was not tampered with. Any devices or media containing data need to be carefully catalogued, labeled, and then sealed away to prevent tampering. Magnetic media should be write-protected to prevent the data from being overwritten.

If all evidence has been properly secured, identified, labeled, and stored, it can be considered solid and admissible in court. A clear chain-of-custody log ensures this process was completed without the possibility of data modification.

Exam Tip

A *chain of custody* ensures that evidence has been handled with the utmost care and lists the persons who have had access to the evidence.

Interview Witnesses

It is possible that, depending on the nature of the incident, you may have witnesses who need to have their statements recorded as evidence. For example, in the case of a physical theft, an employee might have caught sight of an unidentified person in the building. You must take a statement of where she saw the individual and at what time, and she must provide a detailed description. It is also possible that a witness might have noticed screen activity on a server that resulted in the initial incident alarm.

What is most important is interviewing and recording the witness statements as soon as possible after the incident. Over time, the witnesses may forget specific details, and it is important to have as much information recorded as possible while the incident is fresh in their memory.

Track Resources Expended

It is important to track the resources expended on the detailed forensic analysis. While many organizations can easily quantify the amount spent on new computing equipment, there are other expenditures that should be considered as well. For example, how much employee time (or man-hours) was spent on the analysis process? This is considered an opportunity cost, or time that could have been spent on other activities that are central to completing the organizational mission. These hidden costs can easily add up to more than the price of new IT equipment.

Big Data Analysis

Big data presents both challenges and opportunities for forensic analysis. Large data sets are often less structured or even unstructured, as opposed to the rigidly structured format of most modern database systems. Further, the sheer amount of data—the entire point of a big data system—can make forensic analysis daunting in the event of an incident. In addition, sometimes big data comprises result sets from other homogenous databases that may not have compatible structures, and these individual data sources might have to be examined individually, instead of as part of a big data store.

However, there are opportunities present within big data sets. Data may be present within the set that provides clues to a malicious party. Further, due to the lack of structure, it may be more difficult for an intruder to exfiltrate data; there is simply less of a defined roadmap to critical data.

Having access to big data can also give you a strategic view into potential adversary collection priorities and capabilities, and it may set you well on your way to understanding where you can better protect yourself in the future. A savvy analyst will move past solving individual incidents and spot patterns and trends, developing a view of who might be causing problems for your systems and data as well as where they might go next. For example, seeing that attacks generally happen within a certain time period on certain days of the week might lead to an informed supposition of where in the world a malicious organization is located and even if they are corporate or a nation-state.

Any potential tools used within a big data environment should be tested and approved for use within the unique situations presented by such large, unstructured amounts of data; it is too late by the time the incident has occurred.

CHECKPOINT

✓**Objective 2.01: Explain the Importance of Security-Related Awareness and Training** An organization's policies must be communicated to employees through training and documentation to be effective. Training documentation must be easily available via company intranet sites. Use data classification to indicate levels of data confidentiality. Destroy documents to prevent dumpster diving. Create user policies for password management, clean desk initiatives, and personally owned devices. Be wary of social engineering attacks for IM, P2P, and social media applications. Understand the different roles that should have their own in-depth training. Review the types of threat actors and how they vary in capability and intent.

✓**Objective 2.02: Analyze and Differentiate Among Types of Social Engineering Attacks** Perform employee awareness training to educate users on the principles of social engineering. Make sure no one is looking over your shoulder when you're entering sensitive data or login credentials. Be wary of tailgating users passing through an access door behind you. Educate your employees to recognize the characteristics of phishing e-mails and websites. Ignore hoax e-mails and do not forward them.

✓**Objective 2.03: Execute Appropriate Incident Response Procedures** Organizations should have detailed procedures for identification of and response to incidents; these should be written down and thoroughly tested before an incident ever occurs. It is important that first responders know their roles and responsibilities for isolating incidents and performing damage control, notifying the appropriate personnel, and implementing mitigation solutions. These steps should all be documented and the lessons learned should be cataloged for refinement of the procedures.

✓**Objective 2.04: Implement Basic Forensic Procedures** Perform damage and loss control to isolate an incident and prevent it from spreading or causing further damage. To preserve evidence, leave the original system environment intact. Know that a legal hold requires day-to-day procedures to change to support data collection and preservation. Gather information based on order of volatility. Save audit and activity logs, take screenshots, and make a system image for evidence. Use hashing to preserve data evidence integrity. Keep a chain of custody of evidence to prevent tampering.

REVIEW QUESTIONS

1. You have received a call from the legal department to halt regular operations due to pending litigation by a disgruntled former employee. What is this called?

   A. Data collection

   B. Litigation review

   C. Legal policy

   D. Legal hold

2. You are the first responder to a security incident in which a database server has been compromised and has crashed. Which of the following actions should be performed to help preserve evidence of the incident?

   A. Save access logs and a current memory dump.

   B. Restart the system to restore operations.

   C. Perform a backup of the database.

   D. Perform a restore of the database.

3. You are collecting forensic evidence from a recent network intrusion, including firewall logs, access logs, and screen captures of the intruder's activity. Which of the following concepts describes the procedures for preserving the legal ownership history of evidence from the security incident?

   A. Damage control

   B. Audit trail

   C. Escalation

   D. Chain of custody

4. A network administrator has discovered the company's File Transfer Protocol (FTP) server has been hacked. Which of the following items would be the most important to collect and preserve as evidence?

   A. Server memory dump

   B. List of user accounts

   C. List of files on the FTP server

   D. Access activity log

5. You have been contacted by your company's CEO after she received a personalized but suspicious e-mail message from the company's bank asking for detailed personal and financial information. After reviewing the message, you determine that it did not originate from the legitimate bank. Which of the following security issues does this scenario describe?

   A. Dumpster diving

   B. Phishing

   C. Whaling

   D. Vishing

6. During your user awareness training, which of the following actions would be the best security practice for your users to help prevent malware installation from phishing messages?

   A. Forwarding suspicious messages to other users

   B. Not clicking links in suspicious messages

   C. Checking e-mail headers

   D. Replying to a message to check its legitimacy

7. After recent security issues with certain types of development documents being leaked out of the organization, what security policy can you implement to help improve user awareness of what types of documents can be transmitted outside of the organization?

   A. Document security classifications

   B. Clean desk policy

   C. Tailgating policy

   D. Anti-phishing policy

8. A web server recently crashed because of a denial-of-service attack against it. Based on the order of volatility, which of the following pieces of evidence would you preserve first?

   A. Website data

   B. Screen capture of crash error message

   C. Printout of web access logs

   D. Web server configuration files

9. After collecting several log files as evidence for a hacking incident against your web server, what should you do to help preserve the legal integrity of the logs to prove they have not been tampered with?

    A. Print a hard copy of the log files.

    B. Encrypt the logs.

    C. Perform a hash on each file.

    D. Save the logs to backup tape.

10. Threat actors are generally categorized by which of the following? (Choose all that apply.)

    A. Intent

    B. Resources

    C. Internal/external

    D. Nationality

REVIEW ANSWERS

1. **D**   A legal hold is a formal directive from legal counsel that puts the organization into data collection and preservation mode in the event of pending litigation, investigation, audit, or other circumstance where the data may be required.

2. **A**   Any current logs and memory dumps should be saved to make sure you have evidence of all activity during the time of the incident. If you reboot the server to get it functioning again, you can lose valuable log data or data residing in memory.

3. **D**   Keeping a chain of custody requires all evidence to be properly labeled with information on who secured and validated the evidence. This can ensure the evidence wasn't tampered with in any way since the time it was collected.

4. **D**   The activity log will show what times the attacker was performing hacking activities and what those activities were. This evidence might be able to be used in court to help prosecute the attacker if he is caught.

5. **C**   Whaling is a type of phishing attack that is targeted at a specific high-level user. The victim is usually a high-profile member of the organization who has much more critical information to lose than the average user. The messages used in the attack are usually crafted and personalized toward the specific victim user.

6. B To help prevent malware from being installed, it is a best practice to make your users aware that they should never click links in a suspicious message. The link can take the user to a malicious website that could automatically install malware on their computer through their web browser.

7. A By classifying all your documents, you will inform users as to which types of documents are marked "confidential" and must never be transmitted outside of the organization through e-mail, fax, or other communications. Other document types that do not contain confidential information can be marked as "public" and freely distributed.

8. B When collecting forensic data evidence, be aware that certain types of data are more volatile over time. In this case, the error message on the web server should be captured as a screenshot before the server is restarted. The message will disappear, and unless it appears in the logs, you may have no other record of it.

9. C You must be able to prove that the log files have not been tampered with since they were captured. You can create an MD5 hash of the file immediately after the incident to create a "fingerprint" for a message that you can compare to the original file at a later time.

10. A B C Threat actors are generally bucketed using the following attributes: level of sophistication, resources/funding, intent/motivation, and whether they are internal or external in nature.

Business Continuity and Disaster Recovery

	NEWBIE	SOME EXPERIENCE	EXPERT
ETA	3 hours	2 hours	1 hour

Business continuity and disaster recovery constitute a subject often avoided by management personnel because of the additional costs and time required to put together a disaster recovery plan (DRP) that adds little value to the company's bottom line. Unfortunately, if a company is unprepared for natural disasters such as fires, floods, earthquakes, and tornadoes, as well as unnatural disasters such as vandalism, theft, hacking, and malware outbreaks, and a disaster strikes, the final costs of implementing no disaster protection could prove fatal.

The most difficult task is analyzing your company's weaknesses to such risks and identifying the impact each risk will have on your business operations. When it becomes obvious that even a small-scale disaster can send your operations into a tailspin, you must begin planning an overall disaster recovery plan to prevent a disaster from fully impacting your ability to function as a business. A disaster recovery plan must be created so that representatives from each department know exactly what to do if an emergency occurs. Representatives must be trained thoroughly and the procedures documented carefully, and the plan should be tested at least once a year, or whenever company changes require alterations to the original procedures.

Travel Advisory

A disaster recovery plan is a step-by-step plan for recovering your networks and systems after a disaster. It is essential to protect employees, the company's ability to operate, its facilities and equipment, and its vital data.

Protecting your data from corruption, lack of access, or data loss is vital in maintaining your ability to provide critical services to your organization and your customers. As part of a company's overall information security, disaster preparedness, and business continuity plans, redundancy planning is concerned with preventing your systems from downtime caused by failed equipment, interrupted communications, and environmental issues.

Two important steps in this process are identifying critical business processes and their associated systems and components. It is impossible to secure all systems 100 percent; understanding this, be sure that your organization identifies and prioritizes those processes, systems, and components to ensure adequate contingency planning. The key components of redundancy planning are high availability and fault tolerance. Maintaining high availability is the premier goal of most businesses that guarantee access to data and provide host services and content that must be always available to the customer. Fault tolerance defines how able your system is to recover from software or hardware errors and failure. For example, a server with only one hard drive and one power supply isn't fault tolerant: if the power supply fails, the entire server will be rendered useless because there's no power to the system. Similarly, if your file server's hard drive crashes and is unrecoverable, all data on that hard drive will be lost. Fault-tolerant systems are important for maintaining business continuity. This chapter describes the components of business continuity and disaster planning, including the disaster recovery plan, fault tolerance and redundancy, backup policies, and the importance of environmental controls in an organization's security strategy.

Objective 3.01
CompTIA Security+
Objective 5.2

Explain Concepts of Business Continuity and Disaster Recovery

Any disaster, however rare, can be fatal to a business that doesn't prepare for the emergency. Even interruptions on a small scale, such as system or network outages, can quickly incur huge financial costs and a damaged reputation. Many studies have shown that most businesses that suffer a service interruption lasting more than one week are never able to recover and, consequently, go out of business. Critical to a company's preparedness is having a proper business continuity and disaster recovery plan to ensure continuity of operations.

Select the Appropriate Control to Meet the Goals of Security

Ensuring data protection and business continuity in the event of a disaster requires you to utilize these major concepts of information security. Note that these concepts run throughout most, if not all, of the objectives covered within this book. It is important that you consider how you would apply these concepts within any context.

- **Confidentiality** Confidentiality prevents sensitive and private data from being intercepted or read by unauthorized users. Data must be protected in its primary storage location, when it is backed up, and when it is transmitted to another user over a network. Ensuring confidentiality often entails including encryption and access control measures. Confidentiality is important for a BCP/DRP because of the necessity to keep sensitive data protected in the event of a disaster and its subsequent recovery. For example, you could encrypt backup tapes for storage and offsite transport to enforce confidentiality during BCP and DRP operations.

Travel Assistance

For details on encryption, see Chapter 4. Access controls are covered within Chapter 6.

- **Integrity**   Integrity ensures that your data is consistent and never modified by unauthorized persons or manipulated in any intentional or accidental manner. Integrity also includes nonrepudiation methods to ensure information can be trusted from the supposed sender. While data integrity includes the use of proper authentication and authorization security techniques for protecting against data manipulation, it also includes redundancy planning and fault-tolerant systems that protect data from corruption. Common methods of ensuring integrity are hashing, digital signatures, and certificates. To facilitate a BCP/DRP, you should ensure data integrity on backup media through regular testing and validation procedures. In the event of an emergency restore, you should be able to trust that the data is exactly what is expected.

Travel Assistance

For details on hashing, digital signatures, and certificates, consult Chapters 4 and 5.

- **Availability**   Availability ensures that your systems and networks are always operational and providing service to users, minimizing downtime when patching or scanning. Your organization's networks and data must be available to authorized users as required with a minimal amount of interruption. Your disaster recovery and business continuity plans make sure, using redundancy and fault tolerance, that interruptions do not happen, and that if there is downtime, it can be resolved very quickly. In a BCP/DRP, for example, availability might be ensured through the implementation of a cold, warm, or hot site, or through an agreement with an alternate organization.

- **Safety**   Safety first ensures that personnel will be safe, and then that organizational priorities (as listed within disaster recovery and associated plans) will be carried out. Safety considerations often coincide with physical controls such as fencing, lighting, locks, and closed-circuit televisions (CCTV). Documentation contributing to personnel safety includes escape plans and escape routes. Finally, testing should include regular drills and controls testing. Safety in a disaster situation is paramount and can be implemented through fail-safe measures such as doors opening outward for easier personnel rescue and using safer fire suppression methods, such as water.

Travel Assistance	
More information on physical controls is included within Chapter 6.	

Types of Disasters

Many types of disasters can befall a company. Many are small and inconvenient, affecting only a certain part of the company or only one network server. They might affect only communications or software applications. Larger disasters can be devastating, causing the destruction of most or all the company's physical facility. This section describes the different types of disaster scenarios that can affect an organization's operations.

Natural

The types of natural disasters that can occur depend on the location of the company facilities; natural disasters can be the most devastating emergency to affect a business. You must be aware of the types of natural disasters that can happen in your specific geographic area. A fire, flood, earthquake, tornado, or hurricane can destroy your building and its infrastructure within minutes. The only way the company can be truly protected is if its data is regularly backed up and sent to an offsite location. Your company furniture and computer equipment can be replaced relatively quickly, but sensitive company data collected over many years can't.

Human Error and Sabotage

Something as simple as a mistakenly deleted file can cause a company much grief if the data in that file is critical to the business operation. A spilled cup of coffee can render a server unusable within seconds. Human errors and mistakes can be expected and are much more common than natural disasters. Vandalism and sabotage, however, can be quite unexpected but cause great damage. Theft or malicious destruction of company equipment by a disgruntled employee can cause as much damage as any natural disaster. The need for access controls and physical security is emphasized with these types of disasters.

Network and Hacking Attacks

Cyber theft and vandalism are increasingly annoying and dangerous problems for companies, especially those whose business is Internet related. When a company is permanently connected to the Internet, the door is open for unauthorized users to attempt to gain access to company resources. Some malicious hackers simply try to gain access to a system for fun. More-malicious unauthorized users might cause widespread damage within the company's network if they gain access. Some attacks could come from within the network. A security professional will need to analyze threats coming from both outside and inside the network.

Viruses

Computer viruses are special programs able to replicate themselves, and they often perform malicious activities on networks, servers, and personal computers. Viruses can be extremely destructive, causing massive network outages, computer crashes, and corruption or loss of data. Once one computer is infected with the virus, it can quickly spread to other computers and servers on the network. E-mail–based viruses can spread quickly in a short amount of time. Protection against viruses includes the use of special antivirus software at both the personal computer level and the server level, as well as user education about computer virus prevention.

Travel Advisory

Hacking and viruses are probably the most common disasters that befall a business. An e-mail virus can spread so fast it can overload your e-mail servers within a matter of minutes after initial infection.

Recovery Plans

Although the chances of a large disaster, whatever the cause, interrupting or halting business operations are slim, all companies should be prepared for disastrous events. The overall business continuity plan (BCP) is a detailed document that provides an initial analysis of the risks involved to the business because of a disaster, the potential business impact, a disaster recovery plan for restoring full operations after a disaster strikes, and a continuity of operations plan for best continuing operations if disrupted from normal activities by any situation, from a simple outage to an attack. The specific purpose of a disaster recovery plan is to prepare your company with a step-by-step plan to recover your networks and systems. The plan is a technologically oriented part of the overall business continuity plan, detailing specific steps to take to return and recover systems to an operational state.

The process of creating a business continuity plan includes the following phases:

- Creating a disaster recovery team
- Performing a risk analysis
- Performing a business impact analysis
- Performing a privacy impact assessment
- Creating a disaster recovery plan
- Preparing documentation
- Testing the plan
- After-action reporting

Disaster Recovery Team

A *disaster recovery team* is responsible for creating and executing business continuity activities and a disaster recovery plan that outlines the goals for restoring company operations and functionality as quickly as possible following a disaster. The team is also available to provide for the safety and support of the rest of the company's personnel and the protection of company property.

The team should include members from all departments, including management. Including all areas of the company's operations is important because each department has its own objectives and goals, depending on its function. Disaster recovery duties should be included in the job description of each department, even though these duties go over and above regular duties. Designated backup team members should also be assigned in case an original member isn't available to perform the appropriate function.

In a disaster, each team member is responsible for certain priorities and tasks, which could include coordination of other department personnel and contact with outside emergency agencies and equipment and service vendors.

The bulk of the work will be the responsibility of the IT staff, which needs to coordinate the creation of a communications and networking infrastructure, as well as restore all system functionality, including the restoration of lost data.

Risk Analysis

A *risk analysis* identifies the areas of your facility and computer network that are vulnerable to certain types of threats, including disasters. The entire business operation of the company must be broken down and analyzed so the impact of a disaster on a critical business function can be ascertained. At that time, a risk assessment of current mitigations (for example, hardware, software, and policies) should be conducted to determine their adequacy in relation to those threats.

As part of your risk analysis, you examine and identify any areas of your operations that stand out as a single point of failure. For example, you may realize that although you have several redundant web servers that process customer orders, the back-end database is located on a single server. If that single server were to fail or were damaged in a disaster, your web servers would not be able to connect to the database, causing all customer transactions to halt. Through this process, you identify areas where you can replace single points of failure with redundant and fault-tolerant systems.

A risk analysis evaluates the potential impact any type of disaster could have on your company's infrastructure. You need to analyze all possible scenarios in full. For example, in case a flood strikes where your main company building is located, the facility must be carefully examined for areas that would be affected by this disaster. Similar analysis must be made for other potential natural disasters, such as earthquakes and fire, and non-natural disasters, such as software and hardware failure, network attacks, and virus attacks.

Create or obtain diagrams of the facility layout, such as building blueprints, seating plans, network cabling maps, and hardware and software inventories. The effect of each disaster scenario should be more easily ascertained with the aid of these diagrams. When you finish, you'll have a detailed document outlining the possible risks for each type of disaster that might occur. Using this information, you can formulate a business impact analysis that will show how those risks can affect your business functionality.

Business Impact Analysis

A *business impact analysis* outlines your most critical functions and how they'll be affected during a disaster. The analysis will examine the loss of revenue, legal obligations, and customer service interruption that can arise as the result of a disaster. Your most important business functions should be prioritized so that during the disaster recovery process, they receive the attention they need to become operational before any noncritical aspects of the business. Your leadership must take a hard look at what the *Mission Essential Functions (MEFs)* are, meaning those functions that are the most important to complete. For example, if your company is in the business of logistics, the functions of distribution are more critical than, say, the function of employee morale and wellness. While that may sound harsh, getting the distribution systems up and running after a disaster is more critical than the intranet portal supporting the company Christmas party.

After you've determined, in rank order, the MEFs, you can then determine the must-have, or critical, systems that support those MEFs. This is where you'll need to take a cold, hard look at what is critical to operations and what is just "nice to have." It is extremely useful to sit down and have a session with the people doing the work; for example, to use the logistics example again, who are the folks watching shipments move from point A to point B? They are the ones who know intimately how they do their jobs and how long they could be without their systems. Don't make the mistake of asking the IT folks how much money they've spent on different systems and using that as your prioritization schema! The on-the-ground truth from the operational personnel will give you the most reliable information for your prioritization.

Exam Tip
Business functions and their associated systems must be prioritized so that in case of a disaster, they'll be made operational before other less-critical functions and systems.

The business impact analysis should also include timelines on how long it will take to get the company operational again if a disaster occurs. The resources, equipment, and personnel required should be carefully detailed—especially the ability to recover and restore vital company information from backups.

Most important will be examining the total financial loss incurred through certain types of disasters. This isn't only the cost of lost equipment; it's the totality of the loss of life, other property, productivity, and reputation, as well as any injury. If the company isn't prepared, it might not survive a disaster that completely halts its operations. This information can be provided to other managers, who might help fund and organize a disaster recovery plan, based on the statistics of the impact of a disaster. Many companies don't like spending the time or money on disaster recovery, but when the cost of the impact is analyzed and calculated, the ability to be prepared for a disaster will quickly pay for itself when a disaster strikes.

Privacy Impact Assessment

A *privacy impact assessment (PIA)* begins with *a privacy threshold analysis (PTA)*, done to determine if a system is using privacy information, or connecting to one that is. If that is the case, a PIA is required. Your privacy office will begin the process of determining what type of data is being stored, how it is being stored, where it is being stored, and what would trigger a privacy issue. Systems that require a PIA should incorporate increased controls to mitigate the risks of processing and storing privacy data. Keep in mind that different types of privacy data, such as PII and PHI (even different types of PHI), often require additional controls, which should be identified during the PIA. Normally, laws and regulatory guidance dictate how the PIA should be conducted for privacy data as well as the controls that must be in place.

Disaster Recovery and IT Contingency Plans

You must devise disaster recovery and IT contingency plans to establish the procedures that can quickly recover critical systems after a service disruption. Specific tasks are defined and prioritized to aid in the process and define clear objectives that must be met during the recovery phase.

Responsibilities must be clearly defined for those important individuals participating in the recovery as part of the disaster recovery team. Tasks should be divided and assigned to the appropriate people and departments. Everyone must be trained on the specific procedures, and these procedures must be properly documented. Team leaders must be established, and central authorities can guide the recovery process through each of its critical steps.

You also need to decide which aspect of the business is the most critical and must be up and running first if a disaster occurs. Different departments in the company have unique objectives and priorities, but certain functions can be delayed if they don't immediately impact the company's ability to function.

The most important part of the company to get operational is basic communications, such as desk phones, mobile phones, networking connectivity, and e-mail. Until these communication lines are functional, the company's ability to coordinate the disaster recovery effort will be greatly reduced, causing much confusion and chaos. Business-critical items should come next, such as file servers, database servers, and Internet servers that run the company's main applications or anything specifically needed by customers. Most of these responsibilities come under the IT department's contingency plan.

The company's ability to restore full operations as quickly as possible depends on the efficiency with which objectives and goals, outlined in the disaster recovery plans, are met.

Your disaster recovery plans must also contain information on succession planning for key employees. Depending on the type of disaster, specific employees might not be available or could be directly affected by the disaster. You must identify key positions that can be filled in by other employees who can take over and execute the same responsibilities. These positions can be very technical in nature, such as a network administrator, or at the executive level to provide direction during a disaster.

Documentation

Each phase of your recovery plans should be carefully documented, and the resulting document should be readily available to all members of the disaster recovery team. The document should also be safely stored in both hard copy and software form to reduce the potential for damage or loss. In case of a real disaster, a lack of documentation will cause nothing but chaos because no one will know how to get all aspects of the company running again, especially during a stressful and frantic time.

The disaster recovery plan must be precise and detailed so that anyone can follow the instructions without requiring further clarification. Each person on the disaster recovery team will have clear responsibilities and duties that must be performed in the most efficient manner possible.

The plan should include the following items:

- **Notification lists**   A list of people and businesses to notify in case of a disaster.
- **Contact information**   Phone numbers and contact information for employees, vendors, data recovery agencies, and offsite facilities.
- **Networking and facilities diagrams**   Blueprints and diagrams of all networking and facilities infrastructure so it can be re-created on the new site.
- **System configurations**   Configuration information for all servers, applications, and networking equipment.
- **Backup restoration procedures**   Step-by-step information on how to restore data from the backup media.
- **Backup and licensing media**   To reinstall the servers, you will need the operating system software, the appropriate license keys, and the backup media. These should be stored in a safe location so that they are ready and available during the installation process.

Finally, copies of the disaster recovery plan should be stored and secured both onsite and in an offsite facility—especially any designated alternative company site. If a physical disaster strikes your main facility, the plan will be useless if it's destroyed along with the building.

Exam Tip

Be aware of the types of information that should be documented in your disaster recovery plans.

Testing

To complete your disaster recovery plan, you must fully test it to ensure all parts of the plan work as they should. Re-creating a disaster without affecting the current operations of your company might be difficult, but some form of test should be performed at least once a year. One common type of test is a tabletop exercise, which requires the involved parties to sit around a—you guessed it—table and step through a scenario to discern weaknesses in the plan. Conducting this type of test will make participants more comfortable in the event they must conduct the plan, almost like a muscle memory.

Most disaster recovery tests involve the choice of a scenario, such as a fire in a certain part of the building. In the test, your disaster recovery team must consult the recovery plan documentation and execute it accordingly. Depending on the size of the company, it might be feasible to involve only certain departments, but the IT department should always be included because its main responsibilities are the network infrastructure and data recovery. During the testing, every phase should be fully documented using a checklist. Any exceptions or problems encountered during the procedure should be thoroughly documented.

When the test has been completed, the original disaster recovery plan should be reviewed for any procedures that didn't work correctly or that need to be modified because of the test. The plan should be updated with any new information emerging from the testing. Any changes to the existing facilities or infrastructure should initiate a review of the current disaster recovery procedures. Any necessary changes to the recovery procedures should be made immediately to reflect the new environment.

After-Action Reporting

After you have completed your testing, documenting your findings—good and bad—in an after-action report (AAR) allows you to give an honest assessment of the testing, detail the areas that should be improved upon, and the path forward for filling any gaps. Often called a "lessons learned" report, the AAR should be focused on measurement and improvement. Were organizational policies sufficient? Were they followed? What are recommendations for improvement?

Execute Disaster Recovery and Continuity of Operations Plans and Procedures

Disaster recovery and continuity of operations planning are extremely important in preventing downtime for your organization in the event of equipment or communications failure. Your system's ability to recover from a disaster is greatly dependent on the facilities and equipment available if your main facility is heavily damaged or destroyed. Backup equipment and facilities are vital elements in planning for recovery, and each should be examined for both onsite and offsite strategies.

High availability, redundancy planning, and fault tolerance are extremely important factors in ensuring business continuity, and they are implemented at the system and network levels to protect the confidentiality and integrity of data as well as to maintain data availability.

High Availability and Redundancy Planning

The ability to provide uninterrupted service consistently is the goal of maintaining a high-availability system. This initially requires that you identify systems that need to provide services always. Answer the following questions to help you in planning for high-availability systems:

- What is the monetary cost of an extended service downtime?
- What is the cost to a customer relationship that can occur because of an extended service downtime directly affecting that customer?
- Which services must be available always? Rank them in order of priority.

If your company hosts several services required by customers, these services should be given higher priority than your own systems because the service level promised to customers must be maintained always.

Service Levels

Many companies measure their ability to provide services as a *service level*. For example, a web-server-hosting company might promise 99 percent service availability for the systems and services it hosts. The other 1 percent of the time, the systems might be unavailable because of maintenance, equipment failure, or network downtime.

Local Lingo

service level   Specifies in measurable terms the level of service to be received, such as the percentage of time when services are available. Many Internet service providers (ISPs) provide a service level agreement to guarantee customers a minimum level of service. Some IT departments now provide a measured service level to the rest of the company.

The most common examples of servers and services that require high availability and high service levels include the following:

- **Internet servers**   These include Internet services, such as web and File Transfer Protocol (FTP) servers. These types of servers usually require that the information and data stored on them be always available.

- **E-mail**   E-mail is the most commonly used Internet service because all users need and use it. Therefore, mail servers and gateways must maintain high levels of service availability.

- **Networking**   As the backbone of all computer communications, the networking equipment that provides the infrastructure for private and public networks must be always available.

- **File servers**   File servers house all data needed by the users. Without access to this data, users can't perform their job functions.

- **Database servers**   Database servers are typically required as back-end servers to web servers and other applications that use database transactions. Data stored on database servers, just like that stored on file servers, must be always available.

- **Telecom**   Even in an Internet-centric organization, phone and other voice telecommunications systems are still services that require high availability. In the event of a disaster, your voice communications will be of the highest critical priority in order to coordinate disaster recovery efforts.

Reliability Factors

Several industry-standard terms are used in the IT world to refer to the reliability of services and hardware products. These terms are often used in maintenance contracts that identify how long it takes a manufacturer or a service company to repair a failed service or server. They can also refer to service levels provided by a company to customers depending on their services, such as a web hosting company that hosts and services thousands of websites for many customers.

- **Mean time to restore (MTTR)**   Mean time to restore is the average time from the moment of a service failure until when the service is restored. For spare parts for a failed server hard drive, your service contract may state that the web hosting company can provide a new hard drive within four hours, but in other cases, this could be 24 to 48 hours. Also, they may promise that for any failed website or service, the mean time to restore is 60 minutes.

- **Mean time to failure (MTTF)**   This is the time that a device is expected to last in regular service. For example, when you're comparing component prices, one device may have a lower initial price and a lower MTTF, which could mean that your company spends more in the end replacing components if the lower-cost device is chosen for implementation. MTTF assumes the component will *not* be repaired.

- **Mean time between failures (MTBF)**   This is the average time a specific device is expected to work until it fails. A mathematical formula is used to determine how long a specific product should last based on previous measurements of failure rates. For example, a mechanical or electrical device such as a hard drive or power supply may have an MTBF rating of 500,000 hours; after that, it is more likely to fail. MTBF assumes components will be replaced or repaired upon failure.

- **Recovery time objective (RTO)**   This is the maximum amount of time that is considered tolerable for a service or certain business function to be unavailable. Organizations use this as a key factor in their ability to provide specific guaranteed service levels. Different functions and services may have different recovery time objectives. For example, it may be determined that a company website from which customers purchase their products is of the highest importance, and the recovery time objective is set as 60 minutes. These objectives are typically defined in the business impact analysis of the business continuity and disaster recovery plan.

- **Recovery point objective (RPO)**   This is the maximum accepted amount of lost data due to an outage or disaster. This is defined in terms of time, such as one hour. For example, if a database server fails, up to one hour of data can be considered an acceptable loss. These policies are defined in the business impact analysis of your business continuity and disaster recovery plans. This objective can help define other security policies, such as the backup frequency, to make sure that a data backup occurs at least every hour to preserve the RPO.

Spare Equipment Redundancy

Most disasters and disruptions are localized in nature and typically involve only one room or one piece of equipment. Failed hardware, such as blown power supplies, damaged network cabling, failed hard drives, and broken tape backup drives, is the most common type of service interruption. Having spare hardware onsite to fix these small problems is vital to handling these smaller disruptions quickly. Many companies have vendor maintenance contracts that require the vendor to replace failed hardware, but in case of an emergency, the spare parts might not be delivered for many hours or even days. It's critical for hardware components that are commonly prone to failure to be switched quickly with an onsite spare.

The following spare components should always be kept onsite:

- Hard drives
- Redundant array of independent disks (RAID) controllers
- Small Computer System Interface (SCSI) controllers
- Hard-drive cabling
- Memory
- Central processing units (CPUs)
- Network cards
- Keyboards/mice
- Video cards
- Monitors
- Power supplies
- Network switches, hubs, and routers
- Phone sets

It is also highly recommended that you have a contact list on hand for the manufacturers/vendors of your components in the event a replacement part needs to be ordered.

Redundant Servers   In high-availability environments such as e-commerce and financial websites, where servers must be up and running 24 hours a day and seven days a week, a downed server can cause a company severe financial damage. Customers will be unable to make purchases online while the server is down, and critical stock trades or financial transactions cannot take place. In these environments, redundant servers are installed that will take over in the event the primary server is unavailable. For example, an organization with a critical web server can install a secondary identical web server that can be swapped with the primary if the primary is down. If redundant servers are not running concurrently, having spare servers and workstations on hand means that if the primary server goes down, the failed file server hardware can be quickly replaced and the data restored from backup. This is often the preferred method for smaller organizations that do not have the resources or budget to run live redundant systems.

> **Exam Tip**
>
> High availability ensures that a service, such as a web or database server, is always available. Redundancy via live or spare replacement servers is a recommended method of ensuring availability.

Clustering   For more advanced high-availability purposes, the use of *clustering* technology enables you to use several servers to perform the services of one. Clustering greatly enhances load balancing, as the resources of all the servers can be used to perform the same task as one server. For fault tolerance purposes, if one system goes down, one of the other servers in the cluster can take over seamlessly without any interruption to the clients.

Two primary types of clusters are used: active/active and active/passive. *Active/active* means that both servers in the cluster are up and running and actively responding to requests. In the event one server is unavailable, no loss of availability occurs because the other server is still actively responding to requests. In an *active/passive* arrangement, one server is actively responding to requests while the other server acts as a live standby. In the event the active server is unavailable, the other passive server can be triggered into becoming the active server and begin responding to requests.

For major disaster recovery scenarios, failover systems and redundant servers can be kept in buildings of other company locations. For example, a company operating in Los Angeles might have another facility operating in New York. This allows the servers in New York to take over the services offered by the Los Angeles servers if LA suffers an interruption or disaster.

Load Balancing   *Load balancing* simply allows administrators to balance the load traversing a network across several resources in a distributed manner. Load balancing is often used with websites that receive a large amount of traffic, ensuring that the web server is not a single point of failure. Applying the concept of load balancing allows for a failover mechanism in the event one server is lost due to mishap or disaster. This can be implemented in several ways, including clustering.

System Configuration Backups   The use of backups in a business continuity sense involves not only the backup of important data, but also backing up the system files and configuration settings of your server and network equipment.

When equipment failure causes the loss of your server, you not only lose the data and services housed on that server, but you lose all your system settings and configuration as well. Depending on the type of server, these configuration settings can be complex and can take many hours, or even days, to restore. For example, an e-mail server is usually configured with many options and settings that are unique to your location. If the server has failed or is destroyed and needs to be rebuilt, you'll need to reinstall the operating system (OS), install your e-mail server applications, and configure the system properly before you can restore your mail files that were backed up. If you didn't back up your system files, you'll need to recall and enter your system settings manually, which can take up too much time when a high-availability server is down.

Most modern backup applications have disaster recovery options that save important elements of the OS and application configuration files so they can be instantly restored in case of a disaster. If you're recovering a server, you need only install the OS and the required media device drivers for your backup media device to retrieve the rest of your server files and system configuration from the backup media.

Redundant Internet Lines   It might be surprising to learn that many organizations rely on only one ISP to host their connections to the Internet. If any communications issues occur with the Internet line or the ISP itself, the organization's communications are instantly crippled. No users will be able to access the Internet or e-mail, and for companies that have deployed Voice over IP (VoIP) telephony applications, the telephones will not be operational. It is difficult to think that so much time and money can be spent on redundant servers and equipment, while no thought is put into communications redundancy.

It is a best practice to have two or even three completely different ISP services and connections to provide a backup line of communication or to run concurrently with your current ISP line. In the event one of the ISPs or lines goes down, you will still be able to communicate to the Internet via the redundant connection. The ISP lines must be from different companies, or else your supposedly redundant Internet lines will be going to the same point of failure at the same ISP, and if the central router fails at the ISP, both your connections to the Internet will be down.

Many organizations also use redundant ISPs to provide some bandwidth control. For example, critical applications and services can be routed to one ISP, while general company connectivity (such as e-mail or web browsing) can be directed to the second ISP to ensure critical applications receive the maximum bandwidth they require from their own dedicated Internet connection.

Alternate Site Redundancy

In the event of a physical disaster such as a fire or a flood at your main company site, or even a disruption in power or Internet service, you need to plan for alternate facilities (or, in some cases, alternate capabilities) to get your company operational again. In some cases, your original server and networking equipment could be damaged or destroyed, and then a new infrastructure must be created at a new site. For a company with no alternate site in its disaster recovery plan, this could mean many weeks before a facility is secured and new equipment is set up in the new building. The purpose of an alternate site is to have a facility already secured and, in some cases, already populated with a network and server infrastructure to minimize downtime. The choice of alternate sites will come down to how time-sensitive your company's product or services are and how fast you need to be operational again.

Is important to consider where you place your alternate site geographically. For example, for truly mission-critical systems, it is better to have the site be in an area that is not too close to an ocean (missing hurricanes) and not prone to tornadoes, flooding, or other damaging natural weather scenarios. Take, for example, the Cheyenne Mountain Complex in Colorado Springs, Colorado. It's built into the side of the mountain, and its natural attributes, along with a great deal of redundancy that was planned in, is designed to allow missions to withstand any number of natural or man-made disasters.

Distance from your main site is also important consideration, for several reasons. In the event of a crisis, you will want to have maximum speed for your alternate processing, and longer distances make this more difficult. Therefore, many cloud providers have multiple locations that they can fail over to across a large geographical area. Also, it is recommended that an alternate site be at least five miles from any "prime" targets of terrorist activity, such as military installations or major government buildings. Finally, not sharing the same utility grid is smart.

Legal implications are also an issue to be considered, with data sovereignty being one of the most important considerations. Because different nations have different laws governing what can be done with data processed within their borders, it is important to take those requirements into consideration when choosing where to locate an alternate site. For example, the European Union, which encompasses many of the most important data processing centers in the world, has different data processing standards than the United States, with penalties for companies that do not comply. A multinational company that chooses to have a European alternate site may find that it is not prepared to protect the data to the standards set by the European Union. This could set a company up for big problems if it does not comply with the data handling and processing requirements. It truly is a tricky time to be a multinational company that relies heavily on data, especially privacy data.

Alternate Business Practices

Not all alternate considerations are technical; you should also consider people and processes. For example, if you have a system that processes contracting data and it goes offline, an alternate business process could be writing contracts by hand, having them legally reviewed, and then entering them into the system once it's brought back up. Most functions can be done without their information systems. It may be annoying, or even painful; however, understanding how the business can continue, even in the most degraded or disrupted conditions, can mean the difference between recovering the business and closing shop for good.

Hot Site   A *hot site* is a facility that's ready to be operational immediately when the primary site becomes unavailable. All equipment and networking infrastructure the company requires are already in place and can be activated quickly. The equipment duplicates the setup installed in the original building. The hot site facility is usually provided by another company, which hosts your company's equipment. Hot sites should be tested frequently to ensure the switchover runs smoothly and quickly. This is an expensive solution, but for companies that offer critical services, the costs of losing money and customers during an extended downtime warrant the expense of a hot site.

Warm Site   A *warm site* is like a hot site but without most of the duplicate servers and computers that would be needed to facilitate an immediate switchover. The warm site is there to provide an immediate facility with some minimal networking in place. In the event of a disaster, a company will transport its own equipment to the new facility, or if the original equipment is destroyed with the facility, new equipment can be purchased and moved there. A warm site could take several days to restore and transfer data to and bring the business back to full operation, so this option makes sense for companies that don't offer time-critical services. This is the most widely used alternate site option because of its relatively lower price compared to hot sites, as well as its flexibility. The disadvantages of a warm site are that it's not immediately available after a disaster and isn't easily tested.

Cold Site   A *cold site* merely offers an empty facility with some basic features, such as wiring and some environmental protection, but no equipment. This is the least expensive option, but this also means when a disaster strikes, it might be several weeks before the facility and equipment are ready for operation, as almost all the networking and server infrastructure will need to be built and configured.

Exam Tip
Be aware of the advantages and disadvantages of the different types of alternate sites, depending on your environment.

Fault Tolerance

To protect your systems and network equipment and to provide redundancy for maintaining high-availability service, you must implement *fault-tolerant* systems. To make a system fault tolerant, it should contain several redundant components that will allow it to continue functioning if an equipment failure occurs. For example, a file server can be configured with two network cards. In case one network card fails, network communications can continue uninterrupted through the second network card. To ensure data integrity, it isn't enough to implement redundant hardware components, such as power supplies and network cards. The use of fault-tolerant RAID systems is required to allow multiple copies of the same data to be saved across multiple disk media so that data won't be lost if one of the hard drives fails.

Local Lingo
RAID   Stands for *redundant array of independent disks* and defines the concept of using several separate hard drives to create one logical drive. If one of the drives fails, the system can rebuild the information using the remaining disks.

Some fault tolerance concepts must be understood before implementation:

- **Hot swap** Refers to the ability to insert and remove hardware while the entire system is still running. Most types of hardware require that the system be shut down before components are removed or inserted. Hard drives in RAID systems are the most common type of hot-swap device.

- **Warm swap** Refers to the ability to insert and remove hardware while a system is in a suspended state. Although less flexible than a hot-swap device, warm swap means you needn't shut the entire server down to replace hardware components. When the swap is complete, the server resumes its normal operations. Although services are shut down during the suspend period, time is saved by not having to reboot the entire system.

- **Hot spare** Refers to a device already installed in the system that can take over at any time when the primary device fails. There's no need to physically insert or remove a hot-spare device.

The following sections outline the types of system components that can be made fault tolerant.

Hard Drives

Hard drives are partly mechanical in nature. This makes them one of the most common components prone to failure on a server. The hard drives contain all the data, and if the hard drive fails, that data can be irretrievably lost.

> **Travel Advisory**
>
> If a hard drive fails or its data is corrupted, the information it contains can sometimes be retrieved by special hard-drive recovery specialists. However, this recovery process can be both time consuming and expensive.

The most common method of hard-drive redundancy is to use a RAID system. RAID allows data to be spread across two or more hard drives, so if one hard drive fails, the data can be retrieved from the existing hard drives.

RAID can be implemented via hardware or software. Hardware RAID is based on a disk controller that controls the redundancy process across several physical hard drives. Software RAID relies on operating system kernel

TABLE 3.1	RAID Levels	
RAID Level	**Minimum Number of Hard Drives**	**Characteristics**
0	2	Striping only, no fault tolerance
1	2	Disk mirroring
3	3	Disk striping with a parity disk
5	3	Disk striping, distributed parity
6	4	Disk striping, double distributed parity
0+1	4	Disk striping with mirroring

processes to control the RAID redundancy process, and although less expensive, it requires much more CPU processing power to manage the RAID process, and a software problem could put your data at risk compared to a dedicated hardware solution.

Mirroring the contents of one hard drive on another is called *RAID 1*. Several RAID levels can be implemented, depending on the number of disks you have and the importance of the information being stored. Other RAID techniques include *striping*, which spreads the contents of a logical hard drive across several physical drives and includes parity information to help rebuild the data. If one of the hard drives fails, parity information is used to reconstruct the data. Most RAID systems use hot-swap drives, which can be inserted and removed while the system is still running. To increase the fault tolerance of a RAID system, redundant RAID controllers can be installed to remove the disk controller as a single point of failure. Table 3.1 describes the most common RAID levels and their characteristics.

Power Supplies

Because of their electrical nature, power supplies are another important common computer component prone to failure. As the central source of power for any computer or network device, a power supply that fails can instantly render a critical computer system useless. Most modern servers come with multiple power supplies, which are running as hot spares. If one of the power supplies fails, another will immediately take over without an interruption in service. Some high-end servers have as many as three extra power supplies. Many network devices, such as switches and routers, now come with dual power supplies. Replacing a single power supply on such a small, enclosed device would be difficult.

Network Interface Cards

One of the most overlooked fault-tolerant-capable devices in a server system is the network card. Typically, little thought is given to the scenario of a failed network card. In the real world, losing connectivity to a server is the same as having the server itself crash because the server's resources can't be accessed. Many modern servers now come preinstalled with redundant network cards. Extra network cards can also be used for load balancing, as well as being available to take over if another network card fails.

CPU

Although CPU failure is unlikely, failure is still a scenario that requires fault-tolerance capabilities, especially for high-availability systems. Many large-scale server systems have multiple CPUs for load-balancing purposes to spread the processing across all CPUs. Extra CPUs, however, can also be used for fault tolerance. If a CPU happens to fail, another one in the system can take over.

Uninterruptible Power Supply

Although redundant power supplies can provide fault tolerance in a server if one of the power supplies fails, they can't protect against the total loss of power from the building's main power circuits. When this happens, your entire server will immediately shut down, losing any data that wasn't saved and possibly corrupting existing data. In this case, a battery backup is needed. An *uninterruptible power supply (UPS)* contains a battery that can run a server for a period after a power failure, enabling you to shut down the system safely and save any data.

> **Travel Advisory**
>
> Most UPSs come with software that can configure your server to automatically shut down when it detects the UPS has taken over because of a power failure.

Backups

Critical to a company's preparedness is having a proper backup and disaster recovery plan. Without any sort of data backup, a company risks having its entire data store wiped out forever. In most cases, this would cause the company to go under immediately or face a long rebuilding stage until it can become operational again. A well-defined disaster recovery plan is coupled with a backup strategy. Although the expense and planning for such a large disaster can be costly and time consuming because of the dedication of resources and equipment costs, these must be compared to the costs involved with losing the ability to do business for many days, weeks, or months.

Planning

A good backup strategy must be clearly planned, defined, executed, documented, and tested. The first step in establishing your backup strategy is to draft a plan that covers the following points: the type of data to be backed up, the frequency with which backups will occur, the amount of data, and the retention period for the backups.

Type of Data   Your company's data must be separated into mission-critical data and more constant data that doesn't change much over time. Obviously, the most important data is the information the company requires during its daily business activities, especially if this information is something frequently accessed by customers. For example, a database company will ensure that it fully protects its customers' data. If the company loses that data without any procedure for disaster recovery, its business is essentially lost.

Frequency   Depending on the type of data your company stores, a wide range of backup frequency schedules can be implemented. For example, a transactional database used every day by customers would be considered critical data that must be backed up every day. Other files such as OS and application program files that don't change often can be backed up on a lighter schedule—say, once a week. Backup frequency should depend on the critical nature of the data, as well as the costs involved with losing and re-creating data from the same point in time. Some high-end transactional databases, for example, need to be backed up many times a day because of the high rate of transactions.

Amount of Data   The amount of data to be backed up will have a large bearing on the type of backup strategy you choose. Depending on how much information you need to save daily, you might be unable to perform a completely full backup of all your data every night because of the time it takes to perform the operation. To create a backup plan that can meet your objectives, you must achieve a balance between the type of data and the frequency with which it needs to be backed up. Instead of using full backups, you can try other alternatives, such as performing incremental or differential backups on information that has only recently changed.

Retention   You must decide how long you need to keep backed-up data. Depending on the type of business and the type of data, you might need to archive your backup data for long periods of time so it will be available if you need to perform a restore. Other data might be needed only in the short term and can be deleted after a certain period.

> ## Travel Advisory
>
> The legal policy of some companies is to retain information for a certain period before the information must be destroyed. Check with your legal department to create a policy for backup media retention.

Backup Hardware

Several types of backup hardware and devices are available to suit the needs of the backup strategies of most companies. In the past, the most common type of backup system used was magnetic tape. These can be simple devices that contain only one tape drive, or large jukebox tape libraries with robotic autoloaders. Magnetic tape drives and media are flexible and offer relatively inexpensive storage combined with speed and ease of use.

The vast amount of data storage used by today's hard drives that are into the terabyte (TB) territory and the speed required to back up such a vast amount of data are slowly making tape backups a thing of the past. Today's backup systems use hard drives, including removable hard drives, or network-attached storage (NAS) to provide an array of disks to back up your data quickly over the network to secure storage and backup servers. Backup to tape, however, is still popular as a long-term archiving method.

Backup hardware should be routinely inspected for faults. Because of its mechanical nature, tape backup hardware is more prone to failure than typical electrical devices. Magnetic tape drives should be maintained periodically with a special tape to clean the magnetic heads, which become dirty over time. NAS devices need to be monitored for failing hard drives, which should be immediately replaced.

Backup Types

An important part of your backup strategy is deciding what type of backup you'll perform. Depending on the size of all the data you need to back up daily, a full backup of everything every night might be impossible to do. The amount of backup media required and the time needed to perform the backup can render this option unfeasible. The goal is to achieve the most efficient backup and restoration plan possible, depending on your environment and the type of data to be backed up.

Each file on a computer system contains a special bit of information, called the *archive bit*. When a file is modified or a new file is created, the archive bit is set to indicate the file needs to be backed up. When a backup is performed, the archive bit is either cleared or left as is, depending on the type of backup method chosen.

Full Backup   A *full backup* includes all files selected on a system. A full backup will clear the archive bit of each file after every backup session to indicate the file has been backed up. The advantages of a full backup include the fact that all data you selected is saved during every session, so all your system's data is backed up in full. If you need to restore all the information back on to the server, the recovery time is much shorter because it's saved in a specific backup session and can be restored with a single restore operation. For example, if you perform a full backup on Wednesday night and the server crashes Thursday morning, your data loss will be minimal. The disadvantages of using a full backup are that, depending on the amount of data you have, the backup could take up a large amount of media and the time it takes to perform the backup could intrude on normal working hours, causing network delays and system latency.

Incremental Backup   With an *incremental backup*, only those files that have been modified since the previous full or incremental backup are stored. The archive bit is cleared on those files that are backed up. Incremental backups are much quicker to perform than full backups, and they use up much less space on backup media because you're saving only files that have been changed. The disadvantage of incremental backups is that to restore an entire system, you need to restore the last full backup and every incremental backup since then.

Differential Backup   A *differential backup* saves only files that have been changed since the last full backup. In this method, the archive bit isn't cleared, so with each differential backup, the list of files to save grows larger each day until the next full backup. The advantage of differential backups is that to restore an entire system, you need only the last full backup and the most recent differential backup. The disadvantage is that backups will take more time and use more media with each differential backup that takes place.

Snapshots   *Snapshots* allow you to do just that: take a picture of a known-good point in time that will allow you to roll back to a prior configuration at some point in the future. For example, consider if you have a major software upgrade that could radically change the user experience and ability to conduct daily operations. Being able to take a snapshot and then roll back in the event of an unexpected snafu would be exceptionally helpful. There are many contingencies where having that ability to revert and not lose hours, or even days, of rebuilding a system from scratch could keep a business afloat.

Exam Tip
Be aware of the advantages and disadvantages of each type of backup method, considering the environment and availability requirements.

Media Rotation and Retention

Another important factor in your backup plan is determining the length of time that backup media and their data should be retained. Theoretically, you could save every backup you create forever, but this increases costs because of the large amount of backup media you'll need to purchase on a routine basis. Magnetic tape media usually deteriorate over time, and if you use the same tapes over and over, they'll quickly wear out. The integrity of your backups might be compromised if you continue to use the same tapes. Media rotation and retention policies must be defined to form the most efficient and safe use of your backup media. Several methods can be used for rotation and retention, from simple to the most complex.

Son Backup Method   The *son backup method* is the simplest method to use because it involves performing a full backup every day, using the same backup media each time. This method is used only for small backup requirements. The media can quickly wear out and must consistently be replaced. The son method doesn't allow for archiving, and if you need to perform a restore, you can use only the last backup as a source—so if the file you're looking for was deleted months ago, the data can't be recovered.

Father-Son Backup Method   The *father-son backup method* uses a combination of full and differential or incremental backups on a weekly basis. For example, daily media are used for differential or incremental backups from Monday to Thursday, while Friday or weekend media are used to perform full backups that can be archived away as a weekly backup. This method enables you to retrieve files archived from the previous week using the weekly full backup. Additional backup media can be added to the strategy if further archiving is needed.

Grandfather-Father-Son Backup Method The most common backup strategy is the *grandfather-father-son method.* This method is easy to administer and offers flexible archiving. Like the father-son method, daily backup media are assigned for incremental or differential backups. At the end of the week, a full backup is made, which is kept for one month. At the end of the month, a special monthly backup can be made, which is then kept for one year. This method enables you to archive data for at least a year.

Backup Documentation

Your backup plan should be carefully documented so if the primary backup operator is unavailable, another person can perform the backup operator's functions, such as changing backup media, sending backup media offsite, performing restores, and examining backup log files. The document should outline what systems are backed up, how often they're backed up and by what method, and the location and directories of the data. The documentation should also describe any special media labeling used and contact information for any offsite storage facilities. The documentation should be constantly reviewed and updated when new hardware and software are installed. New systems with new data must be added to your backup routine immediately.

> **Travel Advisory**
>
> When adding a new system or a directory/file to a network server, ensure that it's added to your backup schedule.

Restoration

The goal of any backup system is to be able to restore lost or corrupted data from the backup media. It's amazing to think that most companies don't test the backups they've made. The only true way of testing a backup system is to perform routine test restores. Although your backup application logs might show that no problems exist and that backups have completed successfully, a hardware problem could exist with a tape drive or hard-drive storage that causes the written data to be corrupted.

> **Travel Advisory**
>
> One of the most important aspects of a backup strategy is to regularly test backups by performing test restores. Remember that your backups are no good unless you know the information can be restored.

When you're performing regular file restoration, the best practice is not to overwrite any original files of the data you're trying to restore. Instead, create a separate directory and restore the file there. This way, the user can decide which version is required. If the original file and directory have been completely deleted, there's no need for this extra step.

All your backup media should be properly labeled so that in case of an emergency—where time is of the essence—the correct media containing the data can be quickly located and restored.

Offsite Storage

In the event of a disaster at your primary site, such as fire or a flood, any backup media stored there could also be destroyed. All the data that's saved to backup will be lost, and you won't have other backups available. Therefore, you should store copies of the backup media offsite. Offsite storage is an important part of your overall disaster recovery plan. Using an offsite storage facility means that after you successfully complete your backups, they're sent to a different location, which could be another office building or a special storage company facility.

Travel Advisory

In case you want to keep your most recent backup media onsite, you can make two copies of your full backup and then send one of them to the offsite storage company and keep the other. However, creating the extra backup requires extra time and backup media.

When choosing an offsite storage facility, you must ensure it follows the same basic rules of facility security measures that you follow at your own site. You should visit the location where your backup media will be stored to examine the environment. For example, the storage area should be regulated for temperature, humidity, fire prevention, and static electricity prevention. Access control should be strictly enforced so only authorized employees of your company can retrieve backup media from the facility. Depending on the type of data you're sending offsite, you should identify how quickly you'll need access to the media, if this is necessary. The storage facility should allow access at all hours in case you need a backup in an emergency.

Online Backup

With the vast increase in Internet bandwidth speed and capacity, online backup services that back up your data over the Internet are a popular alternative for offsite storage of physical backup media. Client software is installed on your system, and an initial upload takes place of your data. Depending on the amount of data, this can take many days before the full body of data is synchronized. After the initial synchronization, your file system is constantly scanned, and changed files are automatically synchronized over the Internet to a secure server.

Some online servers offer synchronization services that keep only a copy of your data in its current state. There is no way to retrieve a deleted file or a file that was changed two weeks ago but has been modified several times since that initial change. Other services offer version control, where you can restore a deleted file or a version of a file several weeks old.

For security, you must make sure the online backup server stores your data in encrypted form and that all network communications with the service are over encrypted channels such as a Secure Sockets Layer (SSL) connection.

Online backup services are geared toward individual systems or small business servers, and they cannot scale up to handle the vast amount of data produced by a large company or data center. For these larger networks, the same online backup principles can be applied and the data kept securely within the company's networks by synchronizing or backing up data between geographically different sites.

Objective 3.03
CompTIA Security+
Objective 3.9

Explain the Impact and Proper Use of Environmental Controls

Security is often considered as protection against theft, vandalism, or unauthorized access to a company's computer systems. Typically, not enough thought and planning are put into the security of your actual facility, which is the first line of defense for your employees and your company's assets. Threats from unauthorized network access are a great concern, but protecting your facilities from environmental concerns, such as fires and floods, is equally important.

At the minimum, the facility itself must adhere to any local and national safety standards as they pertain to building construction, fire ratings, and electrical code. Many of these issues need to be resolved before and during the time the facility is being constructed.

To protect your employees and any sensitive equipment that resides inside the building, a regulated environment should control and monitor the temperature, humidity, electrical systems, ventilation, and fire-suppression systems.

Facility Construction Issues

Before the foundation of a new company facility is laid, an incredible amount of planning goes into the construction process. Part of that process should involve the physical security and safety of the new facility. Several issues must be considered, often even before the new location is chosen. These main issues include location planning, building construction, and computer room construction.

Location Planning

When planning the location for a proposed company facility, you must consider several factors. Unless secrecy of the facility is desired, the building should be in a visible area and situated comfortably within the surrounding terrain. The building should be easily accessible from major roads, highways, or even railway lines or coastal ports, depending on the type of business. The building facility should have proper lighting for its entrances, both for the security of the employees and for adequate light for security camera recording. Most important, the site should be analyzed with respect to its susceptibility to natural disasters. If the building is in a valley, could flooding occur? Is the building situated in an area prone to tornadoes, hurricanes, or earthquakes? All these factors should be incorporated into an overall site plan.

Facility Construction

After the site has been chosen, the actual construction of the facility must be carefully planned and executed. The construction materials need to be studied for their compliance with local and national safety standards, including fire and structural-strength ratings. Building security must also be a high priority during construction. The following outlines some of the key components of building construction, including some recommendations to enhance security:

- **Walls**   Walls must be examined for fire and strength ratings. For high-security areas, walls might need to be reinforced with stronger materials.
- **Doors**   Doors should be resistant to forced entry and fitted with security mechanisms, such as basic or electronic locks. Emergency doors must be carefully placed for access during an emergency.
- **Ceilings**   Ceilings should be examined for their fire rating, and materials should be made of noncombustible materials. The decision to use a drop ceiling is a balance between security and convenience. Although a drop ceiling is good for cable management, it also inadvertently provides access to other areas and rooms.

- **Windows** Windows should be resistant to shattering and placed to prevent access to sensitive areas of the building. For added security, the windows can be made opaque or reflective so no one can see into them from the outside. Computer screens should face away from the windows so that they cannot be viewed from the outside.
- **Flooring** Flooring should be carefully chosen for its fire rating and should be conducive to a nonconductive, static-free environment.

Computer Room Construction

To preserve the integrity and security of sensitive computer and networking equipment, these components should be housed in a separate, secure, environmentally controlled room. This room should not be accessible by other doors, rooms, corridors, or stairs. Only one secured doorway should exist, through which employees can enter and exit.

Inside, servers and networking equipment are usually stacked in a rack or cabinet that can be secured by a lock. Cabling is typically run up to the ceiling, down through the floor, or high up on the walls using special cable management trays. This prevents people from tripping over equipment or wiring that might be strewn haphazardly over the floor.

The room should also be designed for maximum air ventilation and equipped with environmental controls to regulate both temperature and humidity.

Exam Tip
Ensure that you know the special considerations for computer network room security compared to other parts of the building.

Environmental Issues

Computers and electronic equipment are sensitive to environmental factors such as temperature, humidity, and air and power quality. Imbalances in any of these utilities can result in severe damage to computer equipment, and they can potentially cause even greater perils to both the people and the facilities. Environmental controls must be installed and continuously monitored for proper operation.

Temperature

Sensitive computer and electronic equipment must operate in a climate-controlled environment. To provide a proper operating environment, the temperature and humidity of a computer facility must be carefully controlled and maintained

FIGURE 3.1   Hot and cold aisles

through proper heating, ventilation, and air conditioning (HVAC), and not just your run-of-the-mill home system or wall unit; computer facilities should be equipped with an industrial HVAC to keep the entire room at a steady, cool temperature. Overheating of computer equipment can cause disruption or even total equipment failure. When devices overheat, their components expand and retract, which can eventually damage them permanently. In a computer system itself, several fans circulate the air and cool the components inside.

Hot and Cold Aisles   Using hot and cold aisles is an air circulation technique often employed in large data centers with rows and rows of equipment racks, as shown in Figure 3.1. A cold aisle has the front of the two adjoining rows of equipment facing each other over a vented floor with cool air passing upward, which flows into the front of the equipment racks to cool them down. The backs of each row of equipment face into a hot aisle, where the fans from the equipment racks on each side of the row push out hot air.

Using cool air vents and hot air intakes from the HVAC units creates a constant flow of air to prevent buildup of heat emanating from the back of the equipment racks and allows cool air to flow into the front of the equipment racks.

Humidity

Humidity levels are important to the overall operating health of computer equipment because high humidity can cause corrosion of the internal parts of a system. Low humidity levels create a dry environment where the buildup of static electricity can cause great harm to electronic equipment, so humidity levels should be set between 40 and 50 percent. Static electricity can also be minimized in the environment using special antistatic mats and wristbands, which can be used by technicians who regularly touch the equipment.

Ventilation

The quality of the air circulating through the computer facility must be maintained through the proper use of ventilation techniques. Without proper ventilation, a risk of airborne contaminants occurs. These contaminants could be dust or other microscopic particles that can get inside and clog such critical equipment as the fans, which need to be running to keep the system cool.

Monitoring

The temperature and humidity of your equipment rooms must be constantly monitored to make sure they are maintaining a safe environment for your computer equipment. A failed air-conditioning unit can cause your computer equipment room's temperature to soar immediately, causing equipment shutdown and failure within several minutes.

The monitoring equipment must be able to actively generate alarms so that you will be alerted to a significant change in temperature. This gives you time to quickly shut down systems before they overheat. Individual devices may also have diagnostic tools that can alert you to changes in the temperature of a device.

Electrical Power

Another important environmental concern is the electrical power system that runs your equipment. Electrical power must be provided with consistent voltage levels and a minimum of interference. Even small fluctuations in power can cause irreparable damage to sensitive electronic equipment. Power protection has two aspects: ensuring the consistency and quality of your primary power source, and maintaining the availability of alternate power in a power outage.

Several types of fluctuations can occur:

- **Blackout**   A prolonged period without any power
- **Brownout**   A prolonged period of lower-than-normal power
- **Spike**   A momentary jump to a high voltage
- **Sag**   A moment of low voltage
- **Surge**   A prolonged period of high voltage

To protect your equipment against these different types of perils, you can use several devices. Simple power-surge protectors generally aren't rated for expensive types of computer equipment. Usually, these types of power bars contain some type of fuse or circuit breaker that cuts off the power in a spike or a surge. By the time the breaker cuts in, the moment of high voltage has already been reached and has possibly damaged the equipment that's plugged into the power bar. The recommendation is for most computer systems, servers, and network infrastructures to use a UPS, which works both as a high-end surge protector and during a power failure.

Travel Advisory

Don't plug power bars or high-load peripherals, such as laser printers, into UPS power outlets because they can quickly overload the it.

To provide clean and consistent power to computer equipment, a device called a *line* or *power conditioner* can be used. It plugs directly into the power supply outlet and ensures that the power that reaches the computer equipment is free of voltage fluctuations and interference.

For large organizations with critical high-availability requirements, a more expensive option for backup power is the use of a generator that runs on a battery or fuel. When using batteries, a power generator has a finite time that it can run until the battery power runs out. A fuel-based generator, on the other hand, can be kept operational if it continues to be filled with fuel, and it provides electricity even for very long blackout periods if fuel is available.

Cable Shielding

Network cabling can be extremely sensitive to environmental electrical interference. This type of disruption can cause loss of information, network latency, and the complete disabling of the network. These types of problems are most pronounced in manufacturing environments where computers and networking cabling run side by side with large machines. The following are the most common types of problems that affect network cabling:

- **EMI**   Electromagnetic interference (EMI) is caused by the electrical "noise" created by motors, lighting, and any type of electronic or mechanical equipment. This interference can potentially disrupt communications on network cabling because of the noise in the line that distorts the network signals.

- **Crosstalk** Crosstalk is caused by the electrical signals of one wire disrupting the signals of another wire. Without proper shielding, network cabling is susceptible to crosstalk, especially twisted-pair wiring.
- **Attenuation** As an electronic signal travels, it slowly degrades over a certain distance. This is known as attenuation. The longer a network cable, the more susceptible it is to this type of signal degradation. The rate of attenuation increases when the type of network signaling is using higher frequencies for faster data transfer. Attenuation can also be caused by damaged or faulty network cabling.

To prevent these problems from affecting your network communications, the cabling you use should be properly shielded. Different types of cabling use different kinds of shielding methods.

Exam Tip

Be aware of the different types of interference that can affect network cabling.

Coaxial

Coaxial cabling consists of a special copper-core wire that's surrounded by several layers of protection. The copper wire is insulated by polyvinyl chloride (PVC) or Teflon-based material, as shown in Figure 3.2. This, in turn, is wrapped with a braided shielding material, and then the cable is covered with a protective outer sheath. This cabling is resistant to EMI and, most often, is installed in manufacturing environments because of the large amounts of interference that can result from nearby electrical and mechanical equipment.

FIGURE 3.2   Coaxial cabling

FIGURE 3.3   Shielded twisted-pair cabling

Twisted Pair

Twisted-pair cabling consists of several insulated copper wires, surrounded by a protective sheath. The copper wires are twisted together to protect them from EMI and to balance the crosstalk between the individual wires. Two types of twisted-pair cabling exist: shielded and unshielded. Shielded twisted-pair (STP) cabling contains an extra layer of foil shielding for added protection, as shown in Figure 3.3.

Unshielded twisted-pair (UTP) cabling, which doesn't have this protection, is shown in Figure 3.4. UTP is the most common form of cabling because the extra shielding of STP makes it much more expensive.

Fiber Optic

Because fiber-optic technology uses light as the medium for communication, it isn't susceptible to electromagnetic interference, crosstalk, or attenuation. Fiber-optic cabling is expensive and is typically used in large local area networks (LANs) as the backbone among smaller networks using coaxial or twisted-pair cabling. Figure 3.5 shows a cross section of a fiber-optic cable.

FIGURE 3.4   Unshielded twisted-pair cabling

Outer covering

Optical fiber

Glass cladding

FIGURE 3.5   Fiber-optic cabling

Wireless Networks and Cells

Although no physical wires are involved with wireless communications, wireless networks can still be disrupted in many ways. Because wireless networks use a common frequency band—typically in the 2.4- or 5.8-GHz range—they can suffer from interference from other devices that use those same frequencies, such as cordless phones and microwave ovens.

Another problem is that the overlapping of wireless cells can cause disruptions in communications, especially when a user is tied to a specific access point. An *access point* is a wireless base station that connects the wireless clients to a wired network. A *cell* is a specific area of influence of that access point or other cellular system base station. Users suffer signal degradation as they travel farther from the access point. The ranges for wireless access points are typically 500 feet indoors and 1000 feet outdoors.

> **Local Lingo**
>
> **wireless cell**   A division of wireless networks containing a certain range of frequencies that can be used.

Fire Suppression

Although fire suppression is typically already part of the facility plans, fire suppression for a computer environment can differ from techniques used to protect building structures and their contents. The most obvious difference is that suppressing a fire with water in a computer facility that's filled with many electronic servers, personal computers, laptops, printers, and network devices can be as damaging as the fire itself. Although computer-equipment-approved fire extinguishers are available, other effects of a fire, such as smoke and high temperatures, can also be damaging to computer equipment.

The key elements of fire protection are early detection and suppression. Early detection is a must in preventing fires from escalating from a small, minor flame to a raging inferno. Timing is of the essence, and you can detect a fire in several ways:

- **Smoke detectors**   Smoke detectors are the most common form of warning device. Using optical or photoelectric technology, a beam of light is emitted, and the smoke detector sets off an alarm if it detects a change in the light's intensity. As smoke filters into the unit, it senses the changes in the light pattern.
- **Flame detectors**   A flame detection unit can sense the movements of a flame or detect the energy that's a result of combustion. Flame detection units tend to be more expensive than other options, and they're typically used in high-security environments that require advanced fire-detection techniques.
- **Heat detectors**   A heat detector can detect fires by sensing when a predetermined temperature threshold has been reached. When the temperature from the fire grows to a certain level, an alarm is triggered. Heat detector units can also detect rapid changes of temperature that indicate the presence of a fire.
- **Video monitoring**   A video monitoring system allows you to look for any visible environmental concerns in a computer equipment room, such as smoke or flames that indicate a fire. Full-time video monitoring requires a dedicated security team, and this is typically reserved for protection of larger data centers.

When a fire is detected, a mechanism must be initiated to suppress the fire. A fire can be suppressed in several ways, each with its own positive and negative aspects, depending on the type of fire and the environment of the location.

Water

Water is the most common type of fire suppressant, but for computer facilities that contain a large amount of electrical equipment, water can be damaging. The use of water during an electrical fire can make the fire worse, causing even more damage. Water sprinkler systems usually consist of sprinkler heads that are distributed evenly throughout the area to provide maximum coverage. In some cases, the detection system can be configured to shut down the electrical supply before the water sprinklers turn on.

Chemical-Based Fire Suppression

Older fire suppression units for computer facilities used *halon*, a special fire-suppressing gas that can neutralize the chemical combustion of a fire. Halon acts quickly and causes no damage to computers and electrical equipment. Unfortunately, because of its environmental drawbacks, including depletion of ozone and the possibility of danger to humans when used in large amounts, halon is no longer manufactured. It still currently exists in some building installations, if they were installed before restrictions on halon were put in place.

Several more environmentally safe chemical-based replacements exist for halon, such as FM-200 and argon, which work the same way to neutralize a fire.

CHECKPOINT

✔**Objective 3.01: Compare and Contrast Aspects of Business Continuity** Create a disaster recovery plan that documents your risks, the business impact of a disaster, a contingency plan, succession planning, and network and facility documentation. Don't forget to identify mission-essential functions and associated critical systems. Test your business continuity and disaster recovery plans on a regular basis, and conduct any applicable privacy assessments if privacy data is being processed.

✔**Objective 3.02: Execute Disaster Recovery Plans and Procedures** Consider the security concepts of confidentiality, integrity, availability, and safety to select appropriate access controls before disaster strikes. Perform backups to save and archive critical company data. Full backups are recommended if time and space permit, but if not, use incremental or differential schemes. Test your backups by performing a restore on a regularly scheduled basis. Consider using alternate sites for disaster recovery purposes, taking into account applicable geographical and legal constraints. Maintain high availability of your services by implementing redundancy, data integrity protection, and fault tolerance. Use RAID for disk storage systems. Determine the level of RAID redundancy appropriate to the importance of the data you're protecting. Keep spare parts of common hardware on hand so it can be replaced immediately.

✔**Objective 3.03: Explain the Impact and Proper Use of Environmental Controls** Environmental protection for your computer equipment rooms involves temperature and humidity management, proper ventilation (hot and cold aisles), electrical protection with UPS and power conditioners, and fire detection and suppression. Be aware of electromagnetic interference attenuation with network cabling.

REVIEW QUESTIONS

1. Your chief information officer (CIO) has asked you to evaluate options for an alternate site in the event of a crisis. Availability of data is the main priority, and funding is not an issue. Rank the solutions in the following list:

   a. Warm site

   b. Hot site

   c. Cold site

   d. No alternate

   A. a, b, c, d

   B. b, a, c, d

   C. d, a, c, b

   D. a, d, b, c

2. A business is hosting high-demand content in an earthquake-prone zone. The chief information security officer has asked his leadership to prioritize what should be focused on in the event of a disaster. What should be the highest priority?

   A. Availability of high-demand data

   B. Confidentiality of sensitive data

   C. Integrity of organizational databases

   D. Safety of personnel

3. You are installing a database server that requires several hard drives in a RAID array. In the event one of the drives fails, you need to be able to swap out a failed hard drive with no downtime. Which of the following types of hard drives do you require?

   A. Cold swap

   B. Suspend swap

   C. Warm swap

   D. Hot swap

4. Your company is in the middle of budgeting for disaster recovery. You have been asked to justify the cost for offsite backup media storage. What is the primary security purpose of storing backup media at an offsite storage facility?

   A. So that the facility can copy the data to a RAID system

   B. So that if the primary site is down, the offsite storage can reload your systems from backup at their facility

    C. For proper archive labeling and storage

    D. To prevent a disaster onsite from destroying the only copies of your backup media

5. You have implemented a backup plan for your critical file servers, including proper media rotation, backup frequency, and offsite storage. Which of the following must be performed on a regular basis to ensure the validity and integrity of your backup system?

    A. Periodic testing of restores

    B. Multiple monthly backup media

    C. Purchasing of new media

    D. Updating the backup application software

6. As part of your organization's contingency plan in the event of a disaster, which of the following would be the primary component of the organization to make functional after an initial disaster incident?

    A. Check all file servers and make sure they are running.

    B. Retrieve all backup tapes from the offsite storage facility.

    C. Ensure basic communications such as phone and Internet connectivity are functional.

    D. Ensure that web servers can accept requests from customers.

7. You must ensure that power is always available (24/7) for a critical web and database server that accepts customer orders and processes transactions. Which of the following devices should be installed?

    A. Power conditioner

    B. UPS

    C. Power generator

    D. Redundant power supply

8. You are installing network cabling for the main backbone of a manufacturing facility network. The manufacturing machinery generates a significant amount of EMI. Which of the following network cabling types should you use?

    A. STP

    B. Fiber optic

    C. UTP

    D. Coaxial cable

9. You are performing a risk analysis of the environmental factors for your primary server equipment room. Which of the following environmental issues is most likely to affect an enclosed server room?

   A. Average humidity levels

   B. Cool temperatures

   C. Flooding

   D. High temperatures

10. During disaster recovery planning, you must ensure you have a strategy in place for succession planning. Which of the following concepts describes succession planning?

    A. Replacing key employees who are unavailable during a disaster

    B. Organizing an emergency contact list

    C. Having an alternate hot site facility in place

    D. Availability of onsite spare parts and servers

11. It has been determined that your organization is processing privacy data. Which of the following should be conducted?

    A. Privacy implication assessment

    B. Privacy processing assessment

    C. Privacy impact assessment

    D. Privacy identification assessment

REVIEW ANSWERS

1. **B**   A hot site contains enough networking and server equipment to continue your business operations in case a disaster strikes your primary facility. Warm sites and cold sites contain little to no existing equipment or infrastructure. Having no alternate could risk days or weeks of downtime in a crisis where infrastructure and data are lost.

2. **D**   Personnel safety should always be the highest priority. This can be facilitated using physical controls, such as locks or fire-suppression mechanisms, or through policies and procedures.

3. **D**   A hot-swap device, such as a hard drive, can be inserted or removed without the need to shut down the server. This enables you to retain the availability of the services on that server.

4. **D**   All backup plans should require backup media to be sent to an offsite storage facility. That way, if a disaster destroys your physical location, the backup media will be safe.

5. **A**   Regularly testing your backups by performing a test restore is the only way to ensure that your backup data is valid and the data is intact. If the information cannot be restored, your backup plan is not providing any benefit for a disaster recovery scenario.

6. **C**   The most important part of the company to get operational is basic communications, such as phones, networking connectivity, and e-mail. Until these communication lines are functional, the ability to coordinate the disaster recovery effort will be greatly reduced.

7. **C**   A power generator is required to ensure that there is always power for your server. A UPS battery typically contains only enough power to run a system for about 10 to 20 minutes, while a power conditioner or redundant power supply will not help if there is no power to run them.

8. **B**   Because fiber-optic cabling uses light to transfer information over the cables, it isn't susceptible to electromagnetic interference.

9. **D**   Server rooms can quickly rise in temperature with so many systems running in an enclosed area. At high temperatures, CPUs and hard drives can shut down due to the excessive heat. Most server rooms contain air-conditioning systems that keep the temperature regulated and cooler than normal. If this air-conditioning system fails, the heat can dramatically rise within minutes.

10. **A**   Succession planning makes sure that you have replacements for key employees in the event they are unavailable during the disaster recovery phase. This requires that employees have the same security clearance and can immediately take over the responsibilities of another employee's position.

11. **C**   A privacy impact assessment (PIA) is conducted when privacy data is being stored or processed; when conducted, the PIA will determine what type of data is being stored, how is it being stored, where is it being stored, and what might trigger a privacy lapse. Systems that require a PIA should incorporate increased controls to mitigate the risks of processing and storing privacy data.

Cryptography and PKI

Cryptography and Encryption Basics

	NEWBIE	SOME EXPERIENCE	EXPERT
ETA	3.5 hours	2.5 hours	1.5 hour

Cryptography is the conversion of communicated information into secret code that keeps the information confidential and private. The protection of sensitive communications has been the basis of cryptography throughout history. Modern cryptography performs essentially the same function but with added functionality, such as authentication, data integrity, and nonrepudiation, to accommodate personal and business communications and transactions in the digital world.

The central function of cryptography is *encryption*, the transformation of data into an unreadable form. Encryption ensures privacy by keeping the information hidden from those for whom the information is not intended. *Decryption*, the opposite of encryption, transforms encrypted data back into an intelligible form. Even though someone might be able to read the encrypted data, it won't make any sense until it has been properly decrypted.

The encryption/decryption process involves taking data in *plain text,* which is readable and understandable text, and manipulating its form to create *ciphertext.* When data has been transformed into ciphertext, the plain text becomes inaccessible until it's decrypted. The entire process is illustrated in Figure 4.1.

This process enables the transmission of confidential information over an insecure communications path, greatly decreasing the possibility of the data being compromised. In a file storage system, data is protected by authentication and access controls that prevent unauthorized users from accessing some files. When this data is transmitted over a network, the data can become vulnerable to interception. If the information or the communications channel itself is encrypted, the chance of someone intercepting and deciphering the data is extremely slim.

This chapter details the subjects of cryptography and encryption, including mathematical algorithms, public key infrastructure systems, and encryption standards and protocols.

FIGURE 4.1   Encryption and decryption

Objective 4.01
CompTIA Security+
Objective 6.1

Utilize the Concepts of Cryptography

Today's cryptography involves more than hiding secrets with encryption systems. With the world using more technological means to perform business and legal functions, such as purchasing items from a web-based store, conducting online banking, and digitally signing documents, the need for strong and secure encryption systems to protect these transactions is vital. Security is obviously a key use, but cryptography is also used to promote other ends, such as obfuscation and resiliency, as discussed next.

Information Assurance

Information assurance is a method of protecting information and information systems by providing confidentiality, integrity, authentication, nonrepudiation, and obfuscation.

Confidentiality

Confidentiality is the concept of ensuring that data is not made available or disclosed to unauthorized people. Processes such as encryption must be used on the data, network infrastructure, and communication channels to protect against data interception and disclosure.

Integrity

Data *integrity* is the protection of information from damage or deliberate manipulation. Integrity is extremely critical for any kind of business or electronic commerce. Data integrity guarantees that when information has been stored or communicated, it hasn't been changed or manipulated in transit. The cryptologic function of hashing is often used to create signatures for files that indicate whether a file has been tampered with; if the hashed value does not match the original, the file's integrity has been compromised.

Authentication

Authentication is the concept of uniquely identifying individuals to provide assurance of an individual user's identity. It is the act of ensuring that a person is who he claims to be. Typical physical and logical authentication methods include the use of identification cards, door locks and keys, and network logins and passwords. For modern e-commerce and legal applications, this type of authentication needs to be tightly controlled. Encrypted digital certificates are used to identify users electronically on a network. Encrypted forms of authentication can also be used in smart cards, which are a more secure medium than a typical ID badge.

Nonrepudiation

Nonrepudiation is the term used to describe the inability of a person to deny or repudiate the origin of a signature or document, or the receipt of a message or document. For example, suppose a user is trying to legally prove that an electronic document or transaction did not originate with her. The user could have digitally signed a contract that was transmitted through e-mail, but if the data or transmission wasn't considered secure because of the lack of encryption, the user might legally claim it was tampered with and call its integrity into question. By implementing nonrepudiation processes, a cryptographic system can be considered secure for business and legal transactions.

Exam Tip

A specific type of encryption scheme, algorithm, or protocol may cover only certain parts of the information assurance objectives. For example, certain encryption protocols concern themselves only with authentication, whereas others cover all the objectives of confidentiality, integrity, authentication, nonrepudiation, and obfuscation.

Obfuscation

Obfuscation provides security through obscurity, meaning that data is modified to make it unreadable to a human or a program trying to use it. A good example is when you use your credit card on the Internet; often you will notice that, after your credit card number is entered, it morphs to the format XXXX-XXXX-XXXX-1234. This is to obfuscate the number so that someone eavesdropping in cannot see it and use it; in many cases, the full card number will be sent to the credit card processor, but the last four digits are the only ones kept by the merchant. Although obfuscation cannot be the only attribute you pursue, it certainly doesn't hurt to add it into the mix. However, be aware that the bad guys often use obfuscation as a tool as well; for example, URL shorteners are tools that reduce long, complex URLs into more readily tweeted or e-mailed links. The official McGraw-Hill Education site (mheducation.com) processed through Google's official URL shortener becomes https://goo.gl/whh0g1, which could then be sent to an unsuspecting user. It could be a legit site, but how would he know? This obfuscation is helpful to a genuine user, but provides great opportunity to a phisher, for example.

Algorithms

A system that provides encryption and decryption services is called a *cryptosystem*. A cryptosystem uses a mathematical encryption *algorithm*, or *cipher*, to turn data into ciphertext. A cryptographic algorithm is a complex mathematical formula that dictates how the encryption/decryption process takes place. Because these mathematical algorithms are usually publicly known, the cryptosystem is strengthened with the addition of a secret key, as shown in Figure 4.2.

A *key* is like a password that's combined with an algorithm to create the ciphertext. The encryption can't be deciphered unless the key is used to decrypt it. No one can simply unravel the algorithm to decode the message, because the key is also needed. Depending on the encryption mechanism used, the key might be used for both encryption and decryption, while different keys might be used for encryption and decryption, respectively, for other systems.

The strength of the key depends on the algorithm's *keyspace,* which is a specific range of values—usually measured in bits—that's created by the algorithm to contain keys. A key is made up of random values within the keyspace range. A larger keyspace containing more bits means more available values exist to use for different keys, effectively increasing the difficulty for someone to compromise the system. The smaller the keyspace, the greater the chance someone can decipher the key value.

The strength of the cryptosystem lies in the strength and effectiveness of its algorithm and the size of the keyspace. However, no matter how strong the algorithm, it will be rendered useless if someone obtains the key, so the key must be protected, and one of the methods to do this is to use encryption

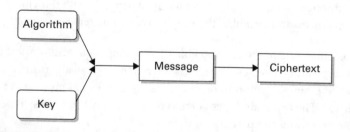

FIGURE 4.2 Cryptosystem using algorithms

protocols for secure key delivery. It is also important to consider the requirements for strength versus performance when deciding which cryptosystem to implement within your organization.

Travel Advisory

Most attacks on encryption center on the interception of keys rather than on attempts to subvert the algorithm, which requires a large amount of processing resources.

Ciphers have two major outcomes: confusion and diffusion. *Confusion* means that the ciphertext output is dependent on several parts of the key, rather than only one. This increases the change in the plain text to ciphertext, and results in a more thorough encryption process. *Diffusion* means that even a small change in the plain text results in a significant change in ciphertext. In other words, changing a single letter of plain text should result in a totally different ciphertext output, not merely a change of only one letter or character. To accomplish both outcomes, there are two main types of ciphers, often used in conjunction:

- **Substitution**   In its most simplified form, a *substitution* cipher takes plain text and substitutes the original characters in the data with other characters. For example, the letters *ABC* can be substituted by reversing the alphabet, so the cipher form will read *ZYX*. Modern substitution encryption ciphers are much more complex, performing many types of substitutions with more than one alphabet. A common, but weak, example of a substitution cipher is ROT13 (which means "rotate by 13 places"). In this cipher, a piece of text is encrypted by replacing it with its pair letter 13 places along in the alphabet. Because it is so easily decrypted, it is not recommended for use in serious contexts.

- **Transposition**   In a *transposition* cipher, the characters are rearranged through mathematical permutations. When used with difficult mathematical formulas, these ciphers can be extremely complex.

Most modern ciphers use a combination of long sequences of substitution and transposition schemes. The data is filtered through an algorithm that performs these complex substitution and transposition operations to arrive at the ciphertext. The two main types of encryption—symmetric and asymmetric—use key values and complex algorithms.

Symmetric Keys

In a symmetric (sometimes referred to as "secret key") encryption scheme, both parties use the same key for encryption and decryption purposes. Each user must possess the same key to send encrypted messages to each other, as shown in Figure 4.3. The sender uses the key to encrypt the message and then transmits it to the receiver. The receiver, who is in possession of the same key, uses it to decrypt the message.

The security of this encryption model relies on the end users to protect the secret key properly. If an unauthorized user could intercept the key, she would be able to read any encrypted messages sent by other users by decrypting the message with it. It's extremely important that a user protect the key itself, as well as any communications in which he transmits the key to another user.

One of the main disadvantages of symmetric encryption schemes is that they don't scale well with large numbers of users. A user needs different keys, depending on the person with whom he is communicating. If the user communicates with a lot of people, the number of keys that need to be distributed and tracked can become enormous. Another disadvantage is that the system needs a secure mechanism to deliver keys to the end users. Symmetric systems can offer confidentiality only through encryption; they offer little in the way of authentication and nonrepudiation.

Symmetric systems, however, can be difficult to crack if a large key size is used. A symmetric system is also much faster than asymmetric encryption because the underlying algorithms are simpler and more efficient.

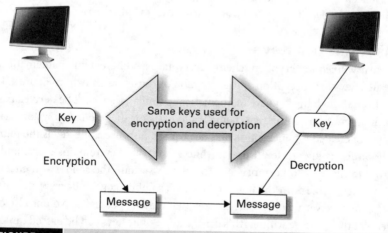

FIGURE 4.3   Symmetric key encryption

Two main types of symmetric encryption can be used:

- **Stream cipher** A stream cipher encrypts data one bit at a time, as opposed to a block cipher, which works on blocks of text. Stream ciphers, by design, are fast compared to block ciphers. The encryption of any plain-text data with a block cipher results in the same ciphertext when the same key is used. With stream ciphers, each bit of the plain-text stream is transformed into a different ciphertext bit using a randomly generated initialization vector (IV; discussed in more detail later in the chapter). A stream cipher generates a key stream that's combined with the plain-text data to provide encryption. RC4 is the most commonly found streaming cipher, and it is used in the Wired Equivalent Privacy (WEP) protocol, which we'll discuss later when we cover wireless protocols.

- **Block cipher** A block cipher encrypts entire blocks of data, rather than smaller bits of data as with stream cipher methods. A block cipher transforms a block of plain-text data into a block of ciphertext data of the same length. For many block ciphers, the block size is 64 bits. Block ciphers use different modes of operation because large streams of data with potentially identical inputs would be less able to provide the required confidentiality or integrity due to their subsequent identical output. These modes of operation and their features are detailed in Table 4.1.

Popular symmetric algorithms include Data Encryption Standard (DES), Advanced Encryption Standard (AES), Blowfish, Twofish, International Data Encryption Algorithm (IDEA), and RC4 (Rivest Cipher).

Asymmetric Keys

In an *asymmetric* encryption scheme, everyone uses different but mathematically related keys for encryption and decryption purposes, as shown in Figure 4.4.

Even though the keys are mathematically similar, they can't be derived from each other. An asymmetric scheme is the basis for the *public key* system. Two keys are created for encryption and decryption purposes: one key is the public key, which is known to all users, while the private key remains secret and is given to the user to keep private. To use this system, the sender will encrypt a message or file with the intended receiver's public key. To decrypt this message, the receiver will use a private key that only he possesses. No one else can decrypt the message without this private key. Public keys can be passed directly among users or found in directories of public keys.

TABLE 4.1		Modes of Operation (adapted from NIST 800-38A and 800-38D)
Name	**Acronym**	**Description**
Electronic Codebook	ECB	A confidentiality mode that features, for a given key, the assignment of a fixed ciphertext block to each plain-text block, analogous to the assignment of code words in a codebook. ECB is vulnerable to replay attacks and has been deprecated.
Cipher Block Chaining	CBC	A confidentiality mode whose encryption process features the combining ("chaining") of the plain-text blocks with the previous ciphertext blocks. The CBC mode requires an IV to combine with the first plain-text block.
Cipher Feedback	CFB	A confidentiality mode that features the feedback of successive ciphertext segments into the input blocks of the forward cipher to generate output blocks that are XORed with the plain text to produce the ciphertext, and vice versa. The CFB mode requires an IV as the initial input block.
Output Feedback	OFB	A confidentiality mode that features the iteration of the forward cipher on an IV (initiation vector) to generate a sequence of output blocks that are XORed with the plain text to produce the ciphertext, and vice versa. The OFB mode requires that the IV is a nonce—a one-time number.
Counter	CTR	A confidentiality mode that features the application of the forward cipher to a set of input blocks, called counters, to produce a sequence of output blocks that are XORed with the plain text to produce the ciphertext, and vice versa. The sequence of counters must have the property that each block in the sequence is different from every other block.
Galois Counter Mode	GCM	GCM provides assurance of the confidentiality of data using a variation of the Counter mode of operation for encryption. GCM provides assurance of the authenticity of the confidential data using a universal hash function. GCM can also provide authentication assurance for additional data (of practically unlimited length per invocation) that is not encrypted.

FIGURE 4.4   Asymmetric key encryption

Another encryption concept related to asymmetric cryptography is that of key escrow. Key escrow involves a third party, such as a government agency or an authorized organization, that holds a special third key on top of your private and public key pair. The third key is used to encrypt the private key, which is then stored in a secure location. This third key can be used to unlock the encrypted copy of the private key in case of loss or the theft of the original key.

Travel Assistance

Key escrow is described in more detail in Chapter 5.

The advantage of this system over symmetric schemes is that it offers a level of authentication. By decrypting a message with a sender's public key, the receiver knows this message came from the sender. The sender is authenticated because, in order for the message to be decrypted with a public key, the private key had to be used to perform the initial encryption.

Exam Tip

Recognize how the different combinations of key-pair encryption methods can provide different levels of information assurance, such as authentication, confidentiality, and integrity.

The main disadvantage of asymmetric encryption is that it can be much slower than symmetric schemes. Unlike symmetric systems, however, asymmetric schemes offer confidentiality, authentication, and nonrepudiation (which prevents a user from repudiating a signed communication). Asymmetric schemes also provide more manageable and efficient ways for dealing with key distribution.

Popular asymmetric algorithms and applications include RSA (named for creators Rivest, Shamir, and Adleman), Elliptic Curve, Diffie–Hellman, and Digital Signature Algorithm (DSA).

Exam Tip

In a symmetric encryption scheme, both parties use the same key for encryption and decryption purposes. In an asymmetric encryption scheme, everyone uses a different (but mathematically related) key for encryption and decryption.

In-Band/Out-of-Band Key Exchange

In-band key exchanges take place within the normal communication channel, whereas out-of-band key exchanges utilize a separate channel outside the norm to authenticate the user. This is to verify that the original channel is not compromised; think of e-mail, banking, or gaming services that require a time-based code from your phone or a token device, and you'll understand the out-of-band concept. Although this helps ensure that a compromise of the original channel doesn't compromise the confidentiality of the communication mechanism, it is susceptible to man-in-the-middle attacks if the out-of-band channel is lost, stolen, or compromised in some way.

Ephemeral Keys

Ephemeral keys are the converse of static keys, in that they are temporary by nature, whereas static keys are semi-permenant (typical life span of a static key is one to two years). Often, ephemeral keys are generated for each execution of the key establishment process and are unique to a message or session. However, they can be used more than once when a sender generates only one ephemeral key pair for a message and the private key is combined with each distinct recipient's public key. The benefit of using an ephemeral key is that if a particular secret key is leaked or compromised, the other messages encrypted by the system remain unreadable because each encryption session generates its own unique keys (see "Perfect Forward Secrecy," next).

Perfect Forward Secrecy

Perfect forward secrecy (PFS) is designed, through the utilization of complex cryptographic protocols, to prevent the situation where a compromise of one secret key or message leads to a compromise of previous confidential messages. For example, if my key were compromised today, perfect forward secrecy would mean that all my previous messages are still secret. Traditional methods assume that the underlying cipher is always secure and cannot be used to recover older plain texts. For example, within Hypertext Transfer Protocol Secure (HTTPS), both the browser and the server exchange information toward an agreement on a secret key. In this process, if a private key is captured by an attacker, that key could be used to decrypt previous messages. PFS works because even if a private key is captured, the session key is truly ephemeral, or used only one time, as discussed previously in the chapter.

Random/Pseudo-Random Numbers and Inputs

Three major types of one-time use numbers are used as inputs into various algorithms: initialization vectors, nonces, and salts. A *salt* is a randomly generated input, often used within hashing schemes (discussed later in the chapter.) As discussed previously, both block and stream ciphers use *initialization vectors (IVs)*, which should be randomly generated to ensure that if the same message is encrypted twice, the cipher text differs between the messages. *Nonces* are, as indicated by their name, numbers used once, and generally for a limited time; nonces are often sequential and sometimes have a salt as an input. Nonces are not required to be random, and they can be pseudo-random in nature; the sequential nature can be helped to check against replay attacks. Nonces and IVs are often used interchangeably as terms, but they have one big difference: IVs must be random, whereas nonces do not.

You may have noticed a common theme in these inputs, in that they are generally dependent on randomly or pseudo-randomly generated numbers. *Random number generators* are self-explanatory in that they are programs that generate numbers that are statistically independent of each other. Truly random numbers are often generated by using inputs that cannot be predicted, such as radioactive decay. While random number generators are most ideal for a scenario requiring a truly random input, they are often considered very inefficient for use, as they generally take longer to produce the number, and they are nondeterministic, meaning that the number cannot be predetermined based on a mathematical equation or set table of inputs. In some situations, such as modeling and simulation, a *pseudo-random number generator* might be preferable due to the speed in which numbers can be created and the ability to determine how a number was generated. Pseudo-random number generators often use a mathematical formula or a set input list to generate the numbers, leading to an ability to replay; for this reason, random numbers are best for highly secure situations.

Steganography

Steganography does not involve algorithms to encrypt data; it is a method of hiding data in another type of media that effectively conceals the existence of the data. This is typically performed by hiding messages in graphics images such as bitmap (BMP) files or other types of media files such as digital music files. Many companies place a watermark (a hidden image) within a company image to be able to prove it is owned by the company in the event it is being used by another company or person. Unused sectors of a hard disk can also be used in steganography. These types of files contain insignificant data bits that can be replaced by the data to be hidden without affecting the original file enough to be detected.

Digital Signatures

A digital signature is an encrypted hash value used to ensure the identity and integrity of a message. The signature can be attached to a message to uniquely identify the sender. Like a written signature, the digital signature guarantees the individual sending the message is who he claims to be. The sender runs a hash function on his message, takes the resulting hash value, encrypts it with his private key, and sends it along with the message. When the receiver gets the signed message, she first decrypts the encrypted hash with the corresponding public key (verifies the sender) and then performs her own hashing function on the message. The calculated hash is then compared against the unencrypted hash, and if they are the same, the receiver knows the message hasn't been altered in transmission.

Basic Hashing Concepts

A *hashing* value is used in encryption systems to create a "fingerprint" for a message. This prevents the message from being improperly accessed on its way to its destination. In the overall information assurance model, hashing is used to protect the integrity of a message and is most often used with digital signatures.

The most commonly used hashing function is the *one-way hash,* a mathematical function that takes a variable-sized message and transforms it into a fixed-length value referred to as either a *hash value* or a *message digest.* This function is "one-way" because it's difficult to invert the procedure, and the procedure is never decrypted. The hash value represents the longer message from which it was created. This hash value is appended to the message that's sent to another user, as shown in Figure 4.5. The receiver then performs the same hashing function on the message and compares the resulting hash value with the one sent with the message. If they're identical, the message was not altered.

FIGURE 4.5   One-way hash appended to a message to protect its integrity

Attacks against one-way hash functions can be prevented by longer hash values that are less susceptible to brute-force attacks. A good minimum starting point for the size of a hash value is 128 bits. The most common problem with weak hashing algorithms is the possibility of *hash value collisions* that occur when two hashed messages result in the same hashing value. When these collisions are discovered, they can be used to reveal the underlying algorithm. *Birthday attacks,* a class of brute-force attacks, are often used to find collisions of hash functions. The birthday attack gets its name from this surprising result: the probability that 2 or more people in a group of 23 share the same birthday is greater than 50 percent. Such a result is called a *birthday paradox.* In encryption terms, if an attacker finds two hashed values that are the same, she has a greater chance of cracking the algorithm with this information.

Another attack to be mindful of is a pass the hash attack. A *pass the hash* attack occurs when an attacker intercepts a hash and uses it to authenticate directly, rather than using the underlying plain text password.

The following sections describe some of the common hashing algorithms in use today.

Message Digest Hashing

Message digest hashing algorithms are used for digital signature applications when a large message must be hashed in a secure manner. A digital signature is created when the digest of the message is encrypted using the sender's private key. These algorithms take a message of variable length and produce a 128-bit message digest.

Exam Tip

Remember that a digital signature is created when the digest of the message is encrypted using the sender's private key.

Message Digest 5 (MD5)

Message Digest 5 (MD5), developed in 1991, is a slower but more complex version of MD4. MD5 is popular and widely used for security applications and integrity checking. For example, downloaded software usually includes an MD5 checksum that the user can compare to the checksum of the downloaded file. MD5 produces a 128-bit hash value using a hexadecimal, 32-character string. Its complex algorithms make it much more difficult to crack than MD4. The algorithm consists of four distinct rounds that have a slightly different design from that of MD4. Vulnerabilities have been found in MD5 in which techniques are used to reverse-engineer the MD5 hash, and Secure Hash Algorithm (SHA) hash functions are often considered better alternatives to MD5 hashing.

Secure Hash Algorithm (SHA)

SHA was developed by the U.S. National Security Agency (NSA) for use with digital signature standards and is considered a more secure successor and alternative to MD5.

Travel Assistance

The NSA website (www.nsa.gov) provides an excellent overview of the history of cryptography for American national security.

SHA produces a 160-bit hash value that is run through the Digital Signature Algorithm (DSA), which adds the signature for the message. The sender encrypts the hash value with a private key, which is attached to the message before it's sent. The receiver decrypts the message with the sender's public key and runs the hashing function to compare the two values. If the values are identical, the message hasn't been altered. Other widely accepted variants of basic SHA (such as SHA-1 and SHA-2) exist, such as SHA-224, SHA-256, SHA-384, and SHA-512, which indicate their larger bit values. SHA is used in several popular security applications, such as Transport Layer Security (TLS), Secure Sockets Layer (SSL), and Internet Protocol Security (IPSec). SHA-1 is considered secure, although published theoretical attacks have been able to break the hash. SHA-2 improves upon SHA-1 through a lack of even theoretical attacks, but is not as widely used because there has been a lack of real-world attacks upon SHA-1. The next version of the standard, SHA-3, was accepted as the winner of the 2012 National Institutes of Standards and Technology (NIST) hash function competition. While NIST acknowledged that SHA-2 was in no imminent threat of being broken, they felt there was a need for a new, unrelated standard. SHA-3 was released to the public in 2014.

RIPEMD

RIPEMD (RACE Integrity Primitives Evaluation Message Digest) is a hash function message digest. Originally based on MD4, RIPEMD comes in several different bit varieties, including 128-, 160-, 256-, and 320-bit versions, although the 256- and 320-bit versions don't necessarily increase security; they only reduce the chance of hash value collisions. The original weak 128-bit version has replaced primarily by RIPEMD-160, but it is slower than and not as popular as SHA-1 or MD5.

HMAC

HMAC (Hash-based Message Authentication Code) is used as an algorithm for message authentication purposes, where the authentication is applied using hash functions and a secret key to create an authentication code value. HMAC is used to authentic a message and provide data integrity. The Message Authentication Code (MAC) is sent along with the message itself so that the receiver can authenticate the sender of the message and verify the integrity of the message contents. The strength of HMAC depends on the size and type of hash it uses, such as MD5 or SHA-1, and the key size.

> **Exam Tip**
>
> Be aware of the different types of hashing algorithms available and their strengths, weaknesses, and applications.

Objective 4.02
CompTIA Security+
Objective 6.2

Use and Apply Appropriate Cryptographic Tools and Products

In a symmetric encryption scheme, both parties use the same key for encryption and decryption purposes. Each user must possess the same key to encrypt and decrypt messages sent to each other.

In an asymmetric scheme, two keys are created for encryption and decryption purposes: one key is the public key, which is known to all users, while the private key remains secret and is kept private by the user to which it is assigned.

Asymmetric encryption schemes are widely used in public key cryptography systems.

Symmetric Encryption Algorithms

This section describes the symmetric-based algorithms.

DES and 3DES

DES is a block cipher defined by the U.S. government in 1977 as an official standard. The actual encryption system used was originally created by IBM. This symmetric cryptosystem uses a 64-bit block size and a 56-bit key. It requires both the sender and receiver to possess the same secret key, which is used both to encrypt and decrypt the message. DES can also be used by a single user for encrypting data for storage on a hard disk or other medium.

After DES was used for many years, the government ceased to authorize it as a standard and moved on to more secure methods of encryption, such as Triple DES (3DES) and the AES standard. Using the same standard with a weak 56-bit key for so long increased the chances for the encryption scheme to be broken.

Travel Advisory

Despite being criticized for published weaknesses, DES-based encryption is still in wide use today. One use is the encryption of digital video disks (DVDs), thus contributing to the increase in piracy of feature films.

Over time, and after tests with multi-CPU systems proved the standard could be broken through brute force, DES encryption was considered insecure. A Double DES encryption scheme was created that contained a key length of 112 bits, but its susceptibility to being cracked wasn't considered much different from the original DES.

Triple DES is a 168-bit encryption standard that's resistant to cryptanalysis because it uses 48 rounds of cryptographic computations. 3DES is considered 2^{56} times stronger than DES. The main disadvantage of 3DES is that encryption and decryption are almost three times slower than with DES.

AES

AES (also often called Rijndael, pronounced *rain-doll*) is the government-defined encryption standard created to replace DES, which was considered vulnerable. The new standard uses a symmetric-block cipher supporting variable block and key lengths, such as 128, 192, and 256 bits. In 2003, the U.S. government stated that the AES encryption standard using 128-bit key lengths could be used for nonclassified documents, while AES using 192 to 256 bits was required for top-secret purposes.

AES itself has not been compromised, but several speculative theoretical attacks have been published. Some attacks, called "side channel attacks," have compromised AES encrypted data, but only because the implementation of the encryption scheme itself was weak, not the encryption algorithm. These cases are rare, and they typically involved attacking an application server using AES that had weaknesses in its timing and caching mechanisms that accidentally leaked data, which led to discovery of the AES key.

Blowfish

Blowfish is a symmetric block cipher that uses 64-bit blocks of data. Its key length is 448 bits, and it uses 16 rounds of cryptographic computations. Blowfish was designed specifically for 32-bit machines and is significantly faster than DES.

Twofish

Twofish is also a symmetric key block cipher that is very like Blowfish, but it uses a block size of 128 bits and key sizes up to 256 bits. Twofish is a free, public-domain encryption cipher and is often used in open-source projects such as OpenPGP.

IDEA

IDEA is a symmetric block cipher that uses 64-bit blocks of data, with a key length of 128 bits. The data blocks are divided into 16 smaller sections, which are subjected to eight rounds of cryptographic computation. The speed of IDEA in software is like that of DES. IDEA is the cipher used in the popular encryption program Pretty Good Privacy (PGP).

RC4

RC4 is a symmetric stream cipher created by RSA Data Security in 1987. With its speed and simplicity, it has been used in popular encryption protocols such as SSL, TLS, and 40-bit and 128-bit WEP (Wireless Encryption Protocol). It utilizes the secure exchange of a shared key. There are weaknesses in some implementations of RC4, such as 40- and 128-bit WEP, and early implementations of WPA. This means you should always use proven technologies for wireless encryption, such as WPA2, which uses Counter mode with Cipher Block Chaining Message Authentication Code Protocol (CCMP) with AES-128.

Asymmetric Encryption Algorithms

This section describes the asymmetric-based algorithms.

RSA

RSA, one of the most popular asymmetric public key algorithms, is the main standard for encryption and digital signatures and is widely used for electronic devices, operating systems, and software applications. The acronym stands for Rivest, Shamir, and Adleman, the inventors of this technique. RSA is also used in many web servers that use SSL, and its algorithm is based on the factoring of prime numbers to obtain private and public key pairs. RSA is used primarily for encryption and digital signatures.

Elliptic Curve Cryptography

Elliptic Curve Cryptography (ECC) provides functionality like RSA, such as encryption and digital signatures. The ECC cryptosystem uses complex mathematical structures to create secure asymmetric algorithms and keys. It was created for devices with smaller processing capabilities, such as cell phones, personal digital assistants (PDAs), and other wireless devices. ECC uses smaller keys than the similar RSA; larger keys need more processing power to compute.

Diffie–Hellman

The Diffie–Hellman Exchange (DHE) isn't an actual encryption algorithm: it's a key agreement protocol that enables users to exchange encryption keys over an insecure medium. Diffie–Hellman groups mandate the strength of the key used within an exchange, with the highest groups providing more security but requiring more time to compute as a result. The Diffie–Hellman protocol depends on the discrete logarithmic formulas for its security. The main vulnerability with the basic protocol is that the key exchange doesn't authenticate the participants. Further enhancements to the Diffie–Hellman protocol, such as the Elliptic Curve Diffie–Hellman Exchange (ECDHE), allow the two parties to authenticate each other through the addition of more advanced technologies such as Elliptic Curve public/private key pairs, digital signatures, and public key certificates. This system is used in the Public Key Infrastructure (PKI).

Travel Assistance
Public Key Infrastructure is described in more detail in Chapter 5.

DSA

The Digital Signature Algorithm (DSA) was selected by NIST, in cooperation with the NSA, as the digital authentication standard of the U.S. government. DSA is based on discrete logarithms and is used only for authentication. The algorithm is considered secure when the key size is large enough. DSA was originally proposed with a 512-bit key size and was eventually revised to support key sizes up to 1024 bits. Because of DSA's lack of key exchange capabilities, relative slowness, and public distrust of the process due to the government involvement in creating it, many people prefer RSA for digital signatures and encryption, but both standards are used widely.

One-Time Pad

A one-time pad is a type of encryption scheme that, when implemented correctly, is considered secure and theoretically impossible to compromise. The pad is generated from random values and uses a mathematic function called an *exclusive-OR (XOR)* to encrypt the plain-text message into ciphertext. One-time pads are secure because they are only ever used once, the pad values are completely random, and the communication of the pad is secure.

Quantum Cryptography

Quantum cryptography is an extremely advanced technique for protecting key distribution through light-based quantum computing. The technique uses the quantum effect of light waves over fiber-optic cable to transmit code within theoretically unbreakable light pulses to distribute a shared key between two users. Unfortunately, the expensive hardware required to support quantum cryptography means it is limited to only the most advanced and secure of environments, such as scientific research or military applications.

Implementing Encryption Protocols

Securing communication between systems is an important part of security that prevents malicious users from capturing data in transit. The following sections outline some of the various encryption protocols and their implementations in communications security.

Wireless Encryption Protocol

For wireless networks, the WEP security protocol provides encrypted communication between wireless clients and access points. WEP uses a key encryption algorithm used to encrypt communications between devices. Each client and access point on the wireless local area network (LAN) must use the same encryption key. The key is manually configured on each access point and each client before either can access the network. Basic WEP specifies the use of up to 64-bit keys (a 40-bit key plus a 24-bit initialization vector); however, 64-bit WEP encryption has been proven to be vulnerable to attack because of a weak algorithm. Most devices now support up to 128-bit encryption (a 104-bit key plus a 24-bit initialization vector), but this, too, this has also been proven to be vulnerable. Because most modern (meaning the last five or six years) access points and other wireless devices now support stronger encryption mechanisms, if your wireless access point supports only WEP, the best thing for you to do is upgrade your legacy equipment to something newer so you can take advantage of better encryption mechanisms. If for some reason you can't upgrade, you should use 128-bit WEP encryption in conjunction with other security controls such as MAC address filtering and network identifiers, along with other security mechanisms, such as IPSec and HTTPS.

Travel Assistance

For more details on wireless security, see Chapter 10.

WPA and WPA2 Security   Wi-Fi Protected Access (WPA) was created as a "quick fix" to issues within the WEP standard until the full implementation of WPA2. WPA can use a preshared key, or it can use an authentication server that distributes the keys. In the preshared key method (also called "Personal WPA"), all devices on the wireless LAN must use the same passphrase key to access the network. The authentication server method (also called "Enterprise WPA") is more suited for environments with hundreds of clients, where using a single passphrase key for each device is not scalable, and the authentication server takes care of key management between the wireless devices on the network. Using WPA, data is encrypted using a 128-bit key that is routinely changed during sessions using the Temporal Key Integrity Protocol (TKIP). With WPA, a single-session key cannot be hacked by the time the protocol changes keys. WPA also provides for improved integrity checking of the data traversing the wireless network to make sure that data cannot be intercepted and changed on the way to its destination. This provides much more protection than the original WEP.

A WPA network, however, is only as strong as the passphrase used. A WPA passphrase can be from 8 to 63 characters long and should be as strong as possible and not based on known dictionary words. It should include numbers, uppercase and lowercase characters, and special characters such as the @ symbol. All devices on the WPA network must share the same passphrase, including all access points. WPA2 is the true replacement to WEP and adds Robust Security Network (RSN) support that includes added protection for ad hoc networks, key caching, pre-roaming authentication, and the CCMP, which uses the AES cipher to replace TKIP. All currently manufactured devices support WPA2 in addition to WPA. If your network devices support WPA2, they should definitely use this type of encryption. However, many older devices do not support WPA2, and you will have to use WPA or some other common encryption method, such as WEP, that can be supported by all your clients. It's a good idea to begin phasing these devices out sooner rather than later.

Exam Tip

You should use the highest level of encryption available for wireless networks, such as WPA2. Older levels of encryption, such as WEP and WPA, have proved to be vulnerable. Use proven technologies such as WPA2 to maximize your security.

Pretty Good Privacy

By default, e-mail protocols such as SMTP, IMAP, and POP3 don't encrypt e-mail messages. This means anyone who might have access to your account, who has hacked the system, or who is capturing the unprotected network traffic can read your private e-mail messages. E-mail messages, once sent, can relay among many e-mail servers until they arrive at their destination. If any one of these servers is insecure, e-mail could be captured and viewed. Users can protect themselves with encryption products or by using digital certificates. Once the e-mail is encrypted, there's no way for an unauthorized user to view the contents of the e-mail. The destination user must also have the matching encryption key so he or she can unlock the message when it arrives.

PGP is one of the most common encryption tools used to protect messages on the Internet, because it's both easy to use and effective. In fact, PGP is so effective that the creator, Phil Zimmermann, was investigated for potentially violating U.S. export laws focused on the export of cryptographic materials. PGP uses its own decentralized type of digital certificates using an RSA-based public key encryption method with two keys: one is a public key you give to anyone with whom you share messages, and the other is a private key you use to decrypt messages you receive. A passphrase is used to encrypt the user's private key, which is stored on the local computer. Each PGP user distributes his own public key, thus creating a "web of trust" with other users. Each user keeps a collection of the other users' public keys on a "key ring." PGP is different from a centralized certificate authority, where one authority is used to authenticate users. Instead, using PGP, users rely on each other to establish trust between other users and their keys.

GNU Privacy Guard (GPG)

GNU Privacy Guard (GPG) is a free, open-source implementation of the OpenPGP standard. Intended as a free replacement for PGP, GPG does not contain any patented encryption algorithms, and it supports many technologies, including DSA, RSA, AES, 3DES, Blowfish, Twofish, MD5, SHA-1, and RIPEMD-160.

GPG utilizes asymmetric keys that are generated by GPG end users. Public keys can be exchanged with other users via Internet key servers. You can also use digital signatures to verify the sender and the integrity of the message.

Travel Assistance
For detailed information on PGP, see www.pgp.com. Note that Symantec purchased the PGP standard. For detailed information on GPG, see www.gnupg.org.

S/MIME

Multipurpose Internet Mail Extensions (MIME) is a specification for transferring multimedia and attachments through e-mail. This specification offers a standard way for all mail clients and mail transfer systems to handle certain types of attachments. For example, if a user sends an audio clip to another user through e-mail, the MIME header will include information on the attachment. When the audio clip reaches the destination user, the user's computer will understand what type of file it is and what application can be used to open it.

Secure MIME (S/MIME) is an extension of the MIME standard that is used for digitally signing and encrypting e-mail using certificates. S/MIME is used for sending confidential e-mail that needs to be secured so that other users can't capture the message and read its contents. By the sender encrypting the e-mail, an unauthorized user will be unable to decipher the contents of the message and its attachments. S/MIME requires the use of public key certificates for authentication and provides message confidentiality and integrity via the user's encryption and hashing algorithms.

SSL and TLS

Although the data on a server might be secured from unauthorized access, the communications pathways between the server and client systems might not be. The SSL protocol enables communication between systems to be encrypted.

Many websites have both secured and unsecured areas. The secured areas might provide access to a financial bank account or a database of personal information, for example. This secured area of the site usually requires user authentication to proceed. To increase security when switching from the unsecured public part of a website to a secured area, SSL encryption is invoked. SSL must be supported by both the web server and the client browser to function. It is also often used in e-mail systems to secure the message communications between mail servers and mail clients.

In an SSL communication, a process known as a digital handshake occurs. The handshaking phase begins when the server sends a message to the client indicating a secure session must be set up. The client then sends its security information and encryption key to the server, which compares the credentials with its own to find the right match. Next, the server sends authentication information so the client knows the web server with which it is communicating is the correct one. This is an important step, because it's possible, through redirection or other methods, that a user can be switched from one website to another without the user's knowledge. So, for example, as you enter your username and password, you might be entering the information into a bogus website that collects this information to perform unauthorized activity with your accounts. This handshake confirms not only that you are who you say you are, but also that the site with which you're connected is the actual site you expect it to be. The SSL protocol uses public key cryptography in the handshake phase to securely exchange symmetric session keys that are then used to encrypt communications for the duration of the session, as shown in Figure 4.6. When the client moves to another website, the encrypted session is closed.

Because of weaknesses when implementing SSL, there have been different exploits that could facilitate man-in-the-middle attacks on the protocol. For this reason, TLS was invented to replace SSL; all versions of SSL are now essentially defunct and have been replaced effectively with TLS. TLS builds on the security of SSL with more enhanced encryption and authentication techniques to secure communications between a client and a server. However, TLS is not interoperable with SSL.

TLS is a widely implemented protocol used to secure connections to websites, e-mail connections between e-mail servers and clients, instant messaging and VoIP applications, and connections to Lightweight Directory Access

Session key

Session key

SSL session

Web server certificate

Certificate authority

FIGURE 4.6   SSL encryption between client and web server

Protocol (LDAP) servers. Cipher suites support the underlying security of both SSL and TLS through the implementation of a combination of authentication, encryption, and MAC algorithms that negotiate the security of the connection. Any number of algorithms can be used, including DHE, ECDHE, AES, MD5, and so on.

Different server implementations of SSL and TLS are possible with the adoption of either strong or weak ciphers. It is important to understand which type of cipher you choose to utilize based on requirements; if strong ciphers are used, weak ciphers should be disabled. Either way, you should research or scan to see what type of ciphers your server implementation supports and make a conscientious decision.

HTTPS

The Hypertext Transfer Protocol over Secure Socket Layer (HTTPS) provides a secure means of communicating HTTP data between a web browser and a web server. All HTTP communications are sent in clear text, so no messages are secure, and they can be easily viewed using a protocol analyzer. This makes HTTP unusable for communications requiring security and privacy, such as web-based banking and other online financial transactions. HTTPS protects the communication channel by using SSL and certificates to provide encrypted and protected communications. When you're connecting to a website that uses a secured channel, the uniform resource locator (URL) begins with *https* instead of *http*, as in *https://secure.website.com*. HTTPS is typically used in banking and online shopping transactions, where the transfer of credit card and personal information must be encrypted to prevent an unauthorized user from stealing the information while it's in transit between the client and the server. When a client connects to the secure site, the web server sends a certificate to the web browser to establish its identity. If the browser accepts the certificate and finds no validation issues with the certificate, SSL is activated between the server and client. This ensures that the website is genuine (it is what it says it is) and that the client is not connecting to a *rogue* site. In many web browsers, a secure site is indicated by a small padlock icon in the application taskbar. HTTPS uses TCP port 443 for communications. Note that HTTPS should not be confused with S-HTTP, another similar implementation that only encrypts the message headers.

IPSec

IPSec is a standards-based suite of protocols that provides privacy, integrity, and authenticity to information transferred across IP networks. It works on the IP network layer to encrypt communications between the sender and receiver. IPSec is most often used to secure virtual private network (VPN) communications over an open network such as the Internet; however, because IPSec operates at lower levels than most application security protocols (such as SSL), it offers greater flexibility in its implementation, because applications do not need to be aware of IPSec to make use of its benefits. IPSec ensures that communications cannot be read by a third party, that traffic has not been modified in transit, and that messages received are from a trusted source.

IPSec uses two types of encryption modes: transport and tunnel. In *transport* mode, IPSec encrypts the data portion of each packet, but not the header. This can be used only in host-to-host communications. *Tunnel* mode, on the other hand, encrypts both the header and the data of the network packet. This is used to host VPN gateway communications, the most common form of virtual private network. The receiver of the packet uses IPSec to decrypt the message. For IPSec to work, each communicating device needs to be running IPSec and share some form of public key. Key management is provided by the Internet Key Exchange (IKE), formerly ISAKMP/Oakley. IKE enables the receiver to obtain a public key and authenticate the sender using digital certificates.

IPSec consists of component protocols, including authentication header (AH) and encapsulating security payload (ESP) headers. The AH is an IP header that is added to a network packet and provides its cryptographic checksum. This checksum is used to achieve authentication and integrity to ensure that the packet has been sent by a specified source and has not been captured and changed in transit. ESP is a header applied to an IP packet after it has been encrypted. It provides data confidentiality so that the packet cannot be viewed in transit. In newer IPSec implementations, the AH functionality is always performed within the ESP header, resulting in a single combined ESP/AH header.

Security associations (SAs) are the basic building blocks of IPSec communications. Before any two devices can communicate using IPSec, they must first establish a set of SAs that specify the cryptographic parameters that must be agreed upon by both devices before data can be transferred securely between them, including the encryption and authentication algorithms and keys.

The primary way of establishing SAs and managing VPN keys is via the Internet Security Association and Key Management Protocol (ISAKMP) and IKE. ISAKMP/IKE is the protocol for performing automated key management for IPSec. The ISAKMP/IKE process automatically negotiates with the remote VPN device to establish the parameters for individual SAs. An SA is established so that all key exchanges can be encrypted and no keys need to be passed over the Internet in clear text. Once the SA is established, a session SA is negotiated for securing normal VPN traffic, referred to as IKE Phase-1 and Phase-2 negotiations. The session SAs are short-lived and are renegotiated at regular intervals, ensuring that the keys are discarded regularly. The same keys are used only for a small amount of time and for limited amounts of data.

SSH

SSH (Secure Shell) is a secure remote-access utility that lets a user log in to a remote machine and execute commands as if they were working at the console of that system. Other remote access utilities such as Telnet are insecure because the data isn't encrypted when communicated. SSH provides a secure, encrypted tunnel to access another system remotely. It is sometimes used as a low-cost alternative to normal VPN communications because of its simple installation and delivery of well-encrypted, secure communications.

SSH uses public key cryptography for authentication, and when a client connects to a system using SSH, an initial handshaking process begins and a special session key is exchanged. This starts the session, and a secure channel is created to allow the access.

Vulnerabilities have been discovered in some versions of SSH, so make sure you are using the latest version. Early versions of SSH were susceptible to man-in-the-middle attacks because a hacker could capture the headers of the handshaking phase to intercept the session key.

Key Stretching

Key-stretching techniques strengthen a weak key, usually a password, against brute-force attacks by increasing the time for testing each potential key. Passwords are particularly susceptible to brute-force or other password-cracking attacks because they are often quite short and are created by humans.

Key stretching works to counteract this by creating an enhanced key—a result of the initial key and a hash function or a block cipher being applied in a loop. This enhanced key should be theoretically impossible (or at least cost prohibitive) to crack through various attacks. The two common functions used for key stretching are the Password-Based Key Derivation Function 2 (PBKDF2) and bcrypt.

Decision Making

Cryptographic algorithms and techniques are considered suitable for use based on different factors, including encryption strength, ease of implementation, high resilience to cryptographic attacks, and the requirement to use a particular cryptographic service provider or crypto-modules. Some methods are more suitable than others, depending on the level of protection required. Other methods may be more suitable due to practicality or resource constraints. In any case, organizations and users must evaluate certain considerations when looking at various algorithms and methods for encryption. As we've discussed throughout the chapter, some algorithms are weaker than others for various reasons, including the use of weak initialization vectors and key sizes. It's important to understand the pros and cons of various algorithms, and to select algorithms that are strong and resilient against attack.

Data States

Data is generally at the heart of what we're trying to protect, and what its state is at any given time makes a huge difference in the protection scheme that should be applied. There are three main states that should be considered: data at rest, data in use, and data in transit. Cryptography is used extensively to protect data at rest—that is, while it is being stored in a file, folder, tape backup, or database. *Data at rest* is inactive in its current state. Most modern operating systems have built-in schemes for protecting data at rest that's resident within its environment (such as Windows BitLocker). *Data in use* is data that is currently being processed through an information system, or data that is being stored in a nonpersistent state, such as memory, whereas *data in transit* is information moving across an internal network, such as a corporate intranet or an external network such as the Internet. It is critical to identify where critical data is residing, what state it currently is in, and whether it is leaving your network, and you should choose an encryption scheme that protects it within all the various states. For example, PII information should be tracked throughout all its states: encrypted while at rest, tracked for its use, and encrypted when sent to highly vetted sources.

Choosing and Implementing the Best Method

Generally, the stronger the algorithm, the better the encryption provided, and the more resilient it will be to cryptographic attack. When you're considering your options, factors such as key length, keyspace, and mode of operation make for stronger encryption. Weak and deprecated algorithms often have common characteristics, including shorter keys and a less complex keyspace. One common flaw is poor implementation. In fact, stronger algorithms can suffer attacks if they are not implemented securely, so taking care here is critical.

Selecting strong ciphers over weak ciphers often isn't the primary consideration, however. The cryptographic method or algorithm that's selected depends on the ability of the operating system, application, or even hardware to support it, or the time that the method or algorithm requires to do its business. For example, devices that have low-power and low-latency requirements, such as embedded medical devices, require cryptographic solutions that balance strength and resource requirements in an efficient and effective manner. (Certainly you wouldn't want your pacemaker to have resource issues!) Resources must be considered alongside security, and understanding the context in which the cryptographic method or algorithm will be used will allow for the correct decision to be made that balances both considerations.

CHECKPOINT

✓**Objective 4.01: Utilize the Concepts of Cryptography** Information assurance protects information and information systems by securing their confidentiality, integrity, authentication, and nonrepudiation. An algorithm is a complex mathematical formula that dictates how the encryption and decryption process takes place. Because these mathematical algorithms are usually publicly known, the cryptosystem is strengthened with the addition of a secret key. A key is like a password that's combined with the algorithm to create ciphertext, and encrypted data can't be deciphered unless the same key is used to decrypt it. In a symmetric encryption scheme, both parties use the same key for encryption and decryption purposes. In an asymmetric encryption scheme, everyone uses different but mathematically related keys for encryption and decryption purposes. Random numbers are often used within algorithms to prevent replay attacks.

✔**Objective 4.02: Use and Apply Appropriate Cryptographic Tools and Products**   A hashing value is used in encryption systems to create a "fingerprint" for a message. This provides assurance that the message has not been accessed and changed on the way to its destination. In the overall information assurance model, hashing is used to protect the integrity of a message and is most often used with digital signatures. A one-way hash is a mathematical function that transforms a variable-sized message into a fixed-length value, referred to as either a hash value or a message digest. Popular hashing algorithms include MD5 and SHA. Use AES-256 and RSA algorithms as secure encryption algorithms. A one-time pad must be used only once, must be truly random, and must be communicated securely. Use WPA2 for encrypting wireless networks, as the WEP and WPA technologies have become vulnerable. Encryption protocols include SSL/TLS and HTTPS for secure web communications and IPSec for VPN communications. Use SSH as an encrypted alternative to Telnet or other mechanisms that use clear text in their communications. Key stretching strengthens potentially weak passwords or phrases by applying cryptographic principles to increase the time costs of password cracking. Different solutions should be utilized based on the state of the critical data: either data at rest, data in use, or data in transit. Finally, you need to understand the different cipher suites available for use, their strengths and weaknesses, and how they can be applied appropriately to meet resource and security requirements.

REVIEW QUESTIONS

1. You have encrypted an e-mail message that is only meant to be seen by the recipient. A hacker has intercepted the message. When he views the message, what does he see?

    A. The plain text of the e-mail

    B. One-way hash of the message

    C. The recipient's certificate information

    D. Ciphertext

2. You have been tasked with implementing information assurance principles within your organization's security and encryption functions. Which of the following isn't a function of information assurance within encryption systems?

    A. Efficiency

    B. Confidentiality

    C. Integrity

    D. Nonrepudiation

3. You have sent your friend a secret, encrypted message. The key you used to encrypt the message is the same key with which your friend will decrypt the message. What type of encryption scheme is used?

   A. Asymmetric

   B. Symmetric

   C. RSA

   D. Diffie–Hellman

4. Which of the following encryption schemes would you use if your company wants to create an invisible watermark hidden within the images on its website to identify the images in case they are used by another company?

   A. One-time pad

   B. Elliptical curve

   C. One-way hash

   D. Steganography

5. Your organization wants you to implement an encryption system that ensures the sender and receiver of the encrypted message use different keys for encryption and decryption. Which type of encryption scheme would you use?

   A. Elliptical curve

   B. Quantum

   C. Asymmetric

   D. Symmetric

6. Which of the following protocols would you use for message authentication and integrity in your encryption systems?

   A. Steganography

   B. Elliptical curve

   C. HMAC

   D. One-time pad

7. You have been asked to implement hashing protocols that have a low possibility of a hashing collision. Which of the following describes a hashing collision?

   A. The greater probability that two or more people in a group of 23 share the same birthday

   B. That the hash values of two different messages are identical

   C. An invalid digital signature

   D. When a 128-bit message digest is mixed with a 256-bit message digest

8. When you connect to a secure website, you are asked to accept the server certificate. What is the function of the digital certificate?

    A. It securely validates the identity of the server and its public key.

    B. It identifies you to a certificate authority.

    C. It provides your ID required by the government to request a public key.

    D. It allows you to assess your web sessions for vulnerabilities.

9. You want to start a secure web session to your banking website to prevent your credentials and financial information from passing as clear text. Which of the following protocols do you use?

    A. DES

    B. SSH

    C. HTTPS

    D. HTTP

10. The following are some of the steps for making a connection to an online banking site in order to conduct a transaction. Put them in the correct order.

    a. A digital certificate establishes the website identity to the browser.

    b. SSL is activated between the client and the server.

    c. The browser accepts the certificate from the web server.

    d. Banking transactions are accepted.

    A. a, c, b, d

    B. a, b, c, d

    C. c, b, a, d

    D. d, b, c, b

REVIEW ANSWERS

1. **D** Clear text is transformed into ciphertext after being put through some type of cipher or encryption algorithm system. The ciphertext is unreadable unless it is decrypted back into clear-text form.

2. **A** Efficiency is not a function of information assurance within encryption systems. The four basic functions pertaining to information assurance are confidentiality, integrity, authentication, and nonrepudiation.

3. **B**   In a symmetric encryption scheme, both parties use the same key for encryption and decryption purposes. Both users must possess the same key to send encrypted messages to each other.

4. **D**   Steganography hides data in another type of media that effectively conceals the existence of the data.

5. **C**   An asymmetric encryption scheme relies on the sender and receiver of a message to use different keys for encryption and decryption. The keys are mathematically related, but they can't be derived from each other.

6. **C**   HMAC (Hash-based Message Authentication Code) is used to authenticate a message and provide data integrity. The Message Authentication Code (MAC) is sent along with the message itself so that the receiver can authenticate the sender of the message and verify the integrity of the message contents.

7. **B**   A collision occurs within a hashing algorithm when the hashed values of two different messages are the same value. Collisions can be used to aid in cracking a hacking algorithm.

8. **A**   A digital certificate is a credential required by PKI systems that can securely identify an organization's server, as well as create an association between the server's authenticated identity and its public keys.

9. **C**   HTTP communications send all data in clear-text form. For secure web communications, HTTPS is a secure means of communicating HTTP data between a web browser and a web server. HTTPS protects the communication channel by using SSL to provide encrypted and protected communications.

10. **A**   When a client connects to the secure HTTPS site, the web server sends a certificate to the web browser to establish its identity. If the browser accepts the certificate and finds no validation issues with it, SSL is activated between the server and client. No other communication can occur between the server and client until the certificate is validated and accepted.

Public Key Infrastructure

	NEWBIE	SOME EXPERIENCE	EXPERT
ETA	2 hours	1.5 hours	1 hour

Traditional cryptography methods based on symmetric key cryptography use the same secret key by both the sender (to encrypt the message) and the receiver (to decrypt the message). Unfortunately, it can be difficult to transmit the secret key securely from one user to another. If an unauthorized user intercepts the key, he can decrypt, read, forge, and modify all messages encrypted using that key. Key management is a challenge for these systems, especially for systems that serve large numbers of users.

Public key cryptography was introduced in 1976 by Whitfield Diffie and Martin Hellman, whose public key protocol was created to solve the key management problem. In public key cryptography, each user receives two keys: the public key and the private key. The private key is kept secret, while the public key can be published for any user to see or use. The problem faced using symmetric keys is solved because no need exists to share a secret key. All transmissions involve only the public keys; no private key is ever transmitted or shared. With public key cryptography, *asymmetric cryptography* is used to exchange symmetric keys. The sender encrypts the message with the receiver's public key. The receiver then decrypts the message with his own private key, as shown in Figure 5.1. The security mechanism is safe if the private keys aren't compromised.

Public key cryptography is efficient and secure, and it scales well with a large number of users, making it ideal for all types of critical personal and business communications and transactions. This chapter describes the core concepts and implementation of public key cryptography, including certificate authorities and the certificate life cycle.

FIGURE 5.1   Public key cryptography

Explain the Fundamentals of Public Key Infrastructure

The *Public Key Infrastructure (PKI)* is a standard infrastructure consisting of a framework of procedures, standards, and protocols, based on public key cryptography. A hybrid of asymmetric and symmetric key algorithms, PKI provides the full range of information assurance objectives for confidentiality, integrity, authentication, and nonrepudiation. The asymmetric keys are used for authentication, and then one or more symmetric keys are generated and exchanged using asymmetric encryption.

> **Travel Assistance**
>
> See Chapter 4 for detailed information on the differences between asymmetric and symmetric cryptography.

A message is encrypted with a symmetric algorithm, and that key is then encrypted asymmetrically using the recipient's public key. The entire message (symmetrically encrypted body and asymmetrically encrypted key) is sent to the recipient. The message can also be digitally signed using digital certificates.

> **Exam Tip**
>
> Public key cryptography uses a hybrid of symmetric and asymmetric encryption systems. A message is encrypted using a symmetric algorithm, and that key is then encrypted asymmetrically using the recipient's public key. The entire message (symmetrically encrypted body and asymmetrically encrypted key) is sent to the recipient.

Digital Certificates

A digital certificate is an electronic credential required by PKI systems that can securely identify an individual, as well as create an association between the individual's authenticated identity and public keys. Common certificate extensions include .der, .pem, .cer, .crt, .p12, .p7b, and .pfx, as various formats and encodings can be used. A trusted party, called a *certificate authority (CA)*, is used to sign and issue certificates. The CA is responsible for verifying the identity of a key owner and binding the owner to a public key. This enables users who have never met to exchange encrypted communications because the authentication is performed by the CA.

Travel Advisory

An emerging best security practice is to "pin" a host with its verified certificate or public key; this creates a trust relationship between you and the site, rather than relying solely in the CAs trustworthiness. Google, for example, has implemented pinning in Chrome.

Each certificate contains a unique serial number, an identity, and public key information for the user, as well as the validity dates for the life of the certificate. Table 5.1 lists different types of commonly used certificates.

Travel Advisory

Certificate extensions are not always interchangeable, due to the different formats and encodings used. Some can be converted from one format to another, however, if required.

Certificate Authorities

A certificate authority is an organization or entity that issues and manages digital certificates and is responsible for authenticating and identifying users who participate in the PKI. This service doesn't necessarily involve a third party; it can be internal to an organization. A CA server can be set up to act as the manager of certificates and the user's public keys.

Third-party CAs are special organizations dedicated to certificate management. Some of the larger companies that offer this service, such as VeriSign and Entrust, have their functionality built into popular web browsers to perform certificate services automatically.

Exam Tip

A certificate authority is an organization or entity that issues and manages digital certificates. The CA is responsible for authenticating and identifying users who participate in the PKI.

TABLE 5.1	Commonly Used Certificates
Name	**Description**
Wildcard	Used to secure multiple first-level subdomains within one domain; one certificate can be used for *.mheducation.com, for example. Cannot be used for both *.mheducation.com and *.mheducation.net.
Subject Alternative Name (SAN)	Used to specify multiple hosts to use the same certificate. Can be used for www.mheducation.com and www.mheducation.net.
Code signing	Used to validate the integrity of code to ensure that it has not been tampered with.
Self-signed	A certificate that is signed by the same organization that it is certifying.
Machine/computer	Used for identifying and controlling which machines/computers are allowed to access network resources within an organization.
E-mail	Used to provide both confidentiality and integrity of e-mail when used with S/MIME.
User	Used for client authentication and encrypting user files.
Root	Used to validate the authenticity of other certificates; sometimes referred to as "trust anchors" and self-signed.
Domain validation	Used within X.509 to validate control of a domain.
Extended validation (EV)	Used within HTTPS to validate domains; obtaining an EV requires a request be made to a CA to prove identity. Can be used for multiple domains but not wildcards.

Some of the actual authentication and identification services for certificates are managed by other organizations called *registration authorities (RAs)*. These organizations offload some of the work from CAs by confirming the identities of users, issuing key pairs, and initiating the certificate process with a CA on behalf of the user. The RA acts as a middleman between the user and the CA, and doesn't issue certificates on its own.

A user will send a Certificate Signing Request (CSR) to a CA to apply for a certificate. To verify the user's identity, the CA and RA will usually require some form of identification, such as a driver's license, Social Security number, address, or phone number. For an organization, the CSR will often require the fully qualified domain name of the server, the name of the organization, and the public key for the organization. Once the identification is established, the CA generates public and private keys for the user. A certificate is then generated with the identification and public key information embedded within it.

Exam Tip

A certificate contains the authenticated identification of a user or organization and their public key information.

Once the user is registered and receives his certificate, he can begin using it to send encrypted messages. When the receiver receives the message, her software can verify the certificate to ensure the message is from the stated sender. Certificates can also be revoked if the certificate's original subscriber information has changed, has been compromised, or is no longer valid.

Travel Advisory

Certificate authorities formally define their policies (from low to high assurance) in Certificate Practice Statements and assign a machine-readable Object Identifier (OID). This is then distributed to anyone who would validate the certificate. An example is S/MIME for secure e-mail: the OID is 1.2.840.113549.1.9.16.

Trust Models

Trust models define how users trust other users, companies, CAs, and RAs within the PKI. These models provide a chain of trust from a user's public key to the root key of a CA. The validated chain then implies authenticity of all the certificates. The following are the most common trust models used in PKI.

Web of Trust

The web of trust is a simplistic trust model that relies on each user creating and signing his or her own certificate, as shown in Figure 5.2. This is the basis for encryption applications, such as Pretty Good Privacy (PGP) or Gnu Privacy Guard (GPG), where no central authority exists. With this model, each user is responsible for authentication and trust, and anyone can sign someone else's public key. When User A signs User B's key, User A is introducing User B's key to anyone who trusts User A. Each user is then considered a trusted introducer in the model.

Third-Party (Single Authority) Trust

A third-party central certifying agency signs a given key and authenticates the owner of the key. Trusting that authority means, by association, that you trust all keys issued by that authority, as shown in Figure 5.3. Each user authenticates

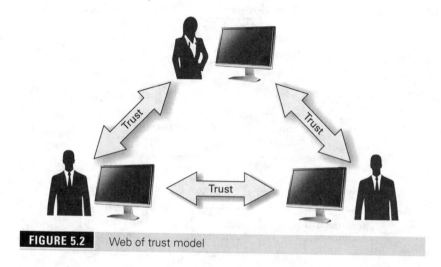

FIGURE 5.2 Web of trust model

the other through the exchange of certificates. The users know the CA has performed all the necessary identification of the owner of the certificate and can therefore trust the owner of the message.

Hierarchical Model

The hierarchical model is an extension of the third-party model, in which root CAs issue certificates to other lower-level CAs and RAs, as shown in Figure 5.4. Each user's most trusted key is the root CA's public key. The trust inheritance can be followed from the certificate back to the root CA. This model allows enforcement of policies and standards throughout the infrastructure, producing a higher level of overall assurance than other trust models. A root certificate

FIGURE 5.3 Third-party (single authority) trust model

FIGURE 5.4   Hierarchical trust models

is trusted by software applications on behalf of the user. Intermediate CAs are subordinate to root CAs and trusted much like the root CAs in that they are delegated authority to issue and validate certificates.

Local Lingo

root certificate   The highest certificate in the hierarchical tree. A root certificate is used to sign other, lower-level certificates, which inherit the trust of the root certificate.

For example, web browsers create trusted connections to secure servers using the Secure Sockets Layer (SSL), using root certificates that identify to the user that this website and its certificate are trusted.

Root CAs are so critical to the trust model that they are often kept disconnected from any network, and are sometimes powered down (offline). Once intermediate CAs have the ability to issue, validate, and revoke certificates, the need to have the root CA available is outweighed by the damage that would be caused by its compromise (potentially requiring revocation of all issued certificates). Keeping the root CA offline minimizes this potential, and the root CA can be brought back online for important tasks such as issuing and reissuing intermediate CA certificates.

Key Management and Storage

Encryption key management deals with the generation, distribution, storage, and backup of keys. Securing encryption keys is an extremely important aspect of encryption and cryptography. Once a key is generated, it must be secured to avoid an unauthorized user discovering the key. Attacks on public key systems are typically focused on the key management system rather than on attempts to break the encryption algorithm itself. No matter how secure or difficult a cryptographic algorithm, the entire process can be compromised by poor key management.

Centralized vs. Decentralized Storage

Keys need to be generated and securely sent to the correct user. The user must then store the key in a secure place so that it can't be accessed by another user. The key can be encrypted and stored on a hard drive, a DVD, a flash device, a universal serial bus (USB) key, or a Trusted Platform Module (TPM). The keys should also be recoverable if they're lost or damaged, or if passwords to use them are forgotten. Key storage is an important aspect of secure key management, which can be centralized either to a server or a third-party service. Key storage can involve both hardware and software storage methods.

In the early days of encryption key management, cryptographic keys were stored in secure boxes and delivered to users by hand. The keys were given to the systems administrator, who distributed them from a main server or by visiting each workstation. This type of administrative overhead for key management could almost be a job itself, and it obviously didn't scale well in large enterprise networks. In today's networks, key distribution and storage are typically performed automatically through a special key management system, such as a key management server, or through a third-party service such as VeriSign or Entrust. Key management can be an extremely time-consuming process for network administrators in a large enterprise network.

Centralized Storage   Most modern encryption infrastructures use a centralized storage system for key management—a single place where all key management occurs. This typically involves a centralized server on your network that takes care of key management for you. The server can issue key pairs, store and back them up, and take care of certificates. A centralized key management system offers several advantages:

- **Administration**   Managing the accounts and keys of users at one centralized location is secure and convenient, relieving the administrator and the users of administrative overhead. Signature verification is automatic because the validity information is co-located with the actual key and other account information.

- **Scalability**   Key management servers are built to scale to any size enterprise network.

- **Integrity**   Keys stored at a server can be easily backed up, eliminating the potential for the loss of a vital verification or an encryption key.

- **Security**   Unlike a decentralized storage system in which keys can be insecure because of lack of user education or due to operating system (OS) vulnerabilities, a key storage server is a secure environment where audited controls are required for access to the physical hardware, and the keys are protected with specialized cryptographic devices.

Exam Tip

Centralized key storage solutions provide greater security and integrity of keys than decentralized solutions. They're also far more manageable and scalable.

Decentralized Storage   A decentralized storage system is typically used by individual users and small networks. Once the user has created her keys, her private key is stored locally on her system or some other secure device. She then sends her public key with a certificate request to a CA. After authenticating the user, the CA sends her a certificate, which is again stored locally.

The advantage for end users is that they're always in control of their private keys and certificates. The users trust themselves with the security rather than trusting a server or a third-party service that might not properly protect their information or could divulge their private keys to other parties such as government authorities.

A decentralized storage method has many disadvantages as well. For example, if the user encrypts data on her hard drive and misplaces her private key, she won't be able to recover any information encrypted with her private key.

Another concern involves users in a corporate network: after a disgruntled employee leaves an organization, he might not reveal the key needed to decrypt information that was protected on the corporate network, thus denying access to the information for other people who need it.

Keys can also be damaged or lost—and if the user didn't properly back them up, those keys will be permanently lost. This means the data the user encrypted will also be lost permanently because no key exists to decrypt the information.

Travel Advisory

Decentralized methods are typically employed by individual users. Centralized types of key storage are used for larger networks of users, for which individual key management would be insecure and time consuming to manage.

Key Storage and Protection

Once a key pair has been generated, the private key must be safely stored to protect it from being compromised, lost, or damaged. The type of security used to encrypt and protect the private key should be as strong as the security used to encrypt and protect the actual message or files. A few methods for protecting the private key can be used, including both hardware and software methods.

The most important aspect of hardware key protection is the ability to protect the hardware itself. Many users store their private keys on their computers' hard disks. Their computers might be part of a network, potentially allowing access to anyone on that network. To prevent this sort of access, private keys are usually stored on removable media that can be more easily protected and can be physically carried with the user. This hardware can be typical media, such as a DVD or a USB device. However, these small media devices can be easily lost or stolen, which is why the stored key should always be encrypted. You can also use a TPM, which is a special hardware chip that is installed within a computer system or device, such as on the system motherboard of a computer desktop or laptop. This protected, encrypted module can store encryption keys that are specific to that system hardware.

Travel Assistance

Trusted Platform Modules are discussed in more detail in Chapter 12.

A private key should never be stored in its plain-text form. If an unauthorized user manages to find the file or steals the device in which the file is located, that user could uncover the private key. The simplest method of protection is to secure the encrypted private key with a password and store it locally on disk or a USB key. The password should be as carefully crafted as your network password so that it can't be guessed easily or discovered through brute-force attack methods.

Exam Tip

A private key should never be stored in plain-text form. It needs to be encrypted and protected with a password.

For enterprise-level networks, the installation of a key management system takes the burden of key storage and protection away from the user and lets the OS or application manage key storage on a centralized server.

An additional method of protection includes the generation of another key pair to be used to encrypt the private key. This key is usually kept with a third party using a type of key escrow service.

Key Escrow

The concept of key escrow has been heavily overshadowed over the years by debates between privacy groups and the government because it concerns the issues of data privacy versus national security. Key escrow involves a third party, such as a government agency or an authorized organization, that holds a special third key on top of your private and public key pair. The third key is used to encrypt the private key, which is then stored in a secure location. This third key can be used to unlock the encrypted copy of the private key in case of loss or theft of the original key. Although the main concern of privacy activists is the possible abuse by the government regarding individual data privacy, the main security issue for most companies is the idea of a third-party entity controlling a crucial part of the company's security infrastructure.

Exam Tip

Key escrow involves a trusted third party that holds a special key in addition to your private and public key pair. This third key is used to encrypt the private key, which is then securely stored. In the event the private key is lost or stolen, the third key can be used to unlock the encrypted copy of the private key.

Another common key escrow entity is the CA, which is responsible for authorizing and distributing certificates and encryption key pairs. As part of your overall security plan, the ability for the CA to protect your information is crucial. CAs are a popular target of malicious hacker attacks because of the valuable information they store. Attacks are usually targeted at the CA's own private keys.

The CA's key pairs are common targets of cryptanalytic attacks that attempt to break weak keys through brute force. CAs should be both secure and practical because their public key might be written into software used by many users. If the key needs to be changed, every user's software will need to be updated to accept the new key.

> ### Travel Advisory
>
> When examining a key escrow service, pay careful attention to its methods of security, including the secure storage and transfer of keys and certificates.

Key Recovery

As the main key to unlocking the encryption on a file or other critical data, the private key must be carefully protected. If the private key is lost or destroyed, nothing that has been encrypted with that key will be accessible. With the storage and backup of private keys, a balance must be maintained between the security of a key and the ability to archive it in the event of the need for recovery.

Unfortunately, the concept of key recovery has been clouded by the issue of government control and the possibility that the government, in the interest of national security, would require a mandatory key recovery system. Such a mandatory key recovery system might enable the government to decrypt private data using key escrow and key management companies. Whatever the outcome of that debate, secure methods of key recovery are available that keep the responsibility and capability of key recovery within the end user's hands.

Recovery Agent   One method gaining in popularity is for a company to maintain protection of the backup of its private keys but to use a third-party company, called a *recovery agent,* to store a unique key that can be used to unlock the backup of the private keys. This system prevents any of the company's private keys from leaving the premises and offers little room for compromising the security of those keys. The private keys are stored on the company's site, while the key to unlock those private keys is stored offsite.

M of N Control   Another method uses what is known as *M of N control,* which refers to a method of storing a private key, protected and encrypted, with a separate unique key. The key used for recovery is split into different parts and distributed to various individuals, called *key recovery operators,* and is usually stored in a smart card or other memory device. To use the recovery key, a certain number of the operators must be present with their part of the key.

> **Travel Advisory**
>
> M of N control can be somewhat difficult to maintain, especially with employee turnover, where new replacements must be entered into the scheme.

The term *M of N control* refers to the number of operator keys that must be present to create the recovery key, such as "2 of 3" or "4 of 7." For example, in a 4 of 7 scheme, a recovery key is split into seven parts and only four of those parts are needed to create the recovery key that will decrypt the backup of the private key.

> **Exam Tip**
>
> *M of N control* refers to the number of keys that must be present to create the recovery key, such as 3 of 5.

Multiple Key Pairs

The issue of using multiple key pairs in a PKI implementation greatly increases both the security and the complexity of data encryption. Using multiple keys directly involves the problems associated with backing up certain types of key pairs for recovery.

In a typical PKI setup, a private key and a public key are generated to be used for encryption and digital signatures. These keys can be used for three basic purposes:

- **Encryption**   To encrypt data to protect its contents
- **Authentication**   To identify users through their public keys and certificates
- **Nonrepudiation**   To make it impossible for someone to deny having signed a transaction or file

The problem with using a single key pair for these functions is that the single key pair can often conflict with the backup and recovery requirements of the organization. A key pair used for encryption should be backed up in case the private key is lost or destroyed so it can be recovered to decrypt the locked data. The backup of the same key pair used for nonrepudiation purposes, however, could be harmful. A digital signature intended to be legally binding can be repudiated if the signer proves it could be invalid because of the existence of another copy of the private key.

To solve this conflict, a dual key pair system can be used that can satisfy all security and backup requirements. One key pair can be used for encryption and decryption, while the second key pair can be used exclusively for digital signatures and nonrepudiation needs. The key pair used for encryption can be safely backed up for recovery purposes, while the second key needn't be backed up, in conformance with nonrepudiation procedures.

> **Exam Tip**
>
> Know the concept of nonrepudiation and how a dual key system can resolve the conflict with key backup.

Key History

Another important concept is the problem of key history. When using multiple keys and discarding old keys in favor of new ones, you might have archived data protected with encryption keys that you no longer use. As part of your key backup strategy, you need to retain copies of keys for encryption still in use on your network.

> **Travel Advisory**
>
> Without some form of key history, you won't be able to recover data files that have been encrypted with older keys you no longer possess.

Objective 5.02
CompTIA Security+
Objective 6.4

Implementing PKI Concepts to Promote Trust

In the overall encryption trust model, all aspects—including users, administrators, the key management server, and any third-party key management company—must be able to trust one another so that the keys and identities of those using the keys are secured. As part of identifying users of keys, certificates are created so users' identities and their public keys can be fully authenticated. If the public keys corresponding to a certain certificate have been compromised, any messages or files that were encrypted might be vulnerable. The only way to ensure the validity of the key is to check the status of the certificate.

Certificates go through a life cycle that identifies how long they're valid, how they are renewed, when they can be suspended and revoked if compromised, and when they can be destroyed when no longer needed.

Certificate Life Cycle

The life cycle protects and secures the certificate mechanism itself because the entire key infrastructure could be undermined if it is compromised. The life cycle of a certificate goes through the following stages, as detailed in Figure 5.5:

1. Certificate is requested.
2. Certificate is issued.
3. Certificate is published.
4. Certificate is received.
5. Certificate is used for intended purposes.
6. Certificate is suspended/revoked.
7. Certificate is expired.
8. Key is destroyed.

If the certificate is renewed prior to being revoked or suspended, the life cycle is extended.

FIGURE 5.5　Certificate life cycle

Exam Tip

Know the various aspects of the certificate life cycle and what
scenarios can cause certificates to be suspended or revoked.

Certificate Requested, Issued, Published, and Received

In the first steps of the certificate life cycle, the user makes a request to a CA for a certificate. In this request, the user must submit certain identity details. A CA cannot issue a certificate without verifying the identity of the requester. As part of the request, the user can generate his own public key pair when he submits his request, or the CA can perform the key generation when the user's identity is established.

If the process is followed correctly, the requester's identity is established and public key pairs are generated; then the CA can issue the certificate, publish it, and distribute it. The user will then receive his certificate, which authorizes him to use the certificate for its intended purpose.

Certificate Suspension and Revocation

A certificate can be suspended and revoked before its expiration date for several reasons. The most common reason for revocation is that the user of that certificate isn't authorized to use it anymore, as in the case of a company employee who quits his job or is fired. Alternatively, the certificate subscriber's data, such as the name of the company, might have changed, or it could have been incorrect on the certificate application. Other reasons for revocation include the problem of a key pair or certificate being compromised. If the private key is lost or compromised, the details in the corresponding certificate will no longer be valid. Immediately revoking the certificate means it can't be used for any authentication, encryption, or digital signature purposes. *Suspension* is a temporary revocation of the certificate until the problem concerning the certificate or the certificate owner's identity can be corrected. A suspension also might be appropriate if, for example, the certificate holder is on extended vacation or perhaps under investigation and shouldn't be allowed use of the certificate during this time. A suspension of a certificate can be undone, but a revocation is permanent.

The owner of the certificate must initiate communication with the CA to begin the revocation process. This needs to be performed in a secure way, through a signed message, in person, or via another authenticated channel. The private key corresponding to the certificate being revoked can be used to authenticate a revocation request, but if the revocation is a result of the key being compromised, the key can't be used to support authentication for a new certificate.

When a certificate is revoked, it's placed on a CA's Certificate Revocation List (CRL), which includes certificates that have been revoked before their expiration date by the CA. A CRL is used by other users and organizations to identify certificates that are no longer valid.

CRLs can be distributed in two main ways:

- **Pull model**   The CRL is downloaded from the CA by those who want to see it to verify a certificate. In this model, the user or organization is responsible for regularly downloading the latest CRL for the most recent list.
- **Push model**   In this model, the CA automatically sends the CRL out to verifiers at regular intervals.

These models can also be hierarchical in nature, in which a specific CRL of a CA is pushed to other sites, where other users and organizations can download it. CRLs are maintained in a distributed manner, but various central repositories contain the latest CRLs from many CAs. Websites and companies that deal with large numbers of secure transactions might need their own local version of a CRL that can quickly be compared to the large number of certificates accepted.

To check the status of a certificate, the CRL can be obtained from the specific CA or from a centralized database of CRLs released by a collection of authorities. To help automate this process, certificate status checks have been built into software applications, such as e-mail programs and web browsers, that automatically check the status of a received certificate. Status checks can also be made manually by checking the website of a CA and entering the serial number of a certificate. The Online Certificate Status Protocol (OCSP) was developed as a more resource-efficient alternative to CRLs. In a similar fashion, a client contacts an OCSP responder that refers to a CA. The OCSP responder returns a signed response to the client ("good," "revoked," or "unknown"); that response contains less information than a typical CRL response, hence the resource savings. OCSP also allows a grace period that enables a user with expired certificates to continue accessing resources for a time after their official expiration. A potential concern regarding OCSP is that it can be vulnerable to attacks through replay; a signed, valid "good" response can be captured and sent later in lieu of a valid response. Also, while more resource efficient than a CRL, OCSP does still require the remote responder be queried for each request, which can slow down the browsing process, particularly for high-volume sites.

The TLS Certificate Status Request extension, more commonly known as *OCSP stapling,* further improves efficiency by allowing the certificate holder to query the OCSP responder itself at set intervals and including ("stapling") the signed response with the TLS/SSL handshake, rather than querying the OCSP responder each time.

A CRL can still be preferred over the use of OCSP if a server has issued many certificates to be validated within a single revocation period. It may be more efficient for the organization to download a CRL at the beginning of the revocation period than to utilize the OCSP standard, necessitating an OCSP response every time a certificate requires validation.

> **Exam Tip**
>
> Know the purpose of a CRL and how it can be used to verify certificates. Understand the strengths OCSP brings as compared to a traditional CRL.

Certificate Expiration

Within each certificate is a specific date for the beginning and ending of that certificate's life cycle. Most certificates are valid for approximately one to three years. The length of time for which the certificate is valid depends on the type of certificate issued and its purpose. A high-security defense contractor might switch its key pairs on a regular basis, meaning the certificates it uses could be valid for a short time.

The purpose of certificate expiry is to protect certificates from brute-force attacks. The longer certificates are in use, the greater the risk that they will be cracked. This is like a password expiry and retention scheme for a network in which users must regularly change their passwords to prevent them from being compromised.

If the certificate will be allowed to expire and not renewed, users should take actions to decrypt any data encrypted with the private key, as well as take any other actions necessary to ensure an "orderly" expiration. Otherwise, if you want to use a certificate after its time of validity is complete, you'll need to renew the certificate. See the upcoming section "Certificate Renewal" for more information.

> **Exam Tip**
>
> Once a certificate has expired, it can't be renewed. A new certificate and key pair need to be generated.

Key Destruction

If a certificate and key pair have been compromised or are no longer in use, the key pair (the private and public keys) should be destroyed to prevent further use. Because the public key has been distributed many times during its lifetime, it can obviously be difficult to destroy completely. Therefore, the destruction of the private key is essential to ensure certificates or digital signatures can no longer be created with it.

Some private keys, however, need to be retained—for example, if they're used for key management or data privacy, such as an encrypted file on a corporate network file server. The private key might need to be maintained as part of a key history so items being stored with an older encryption key can be unlocked if necessary. A balance must be struck between the security need for key destruction and the need to access archived information.

Another aspect of key destruction involves the certificate that validates those keys. If the certificate is still valid, according to its creation and expiry date, then it needs to be revoked by contacting the CA, which will include the certificate's serial number in its CRL.

Destroying the private key can be a fairly simple process, but it must be thorough to ensure that the private key can't be recovered in any way. If the key is simply stored on a local hard disk, it can be deleted. The drawback to this method, however, is that many OSs don't delete the file; they delete only the filename from the disk directory, while the actual file is still stored on disk, so it can be retrieved through a data recovery program such as the Recycle Bin. In some cases, such as if the computer is stolen, an unauthorized user could analyze the hard drive or send it to a special recovery lab that can restore the data still residing on the disk.

To prevent such discovery, many utilities can delete files permanently from magnetic media. Other options include the actual physical destruction of the media itself, whether it is a hard drive, DVD, USB key, or flash memory device.

Certificate Renewal

To continue to use a certificate, the owner must renew the certificate before its expiry date. Typically, the CA will contact the owner when the certificate's expiration date is impending. The certificate owner has the responsibility of renewing the certificate before the expiration date. If this renewal isn't performed before the expiry date, the certificate will become invalid, and anyone trusting the source of that certificate will be unable to transact or communicate with the certificate owner. For companies that rely on certificates for digital transactions, this could be fatal. In addition, a request for a new certificate will need to be issued, which might take time to process before the new certificate and keys are received.

The policies and procedures of the CA must be examined carefully to ensure that certificates are renewed on time, especially because CAs usually require extra time before the expiry date to register the renewal properly. As a rule, you should renew certificates at least 30 days before they expire.

One important aspect of renewal is deciding whether to generate a new key pair to go along with the new certificate. Many CAs, in the process of renewal, merely repackage the certificate with the same public key. Because cryptographic keys can be compromised over time through sustained computational brute-force methods, the longer you keep the same key pair, the more insecure it will become. Therefore, it's extremely important for cryptographic security to generate a new key when renewing a certificate. This might not be so important for an individual who uses encryption only sparingly for personal purposes, but for companies with high-security needs, this is vital.

CHECKPOINT

✔**Objective 5.01: Explain the Fundamentals of Public Key Infrastructure**
Decentralized storage is used by individual users, and centralized storage is used for enterprise networks. Private keys need to be stored securely and, preferably, encrypted with a password. Key escrow companies can store the encryption key that can unlock the encryption on your private key, which is stored at your location. Backups need to be made of keys to prevent loss of data because of lost, stolen, or damaged keys. Keys for digital signing shouldn't be backed up because of nonrepudiation concerns. A dual-pair key system can generate separate keys for encryption and digital signing. M of N control stores different parts of a key distributed among several people, or a third-party recovery agent can be used to store your keys. Only a certain number of key parts are needed to provide the key.

✔**Objective 5.02: Implementing PKI Concepts to Promote Trust** Certificates need to be renewed before expiry; otherwise, a new certificate must be generated. A certificate should be suspended or revoked if the keys related to that certificate are compromised. Check the CRL for certificates that have been revoked, and understand the strengths and weaknesses of using OCSP and new extensions such as OCSP stapling.

REVIEW QUESTIONS

1. An organization is using OCSP to validate certificates within its PKI infrastructure. What is *not* a legitimate response to a validation request?

   A. Good

   B. Validated

   C. Unknown

   D. Revoked

2. For your organization's encryption systems, which of the following should you implement to act as a centralized server to store and distribute your public and private keys?

   A. Key management server

   B. Digital certificate

   C. CRL

   D. Certificate authority

3. To improve the integrity and authentication of your encryption systems, you have contacted a certificate authority to generate which of the following items for you?

   A. Digital certificate and public/private key pair

   B. Public key and a private hash

   C. Private key and a certificate

   D. Secret key for the local encryption server

4. You need to store your company's private key in a safe, secure place. Which of the following would you use?

   A. Save it on a hard drive in plain text.

   B. Seal it in an envelope and store it at your home office.

   C. Encrypt it on a flash memory device.

   D. Store it on a portable USB device in plain text.

5. You have started using a third-party key escrow company to protect your encryption keys. Which of the following do you send to them?

   A. Encryption key to decrypt a private key file

   B. Encryption key to decrypt a public key file

   C. Copy of a public key

   D. Copy of a certificate

6. Your recovery encryption key is split between seven of your coworkers, of which only four are required to be present to decrypt the private key. Which of the following methods are you using for key recovery?

   A. Steganography

   B. Certificate authority

   C. Key escrow

   D. M of N control

7. Put the steps of the certificate life cycle in the following list in their correct order:

   i. Certificate is published.

   ii. Certificate is expired.

   iii. Certificate is received.

   iv. Certificate is requested.

   A. i, iii, ii, iv

   B. iv, iii, i, ii

   C. iii, i, iv, ii

   D. iv, i, iii, ii

8. You have been tasked with contacting your certificate authority and revoking your company's current web server certificate. Which of the following is the most likely reason to revoke the certificate?

   A. You renewed your certificate after it expired.

   B. The previous network administrator who created the certificate was fired.

   C. You installed a new web server.

   D. Your current certificate expires in less than 30 days.

9. You need to look up the details of a certificate that was revoked. Where can you find this information?

   A. Certificate Expiry List

   B. Registration Suspension List

   C. Certificate Revocation List

   D. Registration Expiry List

10. You need to renew your company's certificate for its public web server.
    When should you renew the certificate?

    A. On its expiry date

    B. After it expires

    C. After it's revoked

    D. Thirty days before expiry

11. OCSP _____ improves upon the original OCSP efficiency by including
    a time-stamped, signed response with the TLS/SSL handshake.

    A. pinning

    B. stapling

    C. assigning

    D. synchronization

REVIEW ANSWERS

1. **B**   Within the OCSP framework, the legitimate responses from the
   OCSP responder are "good," "revoked," and "unknown."

2. **A**   A key management server is a centralized storage system that
   takes care of the process of distributing, storing, and backing up keys
   for users of an enterprise network.

3. **A**   When a user's identification is established, the CA generates public
   and private keys for the user. A certificate is then generated with the
   identification and public key information embedded within it. Once
   the user is registered and receives his certificate, he can begin using it
   to send encrypted messages.

4. **C**   Private keys should never be stored in plain text. If they're stolen, an
   unauthorized user will be able to use them to decrypt messages and files.

5. **A**   In a key escrow storage scheme, an encryption key used to encrypt
   and decrypt the private key file is stored offsite with a third party. If
   access is needed to the backup copy of the private key, the encryption
   key needs to be obtained from the third-party company after you've
   been properly authenticated.

6. **D**   In this key-recovery scheme, a prescribed number of the key
   owners must be present with their parts of the key. M of N control
   refers to the number of operator keys that must be present to create
   the recovery key, such as 2 of 3 or 4 of 7. For example, if a recovery

key is split into seven parts, only four of those are needed to create the recovery key that will decrypt the backup of the private key.

7. **D** Within the given steps of the certificate life cycle, the certificate would be requested, published, received, and then expired.

8. **B** The certificate should be revoked because the user assigned to that certificate is no longer with the company. This prevents the user from continuing to use that certificate for encryption and authentication.

9. **C** A Certificate Revocation List (CRL) is published by a CA to show certificates that have been revoked. A verifier can examine the list to check the validity of another user's certificate.

10. **D** Most certificate authorities require that a certificate be renewed within a certain amount of time before the actual expiry date. This provides the CA with enough time to renew the certificate and deliver it back to the client for distribution.

11. **B** The TLS Certificate Status Request extension, more commonly known as *OCSP stapling*, further improves efficiency by allowing the certificate holder to query the OCSP responder itself at set intervals and including ("stapling") the signed response with the TLS/SSL handshake, rather than query the OCSP responder each time.

Identity and Access Management

Access Control

	NEWBIE	SOME EXPERIENCE	EXPERT
ETA	3 hours	2 hours	1 hour

195

Two simple and often overlooked aspects of security are access control and authentication. In many business environments, access involves a single login to a computer or a network of computer systems that provides the user access to all resources on the network. This access includes rights to personal and shared folders on a network server, company intranets, printers, and other network resources and devices. These same resources can be quickly exploited by unauthorized users if the access control and associated authentication procedures aren't set up properly.

Access control refers to permissions applied to resources that determine which users can access those resources. Essentially, access controls ensure that users who are authorized to receive access to certain resources can access them, while users who are unauthorized do not receive access to those same resources. Access control contains all the techniques, policies, and programs designed to ensure that only those entities with a verified need and clearance level for the systems or data in question are able to access it, and all others that don't are denied. Examples include technical access controls, such as permissions, and even physical access controls, such as secured doors and gates. Other types of controls include deterrent (attempting to dissuade unauthorized activity), preventative (averting unauthorized activity), and detective (identifying unauthorized activity). You might choose a compensating control to mitigate risks as best you can when they cannot be completely remediated. Administrative controls put policies and procedures into place to create another layer of protection. *Authentication* goes hand in hand with access control by identifying users to be sure they are exactly who they claim to be. After a user has been authenticated, the resources for which the user has appropriate permissions become accessible. Authentication is a step that comes after a person or entity has identified themselves to the system. When an identity is authenticated, it means that it's verified as being true or confirmed. This may mean comparing the presented credentials with a database to see if they match, or some other verification technique.

As an administrator, you must carefully consider system and network security when creating access and authentication policies. Basic security practices such as login IDs and passwords must be augmented with advanced logical access control techniques, such as the use of long, non-dictionary, alphanumeric passwords (also known as password complexity); regular password rotation and expiration; and password aging. Finally, the protection of personal and shared data resources on network file servers must be maintained using directory and file access control permissions on a per-user or per-group basis.

Access control also pertains to physical access to your organization's buildings or computers. Physical access control is a first-level barrier that prevents unauthorized users from entering your facility or accessing vital company equipment; consider signs, for example, that by their own presence discourage unwelcome intruders and add a level of access control to your organization. Even this inexpensive and low-maintenance measure can pay dividends as a deterrent.

This chapter describes the basic concepts and models of access control, user account and privilege management, and physical access control security.

Explain the Fundamental Concepts and Best Practices Related to Authentication, Authorization, and Access Control

Access control methods determine how users interact with resources and computer systems. Resources must be protected from unauthorized modification or tampering. Access controls must be enforced on a network to ensure that unauthorized users cannot access its resources or the network and computer system infrastructure.

Users and Resources

Your first task is to define who the *users* are and to what *resources* they need access. A *user* in this sense doesn't always mean a specific person. A computer might act as a user when it tries to connect to the resource of another computer system. A *resource* can be anything from a simple text file on a file server, to a network laser printer, to an Internet proxy server. A user of a resource might also be a computer account used by a system to back up other computer systems' resources and data to a tape drive. This *backup* user account must also have its access control defined properly so that it can securely perform its job function.

Just as your users must be carefully defined, the resources offered by your computer network need to be categorized and access controls defined for the resources' security. Your resources must be categorized with the following attributes in mind:

- **Confidentiality**   How confidential is the data from this resource? Should only certain users see it, or should access be open to anyone? An example of sensitive data would be payroll or human resources data. The ability to access this resource should be available only to users from those departments. Confidentiality issues can be secured via access controls.

- **Integrity**   Should users only be able to read from this directory, or can they modify the files within? If the integrity of the data is vital, this resource should have its access permissions set to read-only. For example, a datasheet of released company financials to shareholders should never be modified after distribution. Integrity issues can be addressed via access controls—primarily file and directory security.

- **Availability**   How available should the data be as a resource? Does this data need to be available always or only during certain time periods? Is this information so critical that it must be available whenever a user requests it? Typically, availability decreases with increased security, so the needs of protecting the data must be balanced with the necessary level of availability. Availability issues can be addressed via backups, clustering, and redundancy solutions.

Travel Advisory

In real-world situations, friction can exist between management and the information technology (IT) department over the need for availability versus the need for security. IT departments must emphasize the need for security over ease of availability and balance the requirements accordingly.

Levels of Security

Before a user is allowed access to a facility or resource, three main levels of security must be passed:

- **Identification**   The user must initially identify herself as a valid user for that network, usually with a login username or account name. *Identification,* also referred to as *identify proofing,* ensures that a user (which could also be an application program or process) is who she claims to be. For example, before performing any type of online banking, a customer must identify who she is and have sufficient physical identification, such as bank cards, passwords, personal identification numbers (PINs), and so on, to be able to prove her identity before the process goes any further.

- **Authentication**   The user must then pass the *authentication* phase using her logon username or account number and a password. If these two criteria are matched with the global database of login usernames and passwords stored on the network, the user is authenticated and is granted access to the network. To be authenticated properly, the user must provide proof that she should be using the login name by supplying a password, PIN, or token. If the identity and password or PIN match the central database, the user is authenticated.

- **Authorization**   When a user tries to access a resource, the system must check to see if that user ID is authorized for that resource and what permissions or privileges the user has when using it. Just because a user has been identified and authenticated to a network doesn't mean she should be able to access all resources. If the system determines that the user may access the resource, the user is authorized and allowed access with the privileges she has been granted.

Exam Tip

Be aware of the differences between identifying a user, authenticating, and authorizing. In a secure, access-controlled environment, these terms specifically correspond to different steps in the process.

One more concept you should be aware of is *accounting*, which is the process of logging users' activities and behaviors, the amount of data they use, and the resources they consume. This allows for a trending analysis that enables both planning and control of authorization, both business focused and security focused. Accounting is often grouped with authentication and authorization as the AAA framework, with one server handling all three needs.

Access Security Grouping

Administrators need to visualize the relationships among users and groups and the resources they need to perform their jobs. A network administrator assigning access permissions individually to resources on a per-user basis would likely be inefficient and extremely time consuming. For small networks, this might be a viable option, but for mid-sized and large corporate networks, it would be an

FIGURE 6.1   Organization by job function

unwieldy strategy. Grouping users based on similarities in their attributes is far more efficient. Typically, you can identify groups of users in three main ways: by job function, department, and physical location.

Job Function   Users who perform the same job will most likely need access to the same resources. For example, many financial analysts might need access to the same data directory on a specific file server. By grouping these users into one entity, you can assign the resulting group access to the data without needing to perform this configuration for each user. This model can also be defined hierarchically, as shown in Figure 6.1, where management might have more access to resources than nonmanagement personnel.

Department   Users who belong to the same department in an organization will probably need access to the same data and resources. All employees within a department aren't always working in the same physical location. Because of the virtual nature of many large corporate networks, a sales employee in the United States might need access to the same sales database used by a sales employee in Japan. All users from the sales department can be assigned to the same group: Sales. The network administrator should configure access only to the sales database once for the Sales group, without having to assign access for each individual salesperson. This model is shown in Figure 6.2.

Physical Location   A company could be in a single building, in several buildings, or in different cities and countries. Many companies divide their resources among physical locations; for example, an office in New York might not need access to resources to a file server in Los Angeles. In this way, the security

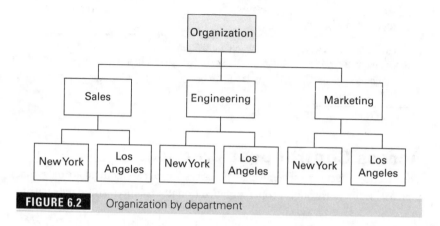

FIGURE 6.2   Organization by department

model can be set up by physical location, where users are grouped depending on the office to which they belong, as shown in Figure 6.3.

In the most efficient security model, data resources are organized based on need-to-know criteria. Resources should be available only to users who need access to that information. In most cases, the users in a sales department wouldn't need access to the data resources of accounting or human resources, for example. Each resource must have its access controls specifically set to allow access only to users authorized for that resource. This also flows down into more granular levels of security, in which a user might have access to read a file but not modify or execute it. For example, an employee assigned to print a directory of documents should need only read and print access to the file; he does not need access to modify or delete. The best practice is to grant only the lowest level of access permissions a user needs to perform his job.

FIGURE 6.3   Organization by physical location

> **Travel Advisory**
>
> When setting up a new network, you should create a user hierarchy based on one of the previous security models. Trying to change the model down the road can be difficult after it is already in place.

Access Control Best Practices

This section discusses several best practices for access control to data that increase security through proper organizational structures and data security principles.

Separation of Duties

To make sure that all employees and management personnel know their roles in the company, the organization's structure should be clear, with positions properly defined with formal job titles and descriptions, definitions of responsibilities, and reporting structures that define the lines of authority.

To increase security and reduce risk from security compromises, part of the effort should be directed toward both a clear organizational structure and a specific separation of duties. A *separation of duties* is intended to prevent one person from having too much power, so that certain actions or groups of actions can't be both performed and verified by one person. For example, one person should not have the ability to perform security-related functions and verify or audit them at the same time. This would enable them to take an action and then cover it up or prevent it from being detected.

To separate duties that involve high-security situations, a certain amount of N-person control must take place. *N-person control* means that to proceed with a certain task, more than one person is required to allow the procedure to take place. In a banking situation, for example, opening the main safe might require the authorization of at least two people, because each authorized person possesses a key and both keys are needed to open the safe. This prevents a single individual from opening the safe without supervision. Like a safe, a computer system must have protected access. The more people involved, the less chance of a single person making a poor security decision that could compromise the entire network. This is also referred to as *M of N control,* allowing that at least M number of N users must be present or participate to authorize or proceed with a task.

> **Exam Tip**
>
> Separation of duties ensures that one individual isn't tasked with both performing and verifying functions—particularly sensitive security functions. N-person control requires that more than one person is needed to allow a specific procedure to take place to ensure that important security decisions are not relegated to a single person.

Rotation of Job Duties

Job rotation provides employees with workforce skills improvement and increased job satisfaction, but it also enhances the security of an organization. Job rotation exposes employees to new skills and opportunities by allowing them to perform different jobs within an organization. Job rotation also ensures better security because no single employee retains the same amount of access control for an area for an extended period of time. This can prevent internal corruption that can occur, for example, when a long-term employee, because of her deep knowledge of an area of duty, takes advantage of the position and security access. Job rotation also boosts accountability when another person takes over a specific job duty and examines potential inefficiencies or evidence of security lapses.

Suppose, for example, that a server administrator and network administrator switch roles. Each administrator has an opportunity to increase her knowledge by applying her security skills and expertise in security procedures to a different part of the organization. The switch also allows each administrator to scrutinize the security aspects of the other role with a fresh perspective.

Mandatory Vacations

Mandatory vacations are a security measure that requires employees to use their vacation days at specific times of the year or requires that they use all their vacation days instead of carrying over unused vacation days into a following year. This policy is most often used to detect security issues with employees, such as fraud and other internal hacking activities, as typically the employee must be present every day to continue to perpetuate or erase the evidence of malicious activities. When a user is forced to go on vacation, his on-the-job activities may be more likely to be noticed and detected because the user is not present to prevent their discovery. When the user is away, the person filling in for him will be able to audit the user's activities and reveal any suspicious behavior. For example, an unscrupulous employee in a financial institution may be performing illegal activities related to customer bank account details and manually cleaning up log files to erase traces of her activity. When she is forced on vacation, this activity may be noticed in the logs because she is not able to cover her tracks while she is away.

Implicit Deny

Implicit deny refers to the security principle of starting a user out with no access rights and granting permissions to resources as required. This principle states that a security policy must implicitly deny all access to provide a fully secure baseline. Only then can the administrator grant a user access to resources.

The implicit deny principle is more secure than starting out with a policy that grants a user default access to all resources and then denies access permissions to certain resources. It is too easy for administrators to overlook several aspects of resources that require access to be controlled and denied as appropriate.

The implicit deny policy should be applied to all aspects of an organization's security, from physical security and access control, to file and resources permissions on a file server, to network firewall and router rules. By starting out with the strongest security policy and then creating access permissions, administrators know that all access is denied by default and each access control permission granted is an exception to that policy.

Exam Tip
Implicit deny means that all access is denied by default and access permissions are granted only to specific resources as required.

Explicit Deny

Explicit deny, as opposed to implicit deny, means that access to a certain resource is explicitly denied to a user or group of users, and that access to that resource cannot be granted to those users even though an allow could be inherited from another policy. For example, if the Human Resources directory has an explicit deny for all users in the Finance group, it will be denied across that group even if some or all the users have gained access through another policy.

Least Privilege

The least privilege principle grants users only the access rights they need to perform their job functions. This requires giving users the least amount of access possible to prevent them from abusing more powerful access rights. For example, a user might need access to certain files to print them for a manager. The network administrator should give the user only enough access rights to read the file and print it, without including privileges to delete, modify, or add information to the file.

The function of management is to decide exactly what a person needs to know or for what areas the person requires access for a position. The network administrator must enact the decision. When in doubt, the network administrator should be cautious and allow only minimal access until someone can authorize more privileges on behalf of the user. Increased privileges should never be handed out at the request of the user who needs them.

Exam Tip

Data access should be based on the least privilege principle, which ensures that users have the minimal access rights available to perform their job function and nothing more.

Access Control Models

Access control models are policies that define how users access data. Access control models also determine the extent or degree to which a user can further allow others access to the data. These policies form a framework based on the security and business goals of the organization. The rules of the framework are enforced through access control technologies. This section covers the main access control types.

Mandatory Access Control

In a mandatory access control (MAC) model, the operating system (OS) is in control of access to data. Most data owners can assign permissions to their own files and share them however they see fit, but OS access controls override any data owner settings. Users have little freedom to adjust access controls, except for specific data under their control. When defined on the system, users are given certain access rights representing a certain level of trust. The data resources themselves also have security classifications that define the level of trust a user must have to access the data. If a user doesn't have the appropriate access rights to use the data, he is denied access. This type of model is centralized and is often used in high-security environments, such as the military or government offices, where access control is tightly guarded through strict OS security policies. Military classification levels such as Confidential, Secret, and

Top Secret are examples of MAC in which specific security access is restricted, depending on the classification of the data, the user's security clearance (or access) level, and the user's need to know.

Discretionary Access Control

Discretionary access control (DAC) enables data creators and owners to specify which users can access certain data. Access to resources is allowed only for authorized users through permissions on the resource. This is the most common model used in Windows and Unix environments in which administrators create a hierarchy of files, directories, and other resources that are accessed based on user privileges and access rights. Resource owners are typically allowed to control who accesses their resources. For example, an individual user can share specific files or directories with users he or she authorizes. This model is a less centralized version of the mandatory access control.

Role-Based Access Control

Role-based access control (RBAC) is also referred to as *nondiscretionary access control*. This centrally controlled model allows access to be based on the role the user holds within an organization. Instead of access being given to individual users, access control is granted to groups of users who perform a common function. For example, many organizations have special "contractor" roles comprising employees who work on a contract basis and are not full-salaried employees; these workers are given less access to certain resources or parts of the network. In an IT department, for example, a user given the role of "backup administrator" might have access to controlling backup and restore operations, but he would not have privileges to add users or assign access permissions, which are reserved for a system administrator. No matter who is assigned the backup administrator role, the access permissions will be the same. Database servers such as SQL servers often use role-based permissions to restrict access to certain portions of the database. Note that role-based access control is often confused with the use of groups in a discretionary access control model; they aren't quite the same. The use of roles is mandatory in an RBAC scheme; there aren't any individual access permissions or rights granted. In discretionary access, the use of groups (often thought of as roles) is purely for the sake of convenience for the administrator; there are still some individuals who can have their own access permissions.

Rule-Based Access Control

Rule-based access control provides enhanced granularity when specifying access control policies and indicates specifically what can and cannot happen between a user and the resource. This type of access control policy is typically defined by an access control list (ACL), such as TCP Wrappers, which specifies a set of rules that must be followed before access is granted. Unlike the DAC method, rule-based access control does not necessarily have to be tied to an authorized identity and could involve access permissions based on network location, content of messages (such as e-mail text or attachments), and other types of content filtering. These rules are typically implemented in network access devices such as routers, firewalls, and content-filtering systems, and they apply to all users, regardless of their identity. Rule-based access control can also use elements such as username or ID, time of day, location, type of access, and so on. For example, user Bob from accounting may only be able to access a certain file between 8 A.M. and noon, but not after that, or is only able to write to one document and only read another one during that same timeframe. Rule elements are typically very specific and restrictive in a well-implemented rule-based access control model.

Exam Tip
Don't confuse the acronym RBAC between discussions of role-based access control and rule-based access control. RBAC refers only to role-based access control. RBAC is never used to stand for rule-based access control!

Attribute-Based Access Control

Attribute-based access control (ABAC) is considered the next generation of access control, even though it has been around for several years. ABAC applies attributes to subjects and objects, and allows or disallows access to objects based on their attributes. For instance, if Susie works in Human Resources, she would have attributes associated with her as a subject (Susie Brown, HR Specialist, HR Department). An object might be, for example, the HR database, with attributes covering its PII data on prospective, current, and former employees. ABAC enables the creation of rules allowing certain subjects (HR Generalists, Specialists, and Managers) to view, edit, or delete PII from the HR database, while others can only update non-PII data. ABAC provides even more granularity and flexibility than RBAC, due to the fact that attributes can be updated and their relationships will be modified automatically. New subjects can be added without new rules.

Implement Appropriate Security Controls When Performing Account Management

Logical access controls are technical components that control user access to resources. These access controls are typically an integral part of an operating system, network security device, or software application to provide user account, password, and access privileges management. By using a strong user account policy, you can greatly diminish the ability of a hacker to break into a user's account.

Account Maintenance

Several policies can be created for account use to strengthen the security of the login process. Some of the most effective restrictions include the following:

- Using appropriate naming conventions
- Limiting logon attempts
- Setting account expiry dates
- Disabling unused accounts
- Setting time restrictions
- Setting machine restrictions
- Using tokens
- Restricting multiple/shared accounts

Using Appropriate Naming Conventions

When you set up and configure a company network, a best practice is to enact some form of standard account naming conventions. A common naming convention is employing a user's first initial and last name, or variations of it, as his account ID. Never use account names that represent job functions: A user account named "admin" is much more likely to attract the attention of an unauthorized user who is trying to hack into a system, because he knows the user ID could be the main administrative account for the network. If he's able to compromise that account, he will have full control over the network. Names such as "human_resources" and "accounting" will also be more likely targets for an unauthorized user.

Limiting Logon Attempts

This parameter sets the maximum amount of incorrect logon attempts before an account is disabled. This is an important feature because many hackers simply repeat attempts at accessing an account using different passwords each time. If no logon attempt restrictions exist, hackers can continue this brute-force attack until the account is eventually compromised. A best practice is to set a limit of three to five failed attempts, after which the account is locked out and the user must contact the administrator to enable the account again.

Setting Account Expiry Dates

Setting an expiry date on a user account will disable it when the target date is reached. This is useful for contract workers who are employed for a limited period of time. When the contract date is reached, the user's login is immediately disabled. By setting an expiry on the account when a contractor is first hired, you won't forget to disable the account because it will be automatically disabled when the expiration date is reached. If the contract is renewed, the account can simply be re-enabled and the expiration date changed.

Disabling Unused Accounts

When an employee leaves the company, his account should be immediately disabled. This is especially important for any employee who is suddenly terminated for any reason. By immediately disabling the account, you deny access to further attempts by that user to access his account. Another best practice is to disable accounts you don't recognize as valid. Unauthorized users could have broken into the system and created their own "dummy" accounts to perform malicious activities unnoticed. If the account is valid, the user will contact you because he can't log in. You can then verify whether the user should have access to the system.

Setting Time Restrictions

If your company operates only during certain hours each day, you can set time restrictions for access to the network. After hours, only a select few users might need access. You can set time restrictions on other users' accounts so that they are able to log in only during operating hours. This will reduce the risk of unauthorized users trying to use an employee's account during off-hours to break into the system.

Setting Machine Restrictions

You can allow logins only from certain machines on the network. Any computer on your current internal network can be set up to prevent anyone trying to access the system using an outside computer or laptop. Machine restrictions are usually set using a computer's network card MAC address, computer name, or the network IP address.

Using Tokens

To provide additional access control and authentication protection, many organizations utilize a system requiring two forms of authentication: In addition to an account name and password, the user requires a hardware or software *token,* such as a special universal serial bus (USB) key, that needs to be connected to her computer before she is allowed access. Certain types of physical tokens, such as RSA SecurID and CRYPTOCard, provide a logical token number that is generated in conjunction with the access control server and must be entered, along with a username and password, before access is granted.

Tokens provide an extra layer of security, because even if an unauthorized user has access to a physical token (if it was stolen from the user, for example), he still requires a username and password to access the system. Similarly, if the unauthorized user knows a username and password he can use, he still needs the physical token to complete the authentication and access control process.

Exam Tip

Be aware of the different types of account restrictions and access control methods that can be used to increase the security of user accounts.

Restricting Multiple/Shared/ Guest/Generic Accounts

There may be legitimate reasons for a user to have multiple accounts; for example, it is a best practice for administrators to have both a user-level and privileged-level account, and to only use the privileged-level account when they absolutely need to conduct business at that level. Likewise, shared accounts can be legitimate in certain scenarios, such as for batch processing.

However, it is imperative to actively track both shared accounts and users who have multiple accounts and regularly validate that their access is required. Further, restricting the access of those users to most resources can limit unauthorized activity, should their credentials fall into the hands of malicious parties.

Guest groups are good idea if you need to allow someone access to your system or network for a limited amount of time, but do not want to give them a full user account (or your user account information—a very bad idea). Guest groups generally allow limited access to specific resources that they need, such as access to networked printers or intranet access for filling out timesheets. When the guest feature is not being used, it's a good idea to turn it off because it can provide a point of unauthorized entry into a system. Service accounts are accounts that a specific application or service uses to interact with the system. For example, if you have an FTP server that interacts with an FTP service, you might use a service account with limited permissions to allow that service to access the system. What this means is that you can apply very tight security controls to the service account, rather than using a general user account to perform the activity (a poor security practice). Finally, policies that require users who have access to so-called generic accounts, such as "root," to only execute single processes using their elevated privileges will mitigate some of the risk of having these types of accounts.

User Access Reviews

Conducting a recertification of user rights is key; this type of review validates a user's rights to access areas (physical or logical) based on his or her roles and responsibilities. For example, a user access review could find that a group of users assigned to a different area of an organization no longer needs access to a sensitive file share; this helps mitigate insider threats. Continuous monitoring of accounts also helps ensure that external threats do not create new accounts for their own nefarious use.

Credential Management

Credential management allows the storage of credentials, such as usernames and passwords, for access to services within a network. Password management, although typically created and enforced by the network administrator, is becoming a special area of network security that should be covered in specific company policies. All users must be aware of the company's rules and procedures for managing user accounts and passwords that allow access to company resources.

Password Policies

Following are some basic, but important, password policies that can be set by the administrator to enforce strong passwords:

- **Minimum length and complexity** The minimum length for a password can be enforced by the network administrator. This prevents users from using small, easy-to-guess passwords of only a few characters in length. The password should be at least eight characters, with more being preferable, and contain a mix of uppercase and lowercase letters, numbers, and special characters.

- **Password history** Most login and password authentication systems can recall a user's last several passwords and can prevent the user from using the same one repeatedly (known as *password reuse*). This technique is often referred to as *password aging*. If this option is available, it should be enabled so that a user's password will always be different.

- **Password expiration** The longer a password has existed, the easier it is for a hacker to eventually discover the password simply by narrowing the options over time. Forcing users to change their passwords regularly can prevent a hacker from discovering a password through brute-force attacks and ensures that if the account password has been compromised, the hacker will lose access the next time the password is changed. Most organizations expire passwords and force their users to change their passwords every one to three months.

- **Password recovery** If a user forgets her password, the administrator must reset it to a secure temporary value and force the user to change that password the first time she logs in. More secure password-recovery schemes include sending a temporary password to the user's e-mail address. This provides some verification of the user's identity because only that user would be able to check her e-mail account.

Domain Accounts and Single Sign-On

In an environment that uses a single sign-on solution, such as a Microsoft Active Directory domain account, the account and password security mechanisms must be strictly enforced because each user will use one account and password to access all file and print resources for the domain. This strengthens security because both administrators and users only need to define, enforce, and utilize a single account and password policy for the entire domain. In the past, users had different accounts and passwords for each resource they needed to access, which usually meant that one or more of these resources was inadequately protected with a weak password. Having an overall domain account and password policy allows administrators to manage the security of these accounts using a single policy and allows end users to remember only one username and password to access any resource.

Federation

Related to single sign-on is the concept of *federation,* often implemented through an enterprise-wide identity management system where a user's identity and associated attributes are carried across enterprise boundaries. This allows a user to log in one time, with his credentials following him through the enterprise and across enterprise boundaries. Federated identities center around the foundational concept of *transitive trust,* where the trust relationship between two domains allows authentication of trusted users across both domains. Transitive trust requires the two (or more) organizations to agree on standards for sharing identity attributes, and for the organizations to accept and authenticate identities based on attributes received from external organizations. A great example might be a university student logging in to his school's portal account and then having access based on his associated attributes to external library or academic publication resources that are granted based on his active student status.

Security Roles and Privileges

Privilege management involves the creation and use of policies defining the users and groups that access company resources, such as data files or printers. To control how users access data, employees need to be logically structured to define access privileges depending on the type of user, the groups to which the user belongs, or the user's specific role in the company.

When designing a company's security infrastructure, you must visualize the relationships among users and groups and the resources they need to perform their jobs. Although assigning access permissions individually to resources on a per-user basis might be viable for small networks, it would be an inefficient and extremely time-consuming strategy for mid-sized or large corporate networks. Grouping users according to similarities in job functions is much more efficient. Beyond this, user security can be designed according to user roles within the company.

User

A single user's access rights and privileges revolve around the data that person creates, modifies, and deletes. In addition to the user's own user access control privileges, he can be part of a group, be assigned a specific role, and be assigned that role's privileges as well. For example, a user can have individual access rights to files in his home directory, but he can also have access to the Sales and Marketing group directory because he also belongs to that group. Furthermore, the user might have an additional role, such as auditor, so he has access to additional resources beyond his user and group access rights.

Group

In this model, several users who need access to the same data are organized in a group. Privileges can be distributed to the entire group of users rather than to each individual user. This is much more efficient when applying permissions and provides greater overall control of access to resources. For example, users who are part of the same Sales and Marketing group would typically have access to and share the same data on a file server and, depending on their location, would share rights to the same printers. Group privileges typically provide additional access rights to users beyond their own individual access permissions to access shared data.

Role

A user might have different security privileges according to his role in the company. For example, a user who is also a database administrator might have extra privileges accorded to that role, on top of or replacing those privileges acquired as a user or part of a group. Predetermined permissions for a role can be created and then applied to users or groups that fit that role.

> **Exam Tip**
>
> Groups are used to designate subsets of static users. Think about a group of system administrators. A role can be applied to that group to designate certain conditions. (Think a day-shift system administrator who only has permissions to access resources between 8:00 A.M. and 5:00 P.M., for example.)

File and Print Security Controls

File and print servers can be involved in much of a user's daily work routine. File servers are used to store the user's data, including personal work files and departmental or company-wide information. Print servers are used to administer print services and print queues, in which a user's print jobs are organized and sent to the appropriate printer.

Security concerns with file and print servers center around authentication and access permissions. File servers should be configured so that no user can access them through the network without first being authenticated via a username and a password. Beyond that, various directories and files, depending on their ownership and confidentiality, need to be secured with access permissions.

Most file servers have directories arranged in hierarchies, typically according to user and departmental or group directories. For example, each user would have her own personal data directory, where only she has access to create, delete, and modify the files and directories within it. This prevents other users from accessing her files. Similarly, the CEO of the company can store her personal and important company files in a personal directory that only she can access.

Typically, some directories are set up as departmental or group directories that provide a separate area for each department to store files to which everyone in that department needs access. For example, a directory could be set up for the finance department that allows each person in the Finance group to access the confidential accounting files in that directory. The access permissions would be set so that no user or department can access that directory except those in the Finance group. Other directories might allow only read-only permissions, such as a directory of company policy and benefit files that all employees need to access for reference but shouldn't be allowed to modify or delete.

This same methodology should be used for printing services. Most printers are configured to allow any user to send print jobs to them. For more confidential printers, such as a printer used in the human resources department, where employment and termination notices might be created, the printer's access permissions would allow only HR department employees to print. The printer itself should also be physically located in a secure area with controlled access. More granular security-access permissions can be set so users can't modify or delete jobs after they've been sent to the printer. Most of these controls are handled by the administrator, who controls the flow and access of print queues.

File and Print ACLs

Several different permissions can be assigned to files and directories on a computer system. This is typically defined in the ACL, which contains a list of permissions granted to users for each resource. Following are the most common Windows permissions that can be assigned:

- **Read**   View or list the contents of a file or directory.
- **Write**   Create and save a new file or write to an existing file.
- **Read and Execute**   View or list the contents of a file or directory and execute accessible files.

- **Modify** Read, write, execute, or delete a file or directory.
- **Full Control** Read, write, execute, modify, or delete a file or directory.

Linux systems have a similar permission structure, based around three groups: owner, group, and all users. Owner permissions apply only to the owner of a specific file or directory, group permissions apply to the group(s) assigned to the file or directory, and all users is self-explanatory. There are three types of permissions:

- **Read** Read a file's contents.
- **Write** Write to or modify a file.
- **Execute** View or execute a file.

Exam Tip

Be aware of the differences between the various access permissions, especially those pertaining to files and directories.

The most basic types of security that can be set at the resource level are full access and no access at all. Using these settings is a bad practice, however, and must be avoided in favor of more granular security. An ACL should be created for every resource and applied for all users. When you first create an ACL for a resource, start with "no access" as the default. This lets you begin with a clean slate, where no access is the default permission. Then add access permissions based on the needs of the user or group, granting only the access permissions necessary to perform their job functions. Never grant Write or Modify permissions unless users need to make changes to a file.

Consider the following example: A sales database is used to keep track of clients and their pertinent information. Employees in the Sales group must be able to read and modify this information as well as delete users from and add new users to the database. The administrative staff will initiate or take calls from clients, and they need access to the database to look up client information. The administrative staff doesn't need access to modify the contents of the client records in the database, however. To perform system maintenance and administration on the database, the Database Administration group needs access to perform all functions, including changing the file attributes of the database file. But the Sales group doesn't want the Database Administration group to delete files or directories. In this scenario, the following access rights should be defined for each group:

User	Access Rights Assigned
Sales	Read, Modify
Admin	Read
Database Admin	Full Control

Travel Advisory

If a user asks to be given access rights to a file or directory, never grant it without first verifying the user's need for the access with his or her manager.

Objective 6.03
CompTIA Security+
Objective 3.9

Analyze and Differentiate Among Types of Mitigation and Deterrent Techniques

Physical access control security differs from computer security. When securing a computer system or network, you're attempting to prevent unauthorized users from accessing the resources of your system. Physical security, however, is implemented to prevent unauthorized users from accessing an environment—anything from the entire facility to a small network closet that contains networking equipment and wiring.

Much time and expense are spent on securing a computer network from unauthorized external access, but typically not enough resources are used on physical security to prevent unauthorized internal access. The possible result of lax physical security and access control includes equipment theft, physical damage and vandalism, service interruptions, and the unauthorized release of confidential data. Physical security is required to protect employees, company data, equipment, and the facility itself.

To secure access to the facility, access systems should be installed to identify employees and control what areas of the facility they can enter. Access control security also includes surveillance and monitoring of company property and the installation of physical barriers to prevent unauthorized intruders from trespassing on a company's property.

Your first line of defense is the security of the perimeter of the facility or the boundaries of its property. It's critical that unauthorized people be prevented from accessing the property or its buildings. This could involve different security mechanisms for use during daily working hours and for use when the facility is closed. Building security includes the use of physical barriers, surveillance, and access control.

Physical Barriers

To deter unauthorized people from accessing a facility, physical barriers, including barricades, can be the most effective form of security. Fencing can close off the perimeter from people who are simply passing by and could be inclined to trespass on company property. Depending on the level of protection required, the fencing can be as simple as a four-foot fence that protects against casual trespassers or animals. Higher fences of at least eight feet should be constructed to make it difficult for the average person to climb over them. For the most protection, barbed wire can be installed at the top of the fence.

Lighting

In the interest of security and safety, all areas of the property—including all the company's buildings and the parking lot—should have proper lighting installed to discourage intruders and provide a safe environment for employees. Floodlights are an effective way to illuminate a large area. The entire lighting system should also be set on a timer, or photoelectric technology can be used to detect outside light levels.

Video Surveillance

To maintain the physical security of the property, surveillance and monitoring devices should be employed. The simplest form of surveillance is the use of common security procedures, such as using security guards. Cameras can be set up throughout the facility, which can be constantly monitored by security guards. Although effective, these options can be costly because of the high price of surveillance equipment and the ongoing wages that must be paid to security guards. Camera surveillance can be coupled with recording equipment that can monitor and record all activity 24 hours a day. If a burglary or vandalism occurs, the culprits could be captured on video, which can then be analyzed to identify the unauthorized intruders. This can be both a detective and deterrent control; the guards monitoring can detect, but if a potential intruder is aware of the surveillance, it certainly can deter.

Camera placement is of primary importance, both in terms of efficiency of surveillance and equipment costs, and at a minimum all entrances, doors, and access ways should be included in the coverage. All people who enter and exit the facility will be recorded on the cameras. In high-security environments, additional cameras are typically placed inside server rooms and other networking equipment areas that form the hub of the communications network.

The use of intruder detection equipment can ensure that a surveillance and monitoring system is proactive by alerting you to suspicious behavior without the need and expense of constant monitoring by security guards. Several intrusion detection technology options are available:

- **Proximity detector**   Senses changes in an electromagnetic field that surrounds a small area or object; when a change is detected, an alarm will sound.

- **Motion detector**   Detects motion in a certain area; most often used in conjunction with floodlights that turn on when motion is detected. The light serves as a warning that an intruder has been detected.

- **Photoelectric detector**   Senses changes in light patterns that indicate someone is in the area. The photoelectric device emits a beam of light that, when disrupted, sounds an alarm.

- **Infrared detector**   Senses changes in the heat patterns of an area that indicate the presence of an intruder.

- **Sound detector**   Senses sounds and vibrations, and can detect changes in the noise levels in an area.

- **Protected distribution**   Protects sensitive cabling from taps or other malicious activity. This can also be monitored by video at critical points.

Travel Advisory

The main drawback of most intrusion detection systems is the large number of false alarms that can occur because of abnormal weather conditions, animals, and improper calibration.

Locks

The most basic and least expensive type of physical-access control is the use of a lock and key. Unfortunately, in large environments, this can quickly become an administrative nightmare because the number of keys that must be distributed for each lock can grow quickly. In addition, employees lose keys, duplicate them, and let other users borrow them. When an employee is terminated, he might not always return his keys, and then every lock should be changed.

Depending on the environment, different types of locks can be used. For perimeter security, a simple padlock on a chained fence might suffice. For more high-security areas, electronic or mechanical locks with programmable keys can be installed. These require a combination or key code to open instead of a physical key.

Travel Advisory

Electronic locks should be linked with the alarm system. In case of a fire or other emergency, the locks should automatically disengage to allow people to leave the building.

Hardware Locks

It's easy for an unauthorized user to walk by an unattended desk or system rack and quickly remove expensive equipment. Not only does the stolen equipment need to be replaced, but the sensitive data saved on that equipment also must be recovered. If the item was stolen for corporate espionage, the results of the theft can be devastating.

Any expensive or sensitive equipment—especially portable items such as laptops, mobile devices, and networking equipment—should be kept out of sight or locked up when unattended. Device locks are available for both desktop computers and portable laptops. A desktop computer can be housed in a lockable cage that would require a great deal of effort to open. Also, alarm cards, which will sound a loud alarm whenever the computer is moved, can be installed in computers. Peripheral devices attached to a computer can be protected with cable traps that prevent their removal. Laptop computers should be fitted with special cables and locks that can securely attach them to a current work area. If the user will be away from a laptop for an extended period, it should be locked inside a desk or cabinet.

Physical access to special network and computer equipment rooms should be secured as carefully as access to company facilities. These rooms are the brains of company operations, concentrating a variety of critical functions, such as network communications, database servers, and backup systems. If an unauthorized user gains access to the central network room, the damage she can cause could be considerable.

The main door to the network or server room should be secured with some type of lock, preferably with some sort of smart access system, as described earlier. Only those employees who need to be in the room to perform their job functions should be allowed access. Inside, servers and other sensitive equipment should be housed within a lockable cage or rack and not left running in an open area where they could be accessed or accidentally damaged. Many types of networking equipment servers come with their own locks that require keys to open them for access.

Man-Trap

A man-trap is a two-tier, physical-access control method with two physical barriers, such as doors, between the person and the resource he is trying to access. A person is allowed access into the first door (sometimes requiring a first authentication), and then when that door is closed, the person is physically caught between doors and must pass a form of authentication to gain entry through the second door. In high-security environments, the person is effectively trapped if he passes the first authentication but cannot be properly authenticated through the second door. The first door will be locked down, and he will not be able to leave until security arrives to examine his credentials. Also, the purpose of a man-trap can be to allow only one individual at a time in, so no tailgating is permitted. Man-traps do exist that have no authentication requirements; they only serve to stop more than one person from entering/ exiting at the same time.

A more basic example of this is a bank whose cash machines are in a lobby between the outside doors and the internal bank doors. To access the first door, the person must swipe his card for that bank. Once inside, the person must use his bank card in conjunction with a PIN to access the automated teller machine (ATM).

Security Guards

You may consider a security guard an "old-fashioned" method of securing access, but simply having personnel who are charged with observing and reacting to threats can be a powerful mitigation to both internal and external threats. Those guards can monitor closed-circuit televisions (CCTVs) and man-traps, and check equipment being moved in and out of the perimeter. Don't discount how valuable having a human for access control can be, even within a highly technical environment.

Access Logs

As part of an overall security plan, access logs should contain the names of all visitors to the facility and the in and out times of their visits. Most organizations have some type of policy that requires all nonemployees to sign in at the front lobby of a building and indicate who they are visiting, including the times they entered and exited. This allows the organization to keep a record of all nonemployees, contractors, and visitors to the building. If any security issues arise, a list is available of everyone who was in the building at that time.

Access logs are also important for highly sensitive areas of an organization such as the main server and telecommunications room that houses the primary system and networking equipment. Each administrator should record his times of entry into and departure from the server room to perform duties or maintenance. Any security issues that arise regarding activities in the server room can be tracked to whoever was in the room at the time.

Most electronic card systems automatically record this information, as employees typically use their ID cards to enter and exit various parts of the building. These electronic logs can be easily obtained and scanned to determine who was at a certain location during times of a security lapse. Manual access logs can still be used for those visitors who are required to enter the controlled access area occasionally but do not have electronic cards for the area.

Personal Identification Verification Card

More advanced personnel-access control techniques include the use of personal identification verification cards. The ID card provides photo identification that can immediately identify the wearer as an authorized user. ID cards should be worn where they can always be seen by other employees. The card should identify the person and his job function. By listing job function, the ID card can be used to quickly determine that person's access clearance into a certain part of the facility. Simple ID cards, however, require the use of security guards and security-conscious employees.

Smart Card

The most common method of personnel access control used today is the smart card. Typically, each employee receives a card with a magnetic strip or computer chip that contains her access information. These cards are swiped in magnetic card readers that are stationed outside important access points, such as doors and elevators. If the card uses a chip, the card is inserted into a card reader. The information on the card is then compared with the security access of the area the person is about to enter. If she doesn't have access to that area, the door won't open.

Travel Advisory

Smart cards should include no company identification. If a card is lost or stolen, the unauthorized user would have no idea from which company or facility the card came.

Another type of access card system is the proximity reader, which doesn't require the physical insertion of a card. The reader can sense the card if it's within a certain minimum distance. The information is read through an electromagnetic field.

The card can also be used as a requirement to log in to sensitive networks and computers. Using a card reader, the computer will not allow you to log in until you have inserted your smart card to verify your identity and access level.

Exam Tip

Smart cards can be complemented with access codes or PINs. In the event the card is lost or stolen, it can't be used for access if the proper corresponding PIN is not keyed in.

Common Access Card

A Common Access Card (or CAC, as it is sometimes lovingly called) is a special type of smart card issued by the U.S. government for a wide variety of its agencies, including the Department of Defense. It is primarily used for military and government personnel as an identification and authentication card for physical access to military and government buildings, and for computer and network access. For example, you would not be able to log in to a military network computer without inserting your card into the card reader for identification and authorization to the resources available for your level of access. The card also contains a digital certificate for a user that allows that user to encrypt messages and perform digital signing.

CHECKPOINT

✔**Objective 6.01: Explain the Fundamental Concepts and Best Practices Related to Authentication, Authorization, and Access Control** Use separation of duties, job rotation, implicit deny, and least privilege principles when organizing your security infrastructure and grouping users and resources into appropriate security groups and zones. In a MAC model, the OS of the network is in control of access to data. DAC allows the data owners to specify what users can access certain data. Privileges can be assigned by user, group, or role in the company. Role-based access control (RBAC) allows access to be based on the role the user holds within an organization.

Rule-based access control is based on ACLs and is not necessarily tied to the identity of a user; it provides access rules that are applied to all users in the organization, based on elements such as desired action, location, time of day, role, user ID, and other factors. Attribute-based access control (ABAC) provides more granularity and scalability by assigning attributes to subjects and objects.

✔**Objective 6.02: Implement Appropriate Security Controls When Performing Account Management** Some of the most effective account restrictions include limiting logon attempts, using expiry dates, disabling unused accounts, setting time restrictions, restricting machine access, and using tokens. Use password policies such as regular password rotation, enforcing strong passwords, and employing password aging to prevent password weaknesses. Each user should have his own personal data directory, where only he has access to create, delete, and modify the files and directories within it. When you first create an ACL for a resource, use no access as a default. This enables you to start with a clean slate, and you can add access permissions based on the needs of the user or group, giving them only enough access permissions to perform their job function.

✔**Objective 6.03: Analyze and Differentiate Among Types of Mitigation and Deterrent Techniques** Physical-access control security includes video surveillance and monitoring, ID cards, locks, man-traps, security guards, cameras, and access logs. ID cards should be complemented with access codes or PINs. In case the card is lost or stolen, it can't be used for access unless the user keys in the corresponding PIN.

REVIEW QUESTIONS

1. Match the permission with its appropriate definition in the following table:

View or list the contents of a file or directory and execute accessible files.	A. Full Control
View or list the contents of a file or directory.	B. Modify
Read, write, execute, or delete a file or directory.	C. Read and Execute
Read, write, execute, modify, or delete a file or directory.	D. Read

2. You are creating an access control model that will allow you to assign specific access policies depending on which network a user is on and not necessarily on the actual identity of the specific user. Which privilege management access control model would you use?

   A. Rule-based access control

   B. Discretionary access control

   C. Attribute-based access control

   D. Mandatory access control

3. You must create an access control mechanism for your server and network room, which houses all your organization's servers and primary networking equipment. Which of the following methods would be the most secure?

   A. Access list

   B. Smart card access

   C. ID badge

   D. Video surveillance

4. You are designing file security for a new file server for your sales department. Each user will have his own private and secure directory as well as a shared group directory. Which of the following should be the initial default access level for each user before you assign permissions?

   A. Full access

   B. Read and Write access

   C. No access

   D. Only Read access

5. You have recently had several laptops stolen after hours when employees leave unattended laptops on their desks after they leave work. Which of the following policies should you implement to increase security and prevent theft?

   A. Enforce the use of cable locks.

   B. Make sure users are logged out of laptops before they leave.

   C. Set a hardware password.

   D. Lock all unattended laptops in a cabinet after hours.

6. Which of the following best practices discourages corruption by ensuring that users do not have the same amount of access and privileges for too long a time?

    A. Least privilege

    B. Separation of duties

    C. Job rotation

    D. Implicit deny

7. Your company has defined working hours for a call center department. There have been several instances of employees using company resources to download Internet content after work hours. Which of the following can you implement to improve security?

    A. Use MAC address filtering to prevent access on suspect computers.

    B. Set access time restrictions.

    C. Shut down all computers after work hours.

    D. Implement job rotation.

8. You have had a rash of hacking incidents where weak employee passwords are being hacked through brute-force methods and unauthorized users are gaining access to the network. Which of the following security policies is most efficient for preventing brute-force hacking attempts on employee passwords?

    A. Password rotation

    B. Password length and complexity restrictions

    C. Password expiration

    D. Limiting logon attempts

9. You have already implemented a password expiration and rotation policy that forces your users to change their password every 60 days. However, you find that many users are simply using their same password again. Which of the following can you implement to improve security?

    A. Password history

    B. Password complexity

    C. Limiting logon attempts

    D. Password expiry

10. A military building uses strict access control where a user must use smart card access to enter the main door of the facility. Then he must meet a security guard at a second door to present an ID badge and enter his PIN number. What security feature is used in this access control mechanism?

    A. Mandatory access control

    B. Implicit deny

    C. Three-tier access control

    D. Man-trap

REVIEW ANSWERS

1. **C D B A**

View or list the contents of a file or directory and execute accessible files.	C. Read and Execute
View or list the contents of a file or directory.	D. Read
Read, write, execute, or delete a file or directory.	B. Modify
Read, write, execute, modify, or delete a file or directory.	A. Full Control

   Be sure to pay attention to how permissions build on each other. Modify, for example, builds on the permission level of Read and Execute by allowing associated users to write and delete a file or directory, as appropriate.

2. **A** Rule-based access control is defined with an access control list (ACL), which specifies a set of rules that must be followed before access is granted. Rule-based access control does not necessarily have to be tied to an authorized identity and could involve access permissions based on network location, content of messages (such as e-mail text or attachments), and other types of content filtering.

3. **B** Smart card access would provide the most security. The server room door will not unlock unless a user inserts her smart card and has the proper authorization to enter the room.

4. **C** You should use the principle of implicit deny, which means that, by default, a user should have no access permission at all unless explicitly permitted. You can then assign Read/Write access for each user to his own home directory and Read/Write access to the shared directory. This ensures you start with the most secure default configuration.

5. **D**   If employees are not taking their laptops home with them, these devices should be removed from their desks and put in a locked cabinet until the users return the next day. Cable locks are useful for security during office hours, but can be cut by a determined thief. Logging out of the laptop or setting hardware passwords can prevent unauthorized access, but will not deter theft.

6. **C**   Job rotation ensures greater security because no single employee retains the same amount of access control for an area for an extended period of time. This can prevent internal corruption, whereby long-term employees, because of their deep knowledge of their area of duty, might be more inclined to take advantage of their position and enhanced access.

7. **B**   By setting time restrictions on network access, you prevent employees from being able to log in and access the network after working hours are complete.

8. **D**   You can limit logon attempts to lock out the user's account if an incorrect password has been entered too many times. Although password length, complexity, rotation, and expiration are helpful security measures, brute-force attacks can most efficiently be stopped by limiting the number of attempted logons.

9. **A**   When password history is enabled, the system can remember a user's former passwords. When the current password expires, the system forces the user to use a new password that is not the same as one of her previous passwords.

10. **D**   When a company uses a man-trap, each user must be authenticated to be able to enter the first door of the facility. When he has entered the first door, it is closed, and the user is physically trapped between the first and second doors. The user must pass an additional round of authentication to gain access through the second door.

Authentication and Identity Management

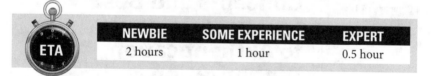

	NEWBIE	SOME EXPERIENCE	EXPERT
ETA	2 hours	1 hour	0.5 hour

To use the resources of a computer system or network or to enter a secure facility, a user must first be *authenticated*. Identification and authentication verify that the user is who he says he is and has the credentials to access these resources. The most common form of authentication requires a username and password, but more secure schemes can use multiple factors to strengthen the authentication process and confidence in the identity and credentials of a user.

Methods such as security cards, tokens, and personal identification numbers (PINs), as well as more advanced techniques such as biometric voice and fingerprint recognition, offer additional forms of authentication. When a user logs in to a system, he supplies a set of credentials or login identifiers that must be matched against credentials stored in an authentication database. If any of the information doesn't match, the user is refused entry or access to the system. Authentication and access control methods are only as efficient as the amount of time and planning spent setting up and configuring the system. The more complex the login process, the more difficult it will be for an unauthorized user to gain access to a system.

This chapter describes the types of authentication models, services, and protocols available that help to provide secure, authenticated access to your networks.

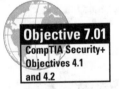

Objective 7.01
CompTIA Security+
Objectives 4.1
and 4.2

Explain the Fundamental Concepts and Best Practices Related to Authentication, Authorization, and Access Services

Before a user can access a resource—be it a network, system, file server, or database—the user must initially *identify* herself as a valid user for that resource. The user must then be *authenticated* using additional criteria that verify the validity of the identity presented by the user. If these criteria are matched, the user is granted access. The following sections describe the basic authentication models and methods that can be used to verify an identity.

Authentication Models

A user-authentication system must be able to confirm a user's identity and level of authorization. Combining three of the following basic authentication components will provide the highest level of assurance in authenticating a user's identity:

- **Something the user *has***   An ID badge or smart card the user possesses. This is also called the *possession factor*.

- **Something the user *knows***   A username, password, or PIN. This is sometimes referred to as the *knowledge factor*.

- **Something the user *is***   A unique physical aspect of the user, such as a biometric characteristic. Sometimes you will see this expressed as the *inherence factor*.

- **Something a user *does***   A unique swipe pattern (often used on mobile devices).

- **Some*where* a user is**   Location-based authentication, using GPS or another geolocation device. This is also known as the *location factor*.

The following sections describe how these factors or multiple sets of factors can be used to identify a user.

Single-Factor Authentication

Single-factor authentication refers to requiring only one factor (such as a password) to authenticate a user. The system compares the password for the account with the database of known usernames and passwords and then authenticates the user if they match. This is the simplest but weakest form of authentication because users' passwords tend to be weak.

Single-factor authentication can also involve a magnetic swipe card or token used to open a locked door. This is also a weak form of authentication, as the card or token can be easily lost or stolen and an unauthorized user can simply use the card or token to access the door without needing to provide any other credentials.

Two-Factor Authentication

Two-factor authentication typically combines two single-factor authentication types, such as something the user knows and something the user possesses. For example, most automated teller machine (ATM) banking transactions require two-factor authentication: the user inserts a physical banking card into the machine and then types a PIN, which is matched with the electronic information contained on the card's magnetic strip. One authentication factor should be physical, such as a smart card or access token (something the user possesses) or a biometric factor (something physically unique about the user), and the second factor should be a password or PIN (something the user knows). Without these two items, no access can be granted.

Multifactor Authentication

Multifactor authentication is the strongest form of user authentication and involves a combination of a physical item, such as a smart card, token, or biometric factor, and a nonphysical item, such as a password, passphrase, or PIN. Typically, the biometric factor is the third and deciding factor used in combination with an access card and password. For example, before he can enter a high-security facility, a user might have to insert a smart card into a door, enter a PIN on a keypad, and then insert his finger into a scanner.

Single Sign-On

In early computer systems, when networking wasn't as available as it is today, each computer contained a set of resources the user could access. To access the resources of a computer system, she used a specific login and password. Each specific computer needed a separate login and password. This was tedious for computer users and administrators alike because of the frequency with which login accounts and passwords needed to be reset for each computer if a user forgot them.

Nowadays, modern networks provide resources that are spread throughout the computer network and that can be accessed by any user from any location. The user can be onsite on her own computer, or she can be logged in from home or on the road by using dial-up methods or via the Internet. With the vast amount of resources that can be contained on a large computer network, the concept of different logins and passwords for each resource has been eliminated in favor of a *single sign-on* to the network; the user must be authenticated only once on the network to access the resources on it. This type of centralized administration is a much more efficient way for a network administrator to control access to the network. User account policy templates can be created and used network-wide to remove the need to configure each user's account settings individually, except for a unique login and password.

An example of single sign-on is a Microsoft Active Directory username and password required for accessing directories, files, and printers on a network, along with Microsoft Exchange mail servers and SQL database servers. Lightweight Directory Access Protocol (LDAP) is also a popular authentication database used for single sign-on purposes. LDAP is discussed in more detail later in this chapter.

Authentication Methods

The methods used for authentication depend on the resources these security mechanisms are trying to protect. Most computer networks rely on a login-and-password system. The use of remote access or virtual private network (VPN) accounts might require the use of encrypted communications beyond the typical user-login-and-password process. Each authentication system must be geared specifically to the circumstances that define a user and resources and how those resources need to be protected. The following sections describe several authentication methods and their components, including remote access authentication.

Remote Access Authentication

Remote access is an important network feature for companies and organizations that require users to access network resources from anywhere offsite. With the evolution of telecommunications, a variety of methods can allow a user to access a network remotely. Early methods included attaching a serial cable between two computers via their serial interfaces. The use of modems enabled users to dial in to a system or network over a common phone line. Modern access methods include complex VPNs that let users access their corporate network from a public network, such as the Internet. Fast home networking technologies have enabled home users to break free of the bandwidth limitations of modems and phone lines to create fast and secure communications channels to remote networks.

The most important factor in securing remote communications is the ability both to authenticate a client to a remote network and to encrypt the communications so that they can't be captured. With the explosive growth of high-bandwidth home networks that communicate over the Internet with remote systems, the need for secure communications is critical.

Each type of communication system depends on the medium used by the client user to connect to the remote machine. A user in a hotel in another country could be trying to access his corporate local area network (LAN) via a public wireless connection. Another user might be connected to the Internet from home through a digital subscriber line (DSL) connection, using a virtual private network to communicate with a remote network. A network administrator might use Telnet or Secure Shell (SSH) to log in to a server remotely from home.

Each remote access method must be carefully examined for security vulnerabilities to make sure that users are properly authenticated to access the network's resources and that communications are encrypted to prevent someone from tapping into the transmitted information.

Dial-Up For many years, the most common way of accessing remote services to a corporate LAN or the Internet was using a dial-up connection via a modem over a common phone line. A modem, short for *modulator-demodulator,* is used to convert the digital signals of a computer to analog for transmission over an analog phone line. A modem at the receiving end converts the signal back into digital for the remote computer. Many companies don't properly protect their remote access services because they think their regular company firewall will protect them. Unfortunately, the firewall protects the network only from traffic that comes from the Internet—not traffic that dials into the network.

Travel Advisory

One of the oldest modem-hacking methods is the use of *war dialing,* in which a malicious hacker uses a program to call phone numbers in quick succession to look for those attached to a modem. Once a number is found, the hacker can dial in to the modem and try to break the authentication to gain access.

For remote access to a network, a client machine initiates a connection to a remote access server. The remote access server is connected to a modem, or to several banks of modems, to provide enough connections for multiple remote users, as shown in Figure 7.1.

When the client and remote modems are connected, the server typically requires some form of authentication, often a username and password, before granting the client access to the network's resources. The authentication system

FIGURE 7.1 Remote access via modem

could be built into the remote access server itself, or it could be a separate service running an authentication protocol, such as Terminal Access Controller Access-Control System (TACACS) or Remote Authentication Dial-In User Service (RADIUS). Additional forms of authentication that can secure communications even more include the use of security tokens, a type of card or token that displays a key code that cycles every few minutes. When synchronized with the server, the token creates another form of authentication that's tied to a user account. Because the sequenced number is cycled with a defined algorithm, the same number can't be used twice within a certain period.

> **Travel Advisory**
>
> Security tokens are combined with traditional usernames, passwords, and PINs; if the token card is stolen, the unauthorized user still needs the other credentials to gain access.

ISDN   Integrated Services Digital Network (ISDN) technology was created to replace the use of common phone lines for network communications. A special ISDN line must be run to your location, and both your client computer and the remote computer must use a special ISDN adapter. Unlike a modem, an ISDN adapter doesn't convert signals from digital to analog and back again; instead, ISDN connects digitally between the two adapters over the ISDN line.

Each ISDN connection is divided into channels:

- **B-channels**   These channels transmit data, such as voice or computer data communications. They can be used individually or combined to create higher bandwidth.
- **D-channels**   These channels transmit control and signal information for managing the transmission of data.

ISDN has generally been passed over in favor of cable modem and DSL communications. These methods are much less expensive and easier to set up and configure because they use the existing cabling infrastructure in the home.

Cable Modem   Using a cable modem is one of the most popular ways of connecting home computers to the Internet. Cable modems are misnamed, though, because they don't operate like a typical modem, which translates signals between analog and digital. A cable modem enables you to connect to your home's coaxial cable lines, which are then connected by common Ethernet cable to your computer's network interface card (NIC).

The speed of cable modem communications decreases when more homes are connected to the same cable line. For example, in most neighborhoods, several homes are connected to the same segment of a coaxial cable run. If many people are using the Internet at the same time, the bandwidth is shared among them, so the individual connections are slower.

The security risk involved with cable modems is that, unlike dial-up connections, the connection to the Internet is permanent and always on until the system is turned off or unplugged from the cable network. If a system is connected to the Internet, it's open to attacks from hackers, who continually scan networks for security vulnerabilities in online systems. The use of a firewall is recommended to secure these connections and protect your computer against these intrusions.

Travel Advisory

Malicious hackers make use of port scanner programs to analyze a bank of IP addresses on a network, looking for open service ports and applications that can be compromised. To prevent a port scanner from viewing your system while you're connected to a cable modem or DSL network, you can install a firewall, which prevents your system from replying to such scans.

DSL DSL is another popular method of connecting a home computer or small business to the Internet. DSL runs over common copper telephone lines but requires the connection to be near a phone company's access point. The closer your system is to the access point, the faster your connection.

DSL can be used for sending voice and data transmissions over the same phone line. Home users can talk on the phone while still connected to the Internet. This type of communication is impossible with normal dial-up modem methods. DSL also differs from a typical modem in that it doesn't require modulating the signal from digital to analog, and vice versa. DSL uses the entire bandwidth of the phone line for digital transmission.

Like cable modems, a DSL network connection is always on until the system is switched off or unplugged from the DSL network. To protect your system, use a firewall.

Remote Access Applications

Remote access applications are used to provide access to a machine from an external client system. The communication that connects the two systems can be anything from a dial-up modem connection, to a direct cable connection, to a TCP/IP network. Typically, these applications consist of server and client components. The server software is installed on the system made available for remote access. Sometimes the client and server computers connect through a simple network or serial cable. The server software is then configured to accept communications as a host server. When the client connects to the server, it must be authenticated before it is granted access.

When connected, the user can remotely control the machine as if she was sitting in front of it on the console. This type of application can create severe security vulnerabilities if it isn't properly secured. This security should include strong authentication and encryption methods.

Telnet Telnet allows you to connect remotely to a system and execute commands as if you were on the console of the system. Telnet provides only basic authentication security, consisting of a username and password on the remote system. Telnet communications are not encrypted but are sent in clear text and can be discovered by a hacker monitoring network traffic.

Telnet use should be limited to communications within an already secure network, but other, more secure methods of remote access that use encryption and stronger authentication methods are recommended.

SSH SSH is a secure form of remote access to a remote computer. Like Telnet, SSH allows you to connect to a remote system and perform commands as if the remote user were on the console of the system. SSH uses a secure, encrypted tunnel to the remote system.

During the initial SSH connection, a special session key is exchanged during the negotiation and authentication. This creates an encrypted secure channel for the communications between the client and the server.

Encrypted remote access solutions such as SSH should always be used in place of Telnet and other insecure remote access utilities.

Travel Advisory

Other utilities that send their information in clear text include remote login (rlogin), File Transfer Protocol (FTP), and remote shell (rsh). Whenever possible, a secure method such as SSH should be used for remote console access and file transfer.

VPN A *VPN* is a secure and private connection over a public network. The connection between the client and the remote network is provided by an encrypted tunnel between the two points, as shown in Figure 7.2.

VPN connection

In addition to remote access, VPNs are used for connecting two remote routers to form a secure wide area network (WAN). For a VPN to work properly, the sender and receiver must be running the same type of VPN, with the same protocols and encryption settings.

The VPN enables the remote user to be connected locally to a public network such as the Internet, while also being directly connected to the corporate network using the encrypted VPN tunnel. This connection can be dial-up through a modem or a direct Internet connection, such as a cable modem or DSL.

The user must first establish her connection to the Internet and then start the VPN software, which creates a virtual connection to the VPN access server on the corporate network. After the connection is negotiated, the client must authenticate itself using a username and password before the VPN will grant access to the corporate network. A VPN is only as secure as the tunneling and encryption protocols used on the connection. Early types of VPNs used older encryption methods, which can be cracked by today's savvy attackers.

Remote Access Protocols

For remote access communications to work, the data must be transmitted using one or several network protocols. These protocols must be able to travel through different networks and different physical infrastructures. A home user who wants to connect his computer to the Internet must use an analog modem, cable modem, or DSL line to connect with an Internet service provider (ISP). Different protocols are needed both to facilitate the transmission of digital data over cable and analog phone lines and to encapsulate TCP/IP (the protocol used for Internet communications) over these mediums.

Exam Tip
Know the advantages and disadvantages of the protocols discussed here, as well as with what types of communications they can be used.

SLIP   The Serial Line Internet Protocol (SLIP) is one of the earliest Internet protocols used for encapsulating IP packets for transmission over serial communications, such as a phone line or serial cable. SLIP can work with most types of protocols, such as Internet Protocol (IP), Internetwork Packet Exchange/Sequenced Packet Exchange (IPX/SPX), and NetBIOS Extended User Interface (NetBEUI), and does not require a static network address; however, SLIP is considered difficult to configure, inefficient, and unreliable. It isn't used much these days and has been replaced by PPP.

PPP   The Point-to-Point Protocol (PPP) is used to enable a connection between two computers using a serial interface, usually over a phone line. PPP is the most popular protocol used by an ISP to enable users to dial in to the Internet network from home using a modem attached to a home computer. The main function of PPP is to encapsulate IP packets and send them over the Internet. PPP is considered much more reliable and easier to use than SLIP because it contains error checking and the ability to run different types of protocols over a variety of media methods. Common authentication protocols used with PPP are Password Authentication Protocol (PAP), Challenge Handshake Authentication Protocol (CHAP), Microsoft Challenge Handshake Authentication Protocol (MSCHAP), and Extensible Authentication Protocol (EAP), which are discussed later in this chapter.

VPN Protocols

The following types of protocols are used by VPNs to tunnel network data over a public network and to provide encryption to protect transmitted data.

PPTP   The Point-to-Point Tunneling Protocol (PPTP) is a Microsoft implementation of secure communications over a VPN. Because PPTP is an extension of PPP, it has become one of the most widely used tunneling protocols and allows network packets to be encapsulated within PPP communications for transfer over another network, such as the Internet.

Previous remote access technologies allowed remote access only through a dial-up modem to the corporate network. Depending on where this user was located, the long-distance charges could be enormous, and sometimes a company would need to create its own expensive toll-free phone service for long-distance dial-in access. Tunneling protocols allow users connected to a public network, such as the Internet (through fast cable modem or DSL service), to create their own private connections to their corporate LANs.

PPTP decrypts and encapsulates PPP packets to create the VPN connection. One major security problem with PPTP is that when a connection is negotiated, the communication is transmitted in clear text. This data can be captured by an unauthorized user who can use the information to try to hack the connection. PPTP connections for VPNs are typically encrypted using Microsoft Point-to-Point Encryption (MPPE), which uses the RSA RC4 encryption algorithm with support for 40-bit, 56-bit, and 128-bit session keys. These keys are changed on a regular basis, which greatly improves security and lessens the chance of the keys being broken.

L2TP The Layer 2 Tunneling Protocol (L2TP) combines the best features of PPTP with the Layer 2 Forward (L2F) protocol created by Cisco Systems. L2TP is most often used with other media technologies, such as Frame Relay.

L2TP consists of two main components:

- **L2TP Access Concentrator (LAC)** The LAC is responsible for terminating the local network connection and tunneling PPP packets to the LNS.
- **L2TP Network Server (LNS)** The LNS is situated on the remote end of the connection and terminates the PPP connection originating from the LAC.

Using the LAC and LNS, the connection can be localized because the L2TP components terminate the endpoints of the PPP connection, as shown in Figure 7.3.

The main difference between L2TP and PPTP is that L2TP can run on top of and tunnel through other network protocols, such as IPX and Systems Network Architecture (SNA), while PPTP can run only on top of IP networks. L2TP, however, doesn't provide any type of native encryption, so it must be

| **FIGURE 7.3** | L2TP deployment |

combined with another encrypted protocol, such as Internet Protocol Security (IPSec). Unlike PPTP, L2TP supports authentication services such as RADIUS and TACACS+ (discussed later in this chapter).

Exam Tip

Understand that neither L2TP nor PPTP is responsible for securing its traffic payloads using encryption or authentication services. Both are only encapsulating protocols that do the heavy lifting of carrying traffic destined for secure networks through untrusted networks such as the Internet. For security services, they rely on other protocols, such as IPSec and MPPE, respectively.

IPSec   IPSec is a suite of protocols used primarily to encrypt VPN communications over the Internet. It provides several security benefits for authentication, data integrity, and confidentiality for remote VPN access.

IPSec utilizes a shared public key encryption method to create an encrypted communications tunnel between two VPN endpoints, including client-to-server and server-to-server connections. The client can remotely connect to a network from anywhere it has Internet access, and all its network traffic is sent through the encrypted tunnel while the IPSec VPN is activated. The connecting client can be authenticated to an authentication service, such as a RADIUS or LDAP server, before the connection is established.

Travel Assistance

For detailed information on IPSec, see Chapter 4.

Objective 7.02
CompTIA Security+
Objectives 3.9
and 4.2

Explain the Function and Purpose of Authentication Services

Your authentication services not only protect your networks for internal users on your wired LAN, but also remote access users who access your network resources over an Internet VPN or wireless network. Protection of the authentication phase of your communications is vital to prevent your users' logins and passwords from being captured. A good remote access method needs to secure the password database and the communications over which the clients send their credentials. The following sections describe some popular authentication services.

> **Exam Tip**
>
> Be aware of the authentication protocols discussed here, including their uses and strengths and weaknesses.

PAP

The Password Authentication Protocol (PAP) is the most basic type of authentication that consists of comparing a set of credentials, such as a username and a password, to a central table of authentication data. If the credentials match, the user is granted access. PAP is most often used with dial-up remote access methods using PPP, such as connecting to an ISP or Remote Access Services (RAS) that supports PPP.

Although the password tables used by PAP are encrypted, the actual communications between the client and authentication server are not, allowing the username and password to be sent over the network in clear text. This can easily be captured by an unauthorized user monitoring the network. Typically used for dial-up authentication, PAP is also the default authentication protocol within Hypertext Transfer Protocol (HTTP). Because of PAP's weaknesses, CHAP is usually used in place of PAP.

CHAP

The Challenge-Handshake Authentication Protocol (CHAP) is much more secure than PAP. Once the communications link is completed, the authenticating server sends a random value to the client. The client sends back the value combined with the username and password credentials, plus a predefined secret, calculated using a one-way hash function. The server compares the response against its own calculation of the expected hash value. If the values match, the client is granted access.

CHAP provides protection against *replay attacks*, which are used by hackers to capture data and then send it again. To prevent this type of attack, CHAP uses an incrementally changing identifier and a variable challenge value, and the authentication can be repeated any time while the connection is open using the new identifiers.

Microsoft has its own version of CHAP called MSCHAP, which extends the functionality of CHAP for Microsoft networks. The latest version, MSCHAPv2, provides stronger security for remote access connections and resolves issues present in earlier versions of MSCHAP.

LANMAN

Windows LANMAN (LAN Manager) is used by older versions of Windows Server (such as Windows NT) for encrypting user passwords for authentication purposes. The hashing system used (LM hash algorithm) is easily subverted via a brute-force attack in which a password can be cracked in only a few minutes or hours.

LANMAN has been replaced by NTLM (NT LAN Manager) in Windows NT 3.1 Server and later operating systems, although LANMAN is still available for backward compatibility. As of Windows Vista, LANMAN is completely disabled, but it can be enabled manually. In general, LANMAN should be disabled if all your systems are running Windows 2000 or later.

NTLM and NTLMv2

NTLM was created as an improvement to the original Microsoft LANMAN implementation and combines challenge/response authentication with message digest hashed passwords that are transmitted between the clients and authenticating servers. NTLM version 1 uses MD4 hashing, while version 2 (introduced in Windows NT Service Pack 4) uses keyed (Hash Message Authentication Code) MD5 hashing and is more secure than version 1.

Since Windows 2000 and the growth of Active Directory–based implementations, Microsoft has implemented Kerberos authentication, but NTLM is still used for authentication purposes in cases where Windows networks are run without Active Directory domains or any other type of third-party authentication service.

Extensible Authentication Protocol

The Extensible Authentication Protocol (EAP) is primarily used in wireless networks, but it can also be used in traditional LANs and remote access methods to extend PPP authentication. The EAP framework provides an extension of the types of authentication protocols that are typically used in PAP and CHAP methods. For example, instead of a simple username and password, additional methods can be used, such as tokens, Kerberos, biometrics, and Transport Layer Security (TLS).

FIGURE 7.4   RADIUS server authentication

RADIUS

The Remote Authentication Dial-In User Service (RADIUS) is the most common Internet standard used for authenticating clients in a client/server environment. When the remote user accesses a network through a remote access device, the user is authenticated by a RADIUS server that compares the user's authentication credentials against those of the server's database. If the credentials match, the user is granted access to the rest of the network. The client's credentials that are sent to the RADIUS server are encrypted to prevent someone from capturing the transmission. RADIUS servers also include accounting and reporting functions that can monitor and log data on each connection, such as packet and protocol types, as well as length of time connected. Figure 7.4 shows an example of how a RADIUS server authenticates a remote access client.

LDAP

The Lightweight Directory Access Protocol (LDAP) is used to look up information in a database for other users and network resources. A *directory* is a database that's often compared to the telephone white pages or the yellow pages because the information can be searched and quickly found within the indexed database. The directory database itself can consist of a wide variety of information, including not only basic user contact information, such as e-mail addresses and phone numbers, but also objects, such as printers and computers. Some directory services are used to configure and control access to every single network resource object on the entire network or to contain a centralized database of logins and passwords. With such a critical collection of network data, security is of prime importance when using directory access protocols such as LDAP.

All LDAP servers have some security controls in place for allowing read and update access to the directory database. Typically, all users can read most of the information held in the database, but only a few users have update privileges.

Large directories usually have multiple information administrators who have access to update only information pertaining to their departments or regions.

For a client to access an LDAP server, it must first be authenticated, unless the server allows anonymous connections. This type of access control allows the LDAP server to decide exactly what that client can access and what information it can update.

Most LDAP servers support the use of encrypted secure channels to communicate with clients, especially when transferring information such as usernames, passwords, and other sensitive data. LDAP servers use the Secure Sockets Layer (SSL) protocol (also called LDAPS, or sometimes also Secure LDAP) for this purpose.

> ### Exam Tip
>
> Remember that LDAP (unencrypted) uses TCP port 389, LDAP over SSL uses TCP port 689, and LDAP over TLS uses TCP port 636.

SAML

The Security Assertion Markup Language (SAML) allows the transfer of information about an individual—specifically, who they are (authentication) and what they have access rights to (authorization)—between identity and service providers. The SAML standard provides three general roles: the principal (typically a user), the identity provider, and the service provider (such as an ISP or an application service provider). The service provider requests information from the identity provider; SAML 2.0 supplies a token containing assertions, or a packet of information about a principal upon receipt. The service provider then decides to allow or deny access to the requested service. If authenticated, the service is provided to the identity (user). Shibboleth furthers SAML 2.0 to provide federated single sign-on across organizations and to control privacy for users through attribute management.

TACACS

The Terminal Access Controller Access-Control System (TACACS) is an older type of authentication protocol that's like RADIUS. A remote access user connects to a network and is authenticated by the TACACS server before being allowed access to the network's resources. Three versions of TACACS have been used:

- **TACACS**   The original protocol, which performs both authentication and authorization.

- **XTACACS**   Extended TACACS, which builds on TACACS by separating the functions of authentication, authorization, and accounting.
- **TACACS+**   This version adds the use of both a username and password for authentication or other authentication methods, such as Kerberos and dynamic passwords, through security tokens. All communications are encrypted.

Unfortunately, the TACACS protocols have several security vulnerabilities, including a weak encryption algorithm. This has decreased its use in favor of the standards-based RADIUS authentication protocol.

Kerberos

Kerberos is a network authentication protocol, prominently used in Microsoft Windows Active Directory (AD) implementations. It is an open standard, supported officially as an Internet standard by RFC 4120. The most current version of Kerberos widely in use is version 5.

Kerberos uses a system based on authentication tickets issued to the authenticated user, as well as timestamps. Timestamps help prevent replay attacks because the tickets expire after a short time and must be refreshed, requiring that the user be re-authenticated and the ticket reissued. Kerberos's timestamps rely heavily on authoritative time sources throughout the network architecture, so many implementations also include a network time server. If clients are outside a certain tolerance for time difference (generally five minutes) between them and the Kerberos server, the users logging in to those clients will not be authenticated.

Kerberos uses several components that you should be familiar with for the exam. First, there is the Kerberos Key Distribution Center (KDC), which is responsible for authenticating users and issuing out session keys and tickets. In AD implementations, the domain controller serves as the KDC. There is also an Authentication Service (AS) and a Ticket-Granting Service (TGS). Although not required to be on the same host, these services frequently are on AD domain controllers in a Windows environment (for simplicity and efficiency's sake), and are part of the KDC implementation.

When a user logs in to the system, the AS verifies the user's identity using the credentials stored in AD. The user is then issued a Ticket-Granting Ticket (TGT) by the AS, which can be used to access resources throughout the domain. The TGT expires after a certain amount of time, so it must be periodically reissued. When a user wants to access a resource in the domain, the

2. AS authenticates and issues the user a Ticket-Granting Ticket (TGT).

1. Client requests authentication.

3. Client needs to access resource and presents TGT to TGS.
4. TGS issues service ticket for the session.

Client/User

5. Server and client communicate using the service ticket issued by the TGS.

Resource Server

FIGURE 7.5 Kerberos implemented within a Windows environment

TGT is presented to the TGS for authentication, and the TGS generates a session key for the communications session between the user and the resource server. This is known as a service ticket, and it's used for the duration of the access to the resource. When a user later needs access to the same resource again, or a different resource, the older ticket is not reused; instead, a new service ticket is generated.

Note that the process just described is specific to Windows AD implementations of Kerberos, but the principles are the same regardless of what operating system and LDAP-based implementation are in use. A network that uses Kerberos as its authentication protocol is called a *Kerberos realm*. Kerberos uses both TCP port 88 and UDP port 88 and uses symmetric key cryptography. Figure 7.5 illustrates the Kerberos process in Windows AD.

OAuth and OpenID Connect

OAuth, originally specified in Internet Engineering Task Force (IETF) 5849 and superseded in IETF 6749, is an authorization framework designed to use secure tokens to allow clients to gain access to resource owners through resource servers that access their information, as well as authorization servers that enable the resource owners to allow or deny the authorization request. OpenID Connect builds on OAuth, allowing a client to perform identity verification and receive information about both the end users and their sessions.

802.1X

The IEEE 802.1X standard is a port-based authentication mechanism for devices connecting to wired or wireless networks. Its goal is to provide a centralized authentication framework for LANs and wireless LANs (WLANs) that includes wired clients, wireless clients, and the wireless access points that connect them to the network.

For wired LANs, 802.1X is implemented on network devices such as switches to provide access control by authenticating connecting clients based on the user or system identity. You can then allow or block network connectivity and apply network access policies based on this authentication.

In WLANs, a client automatically connects to the closest access point and then authenticates to the network by directly communicating with the network's native authentication. Unfortunately, unless the LAN is protected with a strong encryption method, the client can perform certain network functions without authentication, such as ping requests.

Using 802.1X, when a client connects to an access point, the wireless port is set to an unauthorized state so it can't perform any network functions, which include receiving an IP address from a Dynamic Host Configuration Protocol (DHCP) server. The access point then asks the client for authentication credentials. Once received, this data is forwarded to an authentication server running a service such as RADIUS. If the client is accepted as an authorized user, then the client port on the access point is switched to an authorized state and normal communications can commence.

802.1X can be helpful in allowing WLANs to scale upward in size easily while maintaining a centralized authentication system. This authentication, however, should be coupled with a strong communications encryption mechanism to provide full security. Note that networks that use 802.1X not only can authenticate devices such as laptops and workstations but also users, and can easily be integrated into an authentication or directory service such as Active Directory.

Travel Assistance

See Chapter 10 for more detailed information on wireless security.

Certificates (Mutual Authentication)

Certificates are a form of mutual authentication that uses a third party to establish the identity of a user for access control purposes. A certificate is like a digital piece of paper that contains a user's credentials. Digital certificates are used primarily with secure web communications and encryption. Each user needs another user's certificate to authenticate the other user before exchanging secure confidential information.

A user obtains a certificate by registering with a third-party service called a *certificate authority (CA)*. To receive the certificate, the user must supply credentials such as a driver's license, Social Security number, address, and phone number. The certificate authority then issues a certificate to the user, along with the encryption keys she'll be using. This certificate proves the user's legitimacy.

HOTP/TOTP

The HMAC-based One-time Password (HOTP) algorithm can be used to generate the one-time password values often used to authenticate users via an authentication server. This standard was developed as an interoperable, two-factor algorithm to be used across a variety of platforms, both commercial and open source. You will often hear HOTP and variant algorithms referred to as "two-step authentication" within many web applications.

Travel Assistance	
See Chapter 4 for a refresher on Hash-based Message Authentication Code (HMAC) principles.	

The *Time-based One-time Password (TOTP)* algorithm extends the general HOTP concept through the adoption of a time-based factor, generally measured in seconds. Adding the element of time means that even a second's difference will result in a totally different value for the two passwords generated. A few major commercial entities, such as Google and Amazon, have adopted TOTP authenticators as added measures to protect their users. This requires the user to input a username and password combination, and then the user is challenged for a one-time password, generally displayed from a separate device such as a smartphone.

Biometrics

Although typically available only to extremely high-security installations because of the high costs, biometric access control offers the most complete and technologically advanced method for securing access. *Biometrics* uses a unique physical attribute—such as a fingerprint, voice scan, or retinal scan—to identify a user.

Initially, the user requesting access must have the particular attribute scanned so a perfect copy is on file for comparison when the user tries to gain access in the future. These types of biometric systems are complex and sensitive, and they can often result in false permissions and denials for access. These are known as the *false acceptance rate (FAR)*, which is the rate at which a biometric system allows access to an unauthorized individual based on an incorrect identification, and the *false rejection rate (FRR)*, which is when the biometric system incorrectly rejects access to an authorized user. A system that has a high FAR—allowing unauthorized access—is considered to be more dangerous than one with a high FRR, which is generally just annoying due to the unnecessary rejections. The *crossover error rate (CER)* is the rate where the system has been tuned to be precise enough that the FAR and FRR are equal. It is important to note that biometric systems must be constantly calibrated, so repeated measurements of users' biometric data are often required.

The following are the most common types of biometric access systems:

- **Palm/fingerprint scan**   No two fingerprints are alike. A user must place his hand on a biometric scanner that compares it to the palm scan and fingerprints on file for that user. This is the most effective of all biometric methods.

- **Hand geometry scan**   The size and shape of hands vary significantly among different people. Like a fingerprint scan, the user places his hand on a biometric scanner, which measures the length and width of the hand, including the sizes of the fingers.

- **Retinal/iris scan**   A person's retina is a unique attribute, like a fingerprint. The user must place his eye up to a device that projects a light beam into the eye to capture the retinal pattern.

- **Voice scan**   The voice is also a unique characteristic for each user. The user is recorded speaking a set of access words, and the captured voice print can be compared to the same spoken words the next time the user tries to gain access.

- **Facial scan**   A facial scan records the unique characteristics of each user's face, such as bone structure and the shape of the eyes and nose. These characteristics can be captured in the scan and compared to the facial scan on file.

- **Signature scan**   Considered one of the weakest types of biometric security, a signature scan records the written signature of a user and then compares it to subsequent signatures when the user attempts to gain access. Two types of signature scans exist: static and dynamic.

A static scan merely compares the two signatures for accuracy and can't be considered rigorous. A dynamic scan can record the motions of the signature using electrical signals; these unique characters make a dynamic signature scan much more reliable.

Exam Tip

Be aware of the characteristics of a biometric access control system that differentiate it from other traditional access control methods.

CHECKPOINT

✔**Objective 7.01: Explain the Fundamental Concepts and Best Practices Related to Authentication, Authorization, and Access Services** Identification ensures that a user (which could also be an application program or process) is who he claims to be. The user must then pass the authentication phase using his logon username or account number and a password. If these two criteria are matched with the global database of login usernames and passwords stored on the network, the user is granted access to the network. Finally, when a user tries to access a resource, the system must check to see if that user ID is authorized for that resource and what permissions or privileges the user has when accessing it. Two- and three-factor authentication schemes build upon single-factor authentication by combining multiple single-factor authentication types, such as something the user knows (a password or PIN) and something the user possesses (a magnetic swipe card or token).

✔**Objective 7.02: Explain the Function and Purpose of Authentication Services** Remote access via VPN is typically the most secure method because it encrypts communications while ensuring that users are authenticated before being granted access. Other methods include RADIUS, Kerberos, TACACS, SAML, OAuth/OpenID Connect, HOTP/TOTP, LDAP, and certificates. LDAPS offers secure, encrypted authentication to an LDAP server. Biometric systems offer the most complete and advanced methods to identify people through a unique physical attribute, such as a fingerprint, voice scan, or retinal scan, but a balance between the FAR and FRR must be achieved in order to find the CER.

REVIEW QUESTIONS

1. You must set up a secure authentication and encryption method for your remote users. Most users are remote salespeople who connect to the company's networks from home networks or hotel Internet connections. Which of the following methods would you use?

    A. 802.1X

    B. VPN

    C. Kerberos

    D. TACACS

2. You are tasked with creating a high-security authentication system for physical access control to a military installation. Which of the following authentication systems would be most appropriate?

    A. Biometric eye scan

    B. Security badge

    C. Smart card and PIN

    D. Encrypted login and password

3. You are setting up an LDAP server that will provide secure, encrypted authentication services. Which of the following protocols and ports do you use?

    A. LDAP on TCP port 689

    B. LDAPS on TCP port 389

    C. LDAPS on TCP port 689

    D. LDAP on TCP port 389

4. You are at home and have received a call from your office that one of your mail servers is down. You have set up a secure, encrypted remote access method to an administrative computer at your office. Which of the following remote access methods do you use?

    A. HTTP web login

    B. Dial-up

    C. Telnet

    D. VPN

5. You have several home users with Internet access who require remote access to your organization's network. Which of the following remote access and authentication technologies would be the most secure?

    A. Dial-up access to a Kerberos server

    B. A VPN authenticated to a RADIUS server

    C. Telnet access to a local password database

    D. Wireless access to an LDAPS server

6. A web services provider has suggested improving their security through the implementation of two-factor authentication. What would be the most likely authentication method?

    A. TOTP

    B. SAML

    C. ISDN

    D. TACACS

7. You are creating an authentication mechanism for physical access to a high-security government building. The high-security nature of the facility requires at least a three-factor authentication model. Which of the authentication types do you use?

    A. Biometric eye scan

    B. Smart card and PIN

    C. Smart card, PIN, and fingerprint scan

    D. ID badge and password

8. After a user is identified and authenticated to the system, what else must be performed to enable the user to use a resource?

    A. Authorization

    B. Authentication by token

    C. Encryption of network access

    D. Biometric scan

9. SAML implementations have three basic roles: the identity, the identity provider, and the _____.

    A. Internet provider

    B. service provider

    C. authentication provider

    D. authorization provider

10. You are setting up a single sign-on authentication system for a large enterprise network of 5000 users. Which of the following authentication methods would you use?

    A. Local login and password database

    B. Login and password with a security token

    C. LDAP server

    D. Smart card with PIN number

REVIEW ANSWERS

1. **B** The VPN can encrypt your communications while providing authentication to an authentication server. This is especially important for users connecting remotely over the Internet from insecure locations.

2. **A** For high-security installations, biometrics is an extremely secure method to authenticate users based on unique physical characteristics.

3. **C** When you use LDAPS (which uses TCP port 689), the authentication takes place over an encrypted channel to prevent the capture of authentication credentials.

4. **D** The VPN method provides a secure, encrypted channel over the Internet to your organization's private network.

5. **B** By using a VPN to a RADIUS server, you ensure that your communications are encrypted and that secure authentication takes place to the RADIUS server.

6. **A** Time-based One-time Passwords (TOTPs) allow users to log in to a system with a username and password combination and then a one-time token, usually generated from a separate device.

7. **C** For a three-factor authentication model, you need at least three different types of authentication. A biometric eye scan, although extremely secure, is still only a one-factor system, while the other methods (such as a smart card and a PIN) are only two-factor systems.

8. **A** Although a user has been given access to log in to the network, he still needs to be authorized to use a particular resource based on access permissions.

9. **B** The service provider takes the token passed from the identity provider and either accepts and provides services to the user or denies the request and does not provide the services.

10. **C** An LDAP server provides a centralized authentication database that can be used to securely authenticate a user to multiple services on the same network. This is the most efficient and secure method for a large network of 5000 users. Other methods would require tedious configuration and management of each individual user.

PART

IV

Network Security

Securing Networks

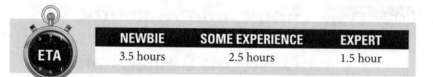

	NEWBIE	SOME EXPERIENCE	EXPERT
ETA	3.5 hours	2.5 hours	1.5 hour

Network security devices and secure network design provide a first line of defense for detection and prevention of attacks at your network border. These security threats can be low-level, network-based threats such as TCP/IP protocol attacks, or they could be high-level application threats such as application content downloaded from the Internet via a web browser. Several network security tools are available, such as firewalls, routers, switches, proxy servers, anti-spam filters, intrusion detection systems, web security gateways, and content filters, which not only detect network threats but also take proactive steps to stop them from entering or leaving your network.

Setting up your network securely requires planning to make sure that your network is safely partitioned into network security zones. By splitting your network into public, private, and high-security zones and then regulating access between these zones with other types of networking techniques, you provide several lines of defense against incoming network attacks. Understanding the areas within your network that need to be defended allows for the implementation of layered security (also known as defense-in-depth), or the application of a combination of different solutions to provide more comprehensive coverage of assets. As the different technologies are discussed, be thinking of how they could be combined to more effectively secure a network than using one device alone.

This chapter discusses the network security devices and secure network design principles that can maximize the ability to detect and prevent network security threats at your network's borders.

Implement Security Functionality on Network Devices and Other Technologies

Objective 8.01
CompTIA Security+
Objective 2.1

Several types of network devices make up your networking infrastructure. At the most basic level, you have routers and switches that form the backbone of your network to make sure that network information can properly flow from its source to its destination. More advanced devices, such as firewalls, proxy servers, web security, and content security servers, analyze the network information for its content to decide what can pass through to its destination and what must be blocked.

Firewalls

Firewalls are like physical security walls situated between an organization's internal network and any external public networks such as the Internet, as shown in Figure 8.1. The firewall protects an internal network from access by unauthorized users on an external network.

The external network can be located on the Internet or may even be another network within the same organization. A network firewall is a critical system in an organization's overall security architecture. The firewall controls and monitors access between different networks by filtering inbound and outbound traffic, manages access controls to requested locations, and typically blocks all services except those explicitly permitted by the administrator.

To configure the firewall, an administrator must set up several rules to use each time on incoming and outgoing network communications. These rules can be general or specific. For example, a firewall can be configured with a

| FIGURE 8.1 | Network firewall deployment |

rule that states that any Hypertext Transfer Protocol (HTTP) traffic can come and go on a specific network. It can also be much more detailed and state that a Simple Mail Transfer Protocol (SMTP) packet destined for a mail server can only come from a specific host. The best practice to use when configuring a firewall for the first time is to implicitly deny everything by default and then create rules to allow the access you need. This ensures you're starting off with the most secure model and working backward to configure the firewall to accept certain types of communications.

Most firewalls log network traffic and activity and activate alarms if anomalous situations are detected. The firewall implements security, authentication, and access controls at multiple levels while remaining completely transparent to internal users. Most firewalls provide the following services and security features:

- **Packet filtering** The firewall server analyzes each network packet destined for inside or outside the network; it can filter out dangerous malformed packets, attacks, and spoofed IP addresses to prevent unauthorized access. Packets are also analyzed and acted upon depending on the rules enabled by the administrator.

- **Stateful and stateless inspection** Stateful inspection of packets ensures that the firewall maintains a record of the connections that pass through and monitors their state from when they are connected to when they close. This ensures the firewall is not only tracing packets but also analyzing the state of the entire connection. Stateless inspection, conversely, does not maintain a record and uses an access control list (ACL) to allow or deny traffic. Depending on the configuration of the access rules, certain actions can be taken when an anomalous change of state occurs (such as a connection hijack).

- **Access and authentication control** The firewall can restrict access to networking services by source and destination IP address, type of service, time/day of the week, and also through authenticated access. Most firewalls have very flexible access control policies that can be fine-tuned by the administrator to secure access for specific users and networks.

- **Application layer filtering** Firewalls can be aware of specific applications and services such as Domain Name Service (DNS) and SMTP e-mail. This allows a firewall to analyze network traffic and apply access rules that are specific to that application. For example, the firewall can act as an application gateway for e-mail servers to help secure the connections between external e-mail servers and your local e-mail servers and clients that send and receive messages. The firewall can detect if these services are trying to be accessed on unauthorized ports for that specific application.

- **Network address translation (NAT)** Most firewalls utilize NAT to map source IP addresses of outbound connections so that those connections appear to have originated from the firewall's address. This allows internal networks to be hidden behind a single Internet IP address with no additional registered addresses required.

Some firewalls now allow the ability to decrypt SSL sessions; although this is helpful from a malware prevention or data loss prevention perspective, it also can present privacy concerns and should be assessed through a cost/benefit analysis.

Routers

A *router* is a network device that connects several networks together and relays data between them, as shown in Figure 8.2. A router usually contains a few network interfaces, where each represents a different network. Smaller companies generally only have one main router, whereas larger companies could have several routers to relay information from all their networks.

Router software contains a lot of the same protections found in firewalls, including packet filtering and access control lists. These enable you to control more carefully the protocols, services, ports, and source and destination of the information that flows through the router. For example, you can configure the router to accept only File Transfer Protocol (FTP) communications to a certain network. Other security features of routers include the capability to protect against spoofing and denial-of-service (DoS) attacks. Routers are different from simpler bridges in that routers operate at Layer 3 of the network, whereas bridges operate at Layer 2.

Switches

A *switch* is a network device used to segment networks into smaller, more manageable sections and relay packets between the segments. Switches can be used for security, load balancing, and performance improvements in a network.

A switch can work at either Layer 2 or 3 of the network and is more intelligent than a network hub, which is a simple device that is used to connect multiple computers to a network backbone. A switch can inspect network packets and determine the source and destination to provide more efficient network flow and prevent network packets from one segment, including broadcasts, from passing on to other network segments and causing network collisions.

You can configure the switch to accept only data from certain mandatory access control (MAC) address ranges to guard against MAC flooding attacks. In this type of attack, network packets are sent with multiple spoofed source MAC addresses, which flood the switch's MAC address tables and cause excessive

FIGURE 8.2   Router deployment

network broadcasts. Layer 2 switches can also provide port security by allowing the ability to limit the number of source MAC addresses to enter a port. When you're using Layer 2 switches, it is important to ensure they are configured to prevent against network loops, where frames can loop indefinitely due to the switches rebroadcasting their traffic repeatedly without the benefit of a time-to-live (TTL) value.

Travel Assistance
Network loops are also discussed in Chapter 9.

Load Balancers

A *load balancer* is a network device that helps evenly distribute the flow of network traffic to other network devices, either in an active-active mode (two or more load balancers distributing the load) or an active-passive mode (where one or more modes lie dormant until needed). In larger networks that process thousands of network transactions per minute, the load balancer spreads the network load between each network device to ensure that network congestion and bottlenecks do not occur, using at least one virtual IP address that is publically available.

Your organization may have several routers on the network border to process incoming network connections and route them to their required destination. If a specific router receives too many network requests at one time, it can cause a bottleneck in processing requests and cause network delays. Other routers may not be receiving enough network traffic and are running at only partial capacity compared with what their resources are capable of.

Large organizations use load balancers with web services distributed among several web servers to provide their customers with enough processing power and resources to respond to thousands of web requests per hour. The load balancer is required to analyze the incoming requests and route the requests evenly between these servers. Also, many load balancers also function as *SSL accelerators*, offloading the resource-intensive process of accepting SSL requests, unencrypting the traffic, and passing the unencrypted traffic on to its destination. This allows for a more robust implementation of SSL across large networks with minimal performance degradation.

Load balancers can perform their functions through scheduling algorithms, such as round-robin techniques where each server in turn is sent a request, or they can use intelligent load-balancing methods (for example, current number of connections and response times) to detect which servers are overloaded and which servers have enough resource capacity to handle incoming requests. Many high-end load balancers work at the application layer to properly load-balance specific protocols and network application services.

Load balancers possess the network security awareness to help prevent DoS network attacks by detecting floods of network packets and preventing them from overloading the devices for which they are balancing network traffic. Also, note that some applications do not work well when load balanced; in this case, *session affinity* subverts the load balancer and sends client requests directly to the specific application server, binding the user's session to that server.

Proxy Servers

A *forward proxy server* is an application, network server, or multipurpose device that accepts and forwards requests from clients to other servers. The proxy server performs this function on behalf of the client. The proxy is typically situated between the clients and the Internet, and it can be used to forward requests for many types of traffic and data transfers, such as web and FTP. This protects the specific addresses of internal clients from being revealed to external servers and allows the proxy server to filter incoming and outgoing requests to prevent attacks and malware from reaching the client systems.

The most commonly used type of forward proxy server is for web browsing. A web client requests a specific uniform resource locator (URL) in its web browser that is sent to the proxy server. The web proxy server forwards the request to the destination website using its own IP address as the source of the request. When the data is retrieved, the proxy server may cache or content-filter the data and then return it to the requesting client. Web proxy servers are used primarily for their caching capability, which boosts web browsing performance by storing content retrieved from an external web server. The next time a client retrieves the same web data, the web proxy can serve the information to the client without sending another request to the external web server. This greatly reduces the amount of bandwidth required to retrieve numerous web requests from an organization and provides significant cost savings. Proxies that do not modify requests, and simply redirect them, are called *transparent proxies,* whereas those that do make modifications are called *nontransparent proxies.* Clients should not be aware of the presence of a transparent proxy—after all, it is meant to be "transparent"—whereas a nontransparent proxy often adds elements to the request.

Conversely, a *reverse proxy server* works on behalf of servers to accept requests from external clients, forwarding them on to the servers behind it. An example of how this might work is if an external client wants to gain access to your web server. Rather than allow that traffic direct access to the web server, the reverse proxy acts as a "go-between," providing cached content for high-demand content, as well as increased protection in the event your web server does not have appropriate security configurations for public use.

All-in-One Security Appliances

With the surge in malware (for example, viruses, spyware, Trojan horses, and back-door programs) directed at user desktops, not only from traditional e-mail spam but also from malicious websites, peer-to-peer file sharing, and social media networks, there is a greater need for all-in-one network security appliances, often termed *Unified Security Management (USM)*. These appliances can offer several layers of security protection against incoming messages from a wide scope of communications mediums.

You can run each type of security service, such as e-mail scanning or web scanning, on a separate network device, or you can integrate these security services to scan multiple network protocols (e-mail, web, social media, Voice over IP [VoIP]) from the same device. Integrated security appliances are very popular and cost efficient for small- to medium-sized organizations, enabling them to scan all their network traffic with a single device.

Data Loss Prevention

Data loss prevention (DLP) solutions require the identification of information that is critical to the organization or considered "sensitive" (either PII—personally identifiable information—or identified as such through classification levels) and then work to ensure that this data doesn't leave the network via a USB device, e-mail, or some other method. In DLP, data is tagged and labeled with metadata denoting its security or sensitivity level as well as attributes that may or may not allow it to leave via various means. Some data might be tagged as OK to leave via USB or encrypted e-mail, but not via unencrypted e-mail. For example, DLP solutions would look for mobile devices that are connected and then monitor (or block) any data transfers of data that has been tagged as such. This can be achieved either through dedicated, on-site appliances or through cloud solutions that funnel data requests to the cloud where the analysis is conducted by off-site experts. E-mail filters can also be created to identify certain sensitive data patterns, such as Social Security numbers, and block e-mails containing that data from exiting the organization.

Malware Inspection

Devices offering *malware inspection* scan the data and/or header of a packet traversing the network, searching for signatures indicating the existence of viruses, worms, or spyware. The device can then make the decision to block the data, alert administrators, or clean the content by removing malicious files and then pass the cleaned content through to the recipient.

Anti-spam Filter

An *anti-spam filter* is a type of network security service primarily targeted to e-mail communications. Anti-spam filters reside between your e-mail gateway and your firewall; they process any incoming and outgoing mail messages before they deliver the messages to their destination.

Anti-spam filters use a variety of techniques to determine if an incoming message is spam or legitimate mail. If the message is determined to be spam, it can be immediately deleted or quarantined by the anti-spam filter before it reaches the client user's mail inbox. Most anti-spam filters have a very high rate of effectiveness against most types of spam, and if configured correctly, they prevent users from ever having to see a spam message in their e-mail.

No anti-spam filter is perfect, and most use a variety of techniques to identify spam messages and prevent legitimate mail from being classified as spam (a false positive). These techniques include the following:

- **Databases of known spam**   The anti-spam filter usually comes with a default database of known spam messages. This is useful for catching the most obvious forms of historical spam, but it cannot identify new types of spam. The default database provides a good base configuration but requires additional anti-spam techniques and training to detect new spam.

- **Blacklists (or block lists)**   There are several types of public blacklists (also called *block lists*) that contain a list of mail server IP addresses that are known to send spam messages. By comparing a connecting mail server to the blacklist, the anti-spam filter can determine whether to block or allow the connection from the mail server if it appears on the list. The list is checked as the mail connection begins, typically using a DNS-based lookup to a blacklist server. Blacklists are not perfect, and very often perfectly legitimate mail servers are accidentally added to blacklists. That is why a variety of methods must be used during the anti-spam message processing to accurately determine if the message is spam or legitimate mail.

- **URL block lists**   Spam messages often contain URLs that, when clicked, take you to a web page that could be malicious in behavior and may contain spyware or malware or else try to trick you into using your login credentials or credit card information for a phishing scam. Much as in the case of blacklists and DNS block lists, the anti-spam filter compares the URLs extracted from a message with a list of known spam URLs.

- **Bayesian filtering**   This is an anti-spam technique that extracts tokens from spam messages and legitimate mail. These tokens are keywords and phrases that are statistically evaluated to determine the likelihood that a message is spam or legitimate mail. Bayesian techniques require scanning of inbound and outbound mail over a period of time to create a valid number of tokens that properly train the anti-spam filter to distinguish spam and legitimate messages.

- **Reputation services**   The next generation of third-party block lists, reputation services track mail servers and score them with a good or bad reputation, depending on the amount of spam and viruses sent from those mail server addresses. An anti-spam filter queries the reputation service when it receives a mail connection, and if the sending mail server has a bad reputation, the filter can drop the connection before any transfer of mail occurs. This improves performance for the anti-spam filter, as it does not have to process any mail because the connection is rejected before any transfer of messages takes place.

Content Filtering

To address privacy concerns and data loss prevention, certain types of organizations (such as financial and medical companies) must now adhere to specific government regulations regarding the release of private data. This means that organizations must take greater control over the outbound content that is transmitted outside their organization's networks.

Several types of rules are in place that must be adhered to by financial organizations to protect the security and privacy of data, such as PCI (Payment Card Industry) compliance. PCI is a compliance policy that defines the minimum amount of security that is required for credit card, debit card, automated teller machine (ATM) system, and other financial transactions. Most major credit card and banking companies are PCI compliant. These compliance rules are primarily based on the storage and transmission of sensitive financial information. For example, a bank must ensure that a private customer's credit card or banking details are not transmitted outside of its networks, or if they must be transmitted, that they are encrypted.

Medical and health providers must adhere to strict rules, such as HIPAA (the Health Insurance Portability and Accountability Act). These rules ensure that these organizations are accountable for the privacy and security of their patients' medical records. Outbound content filtering can ensure that messages with specific identifying information can be blocked from being sent outside of the organization.

An outbound content filter on a proxy server can monitor outgoing e-mails (including deep content scanning of e-mail attachments and web file uploads) to scan the content for patterns of credit card or account numbers. If they are encountered in the message, they can be blocked or quarantined, or policies can be set in place to automatically encrypt the message before it leaves the organization.

URL Filtering

Organizations can filter specific URLs or file types (such as .mp3, .exe, and .zip, for example) to prevent them from being accessed. Examples are adult sites and other types of content that should not be viewed or used on a corporate or public network. URL-filtering software uses a predefined list of sites that are allowed or blocked as required via policies. If a client tries to access a blocked website or file, that client will receive a warning message and will not be allowed access to that website.

There are also third-party public URL-filtering products that contain a list of categorized websites that are most commonly blocked because of their content. These are configurable by the administrator to block specific types of content, such as offensive sites, gambling sites, or even sites that reduce productivity such as shopping sites and social media.

Security Information and Event Management

Until recently, the traditional way to manage logging and monitoring in a network was to sit down at a system and look at the log files generated by the system, reviewing them for any events of interest; however, this is not the most efficient way to manage network monitoring and analysis activities. Another new paradigm that falls under continuous monitoring is *security information and event management (SIEM)*. SIEM solutions comprise an enterprise-level technology and infrastructure that aggregates all the different data points from the network, including log files, traffic captures, SNMP messages, and so on, from every host on the network. They can collect all this different data into one centralized location and allow an analyst to look for correlations related to security and performance issues, as well as negative trends, all in real time, and can automate alerts to analysts based on preset triggers. SIEM infrastructures usually require a multitier setup consisting of servers designated as centralized log collectors, which pass log events on to other servers designated for mass log storage, which are then accessed by devices focused purely on real-time correlation and analysis. When you're using an SIEM solution, it is important to make sure that the time is synchronized between the various devices providing data for aggregation and analysis; otherwise, your trend analysis will be incorrect, providing either false positives or false negatives. Also, because events can generate duplicate data (think of multiple logs across multiple devices), *deduplication*, or the reduction of duplicate events, is important; otherwise, your analysts might be drowning in data.

Note that an SIEM solution requires real-time monitoring technologies. However, just because you're using some of these real-time technologies doesn't necessarily mean you are using an SIEM solution. These solutions unify and correlate all the real-time events from a multitude of disparate sources, including network alerts, log files, physical security logs, and so on. You could still have real-time monitoring going on, but without combining and correlating all those different event sources. A true unified SIEM system is required to do that.

Web Security Gateway

A web security gateway is a more complex device than a simple web proxy caching server. Beyond performing the basic tasks of a web proxy, it provides content filtering and application-level security to protect end users from accessing dangerous websites and downloading files that are infected with worms, spyware, or malware, or else from connecting to servers that host phishing and fraud sites.

These types of application-level security devices provide specialized protection beyond that of a network firewall, which is designed to provide more basic access controls and filtering of all types of network traffic. Web security gateway devices can perform deep inspection of web HTTP traffic to prevent end users from accessing dangerous content and protect them from HTTP-specific script attacks such as cross-site scripting (XSS).

When a user accesses a website, the request is filtered through the web security gateway. The web security gateway contacts the destination website as a proxy for the client and analyzes the files and requests returned from the website. It scans the network traffic for known types of web attacks and analyzes file downloads for malware, such as viruses, spyware, and Trojan horse software. These types of gateways can also scan the text content of websites to search for prohibited words and phrases that indicate inappropriate content.

For a web security gateway to be effective, all end-user web browser clients must be configured to use the gateway as their web proxy. This ensures that all web traffic is filtered through the gateway and processed for security issues before the clients can continue their web sessions. Some web security gateways enforce authentication to allow only clients with authenticated access to traverse the web proxy and access content outside of the private network. The user's web surfing habits can then be tracked to monitor content and bandwidth usage.

Intrusion Detection and Prevention

As a first line of defense for your network security, the implementation of an intrusion detection system (IDS) greatly enhances the security of your network. An IDS can monitor your network activity for suspicious behavior that can indicate if someone is trying to break in or damage your network. By proactively monitoring the network border, the detection system can immediately notify an administrator of the intrusion. Some more advanced detection systems, called *intrusion prevention systems (IPSs),* can attempt to deal with the problem autonomously and either disconnect suspicious network connections or turn off network services that are being attacked.

IDSs can also be either active or passive. In an *active detection system,* intrusion attempts are dealt with immediately by shutting down network connections or services that are being attacked. A *passive detection system,* on the other hand, relies on notification to alert administrators of an intrusion. Active detection deals more swiftly with situations but can cause unwanted behavior if false positives (blocking legitimate traffic) arise. What's more, false negatives can allow unauthorized traffic to flow with an administrator unaware. It is critical to make sure, no matter which type of system you use, that your IDS or IPS is tuned carefully.

A network IDS (NIDS) examines network patterns, such as an unusual number of requests destined for a server or service (for example, an FTP server). The headers of network packets can be analyzed for possible spoofing attempts or suspicious code that indicates a malformed packet. Corrupted packets and malformed data can bring down a web server that's vulnerable to such attacks.

An NIDS typically consists of the following components, as shown in Figure 8.3:

- **Detection agent**   The *detection* agents of an IDS usually are physically installed in a network and are attached to core network devices, such as routers, firewalls, and switches. Detection agents can also be software agents that use network management protocols, such as the Simple Network Management Protocol (SNMP). They simply collect the data passing through the network and send it on to the network monitor for analysis.

- **Monitor**   The *network monitor* is fed information from the detection units and analyzes the network activity for suspicious behavior. This is the heart of the IDS, which collects information from the network, analyzes it, and then uses the notification system to warn of any problems. The monitor can utilize several methods, including heuristic-, behavior/anomaly-, rule-, and signature-based scanning, to detect network threats. These are discussed in more detail later in the chapter.

- **Notification system**   The *notification system* is used for notifications and alarms, which are sent to the administrator. Once the network monitor recognizes a threat, it writes to a log file and uses the notification system to send an alert, such as an e-mail or a Short Message Service (SMS) message, to an administrator. The notification system can usually be configured to allow for a variety of methods of communication.

Server   Workstation

Router

Detection agent

Notification

Network data

Workstation   Network
administration

Alarm
notification

Network monitor

FIGURE 8.3   Network intrusion detection system (NIDS)

To protect the entire network, the IDS is usually located at a central point, such as a main router, switch, or firewall system. An IDS can also be deployed either *in-band* (more often referred to as *in-line*), where all traffic is analyzed (often at the network edge), or *out-of-band,* where only some traffic is analyzed. A detection system can only monitor what it sees, so placing it further down in the system lessens the chance of finding intrusions, especially because your firewall and routers are the entry points to the network. Therefore, an in-line IDS deployment is more secure. This characteristic makes a network-based system generally more valuable than a host-based system because of its capability to detect intrusions at the entrance to the network. The disadvantage of a network-based system is that it can rarely detect intrusions originating from the internal network. This is where also using host-based IDS in your overall security model is important.

Travel Advisory

Network-based intrusion systems also are not effective in monitoring encrypted communications, such as communications over a virtual private network (VPN).

When an intrusion is detected, the system works in either an active or a passive way to alert an administrator of the problem. A passive system will only send warnings and alarms through log files, e-mail, instant message, or SMS message. An active system tries to fix the problem by shutting off certain services or preventing connections from a suspicious host.

Active Detection

An NIDS that uses active detection methods can take immediate steps to halt an intrusion. These types of systems are also called *network intrusion prevention systems (NIPSs)* because they actively attempt to prevent intrusions rather than just detect them. The advantage of this method is that it can attempt to prevent the intrusion from continuing. Active detection prevents the suspicious activity from expanding into actual damage or data loss. This is a great advantage over passive detection systems, which merely log the incident or send an e-mail to the administrator, who might not see the message for many hours before she can perform any preventive actions. By then, it could be too late.

> ### Exam Tip
> A network intrusion prevention system (NIPS) tries to prevent an intrusion from continuing after detecting it.

Network-based active detection systems can automatically reconfigure logical network topologies to reroute network traffic in case of some form of network attack, such as a DoS attack. They can also detect suspicious activity on a network connection and terminate it, logging the IP address to prevent any further connections from that origin. The detection system can also sense attacks on certain ports or services, such as an SNMP port on a router, and shut the port down to prevent any more attacks on it.

The disadvantage of active detection systems is that the occurrence of false positives can cause the system to shut down services or network connections for legitimate requests.

Passive Detection

Passive detection by an NIDS involves alerting an administrator of the intrusion so that he can take the necessary actions to stop it. The system will not take any active steps to prevent the detected intrusion from continuing. The disadvantage of a passive system is that the administrator might not get the alert immediately, especially if he is offsite and not carrying a smartphone or other mobile device. By the time he gets to the system, the damage of the intrusion could have already been done.

Passive methods of detection usually consist of some form of logging utility that logs events as they happen and stores them for later examination or notifies the administrator of high-level warnings and errors. If no type of messaging alert function is configured, the administrator must scan the log files regularly for suspicious behavior.

Exam Tip

Make sure you know the difference between network- and host-based intrusion detection systems, as well as the difference between active and passive versions of these systems and how they mitigate threats.

Monitoring Methodologies

Network monitoring applications such as an NIDS/NIPS are used to monitor and analyze network traffic to detect security threats such as network-based attacks (DoS attacks, ping sweeps, and port scans). When a security threat is detected, the monitoring system logs the event and notifies the administrator or takes immediate steps to mitigate the incoming threat. Different types of monitoring methodologies can be used to detect intrusions and malicious behavior. The following sections describe these monitoring methodologies and their benefits and weaknesses.

Exam Tip

Understand the differences between signature-, behavior/anomaly-, heuristic-, and rule-based monitoring methodologies, including their strengths and weaknesses.

Signature-Based Monitoring Signature-based monitoring systems are like antivirus programs and contain predefined signature databases of known attacks that have appeared previously. Each type of attack can be recognized by its unique characteristics, and a signature is created for that type of attack. For example, signature-based systems can detect popular types of DoS attacks. The signature (if available) can detect this exact information in the network packet and generate an alert to the administrator. These databases are dynamic, and the monitoring program must be continually updated to ensure it has the latest signatures to identify the latest types of threats.

Signature-based systems are powerful and efficient because they rely on the collective knowledge of security vendors, who analyze and collect information on Internet security threats and trends and who update their databases quickly when new threats arise. However, signature-based systems are unable to detect very new attacks whose signatures are not yet available. In this respect, signature-based systems are often used in conjunction with behavior-based systems.

Behavior/Anomaly-Based Monitoring   Behavior-based (also referred to as *anomaly-based*) monitoring systems do not use a predefined database of signatures, but start from a baseline of normal behavior and then monitor network traffic based on these performance profiles and increasingly sophisticated analytics to recognize behavioral anomalies that exceed the thresholds of the normal baseline. Such a monitoring system becomes more effective over time as baseline activity is recorded, allowing the system to detect aberrations to these baselines more efficiently. For example, a sudden burst of incoming connections that is out of character for the network will trigger the monitoring system to generate alerts of the activity and, in some cases, take proactive steps to mitigate the anomalous behavior (which could be a DoS attack) by blocking the attempted connections.

The primary benefit of behavior-based systems is that they easily and quickly adapt to the current environment and can detect new variants of attacks that a signature- or rule-based monitoring system might not recognize. The monitoring system is actively looking for behavior that is inconsistent with the current system baseline profile; therefore, even new types of attacks will be recognized immediately and action can be taken. New attacks are often referred to as *zero-day attacks,* and signature-based monitoring systems might not recognize them as threats.

Local Lingo

zero-day attack   A type of attack that has rarely or never been encountered (such as an unknown virus or a malicious program) and takes advantage of previously unknown weaknesses and vulnerabilities in a software program or operating system. Because the attack is new, no existing defense or signature has been created to detect it.

The disadvantage of a behavior-based system is that it takes some time to build the baseline profile, and until the system learns enough information about the current system, it cannot accurately detect anomalies to that profile; efficiency is built over time. False positives can occur, in which normal behavior is flagged as anomalous because the system has not had time to build its baseline profile to recognize it as normal behavior. Also, the anomalous behavior detected can generate an alert, but the monitoring system can only warn the administrator that the thresholds have been exceeded; the administrator must determine whether an actual attack is taking place and what steps to take to mitigate it. The behavior-based monitoring system doesn't always recognize the type of specific attack, only its symptoms.

Heuristic-Based Monitoring Heuristic-based security monitoring continuously trains on network behavior (similar to anti-spam filters, as described in a previous section). Heuristics uses an initial database of known attack types, but dynamically alters their signatures based on learned behavior of inbound and outbound network traffic. These types of systems are powerful for detecting suspicious behavior that might not be detected by other methods, but they require constant tuning to prevent false positives.

Rule-Based Monitoring Rule-based security monitoring takes more work to match the efficiency and effectiveness of other types of monitoring methods such as signature- and behavior-based systems. Like a firewall, a rule-based security monitoring system relies on the administrator to create rules and determine the actions to take when those rules are transgressed. For example, a rule can be created that will block connections from an IP address if more than 100 connections are attempted from the same IP address within a certain time, such as 30 seconds. This could indicate a DoS attack, and when the rule thresholds are exceeded, the offending connection will be blocked to contain the threat.

Rule-based systems require significant manual initial setup and constant maintenance to keep the rules current and up to date with the latest threats. These factors are handled automatically by a signature-based system, which already contains an up-to-date database of the latest security threats and compares these threats with the behaviors the system is experiencing. The system will then take action as appropriate.

Application-Aware Devices

Most the traditional security appliances we have discussed previously, such as firewalls and IDSs, operate at Open Systems Interconnection (OSI) layers below the application layer. This means that application-specific threats utilizing the application layer will pass through without consideration. Application-aware devices combine the properties of stateful devices and application-layer devices (there are application-aware firewalls, IDS/IPS, and proxies) into a product that can both examine network traffic and identify application traffic, even web applications, and apply rules based on that specific application. Application-aware devices catalog applications approved for use within the network and examine traffic passing to and from them, and can "learn" new applications as they are added to the network. Adopting the qualities of a behavioral device, they can alert to both signatures and anomalies within a network.

Exam Tip

Be sure to understand the differences between traditional security devices, such as stateful firewalls, and application-aware devices.

Protocol Analyzers

Beyond basic network-level and content filtering, protocol analyzers have also become another defense in the security arsenal of organizations that want to prevent attacks and exploits from reaching their server and client systems.

Protocol analyzers (also known as *network sniffers*) can be stand-alone applications or used in conjunction with other network monitoring and intrusion detection applications to monitor and capture network data, right down to the packet and frame level. This allows the network administrator to analyze each frame of network data to look for abnormalities and inconsistencies in network requests and responses that may indicate an intrusion or other malicious application running on the network. Due to the enormous volume of data that floods through a network, it would be impossible for a network administrator to examine each frame passing through the primary network router. Stand-alone analyzers are most useful for detecting isolated problems with specific systems or on a small subnet of clients.

Protocol analyzers can also be used in conjunction with intrusion detection and prevention systems to analyze large blocks of the network and network protocols such as web HTTP and FTP. This deep-level scanning of network data can detect specific behaviors of known exploits or network attacks, such as by detecting anomalous data in an HTTP request. This information can be communicated to the IDS, which will block those network packets from reaching the client. This technique is very like how antivirus or anti-spyware applications detect malicious programs by comparing them to known behaviors based on a signature file. To ensure efficiency, this signature file must be kept up to date with the latest known network and application exploits.

Objective 8.02
CompTIA Security+
Objective 3.2

Explain Network Design Elements and Compounds

Securing a network infrastructure can be a daunting task for a network administrator. Depending on the size and complexity of the network, the administrator must examine the security implications of several interconnected communication systems, from the internal networking equipment of an organization, such as routers, firewalls, and switches, to users who access the organization's network remotely via a VPN.

Compounding the problem are the several types of Internet services that most companies and organizations need to run their business: web services, e-mail, and file transfer servers. These types of applications require special attention regarding security. At the same time, you need to protect your internal network hosts and servers from unauthorized access from the public Internet.

To provide maximum security with the least amount of administrative overhead, the use of security zones is recommended. *Security zones* are created when parts of your network are divided into special separated areas where similar systems and servers reside. By putting all your Internet servers in one zone and your internal network in another zone, you create a protective wall to regulate access between them. This type of topology is created using a firewall, which controls access to the various zones through a rules-based access system.

Other network protection schemes, including the use of NAT, network access control (NAC), virtual local area networks (VLANs), VPNs and remote access, virtualization, and cloud computing, can help you divide the network into more manageable zones to secure access.

Security Zones

Dividing your network into separate security zones lets you create physical and logical barriers between the different areas of your network. These zones enable you to allocate different types of security, depending on the sensitivity of the data and network equipment within that zone. This is the equivalent of setting up fences or walls between different buildings in a facility, which prevent users of one building from entering another building for which they are not authorized. A *firewall*, as discussed earlier within the chapter, is used to set up these zones on the network. The firewall uses a special set of rules to admit or deny network access, as appropriate, such as only allowing FTP traffic to a specific

FIGURE 8.4 Network security zones

server. By setting up the firewall to split the network into different zones, you can more easily create firewall rules to allow access to servers in those zones.

The three main zones into which networks are commonly divided are the external public network, the internal private network, and a demilitarized zone (DMZ), as shown in Figure 8.4.

DMZ

The *DMZ* is an area of the network where a high number of publicly accessed Internet systems should be located. In an overall network security topology, the DMZ is situated between the public and protected zones (private network), as shown in Figure 8.5.

FIGURE 8.5 The DMZ

The DMZ provides a buffer zone between your external network devices, such as a router, and the internal network that comprises your servers and user workstations. The DMZ usually contains popular Internet services—web servers, mail servers, and FTP servers. These services may need to be accessed by those on the public network, the Internet. Your company might use a website that hosts certain services and information for both current and potential clients. A public FTP server on the DMZ might serve files to all users or only to certain clients. Your mail server needs to allow a connection from the Internet to let e-mail be relayed to and from your site and to provide mail access for your own users who might be using the system remotely.

Exam Tip

Know the purpose of the DMZ and how a firewall can be configured to separate these Internet servers from the internal network.

These Internet services, however, should be separated from your internal local area network (LAN). If you were to host a web server on your internal LAN that is accessible from the Internet, you would create vulnerabilities in your network because an unauthorized user might be able to compromise the web server and then have full access to your local LAN. If the web server is on your DMZ and is somehow compromised, the hacker could only get as far as the DMZ because the internal LAN is on another network, protected by the firewall.

Travel Advisory

Many web servers act as a front end for access to database servers, which need to be located on the internal LAN. Care must be taken to make sure that only those ports needed for access to the database are opened by the firewall and that access can only be granted from that web server. If a hacker were to compromise the security of the web server, he might be able to use that as a jumping point to get to the database server on the internal LAN.

Intranet

An *intranet,* or internal network, is a locally available web network that is not accessible from the public Internet. The prefix "intra" specifies this is an internal network. Many companies provide web services that are only relevant to their internal employees and not to the public or the company's customers. These web pages usually contain such services as a directory of contact information for everyone in the company, or they are dedicated to specific departments (for example, human resources or engineering) or are finance web pages dealing with the company's stock and financial plans. Web-enabled applications for internal use give employees access to internal services via a web browser.

The intranet only lets internal employees have access to these web pages because the information they provide can be confidential and shouldn't be accessed by the public, especially rival companies. The web servers that host intranet services are located on the private internal LAN in the overall security zone model to prevent access from both the public and DMZ zones.

Extranet

An *extranet* is an extension of your private network or intranet. An extranet extends outside the body of your local network to enable other companies or networks to share information. For example, an automobile manufacturing company could have an extranet that connects selected business partners so they can access and share specific information on availability and inventories between the networks. These are often referred to as *business-to-business* (B2B) communications or networks because one company uses the internal resources and services of another.

Extranets can open security vulnerabilities in your network unless they are configured properly. Older types of extranets used dedicated communications links between the companies, which are much more difficult for an unauthorized user to penetrate. Now, most extranets use VPN tunnels over the Internet to communicate, which makes them more susceptible to intrusion. To ensure extranet communications are secure, your VPN, encryption, and firewall configuration must be carefully planned to limit the access of an intruder.

Network Security Techniques

Beyond physically dividing the network into zones to secure network communications, several software-based network configuration techniques can aid in securing your network from unauthorized intruders. These enable you to reconfigure the network logically instead of physically, which reduces administrative overhead and removes the need to purchase additional expensive networking equipment.

NAC

Any network is often at its most vulnerable from internal attacks from hosts on its own network rather than malicious entities attacking from outside the network. *NAC (network access control)* enables your network devices to allow or deny access to clients based on predefined access policies in a permanent method using persistent agents that are installed on the device, or using a dissolvable agent that authenticates and then is deleted or "dissolved." NAC policies set out rules for what clients can access on the network and define a minimum set of parameters that clients must adhere to and ensure they are properly configured and "healthy." This helps prevent viruses and worms that have infected a client on your network from infecting other systems by denying the client access to the network based on its status.

NAC policies can assess a connecting host and examine several factors: for example, the computer's operating system and applications patch update level, the existence of antivirus software and the date of its signature files, the existence of network vulnerabilities, and the access rights of the user who is logged in. It then decides whether to limit access to network resources based on these factors. Any clients that do not meet the minimum policy guidelines can be denied access or have severe restrictions imposed on their access, such as the inability to see and use network resources such as file servers.

NAC-aware appliances are typically inserted into the network before major access switches and routers. Ideally, NAC-aware routers and switches can be deployed on your network that remove the need for separate devices and allow your routers and switches to control access policies for your network. With multiple vendors, each with its own NAC support, successful implementations of NAC on your network require that all network infrastructure devices such as routers and switches be from the same vendor, as interoperability with other types of NAC systems may result in incompatibility and blocked access for major portions of your network.

Most NAC methods require an agent to be running on the client. This agent can be permanently installed as a service on the client system; in some cases, agentless solutions, often using Active Directory, can verify the access policy as the user logs in and out of the domain. If someone brings an unauthorized client into your network, these solutions can enforce your network policies, even though the client does not have permanent NAC client software installed.

These methods require some administrative overhead, especially regarding access for other devices (such as printers and other network-aware devices) that do not have operating systems or antivirus software running. Most NAC systems allow you to whitelist (allow full access without scanning the device) based on the system IP address or hardware MAC address.

NAT

NAT (which stands for *network address translation*) is a networking technique that allows private IP addresses on your internal network to be translated into a routable address for communication on the Internet. NAT was initially created to solve the problem of the lack of IP addresses available for private networks to use on the Internet. The number of remaining IP address ranges is scarce, so an alternative method of using already existing addresses was needed. Private networks can make use of special private IP address ranges internally, and when they communicate with the Internet, they can use an external address. Most companies have only a certain number of external Internet IP addresses to use. To work around this problem, a NAT service can be installed, so when an internal client wants to communicate with the outside world, it is assigned an external IP address for that communication. To the outside world, any communications from that internal network seem to come from one external IP address. The NAT service takes care of handling what requests go back to which clients on the internal network, as shown in Figure 8.6.

FIGURE 8.6   NAT (network address translation)

NAT is also important for security because the internal address of the client cannot be accessed from anyone in the outside world on the Internet. If an unauthorized user tries to see what is in that network, that user can only get as far as the external router or firewall. Most routers and firewalls have the NAT service built in to provide this functionality.

One hacking method that's been used to try to compromise a network using a firewall is to "spoof" the IP address to make it look as if the request is coming from the internal network. The NAT service helps prevent these attacks because the addresses of the internal private network are hidden.

Internal Network Addressing

As part of the internal network security zone, the network is typically configured to use private IP address ranges. These standard private addresses can be used by any internal network and cannot be routed externally on the Internet. The following are the private address ranges that can be used:

- **Class A network**   10.0.0.0–10.255.255.255
- **Automatic Private IP Addressing (APIPA)**   169.254.0.1– 169.254.255.254
- **Class B network**   172.16.0.0–172.31.255.255
- **Class C network**   192.168.0.0–192.168.255.255

Exam Tip

Know the standard nonroutable private address ranges for different classes of networks.

Using these private internal network addresses ensures that any internal network communications cannot be communicated externally unless granted access by the organization's network firewall, which uses NAT to convert the internal IP addresses to external addresses that can be routed on the Internet. Note that automatic private IP addressing (APIPA) is used within more recent Windows-based operating systems to self-configure an IP address for a machine when a Dynamic Host Configuration Protocol (DHCP) server is not available.

Subnetting

Administrators can use *subnetting* to break larger networks down into more manageable subnetworks. Subnetting greatly reduces the amount of network "chatter" and broadcasts sent to all systems on a network by isolating this networking activity to specific segments.

Subnetting logically divides the network, regardless of the actual physical layout of a network. The router is the device that creates and controls the border between different subnetworks. The router facilitates communication between the subnets while keeping intersubnet traffic isolated on its originating network. These subnetworks can be physical Ethernet segments or VLANs, where the segmentation is not physical but logical.

Subnetting provides network security by hiding network details from external networks, and it makes sure that networking data for each subnet, especially potentially dangerous traffic such as excessive broadcasting, is isolated on its own segment.

VLAN

A VLAN (or *virtual LAN*) is a type of logical network that exists as a subset of a larger physical network. Smaller networks can be divided into segments easily, with little administrative overhead. Splitting the network into segments allows network data and broadcast traffic to stay on the local segment, without broadcasting data to the entire network. Segmentation of LANs also provides extra security because a user on one LAN will not have access to another one without special permission.

Unfortunately, segmenting a larger network into smaller networks can be tedious and might involve the purchase of extra networking equipment, such as switches and routers, and extra cabling to separate them. This is where VLANs can help because the network segmentation is performed through software rather than hardware. VLANs have the capability to isolate network traffic on specific segments, and even provide crossover functionality to enable certain VLANs to overlap and allow access between them.

> ### Exam Tip
>
> Know how VLANs can increase security and performance in a network, as well as the different ways they can be implemented.

The capability to create VLANs is dependent on the capabilities of your network equipment. Most modern switches and routers support the use of VLANs, which can be enabled simply through changing the configuration of the network device. There are three basic types of VLANs:

- **Port-based VLAN** The port-based VLAN uses the specific port of a network switch to configure VLANs. Each port is configured as part of a specific VLAN. In order for a client workstation to be assigned to that VLAN, it needs to be plugged into that port.

- **MAC address–based VLAN** The MAC address–based VLAN tracks clients and their respective VLAN memberships through the MAC address of their network card. The switches maintain a list of MAC addresses and VLAN memberships, and they route the network packets to their destination, as appropriate. The advantage of MAC address-based VLANs is if clients' VLAN membership changes, they needn't be physically moved to another port. One drawback of this method is that being part of multiple VLANs can cause confusion with the switch's MAC address tables. Thus, this model is recommended for single VLAN memberships.

- **Protocol-based VLAN** A protocol-based VLAN is the most flexible and logical type of VLAN. It uses the addresses of the IP layer to assign VLAN settings, and an entire IP subnet can be assigned a certain VLAN membership.

Figure 8.7 shows an example of a typical VLAN configuration. This network is divided by network subnets configured as part of a certain VLAN. The switches use a port-based VLAN configuration across two floors of a building.

FIGURE 8.7   A typical VLAN configuration

Remote Access

In today's corporate environments, employees need to access the resources of the organization's networks when they are not physically in the building. In the beginning, this was accomplished using modems to connect to a network using a phone line. Modern remote access methods are primarily dominated by encrypted VPN access over the Internet. Remote access offers opportunities for hackers to compromise computer networks that do not install proper security mechanisms for their remote users. By using remote access, an unauthorized user need not physically be at a console inside the organization's physical building. The unauthorized user can be halfway across the world in another country, merely using a simple dial-up Internet connection. To protect these communications from unauthorized access, a security policy must be put in place to provide authentication measures and data encryption for all remote access users. In addition, the use of network monitoring and intrusion detection tools can aid in proactively monitoring the network for suspicious and unauthorized activity originating from remote access.

Modems

The modem was, and still is, an important tool for remote communications. It allows two computer systems to communicate over an analog phone line. Although this is a much slower method than modern VPN and remote access solutions that use broadband Internet access, modems are still in use today as secondary methods of contact, especially for "back-door" access for technical support and administration to critical systems for remote IT staff.

At a minimum, any type of modem access to a network should require authentication before the session can begin, and the session should use encryption protocols. Additional types of authentication—for example, security tokens—are important, especially if the remote access device is stolen.

VPN

A *virtual private network* is a special, encrypted communications tunnel between one system and another. VPNs are used to secure remote access in most modern networks, as shown in Figure 8.8.

A VPN makes use of an encrypted tunneling protocol, such as IPSec, Secure Sockets Layer (SSL), or Transport Layer Security (TLS), to connect networks together. A tunneling protocol allows an existing internal protocol, such as private IP addressing, to be encapsulated and relayed over the Internet to its destination. This VPN link is encrypted to provide secure access to a private network over the public Internet. The VPN link should be protected with strong

FIGURE 8.8 VPN (virtual private network)

encryption and authentication mechanisms to ensure its security. VPNs can be integrated with a wide variety of authentication systems, such as Lightweight Directory Access Protocol (LDAP), Remote Authentication Dial-In User Service (RADIUS), Kerberos, and digital certificates. Another way to protect VPN communications is to allow the VPN to assign IP addresses as the user connects and to allow only these blocks of IP addresses to access the network.

Travel Assistance

For detailed information on how VPNs use SSL and TLS, see Chapter 4. For detailed information on VPN and authentication integration, see Chapter 7.

After connecting to the VPN server, users have a secure channel between them and the network to which the VPN server is attached, enabling them to access network resources. VPN endpoints are typically secured by a *VPN concentrator* device or server that is responsible for managing the encrypted VPN tunnel between a client computer and the main network, or between two branch office networks in different geographic locations. A VPN server consists of a typical network server running VPN software services that manage the encrypted communications tunnel. The VPN server can run other services (such as authentication), but it may connect to other external servers for these services. A VPN concentrator is a specific hardware device dedicated to VPN connectivity. It is an integrated device that manages all aspects of the connection, including the encryption tunnels and authentication of the VPN client. Authentication can be integrated within the concentrator, but it can also connect to external services, such as an organization's LDAP server, to authenticate clients. Newer VPN configurations now automatically connect users to the VPN server rather than requiring a login to the VPN server, and they are "always on," which reduces the risk of users attempting to connect to internal resources without the protections of the VPN and allows for a more seamless user experience.

VPN concentrators can allow for *split tunneling*, meaning that users can access content in different security domains at the same time (for example, intranet resources and the Internet), by only routing the traffic to internal resources through the VPN connection while not allowing connections to the Internet to pass through the VPN. Conversely, full tunneling routes all traffic through the VPN. Split tunneling reduces the bandwidth used by the VPN but also reduces the ability to use content monitoring and to protect users over insecure connections.

Telephony

In most organizations, *telephony* services also come under the information technology (IT) banner because they are just as much a part of the everyday communications of the company as the computer network.

Instead of assigning a direct line for each user, which can be expensive, most large companies prefer to use a phone switch system, such as a private branch exchange (PBX). The PBX allows the company to maintain a certain number of internal and external lines. For example, a company of 200 people might have a PBX comprised of 200 "extentions" that share 50 incoming lines and 20 outgoing lines. It also gives internal users the capability to call each other directly using only three- or four-digit extensions, with the switching handled internally by the PBX and bypassing the external (public) phone lines/switches. A centralized, integrated voicemail system is also usually a part of the phone network. This can generally be accessed from an outside line in case someone wants to check her voicemail while at home or traveling.

Security for phone systems, however, has traditionally been lax compared to that for computer networks. If an unauthorized user were to gain access to the PBX, that user might be able to make expensive long-distance phone calls, all charged to the company. Unauthorized voicemail access can invade the privacy of your individual users and can also be used to glean information for corporate espionage. Important to note is that most phone PBX systems are equipped with a modem to allow remote access for the service technicians from the system vendor. If this modem is not secured with proper authentication systems, anyone might be able to call that number and access the phone system. A good practice is to unplug this modem when it is not in use and plug it in when a technician needs access to the system.

The voicemail system should be configured to allow only secure passwords for user voicemail boxes, with a minimum of six to eight characters, composed of uppercase and lowercase letters, numbers, and symbols. The same rules should also be applied to the PBX administrator account.

VoIP

The last several years have seen an exponential growth in VoIP (or *Voice over IP*) communications, where clients use the TCP/IP protocol to communicate over traditional computer networks. VoIP clients include basic phone services, as well as video conferencing and other types of multimedia applications that are communicated over a network.

The advantage for VoIP services is that the long-distance costs associated with traditional phone networks practically disappear, as phone services can be deployed globally and users can communicate over existing Internet communication lines. A user in an office in New York can call an office associate located in Tokyo using a VoIP phone that communicates over existing Internet and VPN connections between their offices, completely bypassing the traditional phone system network.

Security concerns over VoIP have also grown because it uses the same computer networks as other Internet traffic and is open to the same types of computer vulnerabilities, such as denial-of-service attacks, spoofing, eavesdropping, call interception, man-in-the-middle attacks, and even voicemail spam.

VoIP also offers less availability, since if your Internet connection fails, none of your VoIP phones will work. Most organizations utilize VoIP for specific applications such as video conferencing but continue to use traditional phone networks for most of their users because of the inherent security and high availability.

Telephony communications over a computer network require the same types of security safeguards that are used on traditional networks and must be part of your overall network security infrastructure plan.

Media Gateway

To translate between different types of media—say, PBX telephony or 3G wireless communications—*media gateways* convert the disparate signals into a standard stream. For example, it is a media gateway that provides the analog-to-digital conversion required for VoIP communications, thus facilitating a seamless telephony experience.

Virtualization

Virtualization technology allows computer desktops or servers to host and run additional "virtual computers." Using virtualization technology, a single computer can host multiple instances of an operating system environment, all running on the same hardware. These virtualized environments run as if they were a separate system and can run applications, be networked, operate remotely, and perform almost any type of function that a single computer running a single operating system can perform. Virtualized systems are very popular for cross-OS and application testing that allows software to be run and tested on several different types of operating systems, all on the same server. The concept of virtualization is expanding from the desktop into networking, known as *software-defined networking (SDN)*, which allows greater agility and scalability to meet demand, with less physical overhead.

High-powered servers can run several virtualized systems simultaneously, thus helping to reduce the cost of additional hardware and power resources. In addition, virtual systems provide improved security, high availability, and better disaster recovery by running as separate processes on the same hardware.

Virtualization works by emulating a complete computer system environment by sharing a single system's processors, memory, and hard disks for several individualized operating system environments. These virtual machines run their own separate operating systems and run their own separate applications like a real system. Several different operating system types, such as Linux, Windows, Mac, and Unix, can all run together on one computer in separate virtualized environments while sharing the same hardware resources. Any software crashes or security issues in one virtual machine will not affect another virtual machine running on the same computer.

The advantages of virtualization are that the number of physical systems running in your environment can be consolidated on several high-end servers, allowing several virtualized environments to be running on each server. In large-scale data centers, this can greatly reduce the amount of hardware required and thus the space taken up by the hardware; it can likewise reduce the amount of infrastructure resources required, such as power and environmental controls, thus significantly reducing overall operating costs. In terms of desktop computing environments, administrators can deploy secure desktop and network environments that can be accessed remotely without the need for separate keyboards, monitors, and input devices, thus greatly reducing the number of access points that create security risks.

Cloud Computing

Cloud computing is a technique that allows network services to be distributed from a central web-based "cloud" that can be updated from any device connected to it. Cloud computing provides a distributed service–based model where all aspects of the cloud—from the platform, to the software, to the entire infrastructure—are based on a distributed web service. This differs from the traditional client/server network model, where specific servers host network services and data and client device applications connect to the servers for the applications to work properly.

Most people now use multiple devices to access and manage their applications and data, including computer desktops, laptops, smartphones, and tablet devices. Before cloud computing, each device needed to have its own copy of the data the user wanted to work on. For example, the latest version of a spreadsheet file that the user was working on with his desktop computer had to be transferred to a laptop so that he could work on it as he commuted home. When he returned to the office, the file would have to be transferred back to the work desktop again.

Cloud computing allows the user to save the file to his cloud web service, and the file is automatically synced to all other devices that are connected to the same cloud. With this model, the user always has access to the latest version of the file no matter which device he uses to access it, and the file is stored in a safe location that is also backed up by the cloud service provider.

Cloud computing also allows applications to be run from the web-based cloud, with no need for additional software to be run on the client. For example, word processing and spreadsheet software can now be run as a web-based application instead of a client-based application. The web-based cloud service hosts both the application and the data without the need to store anything local to the client. This allows the user to use any client she wants to access her cloud-based services.

Security and authentication services for cloud-based services are centralized, and each device must authenticate and be authorized before allowed access to the cloud. Device security is critical for protecting access to the cloud. For example, if you lose your smartphone or laptop and you do not have adequate security for accessing the device and its applications and data, such as a password, you risk providing access to your cloud data to the person who finds the device and is able to launch the cloud application.

Everything as a Service

The concept of "Everything as a Service" (EaaS) means that, for a price, nearly anything that a user or company would want to use a computing system for can be delivered to them by a cloud provider through the cloud infrastructure—typically through a thin client or web interface. This requires less upfront investment in hardware and software by the customer, greater scalability, and centralized management for administration and security concerns. Here are some examples of this:

- *Infrastructure as a Service (IaaS)* provides the ability to quickly stand up virtual machines, storage devices, and other infrastructure that would otherwise require the purchase of physical devices.

- *Platform as a Service (PaaS)* provides the framework of an operating system and associated software required to perform a function (for example, the Linux operating system and components needed to run a web server).

- *Software as a Service (SaaS)* allows a customer to essentially lease software, such as applications and databases, thus enabling rapid rollout to the greater user community.

- *Security as a Service (SECaaS)* allows an organization to offload its security monitoring and administration to a third-party provider on a subscription model. Often, this third party is responsible for antivirus, anti-malware, intrusion detection, and other security-focused monitoring services.

Cloud Deployment

Cloud-based technologies can be deployed in several ways—either on-premise, hosted, or cloud—to fit the unique needs of the user or groups of users who will take advantage of it. These include the following:

- *Private clouds* are available only to the organization and can be managed either internally by the organization or externally by a third party.

- *Public clouds* are available to the greater public, with security segmentation between users.

- *Community clouds* are created when two or more organizations create a mutual cloud.

- *Hybrid clouds* combine two or more different types of clouds (such as private and community) to perform specific tasks not easily completed through one standard solution. For example, an organization could utilize a community cloud for its greater workforce but segment a portion of its most sensitive data to a private cloud managed internally.

CHECKPOINT

✓**Objective 8.01: Implement Security Functionality on Network Devices and Other Technologies** Network device security is your first line of defense against network attacks. Use firewalls, routers, and switches to control and secure network traffic. Use forward or reverse proxy servers, application firewalls, and content filters to prevent malicious content from entering your organization's networks. Use content filtering to control outbound content and facilitate data loss prevention. Use IDS/IPS to proactively monitor and respond to network security attacks. SIEM devices can help correlate data points and track trends, alerting you to suspicious activity in real time.

✓**Objective 8.02: Explain Network Design Elements and Compounds** Appropriate network design is critical to securing your network infrastructure. Differentiate your network into security zones to create logical and physical barriers between your networks. Put high-security servers such as web servers and e-mail servers in the DMZ to protect the private network. Use network security techniques such as private addressing, NAT, subnetting, and VLANs to separate networks. Secure remote access with authentication and encrypted VPNs. Use virtualization and cloud computing to simplify and centralize network security administration. A cloud infrastructure can be used to provide a variety of different services such as infrastructure (raw computing power and storage), platforms (operating systems and web server software), and software (applications and databases). Cloud services can be deployed in a few ways—as public, private, or community clouds—or they can be a hybrid of two or more other types.

REVIEW QUESTIONS

1. You have been tasked by your manager with performing an evaluation of the benefits of using virtualization in your quality assurance (QA) testing environment. Which of the following is an advantage of using virtual machines in terms of security and cost efficiency?

    A. It reduces the need to install operating system software updates.

    B. Multiple operating systems can be installed and run in their own separate, secure area on a single hardware device.

    C. It helps secure the hardware from unauthorized access.

    D. Antivirus and other security software only must be installed once.

2. After a security review, it is recommended that your organization install a network intrusion prevention system (NIPS). Based on the current budget, your manager recommends that you install a less costly network detection system (NIDS). What is the primary security difference between an NIDS and an NIPS that you can use to justify the additional costs?

    A. An NIDS system only detects TCP/IP attacks.

    B. The NIPS system actively tries to mitigate an incoming intrusion rather than just detect it.

    C. The NIDS system can raise alarms when it detects an intrusion.

    D. An NIPS system is only host based, not network based.

3. You must install and secure your organization's Internet services, including web, FTP, and e-mail servers, within your current network topology, which uses a network firewall to protect your internal networks. In which security zone of your network should these servers be installed to isolate them from the Internet and your internal networks?

    A. DMZ

    B. VLAN

    C. Internal network

    D. Intranet

4. Match the cloud type to its description.

Combine two or more different types of clouds to perform specific tasks not easily completed through one standard solution	A. Private clouds
Are available to the greater public, with security segmentation between users	B. Community clouds
Are available only to the organization and can be managed internally by the organization or externally by a third party	C. Hybrid clouds
Are created when two or more organizations create a mutual cloud	D. Public clouds

5. Your organization is growing fast, and the number of clients and devices on your network has doubled in size over the last year. To help better partition and secure your network, which networking technology could you use?

   A. NAT

   B. NAC

   C. VPN

   D. VLAN

6. Your organization has a large remote user base, and it is becoming difficult to enable them to access a legacy local application server and share and collaborate on project documents. Which of the following technologies could you use to provide secure, centralized access to these resources?

   A. VLAN

   B. Web-based cloud computing application

   C. Virtualization

   D. VPN

7. Many of your users are downloading MP3 music files from the Internet and using up the company's valuable bandwidth resources. Which technology could you implement to help block the transfer of these files from the Internet?

   A. Content filter

   B. Anti-spam filter

   C. Protocol analyzer

   D. IDS

8. You need to implement a solution that allows your users to browse web content safely and protects the company from legal liabilities regarding the downloading of inappropriate content. Which of the following security devices would you install?

   A. Anti-spam filter

   B. Firewall

   C. Web proxy

   D. Web security gateway

9. Your users are complaining that web browsing is very slow, but your small office cannot afford a faster Internet connection. Which of the following technologies would help improve web browsing performance?

   A. Web proxy

   B. Firewall

   C. Authentication proxy

   D. IDS system

10. You have discovered that a networking security issue might exist between your network firewall and e-mail server, which is accepting connections from an unauthorized external e-mail server. Which of the following network security tools would be best used for examining network traffic between your firewall and your e-mail server?

   A. IDS

   B. Proxy server

   C. Protocol analyzer

   D. Firewall server

REVIEW ANSWERS

1. **B**   Virtual machines all run in their own separate and isolated area on the system as if they were each on a separate physical machine. This greatly increases security because any issues arising in one virtual machine will not affect another virtual system. This also allows multiple operating systems to be installed on the same physical hardware, which saves money by avoiding the need to buy multiple hardware systems.

2. **B**   The NIPS system actively tries to mitigate an incoming intrusion rather than just detect it. An NIPS actively monitors for intrusions and will alert the administrator when one is detected. A network intrusion prevention system goes a step further and tries to actively prevent the intrusion as it is occurring.

3. **A**   The demilitarized zone (DMZ) is a network that typically contains Internet servers and services that are accessible from the outside world but should be isolated from your internal network. The DMZ ensures incoming connections for these services are routed to the DMZ and never reach the internal LAN.

4. **C** **D** **A** **B**   Here are the descriptions matched with the correct cloud type:

Combine two or more different types of clouds to perform specific tasks not easily completed through one standard solution	C. Hybrid clouds
Are available to the greater public, with security segmentation between users	D. Public clouds
Are available only to the organization and can be managed internally by the organization or externally by a third party	A. Private clouds
Are created when two or more organizations create a mutual cloud	B. Community clouds

5. **D**   A virtual LAN (VLAN) is used to segment a network into smaller logical units to aid in security and performance. The virtual LANs are logically isolated from each other to prevent network traffic and unauthorized access.

6. **B**   You could convert your legacy application to a secure, cloud-based web resource that allows clients to remotely access the application and its data from any Internet connection. The data can be easily shared, and multiple users can collaborate on projects.

7. **A**   A content-filtering server can analyze network traffic and block specific file types, such as MP3 music files, from being downloaded. The end users will receive an error when they try to access blocked files.

8. **D**   A web security gateway device is specifically engineered to content-filter HTTP web traffic and prevent attacks on web clients via the HTTP protocol. A network firewall, web proxy, or anti-spam filter would not prevent security issues specifically for HTTP applications.

9. **A**   Web proxy servers are used primarily for their caching capability, which boosts web browsing performance by storing content retrieved from an external web server.

10. **C**   A protocol analyzer is best suited for examining and capturing network packets and frames between the two devices. You would be able to examine the network traffic to determine the details of the unauthorized connection and use firewall rules to block it.

Secure Network
Administration

	NEWBIE	SOME EXPERIENCE	EXPERT
ETA	3 hours	2 hours	1 hour

Securing a network and its systems requires protection against a variety of attacks. These attacks might affect only certain areas of operations, such as an application attack on a specific File Transfer Protocol (FTP) server, or they can disrupt your entire network, such as a denial-of-service (DoS) attack. Some attacks are attempts to gain unauthorized access to a system or to damage one user account or one server. Other attacks try to disrupt the entire network infrastructure itself or prevent customers from accessing an organization's public website.

The purpose of the attack is not the main concern, however: The main concern is how the attacks occurred and how to prevent them from succeeding. By being aware of the various types of protocols, attacks, tools, and resources used by malicious users and understanding them, you can protect yourself and your systems. By knowing where and how to expect attacks, you can enact preventive measures to protect your systems.

Security must also include the network devices, protocols, and communications technologies that enable users to access the network's resources. Network devices such as routers, switches, and firewalls can be compromised, causing potentially much more damage than the simple theft of a laptop computer. Secure network administration means knowing how data flows in your network and how to properly configure your communications devices for maximum security. Not only do you need to be aware of how ports and protocols support critical functions such as routing and switching, e-mail and web traffic, file transfers, and remote access, but also less obvious uses such as time synchronization across the network.

This chapter discusses the various types of networking threats and vulnerabilities and describes the procedures necessary to mitigate them.

Objective 9.01
CompTIA Security+
Objective 2.6

Implement and Use Common Protocols

To understand the types of attacks that can occur against a network, it is useful to know the basic underlying protocols of Internet-based computer networks and the application protocols that use them. You should already be familiar with the Open Systems Interconnection (OSI) model, which divides communications functions among seven layers. Within the model, a layer provides services to the layer above it and receives services from the layer below it. The OSI layers and some common protocols are presented in Table 9.1.

TABLE 9.1	OSI Model Layers and Corresponding Common Protocols
Layer	**Protocol**
Application	HTTP, SMTP
Presentation	MIME
Session	NFS
Transport	TCP, UDP
Network	IPv4, IPv6
Data Link	PPP
Physical	DSL, ISDN

TCP/IP

The *Transmission Control Protocol/Internet Protocol (TCP/IP)* is the most basic communications protocol of the Internet. TCP/IP communications are "point to point," and together the two aspects of the protocol, TCP and IP, manage and route network messages. TCP/IP is a request/connection type of protocol, where a client requests a service from a server—for example, a web browser that sends a request to a web server to retrieve a web page for viewing. These requests use Application layer protocols, such as Hypertext Transfer Protocol (HTTP) in this case, that utilize TCP/IP to work properly. TCP manages how to partition communications and send network messages from source to destination. TCP is responsible for breaking network messages into smaller packages and frames and then reassembling the messages as they are received at the destination. TCP uses error checking and flow control to ensure network messages get to their destination.

A related protocol in the TCP/IP suite of technologies is the *User Datagram Protocol (UDP)*. UDP is connectionless and is used to transport less important data that does not require the error correction or flow control that TCP provides. UDP is fast and is often used for streaming media to allow content to be transported quickly. The *Internet Protocol (IP)* is used primarily for addressing and routing the network packets from the source to the destination device.

IPv4

Internet Protocol version 4 (IPv4) is the standard for all IP communications today and has been in use since the early 1980s. IPv4 is a connectionless protocol where delivery is not guaranteed; it only concerns itself with getting to the next network point between the source and destination network hosts. IPv4 uses 32-bit addressing, which allows for 4,294,967,296 unique IP addresses. These are separated into the different class types (A, B, C, and D), which make use of subnetting and subnet masks to help subdivide networks and facilitate private internal IP addressing.

Travel Assistance

For more detailed information on IP address classes and subnetting, see Chapter 8.

IPv6

The primary issue affecting IPv4 today is that with the exponential increase in public networks and devices, the number of available IP addresses is running out. *IPv6* is the next generation of the IP protocol that seeks to solve the address space issue and also provide additional network enhancements. IPv6 uses 128-bit addressing, allowing for up to 2^{128} available addresses. Although IPv6 and IPv4 are not interoperable, most modern operating systems, such as Windows 10, now support both IPv6 and IPv4 running concurrently.

With the exhaustion of IPv4 addresses imminent, the push to support IPv6 has resulted in rapid implementation by Internet service providers (ISPs) and large companies. Several technologies are available to aid in the transition from IPv4 to IPv6. For example, you can use the IPSec protocol to tunnel IPv6 traffic. Other technologies, such as the Intrasite Automatic Tunnel Addressing Protocol (ISATAP) and Teredo, also allow IPv4 and IPv6 clients to communicate with each other over an IPv4 network by tunneling IPv6 packets within IPv4 traffic.

ICMP

The *Internet Control Message Protocol (ICMP)* is utilized by the TCP/IP protocol for network diagnostics and troubleshooting. ICMP for IPv4 is called ICMPv4. IPv6 also has its own version of ICMP, called ICMPv6.

ICMP is used primarily to determine if a network host can receive network messages. The ping (Packet Internet Groper) utility uses ICMP for this purpose. ICMP is also used by the traceroute utility to check if network packets can be routed from a source to its destination.

ICMP's diagnostic nature means that it is often susceptible to denial-of-service attacks. The diagnostic messages returned from ICMP can abort a connection if they indicate the connection can't be completed. ICMP responses can be crafted to indicate a network issue, even if no issue exists, causing network communications failure. Rate-limiting features of ICMP can also be abused by hackers who craft ICMP messages that indicate network congestion, resulting in the host limiting its data rate even though there are no network congestion issues.

HTTP and HTTPS

The *Hypertext Transfer Protocol (HTTP)* is the primary communications protocol that allows web browsers to connect to and retrieve content from web servers. When a user clicks a web hyperlink, HTTP tries to connect with the associated uniform resource locator (URL). The browser sends an HTTP request to the corresponding web server hosting that URL. The web server returns the content of the website to the browser through HTTP. HTTP is a stateless protocol, meaning that with each communication, the link between the browser and the server is created, and then it's broken when the communication is finished. All HTTP communications are sent in clear text, so no messages are secure, and they can be easily viewed using a protocol analyzer. This makes HTTP unusable for communications requiring security and privacy, such as web-based banking and other online financial transactions.

Internet web servers accept HTTP port 80 requests from client web browsers, and they send back the requested information to the client. Web servers are the most common forms of servers on the Internet, and as a result, they are the most often attacked. An attack can occur in a variety of ways. Some attacks disrupt users from accessing the information on a website. Other attacks spread worms and viruses over the Internet. Some attacks vandalize websites and deface information on web pages or replace it with false information. Most of these attacks take advantage of security vulnerabilities in the web server. The most popular types of exploits include malformed requests, buffer overflow attacks, worms, and DoS attacks.

The *Hypertext Transfer Protocol over Secure Sockets Layer (HTTPS)* is a secure means of communicating HTTP data between a web browser and a web server. HTTPS protects the communication channel by using Secure Sockets Layer (SSL) and certificates to provide encrypted and protected communications. HTTPS uses TCP port 443 for communications.

Exam Tip
HTTP uses TCP port 80, and HTTPS uses TCP port 443.

Telnet

Telnet is a text-based terminal emulation utility that's part of the TCP/IP suite of protocols. It allows a system to connect to a remote host to perform commands as if you were on the console of the remote machine. For Telnet to work properly, the remote machine must be running a Telnet server service, which listens for Telnet requests from other hosts. When the client connects, it must authenticate to the remote system using a username and password specific to that system. Once authenticated, the user can run commands on the remote system as if he were directly on the command console.

Exam Tip
Telnet uses TCP port 23.

Unfortunately, Telnet provides little security other than basic authentication. This means transmissions, including the username and password, are sent in clear text and can be easily discovered by someone monitoring and capturing the communication. To ensure no one can use Telnet to connect to a certain host, the Telnet service should be disabled.

Although Telnet is a basic utility of TCP/IP communications, its use has been discouraged in favor of more secure methods of remote access, such as SSH.

SSH

Just like the Telnet utility, *Secure Shell (SSH)* enables a user to log in to a remote machine and execute commands as if they were on the console of that system. Telnet, however, is insecure because its data isn't encrypted when communicated. SSH provides a secure, encrypted tunnel to access another system remotely. When a client connects to a system using SSH, an initial handshaking process begins and a special session key is exchanged. This begins the session, and an encrypted secure channel is created to allow the access. SSH can also be used in conjunction with other protocols such as FTP to encrypt file transfer communications.

Exam Tip
SSH uses TCP port 22.

FTP

The *File Transfer Protocol (FTP)* is used to upload files from a workstation to an FTP server or to download files from an FTP server to a workstation. By using an FTP application, you can transfer files from one Internet system to another.

A server hosting files runs an FTP server service that awaits file transfer requests originating from clients using FTP client software. Many FTP server sites on the Internet are public in nature and allow anonymous users to log in and download or upload files to their system. Other companies use authenticated FTP servers to enable clients to download engineering or technical support files. To access the server, the client needs to authenticate using a login and password. FTP servers are a widely used resource on the Internet and one of the most popular targets for hacking attempts and abuse.

The main security vulnerability of FTP is that any information passed is in clear, unencrypted text, including the logon information. This means a hacker monitoring the system with some type of packet sniffer can clearly read your login username and password. Secure FTP (SFTP) is a program that uses SSH to transfer files. Unlike the original FTP, it can encrypt both commands and data, so it can't be captured by a packet sniffer.

Exam Tip

FTP uses TCP port 20 for data transfer and port 21 for connection control information.

TFTP

The *Trivial File Transfer Protocol (TFTP)* is a very basic FTP protocol. TFTP is connectionless and uses UDP port 69. Its use is limited to basic network file transfer operations, and it is often utilized for simple purposes such as a boot loader for booting a device over a network. TFTP transmits in clear text and has no encryption or authentication features. This limits its use to basic, low-security applications.

Exam Tip

Remember that basic FTP and TFTP communications, including login and password authentication, are transmitted in clear text. FTPS (TCP ports 989 and 990) or SFTP (TCP port 22) should be used to encrypt the session.

FTPS and SFTP

Basic types of FTP communications are not encrypted, so any login and password information is sent over the network in clear text and can be easily intercepted by a malicious hacker. *FTPS (FTP Secure or FTP-SSL)* software uses encrypted TLS/SSL communications to prevent interception by unauthorized users. You can also utilize SFTP, which is used to encrypt FTP sessions with SSH.

Travel Advisory
Do not confuse FTPS, which uses TSL/SSL, with SFTP, which uses SSH, to create an FTP tunnel through an SSH connection.

SCP

A related protocol for file transfers is *Secure Copy (SCP)*, a utility that secures file copy operations over SSH. SCP is often used as an alternative to SFTP when copying files from one system to another; however, SFTP is preferred because it has more comprehensive features and options than just a simple file copy operation.

Exam Tip
SCP uses SSH (TCP port 22).

DNS

The *Domain Name System (DNS)* provides a way to translate Internet domain names into IP addresses. For example, the website www.example.com can be translated to an IP address of 192.168.1.12. This allows network applications and services to refer to Internet domains by their fully qualified domain name (FQDN) rather than their IP address, which can be difficult to remember and can often change. If a company changes its system's IP address, it can simply update the DNS tables to reflect this. External users will not see a difference, because they will still be connecting to it by name.

DNS servers perform an extremely valuable function on the Internet, and wide-scale communication interruptions can occur if a network DNS server is disabled. Most client machines use DNS each time they try to connect to a network host. The client's DNS server is configured using its network settings, which can be set manually or automatically through services such as Dynamic Host Configuration Protocol (DHCP). Each time a client tries to access a host, such as a website, the local DNS server is queried for the IP address of the domain name. The DNS server translates the name into an IP address, which the client uses to initiate its connection.

DNS servers can suffer from denial-of-service and malformed-request attacks. In a DoS attack, the DNS server is inundated with DNS or ping requests. The load becomes so much that the DNS server cannot respond to legitimate DNS queries. DNS queries to servers can also be manipulated to include mal-formed input that could crash the server. Ensure that your DNS software is the latest version, with the most recent security patches installed, to prevent these types of attacks. Also, look to implement DNS security extensions (DNSSEC), which have been developed to protect this vital tool by enabling DNS responses to be validated, guarding against many types of DNS-focused attacks.

Exam Tip

DNS uses both TCP and UDP port 53. TCP is used for zone transfers between DNS servers, as well as name resolution responses, whereas UDP is used for DNS queries.

SNMP

The *Simple Network Management Protocol (SNMP)* allows you to use network monitoring programs to analyze diagnostic information on network devices. An SNMP agent service runs on the network device, which is accessed by a network monitoring tool. The SNMP agent provides real-time statistics on the device, such as device status, central processing unit (CPU), memory usage, and network activity. The latest release is version 3 (SNMPv3).

The information available from the SNMP agent is organized into objects that are described by a management information base (MIB) file. Each hard-ware vendor typically provides its own MIB file unique to the device, which can then be imported into the network monitoring tool.

SNMP has very basic security that makes use of a type of password system called *community strings*, which are simple passphrases for SNMP to access each device. Most administrators leave the default community string *public* as is, but this opens a vulnerability because anyone knowing the community string can connect to the SNMP-enabled device. SNMP passwords should be immediately changed from the default if set up on the switch.

You can also use an access control list to limit SNMP access to the specific IP address of your network monitoring system.

Exam Tip

SNMP uses UDP port 161. SNMP traps use UDP port 162.

IPSec

IPSec (IP Security) is a standards-based method of providing privacy, integrity, and authenticity to information transferred across IP networks. IPSec works on the IP layer to encrypt communications between the sender and the receiver. It is most often used to secure virtual private network (VPN) communications over an open network, such as the Internet.

> **Travel Assistance**
>
> IPSec and its encryption methods are described in more detail in Chapter 4.

NetBIOS

NetBIOS (Network Basic Input/Output System) is a local area network (LAN) protocol originally created by IBM but widely adopted by the Microsoft Windows platform. NetBIOS is not routable outside of a local area network and must be used with NetBIOS over TCP/IP name mappings to allow Windows-based LAN computers to communicate with TCP/IP-based networks.

NetBIOS is considered a very insecure protocol and is usually blocked from transmitting beyond the local area network to limit its services to local Microsoft Windows clients.

> **Exam Tip**
>
> NetBIOS is a session-layer protocol, but when used over a TCP/IP network, it uses TCP ports 137 (name registration and resolution), 138 (datagram distribution), and 139 (connection-oriented sessions).

iSCSI

The *Internet Small Computer System Interface (iSCSI)* is an IP-based protocol designed to link data storage solutions. It carries Small Computer System Interface (SCSI) commands, a standard designed to link computers and their peripheral (usually storage) devices, and is routable across IP-based networks at short, medium, and long distances.

> **Exam Tip**
>
> iSCSI uses TCP ports 860 and 3260.

Fibre Channel

Fibre Channel is a high-speed network standard designed to connect data storage solutions. Designed originally to connect supercomputing assets, Fibre Channel is now common within enterprise storage solutions within medium to large networks. Fibre Channel over Ethernet (FCoE) encapsulates Fibre Channel traffic over Ethernet networks. In contrast to iSCSI, FCoE cannot be routed across IP-based networks.

RTP

The *Real-time Transport Protocol (RTP)* is used for delivering voice and video services over IP networks. If you've ever used a Voice over IP (VoIP) phone, RTP likely was the underlying protocol that powered it. It is also often used for other services, such as streaming media and teleconferencing. RTP, however, does not inherently integrate encryption, so the Secure Real-time Transport Protocol (SRTP) was developed to provide AES encryption, as well as integrity, authentication, and protection from replay attacks. RTP uses UDP across a wide range of ports, usually between 16384 and 32767, depending on the vendor implementation.

Objective 9.02
CompTIA Security+
Objective 2.3

Identify Commonly Used Default Network Ports

CompTIA Objective 2.3 requires that you're able to troubleshoot common security issues given a specific scenario. But regardless of the scenario, one of the most overlooked problems with securing network activity is that of unknown ports, services, and protocols running on a system. For example, a simple file server might be set up for file sharing, but the server might also be running software such as a web service, the FTP service, and the Simple Mail Transfer Protocol (SMTP) service. Although these running services might not be used on your system, they could create security vulnerabilities because unauthorized users can still connect to the file server using their protocols and ports. By compromising the vulnerabilities inherent in those services, malicious hackers might be able to gain access to the files on that system, bypassing any authentication or access control.

Unfortunately, many operating systems install some of these services by default. For example, someone setting up a Microsoft Windows server might want to use it only for file sharing, but installing the operating system (OS) using the standard default configuration could lead to the system also installing a web server or other Internet services by default. When installing server OS software, you must ensure that you install only the services and protocols you need for the purposes of that system. Deselect or disable any other services that would be installed by default during the installation process.

> **Travel Advisory**
>
> When installing OS and application software, use a custom installation method that enables you to choose which services you want to run. Running the default installation could install many programs and services you do not need. The bottom line: the more software that's running on your systems, the more vulnerabilities that exist.

Before pinpointing a system or network for attack, malicious users often perform *ping sweeps*, in which the ICMP ping utility is used to find a valid range of IP addresses to attack on the network. A ping sweep performs a quick ping of all the devices in a certain IP address range, and if those devices respond to the ping request, the utility logs the address so that the user can then perform more detailed scanning on that address. After the valid IP addresses are found, an unauthorized user can try to find open security holes in a specific system or network using a special type of software called a *port scanner*, which analyzes a system for every service and protocol it is currently using. This is accomplished by looking for open service ports, listening for requests.

TCP/IP Network Ports

A TCP/IP port is a special numerical port used by a service. For example, HTTP web servers use port 80 by default for web surfing. Other services, such as DNS and Post Office Protocol 3 (POP3), use ports 53 and 110, respectively.

> **Travel Assistance**
>
> See www.iana.org/assignments/port-numbers for a full list of network ports assigned by the Internet Assigned Numbers Authority (IANA).

These services are usually waiting for a request, such as a DHCP server waiting for a client request for a new IP address. By scanning these ports, a malicious hacker can determine what types of software and services are running on the server. From there, he can use that information to employ other methods for compromising the security of those services because of software bugs or security vulnerabilities that have not been fixed.

Exam Tip

A port scanner can be used to analyze a system for open TCP/IP ports. For example, a web server that also runs SMTP might show port 80 and port 25 as open and waiting for connections. The port scanner can run through an entire port range looking for common open services.

To protect your systems, the administrator should examine each server carefully and ensure it is running only services and protocols required for its specific function. Any other services should be disabled or uninstalled. In addition, any current services that are required should be examined to ensure that all systems are using the latest versions of the software with the most recent security patches installed. On a Windows system, for example, the administrator can run the netstat command to view any ports on the system listening for requests.

Exam Tip

Know the port numbers of some of the most common protocols and services.

The administrator can run a port scanner on her own system to discover whether any open ports and services are listening for requests. Table 9.2 lists the most common, well-known protocols and services and their corresponding TCP/IP ports.

Travel Advisory

Many service ports listen on UDP as well as TCP. For example, DNS uses TCP port 53 for zone transfers and UDP port 53 for DNS queries.

TABLE 9.2	Well-Known TCP/IP Services and Port Numbers

Service	TCP/IP Port Numbers
DNS	53
FTP (Data)	20
FTP (Control)	21
HTTP	80
HTTPS	443
IMAP (Internet Message Access Protocol)	143
LDAP (Lightweight Directory Access Protocol)	389
LDAPS (Secure LDAP)	636, 689
NetBIOS	137–139
NTP (Network Time Protocol)	123
POP3	110
Secure IMAP	993
Secure POP	995
SMTP	25
SNMP (Simple Network Management Protocol)	161, 162
SSH (Secure Shell)	22
Telnet	23
RDP (Remote Desktop Protocol)	3389

Objective 9.03
CompTIA Security+
Objective 1.2

Analyze and Differentiate Among Types of Network Attacks

Many of the types of attacks that can assault a network and computer system are geared toward specific system accounts, system services, or applications. The most damaging and, obviously, the most popular attacks by hackers involve disrupting the network itself. Because the network is the infrastructure that allows all systems and devices to communicate, disrupting those communication lines can be the most damaging attack a network can suffer.

The following sections outline some popular types of network-based attacks that have been used to intercept or disrupt communications and describe how to prevent them.

> **Exam Tip**
>
> Know these different types of network-based attacks and how to prevent them.

Denial of Service

Denial-of-service (DoS) attacks are well known for their ability to deny access to a web or Internet site, but DoS attacks can be launched against any type of network or system. In a DoS attack, a hacker overloads a specific server with so much data that the server is too busy to service valid requests coming from real clients on the network. System performance slows to a crawl. This affects a website's ability to service legitimate requests because the client will not receive responses to queries. This type of attack can also be performed on entire networks, as the DoS is targeted at the central router or firewall through which all data passes through. The network traffic becomes so high that nothing can get in or out of the network. The DoS attack is more serious than a single-server attack because network bandwidth is being compromised, which effectively denies access to all systems on that network rather than just one. Another type of DoS attack can occur when a wireless network is purposefully jammed, using a jammer that creates noise that interferes with the wireless signal.

Distributed Denial of Service

In a more organized and devastating attack, a *distributed denial of service (DDoS)*, the flood of data originates from multiple hosts simultaneously. The combined effects quickly overload any server or network device. As opposed to a DoS attack with a single origin, with a DDoS attack, a network administrator cannot pinpoint and deny access to one host because the attacks come from multiple hosts distributed throughout the Internet. Usually, these originating hosts are not willfully engaged in the attack. Malicious hackers can secretly install software on an insecure server somewhere else on the Internet and use that remotely to flood another host with data. This effectively hides the true origin of the attack, especially when the IP addresses are spoofed to show different originating addresses than those used in the attack.

Ping Attack

The most common form of attack uses simple TCP/IP utilities, such as ping, the command used to determine whether a certain host (classified as the destination host) is functioning and communicating with the network. A user sends a ping or query packet to the destination host. The destination host sends back a reply that it is indeed working and on the network. In a DoS attack, a malicious user can send a continuous stream of rapid ping attempts, called a "ping of death." The host is then overloaded by having to reply to every ping, rendering it unable to process legitimate requests.

SYN Flood

Another type of DoS attack is the *synchronous (SYN) flood.* SYN is an aspect of TCP/IP that allows systems to synchronize with each other while communicating. One system sends a SYN packet that is acknowledged by another system. The target system then waits for another acknowledgment from the sender.

This process can be abused by a malicious hacker by sending forged SYN packets to a host that is unable to reply to the request because the return address is incorrect. This causes the host to halt communications while waiting for the other system to reply. If the host is flooded with a high number of forged SYN packets, it will be overloaded and unable to respond to legitimate requests.

DoS attacks can be difficult to stop and prevent, but some simple configuration changes on the local routers and firewalls can help prevent them. The simplest way of protecting against ping flood types of attacks is to disable ICMP at the firewall or router level so the host will not acknowledge any ping attempts from outside the network.

Travel Advisory

Turning off ICMP can deprive you of important feedback from network troubleshooting tools because commands such as ping and traceroute use ICMP to function and can provide important network diagnostics information.

Other types of attacks, including SYN floods, are caused by vulnerabilities in the network protocols themselves. Make sure your OS is updated to the latest version by installing any recent service packs and security patches. This ensures that your underlying network protocols do not have any unresolved security issues.

DNS Amplification

A *DNS amplification attack* uses publicly accessible Domain Name System servers to conduct a DDoS on a victim server by flooding the system with the

DNS response traffic. An attacker will send a DNS lookup request to an open, recursive DNS server or DNS resolver with a spoofed source address that is the victim system and not the actual requestor (the attacker). All responses are then sent to the victim; the amplification part comes in through the attacker querying the DNS server for *any* information regarding the zone, which creates a significant amount of information to be "returned" to the victim. When this is amplified across a botnet, with all machines conducting the same activities, the victim server often can't handle the attack and a DDoS occurs.

Flood Protection

Some firewalls and other security products can also actively detect network flood attacks, actively block them and reclaim TCP resources used by the attack, and even try to trace them back to a source. Flood guard defenses can also prevent attacks based on multiple attempts to log in to a network device that can use up valuable networking resources.

Back Door

A *back door* is traditionally defined as a way for a software programmer to access a program while bypassing its authentication schemes. The back door is coded in by the programmer during development so that later she can break into her own program without having to authenticate to the system through normal access methods. This is helpful to programmers because they need not access the program as they normally would in a typical user mode, where they would be forced to enter authentication information, such as a username and password.

In hacking terms, a back door is a program secretly installed on an unsuspecting user's computer so that the hacker can later access the user's computer, bypassing any security authentication systems. This can also be an unauthorized account that is created on the system that the unauthorized user can access later. The back-door program runs as a service on the user's computer and listens on specific network ports not typically used by traditional network services. The hacker runs the client portion of the program on his computer, which then connects to the service on the target computer. Once the connection is established, the hacker can gain full access, including remotely controlling the system. Hackers usually do not know what specific systems are running the back door, but their programs can scan a network's IP addresses to see which ones are listening to the specific port for that back door.

Back-door software is typically installed as a Trojan horse as part of some other software package. A user might download a program from the Internet that contains the hidden back-door software. Antivirus programs can detect the presence of back-door programs. Personal firewalls can also detect suspicious incoming and outgoing network traffic from a computer. Port-scanning software can also be used to identify any open ports on the system, including those you do not recognize. These open ports can be cross-referenced with lists of ports used by known back-door programs.

NULL Sessions

NULL sessions are a type of attack on Windows-based servers in which weaknesses in the NetBIOS networking protocol are exploited to allow a user to create an unauthenticated connection with a Windows server. NetBIOS allows these unauthenticated connections to permit users and devices to browse the Windows network. To the Windows system, the user appears as an anonymous user; however, a malicious user can use a low-level remote procedure call (RPC) and other probing utilities to glean information on services running on the system, attempt privilege escalation, or access user account and password information. Worms have also been known to spread via RPCs in NULL sessions.

Simple registry and access permissions settings allow administrators to prevent anonymous NULL session connections and enforce authenticated access for non-system service-related access. Newer versions of Windows are not generally vulnerable to the risk of NULL session exploitation via default configuration parameters, but older versions of Windows such as Windows 2000 and NT still have these vulnerabilities.

Spoofing

One of the more popular methods for hacking a system is *spoofing* MAC or network addresses, which involves modifying the header of a network packet to use the source address of an external or internal host that differs from the original address. By spoofing the IP address, the hacker can fool the destination host into thinking the message is from a trusted source. The cause of this problem is that the architecture of TCP/IP has no built-in mechanism to verify the source and destination IP addresses of its network packets. A hacker can spoof the IP address to make it look as though a packet is coming from a different location—in fact, it can even be made to look like the IP address of an internal system. While spoofing is an attack by itself, it's more often used to carry out other attacks, as a first step. There are different ways to execute this attack, depending on what your end goal is and how you must fool other hosts. For example, to spoof a MAC address, you could use *ARP poisoning* to make false updates to a host's ARP cache, causing it to communicate by MAC address to an attacker instead of the actual host.

IP spoofing is mainly used by malicious hackers to hide their identity when attacking a network system, especially in a DoS-type attack. By spoofing the IP addresses of the incoming packets, hackers may make it difficult for network administrators to determine the real source of the attacks before they can set up a filter to block out that IP address.

Another use for spoofing is to emulate a trusted internal system on the network. For example, if a local server has an IP address of 192.168.17.5, and it accepts only connections from that network, a malicious hacker can modify the source address of the packet to mimic an internal address, such as 192.168.17.12. This way, the server thinks the packets are coming from an internal trusted host, not a system external to the network, as shown in Figure 9.1.

FIGURE 9.1 A spoofing attack

To help prevent spoofing attacks, your router or firewall might be able to filter incoming traffic to restrict network traffic coming into the external interface. By configuring the filter to prevent external packets originating from internal addresses, you prevent spoofed addresses from entering the network.

Smurf Attack

A *smurf* attack uses a spoof attack combined with a DDoS attack to exploit the use of IP broadcast addressing and ICMP. ICMP is used by networks and through administrative utilities to exchange information about the state of the network. It is used by the ping utility to contact other systems to determine whether they are operational. The destination system returns an echo message in response to a ping message.

A hacker uses a smurf utility to build a network packet with a spoofed IP address that contains an ICMP ping message addressed to an IP broadcast address. A *broadcast address* includes all nodes of a certain network, and messages to that address will be seen by all of them. The ping echo responses are sent back to the target address. The number of pings and echo responses can flood the network with traffic, causing systems on the network to be unresponsive, as shown in Figure 9.2. To prevent smurf attacks, IP broadcast addressing should be disabled on the network router, because this broadcast addressing is used only rarely.

TCP/IP Hijacking

An unauthorized user can effectively *hijack* a network connection of another user. For example, by monitoring a network transmission, an attacker can analyze the source and destination IP addresses of the two computers. When the attacker discovers the IP address of one of the participants, she can knock him off his connections using a DoS or other type of attack and then resume communications by spoofing the IP address of the disconnected user. The other user is tricked into thinking he is still communicating with the original sender. The only real way to prevent this sort of attack from occurring is by installing some sort of encryption mechanism, such as IPSec.

Man-in-the-Middle

A *man-in-the-middle* attack occurs when a person uses a packet sniffer between the sender and the receiver of a communication on the network listens in on or intercepts the information being transferred, modifying its contents before resending the data to its destination. These types of attacks usually occur when

FIGURE 9.2 A smurf attack

a network communications line is compromised through the installation of a network packet sniffer, which can analyze network communications packet by packet. Many types of communications use plain, clear text, and this can be easily read by someone using a packet sniffer. During an encrypted communication, a hacker can intercept the authentication phase of a transmission and obtain the public encryption keys of the participants, as shown in Figure 9.3.

To prevent man-in-the-middle attacks, a unique server host key can be used to prove its identity to a client as a known host. This has been implemented in newer versions of the SSH protocol, which was vulnerable to man-in-the-middle attacks in the past.

Hacker intercepts SSH
encryption host keys and
impersonates the client
and server, or just listens in

Fake
server

Fake
client

SSH

SSH

Client

Hacker
man-in-the-middle

Server

FIGURE 9.3   A man-in-the-middle attack

A related type of attack, *man-in-the-browser*, uses a Trojan horse to exploit vulnerabilities within a web browser to intercept calls to the browser and manipulate them. This type of attack is most commonly seen when attempting to conduct financial fraud online.

Travel Assistance

Chapter 11 goes into more depth about Trojan horses and other malware affecting hosts.

Replay

A *replay* attack occurs when an unauthorized user captures network traffic and then sends the communication to its original destination, acting as the original sender, as shown in Figure 9.4.

To prevent replay attacks from succeeding, you can implement time stamps or sequence numbers. This allows the authentication system to accept only network packets that contain the appropriate stamp or sequence number. If the time stamp is beyond a certain threshold, the packet is discarded.

Xmas Attack

An Xmas network port scan sends a network request to a system with many nonstandard TCP options enabled to look for active and listening TCP ports. This type of network scan sometimes evades detection by a firewall or network intrusion detection system (NIDS) because it uses nonstandard scanning options. It can also identify operating systems based on their response to these

Hacker intercepts the
communication and
forwards the request as if
he were the original sender

Replayed data   Data

Server   Hacker   Client
               reply attack

FIGURE 9.4   A replay attack

nonstandard options. It is referred to as a *Christmas (Xmas) attack* because all
the enabled options in the network frame are like the lights of a Christmas tree
to the scanned device, which responds to these requests (or does not reply,
which can also indicate certain characteristics of the device).

DNS Poisoning

The *DNS poisoning* technique takes advantage of a DNS server's tables of IP
addresses and host names by replacing the IP address of a host with another
IP address that resolves to an attacker's system. For example, a malicious user
can masquerade her own web server by poisoning the DNS server into thinking that the host name of the legitimate web server resolves to the IP address of
the rogue web server. The attacker can then spread spyware, worms, and other
types of malware to clients connecting to her web server. This type of attack
has a great potential for damage, as several thousand clients can be using the
DNS server or its cache of IP addresses and host names, and all of them will be
redirected to the poisoned address in the DNS cache tables.

The malicious attacker can perform this attack by exploiting vulnerabilities
in a DNS server that does not perform authentication or any type of checks to
ensure the DNS information is coming from an authentic source. This information can be passed from one DNS server to another, almost like a worm, and
the rogue address can be quickly spread.

DNS poisoning attacks can be mitigated by ensuring that your DNS server
updates its information only from authoritative sources by proper authentication or the use of secure communications. Most DNS software has been
updated to prevent these types of attacks, and typically, only out-of-date DNS
software is vulnerable to DNS poisoning.

ARP Poisoning

ARP (Address Resolution Protocol) poisoning is a type of network attack in which the ARP cache of systems on the network is modified to point to an IP address with the Media Access Control (MAC) address of an unauthorized user. ARP is used by systems on a network to associate an IP address of a system with its hardware MAC address. The attacker sends spoofed ARP messages to the network and masquerades as another system so that returned network packets will go to the attacker's system and not its original destination. The malicious user can then modify the data in transit or modify the routing information to use the data as a DoS attack against a router.

ARP poisoning and spoofing can be mitigated by using DHCP or other network services that help network clients keep track of the MAC address of connecting systems to detect receipt of an ARP that does not resolve properly. Physical access to the network should also be controlled by disabling unused ports on network switches and hubs and using port security to limit who can connect to the enabled ports.

Domain Kiting

Domain kiting, also known as *domain hijacking*, refers to the practice of registering a domain name, then deleting the registration after the five-day grace period, and then re-registering it to start another five-day grace period. This results in the domain being registered to the user without him having to pay for the registered domain.

The central authority for domain registrations, the Internet Corporation for Assigned Names and Numbers (ICANN), allows a five-day grace period before the registrar must pay for a new domain registration. This helps prevent mistaken domain registrations, typos, copyright infringements, and other issues related to domain name registration.

Some unscrupulous domain *registrars*, the organizations that register domains on a user's behalf, take advantage of the five-day grace period by deleting the registration before the end of the grace period. The domain is then immediately re-registered, and this is repeated, allowing the registrar to register a domain name indefinitely without having to pay for it.

Malicious users or registrars have also been known to do this with recently released domains that have not been renewed (either purposely or accidentally) and effectively own the domain with no chance for the previous owner or a new owner interested in the domain name being able to officially register it.

A similar practice, called *domain tasting*, utilizes this five-day grace period to test certain domains to track the amount of traffic they receive. These domains' names often use common misspellings of popular website domain names.

The domains that receive the most traffic are re-registered every five days to take advantage of the grace period and continue to generate advertising revenue for a domain that has never been paid for. These practices are often performed using fraudulent usernames and addresses of domain registrars, and a single registrar can perform this with hundreds of thousands of domain names.

Legal domain registrars and other Internet advocacy groups have been working with ICANN to try to find a way to curb this activity by forcing fees for every registration, and they have obtained the support of Internet advertising companies, who have started blocking kited domains.

Network administrators with several domains under their control must keep careful track of their domains and their expiry dates to ensure they are properly registered and renewed each time they are close to expiry to prevent the domains from being stolen by another individual or registrar. Many legitimate registrars offer several security features to prevent domain names from being transferred or renewed by a third party.

Typosquatting

Typosquatters (also known as *URL hijackers*) will register domain names that are very like legitimate domains, hoping for an unsuspecting Internet user to make a typographical error, or "typo," that directs them to the squatter's site. Once the user is there, the squatter will attempt to redirect the traffic to a competitor, install malware, or capture passwords that the user enters in to the fake site.

Typosquatters also often attempt to sell their domains to the legitimate site owners at a substantially marked-up price, or earn revenue through advertisements displayed on the illegitimate site.

Client-side Attacks

Often, we think of attacks as those an attacker wages against a remote server and any vulnerabilities resident on that system. However, *client-side attacks* exploit vulnerabilities in client applications, such as web browsers, using a malicious server or malicious data. A malicious website, for example, can exploit vulnerabilities within the client's web browser and facilitate the remote server gaining access to the client machine. Cross-site scripting (XSS) is an example of an attack that uses client-side scripts to target web applications on the victim's machine. If successful, the attacker can gain elevated privileges and access to the system.

Web browsers are not the only vector of attack, however; think of all the client/server pairings that take place (for example, e-mail, FTP, instant messaging applications) and all the code operating behind the scenes to support those operations, and you will begin to realize how many opportunities there are for a determined adversary to take advantage of client vulnerabilities.

Watering Hole Attack

Watering hole attacks are designed to infiltrate a system or network through the exploitation of a secondary system or network. Think of a lion or other predator lying in wait at a watering hole, waiting for a gazelle or other prey, and you'll get the basic idea of this attack. Often, the attacker will insert malware into a website that he believes the target will use (if the target is an organization, then one of the employees) and wait for the target(s) to be exploited via the secondary site. This is often determined based on the organization's mission. For example, if an attacker wanted to target an Internet business that shipped t-shirts to customers, he might determine the shipping company that the business uses and insert malware into its site, expecting the business to be exploited, in turn, after an employee visits the site.

Zero-Day Attack

A zero-day attack is a type of attack that has rarely or never been encountered, such as an unknown virus or a malicious program that takes advantage of previously unknown weaknesses and vulnerabilities in a network configuration, operating system, or application. Because the attack is new, no defense exists to protect against it and no signature has been created to detect it.

Travel Assistance

Chapter 8 has more information on dealing effectively with zero-day attacks.

Malicious Insider Threats

Insider threats may be the deadliest of all prospective threats. Think about how difficult it is for even the most determined attacker to infiltrate a network; she needs to do reconnaissance of the organization to determine potential vulnerabilities, extensive scanning to determine software versions and other pertinent information, and then know how to exploit those vulnerabilities, all without triggering alerts or autonomous systems. The malicious insider, on the other hand, could know these things—what if she is a system administrator? It could be as simple as plugging in a thumb drive or opening a back-access door into the building.

There is no 100 percent guaranteed solution to preventing attacks from malicious insiders; however, employee training and awareness campaigns can help mitigate the threat somewhat. Teaching your staff to report any suspicious behavior, no matter from whom or what it may be, is a great first step. Following up with regular log analysis and access control reviews will also help.

Apply and Implement Secure Network Administration Principles

Securing your network not only requires the use of specific network devices, but also their proper deployment and configuration. The ability of your network devices to provide network border security and prevent inbound threats is greatly diminished if they are not properly set up in a secure manner. The following sections describe how to implement basic secure network administration principles.

Networking Device Configuration

Several key devices within your network can be configured to increase security against attacks and unauthorized intrusion. These devices are your first line of defense, and it is vital that they be secured through proper configuration and management. Your primary networking equipment includes the firewall, routers, and switches.

Travel Assistance
See Chapter 8 for a detailed description of these network security devices and their secure deployment.

Firewall Administration

The firewall is a barrier on your network border that protects your internal networks from external networks such as the Internet. In its default configuration, a firewall will block all network traffic. This is the best practice of *implicit deny,* meaning that anything that is not explicitly defined in an access rule is denied.

This denies all access by default, until you apply access rules for only the specific services required. This way, you start with the strongest base security policy for your firewall configuration and slowly add rules to allow access as required.

To configure the firewall, you must set up many rules to allow incoming and outgoing network communications for specific ports and protocols. These rules can be general or specific. For example, a firewall can be configured with a rule that states that any HTTP traffic can come and go on a specific network. It can also be much more detailed and state that an SMTP packet destined for a mail server can come only from a specific host IP address. Further, rules can be put into place that allow all traffic access to any part of the network unless explicitly denied; however, this can create huge headaches once the list gets large! Make sure you understand the pros and cons of the different methods of denying traffic.

Travel Advisory

Documenting the rules applied to the firewall and why you are implementing them is important. When auditing these later, you might find you are allowing access to services that do not exist anymore and the rules can be removed.

A firewall can be an independent hardware device or a software application running on a computer or server. In either case, the firewall software should always be kept current with the latest versions and patches. This will ensure you are using the most recent software that does not contain known software bugs and security vulnerabilities.

Router Administration

A router connects several networks together and relays data between them, whereas a switch segments these networks into smaller, more manageable sections and relays packets between them. These devices help prevent network traffic from bridging over unnecessarily to another network by separating the networks physically and logically with software (such as with VLANs) to prevent insecure cross-network access or broadcast chatter.

After the network firewall, these devices form the backbone of your network, and their security is critical to making sure your entire network is secure from intrusion and is not vulnerable to network attacks that can slow down or completely stop network communications.

ACL Rules

Most network device software lets you carefully control the protocols, services, ports, and source and destination of the information that flows through the device via packet filtering and access control lists. For example, you can configure a device to accept only FTP communications to a certain network.

Access control lists (ACLs) are used by network devices to control traffic in and out of your network, and can be general in nature or specific to certain types of communications. ACLs are typically used in firewalls to control communications between public and private networks, but they can also be used on internal routers and switches to regulate traffic within the network. An access control list entry usually includes the origin of the network packet, the destination, the protocol used (TCP or UDP), the TCP/IP port used, and whether access is allowed or denied.

The following types of parameters can be controlled using an access control list:

- **Source address**   Specifies the originating source IP address of a packet, whether an internal or external machine or an internal address that it proxies to an external address.

- **Destination address**   Specifies the IP address where the packet is going, which can be internal or external to the network.

- **Port numbers**   Specifies the TCP/IP port number the communication is using. Each type of TCP/IP service uses a standard port.

- **Protocol**   Identifies the protocol being used in the transmission, such as FTP, HTTP, or DHCP, and is usually used in conjunction with a port number that's standard to that protocol or service. This parameter can also be used to define whether the protocol is using TCP or UDP.

- **Permit or deny**   Permits or denies the communication specified in the access control list entry.

The following is an example of code for an ACL entry for a router:

```
permit source 192.168.13.2 destination 10.1.5.25 tcp port 80
```

The syntax used by your network device will be like this entry, but varies from vendor to vendor. In this example, the ACL entry permits TCP traffic on port 80 (the default port for HTTP) from the host 192.168.13.2 to a host on network 10.1.5.25. The destination might be some type of secured web server that needs to be accessed from a web browser client on the source host. This prevents any other system—internal or external—from connecting to that web server, as shown in Figure 9.5.

Workstation
192.168.3.8

Workstation
192.168.13.20

192.168.13.X
Network

TCP port 80
to 10.1.5.25

Access control list
permit source 192.168.13.2
destination 10.1.5.25 TCP port 80

Router

Workstation
192.168.13.2

Workstation
10.1.5.6

Workstation
10.1.5.5

TCP port 80
to 10.1.5.25

10.1.5.X
Network

Web server
10.1.5.25

FIGURE 9.5 Access control lists prevent other systems from connecting to a web server.

Port and MAC Address Security Most network devices allow you to secure the device right down to the port level. For example, a network switch might have 24 port connections that link your client workstations. You can configure the switch to only allow certain devices to use specific ports, and even disable ports that aren't in use to prevent an unauthorized user from simply plugging his device into the port.

You can also configure network devices to accept only data from specific MAC address ranges, which limits access to the switch or port based on the hardware address of the connecting client.

Network Separation

A network can be divided into different physical or logical security zones—for example, a demilitarized zone (DMZ)—to create an inherent barrier against intrusion. The thought is this: Although an attacker might successfully make his way into one part of the network, there are still controls (such as firewalls and IPSs) that he will have to overcome to enter another zone.

Another type of network separation is an air-gap, meaning a system or group of systems that are not connected to the Internet. Very often, Industrial Control Systems (often referred to as Supervisory Control and Data Acquisition [SCADA] systems) are air-gapped from the greater Internet to prevent remote access. Sometimes, air-gapped systems are not even connected to any other systems. This provides another measure of security, though they are difficult to maintain due to the inability to push patches and conduct automated scanning.

Travel Assistance
The DMZ and other security zones are discussed within Chapter 8.

Unified Threat Management

Unified threat management is the evolution of the traditional firewall concept into an all-in-one device designed to act as a firewall, intrusion detection system (IDS), load balancer, data loss prevention (DLP) device, and filter for spam and malware. Although combining these functions into one device eases the management load on administrators, it is also a single point of potential compromise or network latency.

Travel Assistance
For more detail on all-in-one security devices, see Chapter 8.

Network Device Threats and Risks

Several weaknesses can be exploited in your network devices, and various threats can compromise them. These include weak passwords and account security, software and firmware vulnerabilities that lead to unauthorized access, and direct network attacks on the devices themselves.

Weak Passwords

Like servers and workstations, network devices control access via login credentials, and it is critical that the accounts and passwords used are secure. Passwords to critical network devices must be very strong to prevent unauthorized users from connecting to a device and attempting to log in and guess the password or use some other brute-force method. Select a "strong" password that is, at minimum, eight characters in length and includes both uppercase and lowercase letters, numbers, and special characters such as the @ symbol. Passwords should never be written down. If necessary, password and account information can be stored on an encrypted universal serial bus (USB) key and stored in a locked safe only accessible to authorized users.

> **Travel Assistance**
> More information on password attacks is located in Chapter 14.

Default Accounts

Most network devices have a preinstalled default administrative account, usually called *admin* or *administrator*. Because an unauthorized user can easily guess this account name and use it to try to log in to the device, you should disable this account and create another account with administrative rights and with an account name that does not represent its function. If your team consists of several administrators, you might use their names or other identifying information to help audit access and configuration changes to the device. Any guest accounts or other accounts with diminished access rights should also be disabled.

Transitive Access and Privilege Escalation

Transitive access refers to elevated access permissions that have been passed on to another user. It is possible that through misconfiguration of your network device access rules, you inadvertently allow access to users based on access rules that are too wide in scope and thus allow transitive access. For example, you may create an access rule that allows network access to a specific web server, but because the rule is general and not well defined, you've allowed access to all TCP/IP ports and protocols for that host, when all that was required was HTTP port 80. Make sure that when you create access rules and permissions, they only allow what is required for the specific service, right down to the TCP/IP port and protocol and between specific source and destination IP addresses.

Another aspect of unauthorized access is *privilege escalation,* which refers to the practice of exploiting coding bugs that exist within software. In certain situations, it can be possible for an unauthorized user to gain more privileged access to a network device by taking advantage of a bug exploit to bypass the device security and perform commands with higher-privileged access than expected.

Vulnerabilities that typically lead to privilege escalation scenarios are most often found as buffer overflow attacks, where conditions and boundaries are not properly checked on user-entered fields in a network device's firmware or operating system and allow highly privileged command execution. If a documented exploit is found in a network device's firmware or OS, a patch must be installed (if available) to fix the bug to prevent proof-of-concept exploits from turning into real security threats. You must be diligent in making sure the network device software is running the latest patch level so that all known bug fixes are deployed.

Network Loops

A *network loop* occurs when there is more than one network path between two network hosts. For example, a user might accidentally connect two ports on a network switch together or improperly connect two network switches together. The confused switch starts broadcasting on all ports and eventually floods the network because the broadcasts are constantly looping.

Many network devices now come with loop protection to detect these scenarios and take active measures to isolate the looped ports and prevent the broadcasts from bringing down the network.

Network Device Hardening

One of the most important steps in securing your network and systems is to make sure that the devices that form the infrastructure of your network are examined for security vulnerabilities. Several aspects of networking devices can create many security holes if not properly examined or configured, including firmware, configuration, and log files.

Secure Remote Access

Most network devices can be configured remotely over the network. However, this creates a security vulnerability if the method used to remotely configure the device is not properly authenticated or secure. If possible, insecure remote access methods, such as the use of Telnet or basic HTTP to connect to a device, should be disabled. This will prevent users from accessing the device unless they use secure methods such as SSH or HTTPS, or are physically attached to the device with a network cable. For deeper security, enable access only for the IP address of the client from which the user is connecting.

Device Placement

When designing an effective network architecture, not only do you need to carefully consider the fundamental networking technologies such as routers and switches, but also security devices such as intrusion detection/prevention systems, sensors, data collectors, taps, firewalls, content filters, and correlation engines. It is important that they are put in the appropriate place to gather, analyze, and make decisions on data moving in and out of your network. For example, an IDS can be deployed either in-band, where all traffic is analyzed (often at the network edge), or out-of-band, where only some traffic is analyzed. A detection system can only monitor what it sees, so placing it further down in the network lessens the chance of finding intrusions, especially because your firewall and routers are the entry points to the network.

> **Travel Assistance**
>
> For more information on how device emplacement is important to network security, see Chapter 8.

Disable Unused Services

The administrator must examine the configuration settings of a network device after installation to make sure that the default configuration is suitable for the network's security needs. The administrator should enable secure settings and disable any options or services that are not required by the current deployment.

Optional services can create security vulnerabilities. For example, in many network devices, SNMP is enabled by default to allow the device to be examined by network monitoring equipment. But SNMP has been known to contain several security vulnerabilities and sends its data in clear text, so disabling its use is best. SNMP also makes use of a type of password system that employs *community strings,* which are used as simple passphrases for SNMP to access each device. Most administrators leave the default community string *public* as is, but this opens a vulnerability because anyone who knows the community string can connect to the SNMP-enabled device. SNMP passwords should be immediately changed from the default if set on the devices.

Exam Tip

Remember that SNMP has been known to contain many security vulnerabilities and should be disabled if it is not required, as it is often enabled by default on network devices. The default *public* community name string should be changed when SNMP is installed.

Another protocol used for network diagnostics, ICMP, is employed by utilities such as ping and traceroute. Enabling ICMP leaves a network device open to DoS attacks that can quickly disable a router and cut off the communications flow for your network. ICMP can also be used to identify systems that are live and accepting connections, which can lead to them being attacked. If you do not require the ICMP service, it should be disabled.

Employ DDoS Mitigation

To combat DDoS attacks or even service degradation, an administrator can employ DDoS mitigation tools to ensure a higher level of service reliability. For example, Content Delivery Networks (CDNs) consist of multiple, often globally disparate and distributed servers that deliver incoming requests for content, often based on geographic location or another factor that determines the optimal location. Not only do CDNs provide accelerated content in the best scenarios, they also allow administrators to move distribute DDoS traffic across multiple servers, in an adaptive manner, mitigating the focused attack. When carried out effectively, DDoS mitigation tools can keep the target web server completely available and serving content as if nothing even happened.

Firmware/OS Updates

Firmware is software that controls the functions of the network device—like a device OS. Firmware is typically encoded in flash memory and can be updated, just like any other software application. You simply obtain a newer version of the release and then install it into the device's flash memory.

Like any other OS or application software, the system should be running the most recent version with the latest security and bug-fix patches installed. Some firmware updates also include additional security functionality that was not in previous versions. For network devices such as firewalls and routers that form the first line of defense in network security, you should regularly update the firmware or operating system to maintain maximum security.

Log Files

You should examine the log files from your network devices on a periodic basis to check for any system or security issues. The logs for your network devices will be very large because they record all activity of connections that are passed into your network or are blocked. It is useful to filter the logs to blocked connections to see if you can identify any pattern to known network attacks. Examine the logs to look for any anomalies that can indicate a security issue such as a hacking attempt or unauthorized configuration change.

CHECKPOINT

✔**Objective 9.01: Implement and Use Common Protocols** You should understand the layers of the OSI model and which protocols operate at those layers. You should know the basic protocols, such as TCP/IP, ICMP, HTTP/S, Telnet, SSH, FTP/SFTP/FTPS, SCP, DNS, SNMP, IPSec, and NetBIOS, and understand how they communicate and what their security vulnerabilities are.

✔**Objective 9.02: Identify Commonly Used Default Network Ports** To protect your systems, you should examine each server carefully and ensure it is running only services and protocols required for its specific function. Well-known protocols and ports include HTTP (80), HTTPS (443), Telnet (23), SSH (22), FTP (20, 21), DNS (53), SNMP (161, 162), NetBIOS (137–139), SMTP (25), POP3 (110), IMAP (143), LDAP (389), LDAPS (636, 689), NTP (123), Secure IMAP (993), Secure POP (995), and RDP (3389).

✔**Objective 9.03: Analyze and Differentiate Among Types of Network Attacks** Understand and know how to prevent the different types of network attacks, such as denial-of-service attacks, ping and SYN floods, DNS amplification, back doors, null sessions, spoofing, smurf attacks, hijacking, man-in-the-middle/man-in-the-browser attacks, replay attacks, Xmas attacks, DNS and ARP poisoning, domain kiting, typosquatting, client-side attacks, watering hole attacks, and attacks by malicious insiders.

✔**Objective 9.04: Apply and Implement Secure Network Administration Principles** Several weaknesses and threats can compromise the devices on your network, such as firewalls, routers, and switches. These threats include weak passwords and insufficient account security, software and firmware vulnerabilities that lead to unauthorized access, and direct network attacks, such as denial-of-service attacks, on the devices themselves. Make sure devices are placed properly within the network and at the network's edge to ensure best coverage and maximum utility of tools. Use access control lists to control traffic into and out of your devices. Network separation allows for the division of the network infrastructure into zones that can be secured to different levels. Understand how all-in-one solutions, such as unified threat management, work to mitigate a variety of threats.

REVIEW QUESTIONS

1. You need to set up a secure FTP server to allow your company's clients to upload their files. Which of the following FTP protocols would you use?

   A. SFTP

   B. FTP

   C. TFTP

   D. FTP over HTTP

2. You want to secure one of your network switch segments to only allow access from specific clients on the development network. Which of the following should you implement?

   A. Use a VPN for the development network.

   B. Create a firewall rule to restrict access to the switch ports.

   C. Create a VLAN for the entire development network.

   D. Restrict the switch port access to the MAC addresses of the clients.

3. The rule to block SNMP access to a router with IP address 10.1.5.25 is

   _____.

4. It is discovered that your primary router has a serious software vulnerability that makes it susceptible to denial-of-service attacks. What should you do to resolve the issue?

   A. Disable SNMP.

   B. Disable ICMP.

   C. Enable flood protection.

   D. Update the firmware.

5. Your web server is being flooded by a denial-of-service attack. Using a network analyzer, you see that there are IP broadcast replies being sent back to the address of your server from multiple addresses. Which type of network attack is this?

   A. Man-in-the-middle

   B. Back door

   C. Smurf

   D. DNS poisoning

6. When you're creating firewall rules, which of the following principles should be applied to maximize security by blocking all traffic and only allowing access as required?

   A. Implicit deny

   B. Explicit deny

   C. Unauthenticated deny

   D. Denial of service

7. During a denial-of-service attack, a network administrator blocks the source IP with the firewall, but the attack continues. What is the most likely cause of the problem?

   A. The denial-of-service worm has already infected the firewall locally.

   B. The attack is coming from multiple distributed hosts.

   C. A firewall can't block denial-of-service attacks.

   D. Antivirus software needs to be installed.

8. You have just performed a security port scan on your e-mail server. Which of the following services and ports that appeared in the test as open and accepting connections should be disabled?

   A. TCP port 21

   B. TCP port 25

   C. TCP port 110

   D. TCP port 143

9. Your network router can be remotely configured through a web browser. Which of the following would be the most secure method for remote access?

   A. FTP over HTTP connection

   B. HTTP connection

   C. Telnet

   D. HTTPS connection

10. A few systems have been infected with malware; log analysis indicates the users all visited the same legitimate website to order office supplies. What is the most likely attack the users have fallen victim to?

   A. Replay

   B. Watering hole

   C. ARP poisoning

   D. Domain kiting

REVIEW ANSWERS

1. **A** SFTP is used to encrypt FTP sessions with SSH (Secure Shell). The other methods (FTP, TFTP, and FTP over HTTP) are not secure and communicate in clear text.

2. **D** You should enable MAC address security on your switch ports to only allow the hardware addresses of the specific clients on the development network to access those ports.

3. **deny 10.1.5.25 udp port 161** ACLs are used to control traffic in and out of your network. The ACL rule to block SNMP access (port 161, UDP) to a router with IP address 10.1.5.25 would be deny 10.1.5.25 udp port 161.

4. **D** If a documented vulnerability is found in a network device's firmware or operating system, it should be updated or a patch applied to fix the bug to prevent the device from being compromised.

5. **C** A smurf attack uses a spoof attack combined with a DDoS attack to exploit the use of IP broadcast addressing and ICMP. By spoofing the address of the web server in an IP broadcast, the attacker causes all the replies from other systems on the network to the broadcast to be sent back to the web server, causing a denial of service.

6. **A** Implicit deny means that anything that is not explicitly defined in an access rule is denied. This denies all access by default, until you apply access rules for only the specific services required.

7. **B** A distributed denial-of-service (DDoS) attack comes from multiple geographically distributed hosts, making it difficult for the network administrator to block it.

8. **A** TCP port 21 (FTP) is not required on your e-mail server, and it should be disabled to prevent hackers from connecting to the e-mail server on this port.

9. **D** Of the options listed, the most secure would be the HTTPS connection.

10. **B** The users most likely fell victim to a watering hole attack. The third-party supplier could be hosting malware with your organization as the target.

Securing Wireless
Networks

	NEWBIE	SOME EXPERIENCE	EXPERT
ETA	2 hours	1.5 hours	1 hour

An aspect of network security that is often ignored but can provide direct access to your organization's networks is the use of wireless communications. Without proper security procedures, any person with a wireless device can connect to your network and eavesdrop or access private data by bypassing the traditional security defenses used in wired local area networks (LANs). A firewall or router with maximum security configured for your wired LAN will not stop a hacker who is able to access your network from an unencrypted and insecure wireless access point.

From the end-user perspective, the popularity of wireless devices and the wide availability of free and open public wireless access mean that users can access the Internet anywhere at any time. For users to be able to check their e-mail, manage their finances, perform their work, or just browse the Web can be an incredible boost to personal and business productivity, but this easy access to the Internet can also create the potential for deep security and privacy threats. Using your wireless device, such as a laptop, on an open, unencrypted network could mean your passwords and private data are being transmitted in clear text and could be captured by hackers monitoring these networks.

Wireless security is an important part of your overall network security strategy and design. Strong wireless security not only protects your networks from unauthorized intrusion, but also protects your users from having their authentication credentials and sensitive data intercepted when they use wireless devices.

This chapter provides an overview of wireless networks and their function and design, describes the different wireless and encryption protocols, and provides detailed information on wireless threats and the security techniques to mitigate them.

Objective 10.01 CompTIA Security+ Objectives 2.1 and 6.3

Implement Wireless Networks in a Secure Manner

One of the greatest changes in networking technology is the phenomenal growth and penetration of wireless communications. Wireless networks use radio frequency technology to transmit data through the air, effectively bridging the gap between data connectivity and user mobility. Wireless networks allow the mobile world to reach the Internet, not only with laptop computers, but also with other telecommunication devices, such as smartphones, wireless-enabled tablets, and many other devices.

Wireless connectivity lets users perform their daily computing functions, such as checking e-mail, scheduling the calendar, and browsing the Internet, without physically plugging into a network. Wireless applications also extend into the business world, where inventories are taken by handheld devices and entire floors of a building are set up with wireless networks to enable mobile users to move their laptops and other wireless devices from room to room without the encumbrance of wires.

The popularity and explosive growth of wireless networks, however, have also introduced increased concerns for the security of wireless data. More so than for traditional wired networks, wireless security heavily involves the use of encryption technologies, coupled with traditional security mechanisms such as access control and authentication.

Wireless security depends on the different types of wireless network configurations available and the types of devices that will connect to them. The following sections discuss the various wireless network technologies and their topologies, as well as the protocols, hardware, and software that make them work.

Wireless LAN Technologies

Wireless LANs (WLANs) use electromagnetic airwaves to transfer information from one point to another without the need for a physical connection. To communicate these signals, the sender and receiver need to be tuned to the same radio frequency. The receiver tunes in one radio frequency, rejecting all others. WLANs can comprise a range of technologies, each with its own set of strengths and limitations.

Narrowband Technology

A *narrowband* system transmits and receives data only on a specific radio frequency. The signal frequency is kept as narrow as possible—large enough to communicate only the required information. Crossover between communications streams is prevented through separate channel frequencies. The radio receiver filters out other radio signals, accepting only those on its designated frequency. The disadvantage of narrowband technology is that a Federal Communications Commission (FCC) license must be issued for each site where it is employed.

Spread-Spectrum Technology

Most WLAN systems use spread-spectrum technology to transmit their information. *Spread-spectrum* technology is a wideband radio-frequency technique used to ensure reliable and basic security for communications systems.

More bandwidth is consumed than in a narrowband transmission, but spread-spectrum technology produces a stronger signal. Three types of spread-spectrum radio exist:

- **FHSS** *Frequency-hopping spread-spectrum* uses a narrowband carrier that changes frequency in a pattern known to both the transmitter and the receiver. When they're synchronized, a single logical channel is maintained. FHSS uses a lower data rate (3 Mbps) than DSSS systems, but can be installed into virtually any location without fear of interference interrupting its operation. FHSS is used by the Bluetooth standard.

- **DSSS** *Direct-sequence spread-spectrum* generates a redundant bit pattern for each bit to be transmitted. By using these bit patterns, transmissions can be easily recovered if interfered with or damaged, without the need for retransmission. DSSS delivers higher speeds than FHSS and is used by the 802.11b wireless standard.

- **OFDM** *Orthogonal frequency-division multiplexing* transmits large amounts of data by breaking up the main signal into smaller subsignals sent at the same time over different frequencies. This prevents transmission interference and crosstalk between signals while maintaining a high data rate. OFDM is used by the 802.11a, 802.11ac, 802.11g, and 802.11n standards.

Infrared Technology

Infrared (IR) systems use high frequencies, just below visible light in the electro-magnetic spectrum, to carry data. Like light, IR transmissions can't go through solid objects, and IR is mostly used for short, line-of-sight communications between devices. Infrared technology is rarely used in wireless network applications. Instead, it is geared more toward implementing fixed networks for allowing devices to communicate with each other when in line of sight of their IR ports.

Wireless Access

In a typical WLAN setup, a device called an *access point* is connected to a wired network from a fixed location using standard LAN cabling. The access point acts as a gateway, connecting the wireless and the wired LANs together. A single access point can support a small group of users and can function within a range up to several hundred feet. The access point is usually mounted at the top of a wall or ceiling to provide maximum coverage for the wireless area. The access point and wireless devices usually contain an antenna that can be extended to aid in signal reception. "Fat" access points have the equipment required to handle clients autonomously, in a standalone manner, whereas "thin" access points are essentially a radio and antenna managed remotely by a separate wireless controller that provides switching functionality. Fat access points are more expensive and must be configured separately, whereas thin access points allow for more scalability and centralized management. Many WLAN controllers also do double-duty as network security devices, providing firewall and IDS functionality.

To access the WLAN, the user can use a regular PC with a special WLAN adapter, a laptop computer with a wireless PC card, or even a handheld device such as a smartphone. The wireless adapter appears to the operating system of the computer or device as a typical network adapter.

Site Surveys

The *site survey* is a physical examination and review of your current network environment. An initial site survey should be performed before installation of a wireless network to ensure the environment will be conducive to wireless communications. The survey can also help determine the best placement and coverage for your wireless access points. When your wireless network is in place, you can use site survey software to scan and test your wireless network to examine its power and range. The following sections outline several important issues to examine for the site survey.

Physical Environment Your physical environment can greatly affect the performance of your wireless network:

- Clear or open areas provide better radio range than filled or closed areas.
- Metal physical obstructions can hinder the performance of wireless devices. Avoid placing these devices in a location where a metal barrier is situated between the sending and receiving antennas.
- Radio penetration is affected by the materials used in the building construction. Drywall construction allows greater range than concrete blocks, whereas metal construction can hinder and block radio signals.

Antenna Type and Placement Access points are limited by range—from 100 meters indoors to 500 meters outdoors—depending on the physical environment. In large wireless environments, multiple access points are needed to provide a wide coverage area for the clients. The access point ranges must overlap, so network connectivity will not be lost roaming from one access point to another.

Antenna and access point placement are important to make sure they are not close to any other electrical wires or devices (especially those that broadcast on a similar frequency) where interference can cause a loss of wireless signal. Access points should be positioned at a high, central point of the area that they are servicing to ensure the widest, most unobstructed coverage.

In smaller LAN-based access points, the antenna is attached directly to the device and cannot be moved away from the device. Extend the antenna to its maximum length to ensure a strong signal. Antennas that can be attached to access points with a cable should still be located as close as possible to the access point. The longer the cable, the more chance that signal attenuation or electromagnetic interference (EMI) can occur.

> ### Local Lingo
>
> **Attenuation**   Describes how an electronic signal becomes weaker over greater distances. This applies to both cable and wireless signals.

Many wireless access points use *dipole* antennas that split the signal wire into two wires that provide omnidirectional coverage, with the wireless signal radiating outward in all directions. With 802.11n networks, you can use *MIMO (Multiple Input Multiple Output)* technology, which uses multiple sending and receiving antennas to boost the power and range of the network. All devices on the network must support MIMO to use its multipath benefits. Older hardware uses only a single in/out path.

> ### Exam Tip
>
> Antenna placement is a key factor in ensuring maximum range and power for your wireless network. Be aware of the different issues that affect antenna placement and how to improve wireless network reception.

Power Level Controls   Wireless devices have the capability to limit their power level to control the range and speed of wireless access. This is useful for security purposes if you know you can limit the range of your access point coverage to just the needed areas of your location. This prevents casual, unauthorized access from a longer distance (such as a hacker outside your building).

Exam Tip

War driving is a technique used by hackers to access unsecured wireless networks. By driving around near a company's physical premises, they can scan for unprotected networks.

You may also need to boost the transmit power of specific access points if their range is not reaching difficult points in your physical location where wireless clients experience issues communicating with the network.

The problem with adjusting your power settings is that this also affects your effective data speed on the wireless network because changes to the power and range affect the signal-to-noise ratio, which can lower speeds. For example, setting the power output on your access point to 50 percent instead of 100 percent will decrease the range of your wireless network, but it may also affect data speeds and connection strength for those connected to the network. In many cases, setting the transmit power too high can increase signal noise and data loss, and it may even contravene local rules and standards for signal broadcasting.

Site Survey Software   You can use specialized software for your access points that scans your wireless network and records signal strength and interference levels, depending on your location within your premises. You can run the software on a laptop and walk around your building to look for zones with a low signal strength or high interference. Using this information, you can rearrange your access point and antenna placement, as well as modify your wireless network settings to increase range and power to these low-signal zones.

WLAN Topologies

WLANs can be as small and simple as two PCs or laptops networked together through their wireless interfaces. This type of peer-to-peer (P2P) network requires little configuration and administration, and the wireless devices would only have to be within range of each other to communicate. No intermediary access points or servers are needed on this ad hoc network. Each client would have access only to the resources of the other client.

Networks that are more complex can encompass many access points, connected with many different wireless PCs, laptops, or handheld devices. Installing an access point can extend the range of a small wireless network, effectively doubling the area in which the devices can communicate. The access point is directly connected to a wired network, so any wireless clients accessing that access point can communicate with the resources of the wired LAN through

| FIGURE 10.1 | A typical WLAN configuration |

the access point. Resources on the wired network that wireless clients might access include file servers, mail servers, and the Internet. Figure 10.1 shows an example of a typical configuration for a WLAN access point.

An access point can accommodate many clients, depending on the number and the type of bandwidth transmission required. Typical access points can handle up to approximately 50 client devices. The disadvantage is that the more users connected to the access point, the less bandwidth that's available to each client.

Wireless Protocols

Just like regular networked LANs, WLANs run on specific networking protocols—but optimized for use with wireless communications. As wireless networks began to proliferate, several competing wireless protocols were released that weren't always compatible with each other. A wireless device using one type of protocol might be unable to access a WLAN using an entirely different protocol. The most popular protocol for wireless devices currently in use is the Institute of Electrical and Electronics Engineers (IEEE) standard 802.11n, followed by the older standard 802.11g. The following sections outline some of the most common wireless protocols.

Wireless Access Protocol

The *Wireless Access Protocol (WAP)*, not to be confused with a wireless access point, is a specification that provides the delivery mechanisms for transmitting content information to wireless devices. WAP supports the use of Wireless Markup Language (WML) instead of Hypertext Markup Language (HTML) to send web data to older wireless devices for which the web content must be stripped down to work. This is increasingly not required with modern smartphones.

Security for WAP is handled through the Wireless Transaction Layer Security (WTLS), which provides authentication and encryption functionality like Secure Sockets Layer (SSL) in typical web networking. The wireless client and the server must be authenticated for wireless transactions to remain secure and to provide encryption. WTLS resembles SSL in that both rely on certificates on the client and server to verify the identities of the participants involved.

Exam Tip

Know that WAP security for wireless networks is performed via Wireless Transaction Layer Security (WTLS).

Unfortunately, WAP hasn't caught on as strongly as other wireless protocols and architectures because it's limited to smaller handheld devices, a fact that restricts its usefulness with higher-bandwidth wireless solutions.

Bluetooth

Bluetooth wireless technology is designed to enable and simplify wireless communication between small, mobile devices. To implement wireless methods that eliminate the need for proprietary cables, Bluetooth attempts to allow connectivity between any devices, including peripherals such as cameras and scanners. For example, no cables are needed to transfer digital photographs between a camera and a PC, or to transfer data between an address book program on your PC and your smartphone, because the communications can be performed using Bluetooth wireless. Bluetooth has low power consumption and transmits via common radio frequencies (2.4 GHz). Configuration is usually performed dynamically in the background, allowing seamless communications between Bluetooth wireless devices.

Bluetooth also enables devices to form small wireless networks called *piconets,* which are established using a radio transceiver embedded within each Bluetooth device. This is designed to operate in a noisy radio environment and to provide a fast, robust, and secure connection between devices. The range for Bluetooth, however, is much smaller than typical wireless networks, allowing for a link range between 10 cm (about 4 inches) and 10 meters (about 33 feet), because typical Bluetooth connectivity is used between one device and another. Figure 10.2 illustrates how a Bluetooth network works.

Smartphone   Tablet

Laptop

Scanner   Video camera

FIGURE 10.2   Bluetooth network

802.11

IEEE 802.11 refers to a family of specifications developed for WLAN technology. 802.11 specifies an over-the-air interface between a wireless client and a base station, or between two wireless clients. The IEEE accepted the specification in 1997.

Several specifications are included in the 802.11 family:

- **802.11** Applies to WLANs and provides 1- or 2-Mbps transmission in the 2.4-GHz band using either FHSS or DSSS.

- **802.11a** An extension to 802.11 that applies to WLANs and provides up to 54 Mbps in the 5-GHz band. 802.11a uses an OFDM encoding scheme, rather than FHSS or DSSS.

- **802.11b** Also referred to as 802.11 High Rate or Wi-Fi, this extension to 802.11 applies to WLANs and provides 11-Mbps transmission (with a fallback to 5.5, 2, and 1 Mbps) in the 2.4-GHz band. 802.11b uses only DSSS. It was a 1999 ratification to the original 802.11 standard, allowing wireless functionality to provide performance comparable to the Ethernet 10BaseT standard, which runs at 10 Mbps.

- **802.11g** Applies to WLANs and provides 54+ Mbps in the 2.4-GHz band.

- **802.11n** Applies to WLANs and operates on both the 2.4-GHz band and the 5-GHz band. It can provide from 54 Mbps to 600 Mbps with the use of four spatial streams at a channel width of 40 MHz. 802.11n uses OFDM and can utilize MIMO antenna technologies to boost power and range.

- **802.11ac** The newest standard, 802.11ac has a maximum throughput of 1 Gbps in the 5-GHz band. This increase improves performance to support the increased requirements of streaming services (such as video, audio, and gaming). It also uses OFDM.

Travel Assistance	
For detailed information on the IEEE wireless standards, see http://standards.ieee.org/wireless/.	

Currently, the 802.11n standard is the most popular for home and business wireless users. However, many 802.11g wireless devices and access points still exist and interoperate with 801.11n networks. The popularity of wireless networks has created the need for even better security for WLANs, both at home and in the workplace. Without any type of security mechanisms, WLANs can be easily compromised; with no mechanisms for authentication or encryption configured on the WLAN, an unauthorized user can simply bring her own wireless laptop or wireless device into the range of the WLAN for instant access.

> **Travel Advisory**
>
> With the proliferation of home networks with high-speed Internet connections, many users have also added wireless systems to their home networks. When proper wireless security measures are not implemented, unauthorized users can access a nearby network without subscribing to the service and perform illegal activities, using someone else's home network so that these activities cannot be traced back to the hacker.

Securing Wireless Networks

Securing a WLAN with as many layers of security as possible is extremely important. The following methods can collectively be used to secure access to 802.11 networks:

- Access point security
- A service set identifier (SSID)
- Media Access Control (MAC) address filtering
- Encryption
- A secure virtual private network (VPN)
- A personal firewall
- Captive portals

Access Point Security

Security for a WLAN begins at its primary points of access, and the security configuration of the wireless access point is of critical importance to the network administrator. Most access points allow administrative configuration to be performed wirelessly; however, this creates a security risk, because any user with wireless access can attempt to access the configuration via brute force or other account-cracking methods. If possible, configuration should be limited to a wired connection, and the administrator's machine must be physically cabled to the access point to perform these tasks. Remote configuration should be disabled if wired access can be performed on the access points. If wireless configuration must be used, network administrators should be sure that this occurs over encrypted channels such as Hypertext Transfer Protocol over Secure Socket Layer (HTTPS) and SSL (though deprecated), or TLS.

The administrator's username and password must be secure, like any username and password used on an important server or router on the network. This includes modifying the default "admin" account name (if possible) to something less recognizable and using a secure password of at least eight alphanumeric characters, including uppercase, lowercase, and special characters.

At this point, several security features can be enabled for the entire WLAN, as discussed in the following sections. Ensure that all access points have the same configuration; otherwise, you might leave one of your access points with security weaknesses and vulnerabilities that can be exploited. For example, if you forget to disable SSID broadcast on one of your access points, this allows unauthorized users to attempt to access the network using the SSID name.

Service Set Identifier

The simplest wireless network access control is the use of a network identifier or name. This *SSID* can be set up on a single wireless access points or a group of wireless access points. It provides a way to segment a wireless network into multiple networks serviced by one or more access points. This is helpful in companies that are separated by departments or physical floor locations.

To access a network, client computers must be configured with the correct identifier. For roaming users, multiple identifiers can be enabled on their wireless devices, giving them access to different networks as required. This type of security is minimal, however, because it simply employs a network password, which could easily be compromised by word of mouth or through access points that broadcast the network name.

> ### Travel Advisory
>
> Many access points advertise their SSID by default. For security reasons, check the settings of all your access points to disable this feature. The disadvantage of disabling broadcasts, however, is that new clients cannot see and connect to the network if they do not know the SSID name. It is a standard practice to disable SSID broadcasting, but at the same time, anyone who wants to crack a wireless network knows that even with SSID broadcasting disabled, the network is detectable with basic hacking tools.

MAC Address Filtering

Access points can be identified with network names and passwords, but a client computer can be identified by the unique MAC address of its wireless network card. Access points can be configured with a list of MAC addresses associated with the client computers allowed to access the wireless network. If a wireless client's MAC address isn't included in this list, the wireless client isn't allowed to connect with the access point and the network. This is a much better solution than using network identifiers alone, but maintaining the list of client MAC addresses can quickly become a daunting task with larger networks. In addition, each access point must be configured individually so each node contains the same list of addresses. This type of security is best suited to small networks because the administrative overhead quickly limits its scalability.

MAC filtering is not considered an effective security measure, simply because wireless sniffing can give an attacker the legitimate allowed MAC addresses he needs to connect, which can then be easily spoofed. Like turning off SSID broadcasting, it is better than doing nothing, but is not very effective in preventing attacks. That's where other security methods, such as using a secure protocol like WPA, come into play.

Exam Tip

You can enable MAC address filtering on access points to control which clients can (or cannot) access the network, but understand that it is the bare minimum of security measures and can be easily defeated.

Encryption

The *Wired Equivalent Privacy (WEP)* security protocol is an IEEE 802.11 standard for encrypted communication between wireless clients and access points. WEP uses the RC4 key encryption algorithm to encrypt communications before they are transmitted over the wireless network. Each client or access point on the WLAN must use the same encryption key. The key is manually configured on each access point and each client before they can access the network. Basic WEP encryption has been proven vulnerable to attack because of the weak 40-bit RC4 cipher, and even 128-bit WEP encryption is easily cracked. Most devices now support up to 256-bit encryption. If your devices do not support WPA (described in the next section), they should use 256-bit WEP encryption in conjunction with the MAC address filtering and network identifier methods described previously. A better option, however, is to upgrade older devices so they can support more robust security protocols, such as WPA and WPA2.

Exam Tip

Know that the highest level of encryption available, such as WPA or WPA2, is best to use. Older levels of encryption, such as WEP, have proven to be vulnerable.

WPA and WPA2 Security

Wi-Fi Protected Access (WPA) is the most recent and secure form of encryption for wireless networks and was created to fix several weaknesses in the WEP standard. WPA2 is the 802.11i standard, an amendment to the 802.11 standard to improve encryption security. WPA requires either no authentication (open), authentication to a RADIUS server (WPA-Enterprise), or the use of a pre-shared key (WPA-Personal, or WPA-PSK [for pre-shared key]). Originally conceived for personal or small business networks, WPA-Personal can be used to mutually authenticate wireless client devices and wireless access points. The pre-shared key method means that all devices on the WLAN must use the same passphrase key to access the network. WPA-Enterprise is more robust, but complex and hard to use, and was developed for larger infrastructures, requiring the use of the 802.1X authentication protocol. It is more suited for environments with hundreds of clients, where using a single passphrase key for each device is not scalable, and the authentication server takes care of key management between the wireless devices on the network.

With WPA, data is encrypted using a 128-bit key that is routinely changed during sessions using the *Temporal Key Integrity Protocol (TKIP)*. TKIP ensures that packets are always relayed with a unique key. This ensures that a single session key cannot be hacked by the time the protocol changes keys. WPA also provides for improved integrity checking of data traversing the wireless network to ensure it cannot be intercepted and changed on the way to its destination. This provides much more protection than the original WEP protocol; however, TKIP is cryptographically like WEP and is vulnerable to many of the same attacks. WEP and TKIP are no longer supported by the Wi-Fi Alliance.

A WPA network is only as strong as the passphrase used. A WPA passphrase can be from 8 to 63 characters, and it is recommended that this passphrase be as strong as possible and not based on known dictionary words. It should include numbers, uppercase and lowercase letters, and special characters such as the @ symbol. All devices on the WPA network must share the same passphrase, including all access points.

WPA2 is the most recent version that replaces WPA with a stronger 256-bit encryption and adds Robust Security Network (RSN) support that includes added protection for ad hoc networks, key caching, pre-roaming authentication, and the Counter Mode with Cipher Block Chaining Message Authentication Code Protocol (CCMP). CCMP utilizes the Advanced Encryption Standard (AES) cipher to replace TKIP. It is a block cipher using a 128-bit key and is secure against the bulk of attacks currently directed against wireless networks.

All currently manufactured devices support WPA2 in addition to WPA, using AES. If your network devices support WPA2, they should use this type of encryption. However, many older devices do not support WPA2, and you will have to use WPA or some other common encryption method that can be supported by all your clients.

Wi-Fi Protected Setup

Although not a security standard, *Wi-Fi Protected Setup (WPS)* should be discussed so that you better understand its role within a wireless network. WPS was designed to allow less technical users to more easily set up a wireless network and associated peripheral devices. For example, a WPS-enabled router might only require the home administrator to hold down a button combination on the device to sync to the network. This is perceived as easier for an inexperienced user to implement than a passphrase. However, there are attacks, discussed later in the chapter, that have shown the WPS standard to be quite insecure.

802.1X

802.1X is an IEEE standard, just like the 802.3 Ethernet standards and 802.11 wireless networking standards, but it is not a wireless standard per se. Although 802.1X is probably most seen on corporate wireless networks as the preferred form of authentication, it can be used in wired networks as well. This makes it easier for wireless and wired networks to interoperate, because they can use the same authentication methods and can connect to each other quite easily. 802.1X is called a *port-based* access control method, and can use a wide variety of different security protocols. In that respect, it's more of a security authentication framework than a protocol itself, because it allows various protocols to be used for authentication.

Remember from our discussion of WPA and WPA2 that they both can use pre-shared keys for the personal versions of their implementation, or 802.1X for the enterprise implementation. This is the context we're speaking in now. When using this type of enterprise implementation, not only can you authenticate WPA and WPA2 devices, but you can also require the users themselves to authenticate with the network they are connecting to. This makes it so that not only are you certain unauthorized devices can't connect to the network, but the user operating it must be authorized as well. 802.1X can use several different types of authentication protocols, including the Extensible Authentication Protocol (EAP), and its variants, which we'll discuss in the next section.

Wireless Authentication Protocols

While encryption protocols such as WEP, WPA, and WPA2 focus on the encryption of the communications link and data for wireless networks, there is still the need to provide a secure authentication function for accessing wireless networks. The protocols in the following sections are popular methods for the transmission and security of authentication data within standard wireless encryption protocols.

EAP

The *Extensible Authentication Protocol (EAP)* is used primarily in WEP-, WPA-, and WPA2-based wireless networks for securely transporting authentication data, but it has also been used previously for remote access authentication to local area networks.

EAP separates the message exchange from the authentication process by using a different exchange layer, and it provides a module-based infrastructure that supports several different types of authentication methods. Microsoft Windows uses EAP to authenticate remote access, VPN, and site-to-site connections over Point-to-Point Protocol (PPP). With this method, you can use most standard authentication servers, such as Remote Authentication Dial-In User Service (RADIUS) or Kerberos, to authenticate connections.

Although EAP provides a very flexible authentication infrastructure, one of the major issues with EAP is that part of the initial exchange is transmitted in clear text, including authentication credentials and results. For WEP, WPA, and WPA2 wireless networks, EAP authentication occurs before any wireless transmissions are encrypted.

EAP has been extended with other protocols to help improve security, such as EAP-TLS and EAP-TTLS, which utilize Transport Layer Security (TLS), and to support the use of authentication with client certificates. This means that even if a hacker could obtain a user's authentication credentials, he still would not be able to access the wireless network without the client's private key, which establishes the encrypted session. EAP can also be used in combination with RADIUS and 802.1X to provide a federated wireless network; this has been implemented widely across the educational sector via eduroam, allowing wireless users across a campus to roam freely across more than 10,000 locations globally.

LEAP

The *Lightweight Extensible Authentication Protocol (LEAP)* was created specifically by Cisco Systems, Inc. LEAP was developed to address some of the security issues of EAP, while still providing its flexibility of authentication methods. LEAP provides its authentication using its own version of MS-CHAP (the Microsoft version of the Client Handshake Authentication Protocol, which is insecure) to a RADIUS server. LEAP uses frequent changes to a WEP encryption key and client reauthentication to prevent the current key from being in use too long. Due to general weaknesses in the WEP key itself, LEAP has been largely replaced by PEAP, LEAP-TLS, and Cisco's own replacement, EAP Flexible Authentication via Secure Tunneling (EAP-FAST).

PEAP

The *Protected Extensible Authentication Protocol (PEAP)* is a protocol that uses TLS to transport EAP within an encrypted communications tunnel over a wireless connection. This has advantages over EAP-TLS, a similar protocol, because there is no need for a client certificate.

With PEAP, an encrypted tunnel is formed to a server using TLS and a server-side certificate. This provides for secure key exchange between the client and the server, which then allows for normal EAP authentication methods for the client authentication stage.

VPN Wireless Access

For larger networks with high security requirements, a VPN wireless access solution is a preferable alternative or addition to the other solutions discussed. VPN solutions are already widely deployed to provide remote workers with secure access to the network via the Internet. The VPN provides a secure, dedicated tunnel through a public network such as the Internet. Various tunneling protocols are used in conjunction with standard, centralized authentication solutions using a login and password.

The same VPN technology can also be used for secure wireless access. In this application, the public network is the wireless network itself. Wireless access is isolated from the rest of the network by a VPN server and, for extra security, an intermediary firewall. Authentication and full encryption over the wireless network are provided through the VPN server. The VPN-based solution is scalable to many users. Figure 10.3 illustrates the architecture of a VPN-based wireless network.

| FIGURE 10.3 | A VPN-based wireless network |

Personal Firewall

In addition to the overall wireless network security, all wireless PCs and mobile devices should be equipped with personal firewall software protection. Like home computers with permanent cable modem or digital subscriber line (DSL) Internet access connections, wireless clients can be vulnerable to attacks by unauthorized users accessing the same network. The personal firewall software can be used to protect the roaming user's confidential local data against many types of possible attacks for both incoming and outgoing connections.

> ### Exam Tip
>
> Be aware of the advantages and disadvantages of the wireless access security solutions discussed in this chapter. Depending on the type of network and the scope of security required, some of these solutions won't be acceptable, or they'll need to be augmented by other methods.

Captive Portals

Have you ever tried to access a hotel website and been presented with a page asking you to log in with your name and room number? If so, you've experienced a captive portal. *Captive portals* are designed to halt a user before accessing a wireless network by trapping packets until a web browser is opened, where the portal opens for entering credentials or payment information. The user will generally be unable to perform any functions, such as web browsing, until she has successfully passed the portal.

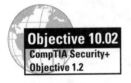

Analyze and Differentiate Among Types of Wireless Attacks

Objective 10.02
CompTIA Security+
Objective 1.2

The following sections describe some common security issues with wireless networks.

Data Emanation

In its most basic form, *data emanation* occurs when any sort of data is transmitted over an electromagnetic medium. For example, when electricity passes through a cable, it creates an electromagnetic field that can be detected and measured. In communications, you could capture data emanation from a message and use it to rearrange the electronic signal to reveal the original communication.

This is a serious issue in wireless networking, as unprotected and unsecured wireless communications can be easily intercepted and an unauthorized user can steal usernames, passwords, and sensitive private data. All information on an unencrypted WLAN is transmitted in clear text, and any wireless user can use a protocol analyzer or sniffer application to view the data traversing the WLAN. All WLANs should communicate using secure encrypted channels to prevent eavesdropping from unauthorized users. The actual equipment for the wireless LAN, such as access points and other wireless devices, must also be physically secure.

Jamming

Occasionally, a wireless network will experience interference from another wireless device, such as a baby monitor or cordless telephone, causing interference with each other. This interference can interrupt wireless network transmission and reception. For the most part, this interference is unintentional; however, *jamming* is a form of intentional interference on wireless networks, designed as a denial-of-service (DoS) attack. This type of attack is conducted by overpowering the signals of a legitimate wireless access point, typically using a rogue access point with its transmit power set to very high levels. However, other electronic devices can be used to intentionally create interference or jamming in wireless networks as well, including some very specialized devices that can be acquired from the Internet. The only way to really prevent jamming and interference is by proactively looking for sources of wireless signals that are not coming from the corporate wireless network. The sources are usually in the same frequency range, and may come from malicious wireless clients or rogue wireless access points.

Bluetooth Vulnerabilities

Several vulnerabilities in vendor implementations of Bluetooth have allowed unauthorized access to personal data on cell phones and computer devices. Bluetooth can also be susceptible to unauthorized messages, a practice called *bluejacking*. An unauthorized user can send unwanted messages to another Bluetooth device in range of the originating device. This has most often been used for Bluetooth spam advertising, in which a Bluetooth device such as a smartphone suddenly receives a text message containing the spam message. Bluejacking is relatively harmless and a nuisance, much like spam e-mails, but there is the potential for harmful media to be transferred from one device to another.

A more serious Bluetooth vulnerability is called *bluesnarfing*. Many Bluetooth phones and devices use a discovery mode that allows a hacker to detect and connect automatically to other Bluetooth devices, much like a WLAN.

Without proper authentication, an unauthorized user can connect to an unprotected Bluetooth device and access any data stored on it. If an unsuspecting user leaves his device in discovery mode, it is not protected from access by other Bluetooth devices in the vicinity.

Bluetooth defines three security modes:

- **Nonsecure mode**   No security features are enabled.
- **Service-level security mode**   Application security policies are used, in which the actual applications on the wireless device are responsible for security.
- **Link-level security mode**   The most secure of the three modes authenticates the actual communications link before data transmission can begin. Data encryption can also be performed in this mode once the link is authenticated. Authentication allows the devices to decide whether a connection will be formed based on available identification at the hardware level. Once the link is established, additional security might be applied to the data transmission using encryption. Stronger encryption can also be enabled at the software level, if needed.

Exam Tip

Remember that bluesnarfing is a serious Bluetooth security threat, and link-level security is recommended to protect the communications link and transfer of data. Bluetooth should be disabled if you are not using it.

Near-Field Communication

Near-field communication (NFC) is a standard used primarily in mobile devices to facilitate easily accessed communications between two or more devices by bringing them into proximity (likely touching them together). This is often used within applications to send pictures, contacts, and other media between compatible devices. However, while the range of NFC is quite limited to the immediate proximity of the devices, the standard itself is essentially an emanation and is quite vulnerable to eavesdropping and man-in-the-middle attacks by anyone within that same vicinity. NFC uses RFID technologies, and unfortunately is vulnerable to several types of attacks. These attacks include eavesdropping by another NFC device, man-in-the-middle attacks, and relay attacks (relaying modified information back and forth from the victim's device, pretending to be the victim). Many WPS-enabled devices also use NFC, making wireless hacking of WPS-enabled networks trivial.

War Driving

Many corporate WLANs and home-based wireless networks are set up and configured with no encryption or access control. Hackers have been known to roam neighborhoods with a large corporate presence and use simple laptops with wireless connectivity to connect to unprotected WLANs and access their resources. This is called *war driving*. Several programs are available that allow unauthorized users to scan an area for open and unprotected wireless networks. After accessing the network, the user can attempt several types of attacks, such as eavesdropping and sniffing the wireless data, or accessing and capturing the data on other wireless devices on the network.

Administrators can lower the susceptibility of their wireless networks to war driving attacks by encrypting their networks and disabling the broadcast of their SSIDs. These and other techniques are discussed earlier in the section "Securing Wireless Networks."

Access Points (Evil Twin)

With wireless networks, much of the typical physical security that prevents someone from plugging into a network is unavailable. Anyone within the vicinity of a WLAN can connect to it easily using a laptop or other wireless-equipped device. Unauthorized users can also set up their own wireless access points to which unsuspecting users connect and transmit sensitive and private data, including username and password credentials, directly on the hacker's network. Sometimes called *evil twins*, often these access points are set up with legitimate names (for example, as a Wi-Fi hot spot for a popular network carrier). The wireless access is typically set up as password-free and unencrypted, and an unsuspecting user could connect and use her banking or credit card details, which are then stolen by the hacker for the purposes of identity theft and fraud.

You can prevent rogue devices and access points from connecting to your wireless network by setting a unique SSID name and encrypting the network, since any rogue access points and devices will require the SSID name and encryption passphrase to connect to the network. In certain cases, MAC address filtering can also be used to allow only certain hardware addresses access to the network; however, this is not practical for networks with hundreds of wireless clients. Your networks should be routinely scanned for evidence of rogue access points or devices using wireless scanning tools such as NetStumbler; just walking the area with a laptop scanning for access points can help you determine which legit (and not-so-legit) points you have.

Exam Tip

Be sure not to connect to WAPs that don't require authentication or that sound "similar" due to similar SSIDs. They very likely are rogue access points.

Local Lingo

MAC address   MAC stands for Media Access Control. A MAC address is a unique hardware address assigned to network interface cards. This address is expressed in hexadecimal format.

As an end user accessing a free rogue access point, your only protection is to always use secure, encrypted websites via SSL when using an open wireless access point you are unfamiliar with, or use a VPN connection when you are connected to the access point. This way, if you happen to be connected to a rogue evil twin access point, your information remains encrypted and undecipherable to the hacker. Be careful when connecting to wireless access points advertised as a popular wireless provider, and make sure that the page is legitimate before entering any type of authentication or payment card details.

Deauthentication and Disassociation

Deauthenticating (sometimes known as *disassociating*) a wireless host from the access point forces the client to reconnect and exchange the wireless key. There are different methods and desired ends for conducting this type of attack; if it is successful, an attacker can either join or intercept traffic from the wireless network (man-in-the-middle), or prevent an authorized client from associating back to the legitimate network, essentially performing a denial of service (DoS).

War Chalking

War chalking is the act of marking a physical area, such as the wall of a building or sidewalk, with symbols that indicate a free and open wireless access point is active in that location. War chalking was more popular in the earlier days of wireless access when local Wi-Fi access points (hot spots) were few and far between. It indicated to a mobile user that she could connect her wireless device to an open access point in that area if she needed to quickly access the Internet.

This is an outdated practice in an era of almost full wireless or mobile data access coverage, but it can still present a security risk, primarily if the indicated access point is a rogue evil twin where the network traffic will be monitored by a hacker looking for authentication credentials and credit card numbers.

Packet Sniffing and Eavesdropping

On an unencrypted open wireless network, any hacker can use a packet sniffer or network eavesdropping tool to analyze wireless network data as it passes through the network. The hacker can use this information to obtain authentication credentials of users, including usernames and passwords, and sensitive financial information such as credit card and bank account numbers. The hacker could also initiate a man-in-the-middle attack, where data is modified en route to its destination. For example, the hacker could spoof the sender or destination address, or even a network MAC address to emulate another host.

To prevent packet sniffing and eavesdropping, the wireless network must be encrypted with a strong encryption technique. While security measures such as SSID names, disabled broadcasting, authentication, and MAC address access control can help prohibit unauthorized access, only by encrypting the data can you make it indecipherable to those who are monitoring network traffic.

Replay Attacks

Much in the same spirit as traditional replay attacks, wireless replay attacks occur when an unauthorized user captures network traffic and then sends the communication to its original destination, acting as the original sender.

Travel Assistance	
For more detailed information on replay attacks, see Chapter 9.	

WPS Attacks

As discussed previously, WPS was implemented for ease of use, not security. There are attacks that utilize an active WPS implementation to compromise more computing assets. For example, the Reaver tool conducts a brute-force attack against a WPS registrar personal identification number (PIN), usually residing on an access point. If the attack is successful, it will then recover the WPA or WPA2 passphrase for the access point.

Brute-force attacks against WPS can be mitigated by using a time-out period for the WPS-enabled device that disables the PIN. Mitigating WPS attacks is further complicated by the fact that in many WPS-enabled devices, disabling the WPS feature does not result in the feature being disabled—it only "appears" disabled to the user. The device would still be vulnerable to attack.

WEP/WPA Attacks

There are many attacks against networks utilizing WEP, such as dictionary-based attacks that passively analyze traffic and build a dictionary file, or that utilize an open-source dictionary file that looks to break the key. Other attacks can look to decrypt traffic at the access point. The most serious against WEP is the IV attack.

IV Attack

On wireless networks encrypted with WEP, the WEP encryption technique uses a special 24-bit *initialization vector (IV)* that is combined with its 40-bit WEP key to encrypt each network packet. This extends the life of the WEP key, as the IV changes with each transmission. WEP has proved to be an insecure protocol, and coupled with a short 24-bit IV factor that is sent in clear text, it could enable a hacker to discover the IV through repetition. In very large and busy wireless networks, the IV itself can be repeated in a space of hours. The hacker can then use various utilities to decrypt subsequent packets that were encrypted with the same IV key stream. This makes it possible to not even need to decrypt the WEP key to decrypt packets.

This type of attack has become less common as WEP is replaced by stronger encryption methods such as WPA2.

TKIP Attack

WPA networks are not impervious to attack. WPA networks utilizing TKIP are vulnerable to attacks that decrypt and recover portions of the data, such as the Beck–Tews and Ohigashi–Morii attacks. While the size of the data decrypted can be somewhat negligible (between 12 and 596 bytes), an attacker can use the retrieved information to conduct further attacks on the network. These attacks can be mitigated through use of WPA2 combined with AES.

WPA2 Attacks

WPA2 attacks are also possible if the WAP uses a weak passphrase ("password," for example). Cracking WPA2 is done by deauthenticating the client and WAP, forcing them to reestablish connections by performing a four-way handshake.

If you can capture a full handshake (which is very easy to do with the command airdump-ng after deauthenticating them), then it's only an issue of cracking an easy-to-guess password, because you capture the key as well during the handshake. Password length and complexity are the keys to securing WPA2.

CHECKPOINT

✔**Objective 10.01: Implement Wireless Networks in a Secure Manner** More so than security for wired networks, wireless security heavily involves the use of encryption technologies, coupled with traditional (wired) security mechanisms such as access control and authentication. Wireless networks should use WPA or WPA2 encryption with a strong passphrase. Also, you should disable SSID broadcasts and use a unique SSID name, as well as use MAC address filtering if possible. In addition, you should have access points that are properly secured with a strong password for administrative configuration, with remote configuration disabled. Captive portals require a user to authenticate (and often pay) through a web browser before they can use the network.

✔**Objective 10.02: Analyze and Differentiate Among Types of Wireless Attacks** Data emanation causes unauthorized access to authentication credentials and unencrypted sensitive data. Jamming is a form of intentional interference on wireless networks, designed as a denial-of-service (DoS) attack. Hackers use war driving techniques to drive around looking for open, unencrypted Wi-Fi networks. A rogue "evil twin" access point masquerades as a legitimate wireless access point to trick users into communicating sensitive information over a network completely under the control of a hacker. War chalking identifies open Wi-Fi hot spot locations by marking physical locations with symbols. Hackers can use packet sniffers to eavesdrop on unencrypted wireless networks to discover authentication credentials and sensitive data being passed in clear text. WPS attacks can utilize tools such as Reaver to compromise the access point passphrase through a number of issues with WPS. IV attacks focus on the weak, 24-bit initialization vector that is used to help strengthen WEP keys, and which can then be used to break the WEP key. TKIP attacks focus on decrypting small portions of data that can be used to create more damaging attacks.

REVIEW QUESTIONS

1. Match the WLAN term to its definition.

Uses a narrowband carrier that changes frequency in a pattern known to both the transmitter and the receiver	A. Frequency-Hopping Spread-Spectrum (FHSS)
Transmits large amounts of data by breaking up the main signal into smaller subsignals sent at the same time over different frequencies	B. Direct-Sequence Spread-Spectrum (DSSS)
Generates a redundant bit pattern for each bit to be transmitted	C. Orthogonal Frequency-Division Multiplexing (OFDM)

2. You have set up a wireless network for your small office of 50 users. Which of the following encryption protocols would you implement to ensure the highest level of encryption security?

    A. WAP

    B. WPA

    C. WEP 128 bit

    D. WPA2

3. You are connecting to a secure, encrypted wireless network. During the initial connection phase, you are asked to enter a passphrase. Which WPA encryption method is in use on the network?

    A. WPA-EAP

    B. WPA-TKIP

    C. WPA-PSK

    D. WPA-Enterprise

4. You are setting up new Bluetooth-enabled mobile phones for your executive team. You should enable _____ to prevent bluesnarfing.

5. You are setting up a new wireless security network for your small office. You have set the SSID of the network to a secure value. Which other action can you take to enhance SSID security?

    A. Enable SSID broadcast.

    B. Enable SSID tunneling.

    C. Disable SSID snarfing.

    D. Disable SSID broadcast.

6. Which of the following types of wireless attacks utilizes a weakness in WEP key generation and encryption to decrypt WEP encrypted data?

    A. IV attack

    B. War driving

    C. PSK attack

    D. Eavesdropping

7. To further secure your wireless network, you implement MAC address filtering. Which of the following statements describes the wireless network behavior after you do this?

    A. It allows wireless access only for specified MAC addresses.

    B. It prevents wireless access only from specified MAC addresses.

    C. It encrypts only specified wireless device MAC addresses.

    D. It encrypts only MAC addresses not specified.

8. After checking the signal strength of a specific floor of your building, you realize that two of the farthest offices on the floor have very poor signal strength. Which of the following actions can you perform to provide a cost-effective solution to increase signal strength to that part of the building?

    A. Disable encryption to speed up the network.

    B. Add another access point.

    C. Use a cable to extend the antenna range of the closest access point.

    D. Switch to the 5-GHz band instead of 2.4 GHz.

9. You are installing a wireless network in a manufacturing facility. Which of the following aspects of the wireless network do you concentrate on to prevent security issues with EMI?

    A. Use of WPA2 encryption

    B. Use of 802.11g or 802.11n

    C. SSID network name

    D. Access point and antenna placement

10. Access points generally have a range of from _____ indoors to _____ outdoors.

REVIEW ANSWERS

1. **A** **C** **B**

Uses a narrowband carrier that changes frequency in a pattern known to both the transmitter and the receiver	A. Frequency-Hopping Spread-Spectrum (FHSS)
Transmits large amounts of data by breaking up the main signal into smaller subsignals sent at the same time over different frequencies	C. Orthogonal Frequency-Division Multiplexing (OFDM)
Generates a redundant bit pattern for each bit to be transmitted	B. Direct-Sequence Spread-Spectrum (DSSS)

2. **D** WPA2 is currently the strongest level of encryption security available for a wireless network. WPA2 replaces the weaker WPA and adds RSN support that includes added protection for ad hoc networks, key caching, pre-roaming authentication, and CCMP, which utilizes the AES cipher to replace TKIP.

3. **C** WPA-PSK uses a pre-shared key passphrase that requires all devices on the wireless network to use the same passphrase to access the network. WPA-Enterprise uses an authentication server to perform key management and exchange for all wireless clients.

4. **link-level security** Bluesnarfing is a hacking method in which an unauthorized user can connect to unprotected Bluetooth devices and access any data stored on them. Enabling link-level security authenticates the actual communications link before data transmission begins. Data encryption can also be performed when the link is authenticated.

5. **D** By disabling SSID broadcast, you ensure your access points will not advertise the SSID they are using for wireless clients to connect. A user would require prior knowledge of the SSID before he could access the network.

6. **A** The IV (initialization vector) attack uses the weakness in the 24-bit generated IV that is paired with the WEP encryption key. The IV can be discovered over time on busy networks that use repeated IV values, which can then be used to decrypt the cipher stream without the hacker knowing the WEP key.

7. **A** A list of authorized client MAC addresses must be configured on each access point for the network. If any client tries to communicate with the access point and its MAC address isn't in the list, it will be denied access.

8. **B** You can use a cable and an external antenna to extend the range of your closest access point to the office with the low signal. This is an easy and inexpensive solution rather than purchasing and installing a new access point.

9. **D** You need to make sure that the antenna and access point are not placed close to any other electrical wires or devices (especially those that broadcast on a similar frequency), where electrical interference can cause a loss of wireless signal.

10. **100 meters to 500 meters** Access points are limited by range—from *100 meters* indoors to *500 meters* outdoors—depending on the physical environment. In large wireless environments, multiple access points are needed to provide a wide coverage area for the clients. The access point ranges must overlap, so network connectivity will not be lost when a user roams from one access point to another.

Host, Application, and Data Security

Securing Host Systems

	NEWBIE	SOME EXPERIENCE	EXPERT
ETA	4 hours	3 hours	2 hours

Although your communications networks are the primary origins for external threats to your internal systems, you must also dedicate resources to the security of your organization's host systems on the network. System administrators must be aware of the numerous threats and risks to their server and client systems that originate within your networks. Malicious software such as viruses, worms, Trojan horse programs, and logic bombs can wreak havoc on an unsecured server or client system, while up-and-coming ransomware and crypto-malware require a decision to be made: pay or risk losing your data permanently.

Host security includes using a strong security baseline and making sure all operating system and application software is up to date and that all user accounts and passwords are as secure as possible. Diverse, specialized host security software is also required to scan and monitor the system for dangerous malware and attempts at intrusion.

In addition to more traditional system security, mobile devices are also a cause for concern. Due to their portable nature, mobile devices are a prime risk for theft, and these devices must be secure to prevent unauthorized access and loss of confidential data. In addition, malware can be transmitted by a universal serial bus (USB) key or external hard drive to the system just as easily as malware can be spread via e-mail or the Web. This chapter explores various security threats and risks for host systems, including software threats such as malicious programs (viruses, worms, Trojan horses, and so on), system peripherals and removable storage, and account and password threats. It also describes host security hardening techniques.

Objective 11.01 Analyze and Differentiate Among Types of Malware

Systems security means not only securing sensitive data against unauthorized access, but also protecting the integrity and existence of that data from malicious users and software. Most companies use security resources, such as security guards and cameras, to prevent unauthorized physical access to their equipment and facilities. Organizations must also protect themselves from threats originating from the numerous technological pathways that can potentially provide unauthorized system access. Damage from virus attacks or unauthorized access gained via back-door or Trojan horse types of programs can be catastrophic. A simple worm attached to an e-mail message can cause mail and network systems to grind to a halt. Other viruses contain payloads that destroy or damage information that might never be recovered if a backup plan is not in place. System administrators must be aware of the numerous types of system software attacks as well as know how these attacks enter the system and what can be done to rectify the issue if they infect a system. First and foremost, proactive protection in the form of knowledge and user education is critical in dealing with these types of threats.

Viruses

Viruses are probably the most common and prevalent type of system attack. A *virus* is a computer program that requires user intervention (such as clicking it or copying it to media or a host) within the affected system, even if the virus program does not harm the system. Most computer viruses self-replicate without the knowledge of the computer user.

Similar to a human virus, computer viruses can be passed along from one system to another—via e-mail messages, instant messaging, website downloads, removable media, and network connections. Enormous amounts of expense and time can be required to clean up and restore operations after a virus attack. Some companies take many days, or even weeks, to get back to full operations after their systems have been infected with a virus. For certain time-sensitive businesses, a virus infection can be fatal to the entire computer system and company operations.

Types of Viruses

Viruses come in a variety of forms, with different locations and methods of infection and payloads of varying severity. The following sections outline some common virus types.

Boot Sector Viruses   *Boot sector viruses* infect the boot sector or partition table of a disk. The *boot sector* is used by the computer to determine what operating systems (OSs) are present on the system to boot. The most common way a boot sector virus finds its way into a system is through an infected disk or removable media device that is inserted into the computer. After infecting the boot sector, the virus will not allow the system to boot into the operating system, rendering the computer useless until the boot sector is repaired.

The best way to remove a boot sector virus from a system is to boot the system using an antivirus or similar emergency recovery media. This lets you start up the computer with basic start-up files, bypassing the boot sector, and then run the antivirus program on the recovery media.

Companion Viruses A *companion virus* disguises itself as a legitimate program, using the name of a legitimate program but with a different extension. For example, a virus might be named *program.com* to emulate a file called *program.exe*. Typically, the virus runs the legitimate program immediately after installing the virus code, so it appears the system is performing normally. Some viruses replace the original legitimate file with their own version that performs the same tasks and includes new malicious code to run with it.

File Infector Viruses *File infector viruses* generally infect files that have the extension .com or .exe. These viruses can be extremely destructive because they try to replicate and spread further by infecting other executable programs on the system with the same extension. Sometimes, a file infector virus destroys the program it infects by overwriting the original code.

Travel Advisory

If your computer is afflicted with a file infector virus, do not attach it to a network because it could start infecting files on other workstations and file servers.

Macro Viruses A macro is an instruction that carries out program commands automatically within an application. Macros are typically used in popular office applications such as Microsoft Word and Excel. A *macro virus* uses the internal workings of the application to perform malicious operations when a file containing the macro is opened, such as deleting files or opening other virus-executable programs. Sometimes, these viruses also infect program templates that are loaded automatically by the applications. Each time the user creates a file using the default template, the macro virus is copied to the new file.

Memory-Resident Viruses When a system is infected by a virus that stays resident in the system memory, the *memory-resident virus* will continue to stay in memory and infect other files that are run at the same time. For a memory-resident virus to spread, the user must run an infected program that, once activated, inserts the virus into system memory, where the virus examines each new program as it is run and, if the program is not already infected, infects it.

Stealth Viruses A *stealth virus* hides itself from virus protection software by encrypting its code. Stealth viruses attempt to cover their trail as they infect their way through a computer. When a stealth virus infects, it takes over the system function that reads files or system sectors. When something or someone attempts to access the corrupted file, the stealth virus reports that the original file is there. However, the original information is gone and the stealth virus has taken its place.

Armored Viruses *Armored viruses* are designed to make detection and reverse engineering difficult and time-consuming, either through obfuscation (hiding in one place and attempting to trick antivirus programs or researchers into believing they reside elsewhere) or through techniques that add substantial amounts of confusing code to hide the actual virus code itself. While armored viruses are often quite good at what they are designed to do, they are significantly larger than necessary, which makes their presence easier to detect.

File Types That Commonly Carry Viruses

Some types of files are susceptible to virus infections because they are common to certain types of computer systems and applications. The following are a few of the most common types of program files targeted by viruses:

- **.bat** An MS-DOS batch file contains a series of commands for the OS that are executed automatically in sequence.

- **.com** MS-DOS command files usually execute within a command shell interface, or they can be executed from a user interface such as Windows. Most early computer viruses were created as .com files because the main DOS program files were in this form.

- **.doc/.docx** These file extensions are associated with Microsoft Word. Along with Microsoft Access and Excel files, files with the .doc or .docx extension are susceptible to macro virus infection.

- **.dll** A dynamic link library (DLL) is a library of executable functions or data that can be used by a Windows application. Typically, a DLL provides one or more functions, and a program accesses these functions.

- **.exe** An executable file is most commonly found on MS-DOS and Windows OSs.

- **.html** The .html or .htm extension is used for a document written in Hypertext Markup Language (HTML) coding that can be opened by web browsers.

- **.mdb** This file extension is associated with a Microsoft Access database. As with Word and Excel files, the .mdb file is susceptible to macro virus infection.

- **.scr** This is the default file extension for Microsoft Windows screensavers. Because screensavers are popular items to copy to other users, .scr files are typically easy targets for viruses.

- **.vbs**   Files with the .vbs extension are for Microsoft Visual Basic Scripting, a subset of the Visual Basic programming language. This powerful language can create scripts that perform a wide variety of functions, such as control applications and manipulate the file system. VBScript is powerful and can be used to create malicious code.

- **.xls/.xlsx**   These file extensions are associated with a Microsoft Excel spreadsheet. As with Word and Access files, .xls and .xlsx files are susceptible to macro virus infection.

- **.zip**   This extension is used for a compressed file that contains one or more other files. ZIP files are compressed to save space and to make grouping files for transport and copying faster and easier. ZIP files must also be checked by antivirus software to ensure that the files in the archive are not infected.

Exam Tip

Be able to recognize which types of files are most likely to carry a virus.

Polymorphic Malware

Polymorphic malware changes with each infection. These types of viruses were created to confuse virus-scanning programs. These viruses are difficult to detect by scanning because each copy of the virus looks different from previous copies.

Metamorphic Malware

Metamorphic malware can recompile itself into a new form, and the code keeps changing from generation to generation. Metamorphic malware is like polymorphic malware because both types can modify their forms. However, a metamorphic virus does not decrypt itself to a single constant virus body in memory, as a polymorphic virus does. A metamorphic virus can also change its virus body code.

Keyloggers

Keyloggers do just that: log a user's keystrokes for various purposes. This can be accomplished using a hardware device that is often discreet enough to blend in with the various cords running to and from peripherals—picture a small pass-through between the keyboard and its USB port, for example—or software that runs in the background. Keyloggers can be used by suspicious spouses, stalkers, or hackers looking to gain sensitive information, such as login credentials or credit card information, and are often installed by Trojans. While antivirus can often spot a software keylogger, hardware keyloggers can be almost undetectable.

Trojan Horses

Trojan horse programs are named from the ancient myth in which Greek warriors invaded the gated city of Troy by hiding inside a gigantic wooden horse. Once inside the city gates, the warriors leapt out from inside the horse and attacked the surprised inhabitants, winning a decisive battle. A Trojan horse program hides on your computer system until called upon to perform a certain task. Trojans are usually downloaded through e-mail attachments, websites, and instant messages. They are usually disguised as popular programs such as games, pictures, or music. When the program is run, it usually appears to the victim user as if nothing has happened, but the Trojan has secretly installed itself on the user's computer.

Remote Access Trojan

Remote Access Trojans (RATs) leave a back door that allows a hacker access to the client computer that bypasses any authentication. The RAT runs a service on the victim's computer and opens a port (such as TCP/IP port 12345 in the case of the NetBus Trojan software) on the system to which the attacker can connect when he runs the control application from a remote location. When connected, the attacker has full access to the infected system. Antivirus programs can detect the presence of RAT programs. Personal firewalls can also detect suspicious incoming and outgoing network traffic from a computer. Port-scanning software can also be used to identify any open ports on the system, including those you do not recognize. These open ports can be cross-referenced with lists of ports used by known back-door programs.

Travel Advisory

A firewall can detect suspicious incoming and outgoing network traffic from your computer. If you do not recognize a program, it could be malware communicating out to the network.

Logic Bombs

Although it can be running on a system for a long time, a *logic bomb* program will not activate until a specific trigger, such as reaching a specific date or starting a program a specific number of times, is set off. Logic bombs can be highly destructive, depending on their payload. The damage done by a logic bomb can range from changing bytes of data on the victim's hard disk to rendering the user's entire hard drive unreadable. Logic bombs are distributed primarily via worms and viruses; however, cases of malicious programmers inserting code into a trusted application that will trigger later have been documented. Logic bombs can be difficult to detect because most logic bombs are simple scripts that are inert (not executed and not memory resident), until executed by the event, and there may be no indication that the logic bomb is present for hours, days, months, or even years before it releases its malicious payload. Most antivirus software can detect the most common types of logic bombs; however, if a logic bomb is hidden within a trusted application, it may be difficult to detect its presence until it is too late. For software development companies, all code must be peer-reviewed before the application is released to ensure that a single malicious programmer cannot insert hidden logic-bomb code.

Worms

A computer *worm* is a self-contained program (or set of programs) that can self-replicate and spread full copies or smaller segments of itself to other computer systems via network connections, e-mail attachments, and instant messages. Compare this to viruses, which cannot self-replicate, but instead depend on the sharing of their host file to spread. Worms are most common in various types of networking application servers such as e-mail servers, web servers, and database servers. The explosive increase in worms within e-mail attachments and instant messages has caused antivirus companies and messaging software companies to reevaluate the functionality of their applications to prevent the spread of messaging-based worms. A user receives an attachment to an e-mail or an instant message that contains a malicious worm. When the attachment is opened, the worm infects the user's computer and then replicates itself by sending copies of the same e-mail or instant message to everyone in the user's address book. Each user, in turn, sees a message arrive from someone familiar and automatically opens the attachment, thinking it is safe. These types of worm infections can spread quickly and can bring down an e-mail server in a matter of minutes. Application server vendors have taken steps to prevent these types of worms from spreading by patching their applications to prevent malicious attachment code from executing.

Adware and Spyware

Adware (advertising software) and *spyware* are potential software threats that are not always considered security risks. Many free or low-cost software programs are often supported financially by embedding advertising content within the applications themselves. Although this provides a modest revenue stream for the software developers, it also opens the door to potential security threats, such as compromised private and personal data. Even software as simple as a downloadable screensaver may contain adware or spyware that installs code to deliver advertising to the user and/or collect personal information for use in targeted advertising. In addition to the nuisance of the advertising (which is not easily disabled) is the threat that the program itself is sending the user's personal information back to the advertiser. This information can include web surfing habits, key logging, online purchases, and personal contact information such as e-mail address, home address, and credit card details. This personal information can be used directly by the advertiser or sold to other companies that will also use or distribute the personal information.

Spyware is not necessarily involved with advertising, and it can be installed by any type of software application, even trusted, popular application and entertainment software. Spyware typically tracks the user's habits while using an application, such as a music player that relays the user's musical preferences back to the application vendor. This information can then be compiled by the vendor and sold to third parties such as record companies. Many types of antivirus and personal firewall software can detect and clean software designated as adware and spyware. It is critical that end users run some type of security software on their computers and regularly scan their hard drives for evidence of adware and spyware programs that are secretly sending personal data from the computers to advertisers. User education is also important to advise users not to download non-work-oriented software that may contain adware or spyware, such as games, screensavers, entertainment, or social media software, to a networked company computer.

Ransomware

Ransomware is designed to lock users out of their system until a ransom is paid. Ransomware generally enters the system much like a conventional piece of malware in a downloaded file or e-mail attachment. Once present, it either encrypts the system files or simply blocks access to the user interface and plays on user fear or embarrassment to extort the desired funds via a web page or text file, often for hundreds of U.S. dollars per machine.

Early ransomware often displayed a page or message claiming to be from law enforcement or the operating system vendor, purporting the software on the machine to be illegal and demanding a fine be paid. Based on the geographical location of the user, the ransomware would shift its language settings, showing an initial amount of finesse.

More recent types of ransomware, such as Cryptolocker and WannaCry, also referred to as *crypto-malware*, encrypt user files and require payment within a timeframe, often through a digital currency such as bitcoin. If the ransom is not submitted, the malware claims that the key will be destroyed and the files can never be unencrypted. You can imagine, then, that the spread of this type of ransomware within an organization could potentially cause quite a headache for IT staff, who don't wish to bow to malware authors but also stand to lose a substantial amount of data. Anti-malware solutions and securely backing data up on a regular basis are almost the only ways to combat this type of malware.

Rootkits

A *rootkit* is a type of back-door program that is inserted into application software and allows a remote user *root* access (administrator access) to the system on which the software is installed, without the permission or knowledge of the user. This access potentially results in full control over the target system. Although rootkits are usually related to malware and Trojan horse types of malicious software, they are also becoming more common in trusted applications that are potentially used by millions of users. For example, a well-known entertainment company was found to be distributing rootkits on its music CDs. This software was installed on a user's computer while the music CD was played on the system. This software installation was not disclosed to the user, and the software (primarily used for digital rights management of music copyright) allowed root access and control of the computer system for anyone aware that the software was installed. After the issue was widely publicized on the Internet, the company quickly intervened to ensure that this software was no longer distributed with its music CDs. Rootkits are not always installed by application software. They can be distributed via firmware updates for a hardware device, embedded into the primary operating system kernel (kernel rootkits), and included on application software libraries such as DLL files. Rootkits do not spread like a worm or virus; they typically infect one system only. However, rootkits themselves are typically spread as the payload of replicating worms and viruses. Several types of rootkits exist, including the following:

- **Firmware rootkits**   The rootkit is embedded within the firmware of a device, such as a computer peripheral or network device. The rootkit is always available because it is embedded within the firmware of the system and is always activated when the device is running.
- **Kernel rootkits**   The rootkit is embedded within the operating system core itself. This effectively hides the rootkit because it runs as a hidden process and can rarely be spotted by checking active processes on the system.

- **Persistent rootkits**　The rootkit is enabled when the system starts and will not turn off unless the system is shut down. This type of rootkit is often installed and activated within the Windows Registry and is run each time the system boots.
- **Application rootkits**　The rootkit is activated and run in current system memory only when a specific application is launched, and is not persisted when the system is shut down and restarted.
- **Library rootkits**　In software applications that use code library files, such as Windows DLLs, the rootkit can intercept specific system and application programming interface (API) calls and replace them with its own code.

Some antivirus software applications can detect the presence of rootkits; however, they may be difficult to clean from a system, especially if they are embedded in the kernel or boot sectors of an OS. In such cases, it is often the safest and most secure practice to reinstall the system to ensure that any rootkit code is deleted.

Botnets

Botnet is short for *roBOT NETwork*. A *bot* is typically any type of computer system that is attached to a network whose security has been compromised and that runs malicious software completely unknown to the system users. Botnets (often called "zombie" computers) are typically used for *distributed denial-of-service (DDoS)* attacks, in which hundreds or even tens of thousands of computers are overtaken and programmed to send network attacks to a single target site. Botnets can also be used to send out large amounts of spam, adware, spyware, and malware. An infected computer (which is typically infected by a worm, virus, or Trojan horse) that is made part of the botnet might not show any initial effects. It is only after the computer is remotely "turned on" to start its attack on another computer that the compromise becomes apparent. Typical symptoms include slow responsiveness and large amounts of network packets being sent from the infected system.

Because compromised servers are controlled by the botnets and are typically not under local control, and because of servers' distributed nature (which means the affected servers could be located anywhere in the world), it can be difficult to mitigate the effects of these types of coordinated attacks. It is also very difficult to plan for future attacks. Although the originating addresses of the systems in the botnet can be blocked, other compromised systems can be easily added to the botnet to continue the attack from different addresses. Nevertheless, regular investigations of system activity and frequent antivirus scans can help prevent a system from becoming infected with a virus or worm and becoming a bot within a larger botnet.

Carry Out Appropriate Procedures to Establish Host Security

The following sections describe the procedures an administrator should take when securing server and workstation operating systems and applications, and creating and deploying a security policy across all systems in the network.

Physical Hardware Security

At the most basic level, securing a computer requires that it can't simply be walked out of the building. Depending on the level of security desired, you might consider implementing cable locks that secure the machine to a desk or cabinet. Both desktop and laptop systems generally have a standard slot that fits a simple cable lock.

More secure environments might want to lock the systems themselves up after use; a safe or locking cabinet provides a high level of hardware security, but at the sacrifice of inconveniencing the user. Users within this environment will need to retrieve the systems, use them for their daily activities, and then lock them back up, either daily or even when walking out of the room.

Availability concerns can arise if your cabling is susceptible to EMI; remember that electromagnetic interference (EMI) is caused by the electrical "noise" created by motors, lighting, and any type of electronic or mechanical equipment. This interference can potentially disrupt communications on network cabling because of the noise in the line that distorts the network signals. Be sure to use cabling that properly shields you from EMI, such as shielded copper or fiber optic, when possible.

Consider *control diversity* in your choices, making sure that your controls protecting your hosts are not only technical in nature, but also mitigate identified physical threats and administrative concerns. This helps with your "defense-in-depth" approach.

Travel Assistance

Cabling choices are covered in more depth within Chapter 3. More information on locks is available within Chapter 6. Information on other hardware security measures is available within Chapter 12.

Supply Chain Risk

What if you securely configured all your software, and made sure that the hardware that you bought was capable of performing well and providing the needed security, but it still wasn't enough to protect against embedded code and back doors? The National Institute of Standards and Technology (NIST) SP 800-161 states that *supply chain risks* "may include insertion of counterfeits, unauthorized production, tampering, theft, insertion of malicious software and hardware, as well as poor manufacturing and development practices..." Adversaries at the nation-state level can introduce such risk, as well as manufacturers simply wanting to gather information and covertly send it back to themselves, even for benign reasons such as crash analysis.

The way to combat supply chain risk is to know which of your hardware and software that contains information or communications technologies and and then work to reduce the risks they pose. This is known as *supply chain risk management*. However, this management becomes exponentially difficult when you realize that the average computing system, for example, combines hardware, software, and firmware from potentially dozens of different vendors. The motherboard, optical drive, hard drive, and memory are all likely from different suppliers, not to mention the software from the OS onward. These each, in turn, likely have components sourced from other suppliers.

In more secure environments, especially those where the data is extremely sensitive, doing your best to learn about where the components came from can increase your trust that your hardware or software isn't selling you out. One option is to use *roots of trust*, which are described by NIST as "highly reliable hardware, firmware, and software components that perform specific, critical security functions.... [Roots] of trust provide a firm foundation from which to build security and trust." Roots of trust are inherently trusted by the other hardware and software, with the higher layers in the model trusting the lower, foundational levels, so it is critical that those roots be as secure as possible. These are often hardware components such as a trusted platform module (TPM). Another option is to use a trusted manufacturer that allows better visibility. Finally, when you have these roots of trust in place, it's a good idea to stockpile these items to deal with a crisis, so as not to be forced to rely on less trusted components to maintain availability.

Travel Assistance
More detail on trusted platform modules is located within Chapter 12.

Host Software Security Baseline

A *security baseline* is a minimum standard that each system and application must meet to supply the absolute minimum level of protection against security vulnerabilities and to mitigate threats and risks. Security baselines are created to provide assurance that all aspects of operating system and software applications are running at a specified base level of security.

To establish initial baselines, specific security requirements of your environment and a history of past security vulnerabilities in your systems and applications should be compiled. You can also gather information from industry security standards, associations, and organizations of systems administrators. This information helps ensure that your operating systems and applications are all running the latest software updates, patches, and hot fixes that minimize the risks of known software exploits. After these baselines have been compiled and configured specifically for your environment, they must be implemented across the network and updated regularly to ensure maximum-security efficiency for all systems in your organization.

Security templates and *policies* provide a documented minimum configuration baseline for all your server and workstation operating systems and applications, as well as more secure configurations for environments (such as classified hosts) that require a higher standard. When a server or workstation is first installed, the template must be applied so that the system meets the minimal version and security update policies, as outlined by the organization.

Security configuration guides, such as the U.S. Defense Information Systems Agency (DISA) Security Technical Implementation Guides (STIGs), provide a checklist-based approach to securely configuring different types of systems, including all sorts of hardware and software. Don't think of government guides only, though; there are many nonregulatory and industry best practices that can lead the way. Although many of these documents are written for specific devices and applications, there are some available for more general purposes, such as securely configuring personal social media accounts, webmail usage at home, and operational security, that offer your personnel comprehensive coverage of security issues that span both the workplace and the home. While security configuration guides might not be mandatory for every organizational context, it is important to determine if yours should require certain guidelines, particularly if you work inside the government or in the healthcare industry. If you're interested in better configuring your system and keeping up to date with best practices (as you should be), check out the openly available guides as they provide a wealth of knowledge gained through many years of practical, real-world security experience. Configuration compliance can be validated using a checklist, or, more ideally, a configuration compliance scanner that can be automated.

Organizations typically have separate security policies that cover different organizational groups, such as development, sales, human resources, IT, and so on. This ensures that the security issues specific to a certain organizational department are treated in separate policies. For example, a server in the human resources department may have much stricter security policies and baselines than a server in the sales department. The human resources server contains confidential data about employees and, therefore, causes greater security concerns for the privacy and integrity of the data than a file server containing sales and marketing information.

Operating System Hardening

The OS is the primary software that controls how your system works and how it interoperates with your hardware. The OS is the most critical part of your computer system. *Operating system hardening* refers to keeping the OS and applications current through regular updates and critical software patches, and removing unnecessary software services from the system. This is true no matter the type of operating system, including those residing on your network devices, servers, workstations, appliances, kiosks, and mobile devices. Despite having been tested before being released, every OS experiences some software bugs and security vulnerabilities after release. New versions of the software or bug fixes and patches are released to correct these issues, and you should make sure that these are installed on the system as soon as possible. You must also be aware of any types of operating system vulnerabilities in virtual machines installed in your environment that run multiple types of operating systems on the same hardware platform. In addition to software updates, many other areas of your OS need to be examined for security vulnerabilities, including setting configuration options, examining available running services, and securing file systems.

Trusted Operating System

Some organizations have resorted to using a *trusted OS,* or operating system that has met a set of standards such as the Common Criteria. These standards validate the security posture of an OS, sometimes only on particular hardware. Trusted OSs are often required within high-security environments such as government systems.

Trusted OS configurations are not necessary in lower-security situations and may create situations where hardware and OS software are difficult to upgrade on an appropriate schedule.

Operating System Updates

Your OS software should be operating at the latest release version with the most recent security patches applied. OS vendors regularly release software updates, which are often rolled into larger software packages called *service packs* or *updates.* Smaller bug fixes or patches that fix critical security vulnerabilities (often called *hot fixes*) are usually released quickly so administrators can patch their systems before hackers can take advantage of the vulnerability. Vendors usually provide these patches and service packs as downloads from their websites. Some OSs have automatic system update functions that can periodically connect to the vendor's website and download the latest versions of software components. Some vendors release an update DVD or Internet download every few months that contains all the latest patches and bug fixes since the last version. It is especially important that you perform this software update procedure just after a new system has been installed. The OS installed on a computer is often the original version that shipped with the hardware; since that time, several service packs and patches have probably been released.

Travel Advisory

Even if you just installed a service pack for your OS, you need to install any security patches released after that service pack to be completely current and fully protected.

Patch Management

In organizations with hundreds and often thousands of workstations, it can be a logistical nightmare to keep all the operating systems and application software up to date. In most cases, operating system updates on workstations can be automatically applied via the network. However, administrators must have a clear security policy and baseline plan to ensure that all workstations are running a certain minimum level of software versions.

Before you install any update or patch onto networked systems, it should first be installed on a server in a lab environment. In some cases, software updates have been known to fix one problem but cause another. If no lab system is available, you can patch a server after business hours, constantly monitoring that server and having a back-out plan in place to remove the update if something should go wrong.

BIOS and UEFI Security

The *Basic Input/Output System (BIOS)* of a host system contains the program code and instructions for starting a computer and loading the OS. BIOS software can be updated when new hardware support and device drivers are required. BIOS software updates may also contain bug fixes and security enhancements that prevent problems in the BIOS code from being exploited and causing a system to be compromised; the BIOS of servers and clients should be updated to the latest version. Most BIOS programs also contain a basic password feature that allows the network administrator to assign a password to the BIOS system that must be entered before any BIOS changes or updates can occur. This provides an additional layer of security to prevent unauthorized access to the BIOS software or the primary system settings. Administrators should be aware that unauthorized users could also boot a system (if they have physical access to it) using Live CD or DVD media that can boot their own OS and bypass the actual BIOS and OS of the computer. The disc contains a minimal OS software environment and does not boot any code from the system hard disk. From the disc's OS, an attacker can access the host system and its hard disk.

Although it's often still referred to as the BIOS, more modern systems, including Mac computers and Windows PCs after Windows 8 use the *Unified Extensible Firmware Interface (UEFI)* to boot, which can either be loaded from flash memory, a network share, or a hard drive. UEFI has several improvements over traditional BIOS, including better performance and increased security features. One of these is *secure boot,* which is designed to prevent malware from modifying or replacing the boot loader by checking the certificate resident within the bootloader; if it has been tampered with, UEFI secure boot prevents the system from booting.

Services and OS Configuration

After you've installed an OS, configuring the many administrative and security-related options can increase your system security. Other options might make your system more vulnerable to attack—that's why installing or enabling only the necessary options for a system is critical. By enabling unnecessary options, you create potential vulnerabilities for unauthorized users to exploit. The system should also be investigated for ports and services enabled by default that are not required, and this is especially important when you are enabling services to be run on your system. Examples of services that might not be needed but that could be running are file- and print-sharing services and Internet services such as the Hypertext Transfer Protocol (HTTP), the File Transfer Protocol (FTP), the Simple Mail Transfer Protocol (SMTP), the Domain Name System (DNS), and the Dynamic Host Configuration Protocol (DHCP).

If the system you are configuring does not need to share files, the server service should be disabled so that no one on the network can connect to a network share on that system. Enabled Internet services can cause a variety of security vulnerabilities by opening network ports on your system to which unauthorized users can connect. For example, enabling web server services on your system enables hackers to connect to your system by issuing HTTP requests to the server, where they can attempt a variety of attacks to gain access or to disrupt communications. Remember that it's always better to configure a system to have the least amount of ports and services enabled, or *least functionality,* to minimize the attack surface available to a malicious actor. Also, although backward compatibility with older OSs and software sounds like a safe bet, it exposes you to *downgrade attacks,* which force a system to revert to an older or less-secure mode of operation. Removing backward compatibility helps prevent these attacks.

> ### Exam Tip
>
> Services that are not required by the system should be disabled or removed, while existing services should be configured to provide maximum security.

File System Security

For file servers that share files with other users and computer systems, the file system in use must properly address security concerns for locking down file sharing. Older types of disk file systems, such as File Allocation Table (FAT), do not provide the same security as NT File System (NTFS) on Microsoft systems or ext3 on later Linux. Newer file system formats allow for greater access controls, such as specific security permissions for files and directories. Some file systems also provide encryption capabilities so no one can read the contents of a system without the proper key to decrypt it. Another aspect of file system security is how access permissions are configured for files on the server. Without proper access control, users can read or modify files that could be confidential in nature. Protection is critical for OS files that contain administrative programs and sensitive configuration programs. Access to system files should be granted only to system administrators, and user files should be stored on a separate disk or partition to ensure these system files are not accidentally accessed or removed. Each user should have a separate home directory to which only he or she has access. Group or department directories should be set up for files that must be shared among groups.

System User Accounts and Password Threats

Although the most common form of system authentication is a login and password procedure, this is also considered one of the weakest security mechanisms available. Users' passwords tend to be weak because users use common dictionary words or personal information that can be easily guessed by an unauthorized user. Often, a user's password is the name of a spouse or a pet or a birth date. Or the user may reveal passwords to others or write them down in conspicuous locations, such as a note taped to the computer monitor. Most operating systems come with a default administrative account called *admin,* *administrator,* or another similarly obvious name that points to this account as being necessary to manage and administer the system. For example, the *root* account is still the primary account that's been used for decades for full access to a Unix system. Most malicious users and attackers look for the admin or root account of a system or device as the first account to be compromised. It is a best practice for network administrators either to disable or rename default or administrator accounts, or, if that is not possible, to create an alternative administrative account with equal access rights and name it something inconspicuous. This ensures that a malicious user cannot automatically try to log in using the well-known account names for the admin user. It is a regular practice to use separate logins for each administrator to ensure that any admin account actions can be properly logged and audited. Generally, network administrators should never name accounts after their job function, such as *admin, backup, databaseadmin,* and so on. Enforcing the use of strong passwords, which are not based on dictionary words or personal information but include the use of alphanumeric characters and uppercase and lowercase letters, greatly diminishes an unauthorized user's ability to guess a password.

Passwords are usually attacked in two ways: online or offline. In an online attack, the attacker attempts to log in as a user by guessing the user's password. If the attacker has the password already, or can effectively guess the password based on knowledge of the person, this might work. However, this is usually the most ineffective and inefficient type of attack, because most systems are configured to automatically lock the user account after a certain number of unsuccessful login attempts. In an offline attack, the (generally hashed) database of user credentials is usually stolen to be attacked offline by being loaded on to a system where the attacker has a variety of tools. If the attacker has the hashed passwords, he can wage different attacks against them, such as brute force or dictionary attacks. Remember that hashing is a one-way function that is not intended to be decrypted, and that it is mathematically difficult to find two different pieces of plain text that, when subjected to the same hashing algorithm, produce the same identical hash. When this does occur (and, although extremely rare, is theoretically possible), it is called a *collision*, and can be used in a so-called *birthday* attack, which attempts to just find a piece of plain text that supplies the same hashed value, no matter what the original plain text might have been.

A *brute-force attack* is the most basic type of password attack. In this attack's simplest form, an attacker might repeatedly attempt to guess the user's password. A more effective way would be to simply start at the beginning of the character set and try all possible combinations, in order, until the attacker eventually finds the correct combination of characters and password length. This obviously would take a very long time for a person to accomplish on his own; however, improved hardware and software has reduced the time of performing brute-force attacks. Even with the best hardware and software, though, brute-force attacks could theoretically take several hundred or more years to go through every permutation.

More effective and efficient, a *dictionary attack* uses dictionaries, or lists of common words across various types of organizations, languages, and other words that might be used for passwords, as well as common substitutions, such as using the @ symbol in lieu of the letter *a*. *Rainbow attacks* are a variation on a dictionary attack that, instead of trying to guess the password, use precomputed hashes (called *rainbow tables*) developed by software that can process huge lists of words and spit out their hash, which is then added to the rainbow table's file. The attacker then compares the rainbow table to the password hashes he obtained illicitly, looking for matches.

To ensure the usefulness and efficiency of a login and password procedure, you must create and strictly follow account and password policies, such as enforced password expiry and rotation after a specific period.

Travel Assistance

For detailed information on user account and password security, see Chapter 6.

Management Interface Security

Access to servers should be restricted to authorized individuals, such as the network administrator. Servers should be stored in a locked room with controlled access and locked in some type of cage or rack to prevent passersby from being able to access the console or the server equipment itself. The server console should be password-protected so only authenticated users can physically access the server or attempt access through a network connection. Any cables, including network, keyboard, and mouse connections, should be secured and be as short as possible to prevent devices such as a keystroke logger or network sniffer from being introduced into the connection. Remote management access over the network to a host must be secure so that only the network administrator can access the remote management console through a special management application or a web browser. Most management programs allow you to restrict remote access to specific workstations using an IP address or Media Access Control (MAC) hardware address. Authentication must also be enabled to force a user to authenticate as an administrative user before he can access the management console. Web connections should always use HTTPS (HTTP over SSL) to encrypt management access communications. When a host management console is left unattended, the user should log off and lock the computer with a password. This prevents passersby from being able to access the systems of others and gaining access to restricted network resources. Many operating systems include the ability to autolock the host or time out a web session after a certain period of inactivity.

Host Internet Access

Most users have access to the Internet to send and receive e-mail and instant messages, and to access information they need to do their work. Although most networks are secured from outside intrusion through routers and firewalls, several security vulnerabilities can be created by users inside the network. At the office, users often download and install applications that should not be operating on the company network, such as chat, file-sharing, and music-sharing programs. Unfortunately, these applications can contain security vulnerabilities that allow access to unauthorized users outside the company via unique service ports that the company firewall might not be blocking.

Beyond the security vulnerabilities, user interaction with external Internet users can result in viruses or Trojan horse programs being downloaded, which allow back-door access to the user's computer. To protect against the use of these programs, the network administrator should block the service ports accessed by these programs on the main network firewall so that they cannot communicate with the Internet. The administrator can also assign access rights to users on their computers that deny them the ability to install any type of software that is not already loaded on their system.

Some users also download questionable content from the Internet, such as pornographic materials or other objectionable content, onto their office computer. This presents a legal problem for the company, as many companies have been sued for allowing such access. To prevent this activity, network administrators can install special web filter programs that block access to these sites. These filters use a list of known objectionable sites that is compared to the websites users try to access through their web browsers. These lists can also contain well-known phishing, spyware, and malware sites, which can also be blocked accordingly.

Travel Assistance
For detailed information on firewalls, content filters, and web security gateways, see Chapter 8.

Software Access and Privileges

All software on the workstation should be kept current with the most recent patches and upgrades to remove security vulnerabilities from previous versions.

The administrator should ensure that users have only the access privileges they need to perform their job functions. For example, any system functions that enable changes to be made to the network address of a computer—or any other type of system change—should be off limits to a regular user and accessible only to the administrator. Regular users should not be able to access any application or configuration programs other than those required for their jobs. The most efficient way of preventing certain system functions from user abuse is to enact network-wide security policies that are automatically set for each workstation on the network. This can save considerable time because an administrator does not have to visit each workstation and block out items one by one.

Peripherals

Although certainly the bulk of your efforts will go toward securing the hosts, don't forget the peripherals that are connected to your system. As mentioned earlier, hardware keyloggers can pass your sensitive information almost undetectably, but more benign items, such as wireless keyboards and mice, can pose their own threat of attacks based on their wireless connectivity. Therefore, it is considered a best practice to not use these in a secure environment, and to stick to their wired counterparts. Displays have their own vulnerabilities as well; for example, they can suffer from issues related to leaking electromagnetic emanations, especially the older CRT models; an attacker can use those emanations to "read" the sensitive information on the screen. If this is a concern, special testing can be done to check for emissions. Although more modern displays are less prone to emanation issues, in a highly secure environment it's a good idea to choose your equipment carefully, such as using National Security Agency– or Canadian TEMPEST–approved equipment, to be sure that an attacker cannot use those emanations to "read" the sensitive information on the screen.

Have you ever considered your printer or multifunction device (MFD) as a threat vector? You should, because an unsecured printer can provide access into your network in the same way an unsecured host might. Printers often connect via Ethernet into the same networks that your more traditional hosts connect, and often have no or very minimal security controls applied. Modern multifunction devices can be configured to require passwords or two-factor authentication, and if you have implemented this within a more secure environment, it's a great idea that you check out a secure configuration guide for printers. If you see any odd behavior coming from your printer, such as refusing to print or unknown content being printed, don't just assume that your printer is misbehaving; it could be an attack against an accessible printer.

Mobile devices will be covered later in this chapter, but other devices that you should be on the lookout for include portable hard drives, SD cards, digital cameras, flash drives, and other external storage devices—some are even Wi-Fi enabled—that can be used to remove your organization's precious data from a host or network device. This is a great time to have your data loss prevention (DLP) solution scanning, blocking, and reporting these connections.

Host Security Applications

A wide variety of security software can be installed on your system to protect it against various types of security threats, such as viruses, spyware, malware, e-mail spam, access intrusion, network attacks, and web browsing threats. The following sections describe some of the types of solutions that can be implemented to help protect your system.

Whitelists or Blacklists

Whitelists prevent applications from executing by checking each potential execution against a list of applications that have been granted execution rights. If the application can execute, it can proceed as planned. If not, it is terminated. Often, whitelisting solutions will check the hash of the potential application against the known-good hash to ensure that the application isn't maliciously claiming to be the legitimate version.

Conversely, *blacklists* are the method used by most anti-malware vendors; they require maintaining a list of "known-bad" applications, or just applications that the administrators don't wish to have choking the available bandwidth or worse (think video games, bitcoin mining, and so on). Applications that don't appear on the blacklist can execute.

There is no definitive answer as to which method is better; you could argue that blacklisting is better because of the intricate nature of enterprise systems and the number of applications required to support daily operations. In a blacklist situation, these applications would be more likely to execute as planned. However, proponents of a whitelist solution argue that it only takes one malicious program slipping through the blacklist to wreck an organization, and that it is better to put the time and effort into developing a whitelist. It is a good idea to go over both scenarios with the leadership of the organization and make an informed choice of how to proceed.

Antivirus and Anti-spyware Software

To protect your systems from being infected by viruses, spyware, and other types of malicious code, antivirus systems should be installed in all aspects of the network—from desktop computers to servers and firewalls. Because viruses and spyware can enter a company network in a variety of ways, such as by a user bringing in a USB key from home, from e-mail attachments, and from Internet downloads, antivirus protection should be set up for all these different types of access points. Antivirus protection should be set up on every server, desktop, and laptop in the system and should include scheduled updates of virus signature files (discussed in more detail later in this section) from a central antivirus update server. This can protect both the computers and the networks to which they connect, as well as provide a first level of defense to prevent viruses from spreading to the network.

Protecting just the end-user systems is not enough, however. All servers should be protected to prevent viruses transmitted from a desktop system from spreading to any of the server systems. The reverse situation is also a great concern: If a common file on a server is used by all company systems, simply accessing the infected server file can also infect them. Most viruses and spyware enter a system from e-mail attachments and Internet downloads that come from outside the company. E-mail servers that send and receive mail should be protected with special antivirus software that can scan incoming e-mail for attachments with viruses. The virus is either cleaned or quarantined, or the message is deleted, and then notification e-mails are sent to the source and recipient to warn about the existence of the virus.

Travel Advisory

When installing antivirus software on an e-mail server, be certain you install the version of the software that examines incoming mail and attachments. Normal antivirus protection only prevents viruses in normal program files outside the e-mail system.

Many types of network firewalls or other types of network-perimeter devices can be set up with virus-protection software that scans files being downloaded from the Internet. With the amount of traffic that goes through a firewall, this type of protection can slow down the network considerably, so be aware and evaluate your system needs carefully.

Although there are advantages to this all-in-one approach, such as standardization and the ability to update products more efficiently, in some instances it may be better to have different products from different security vendors on a host. *Vendor diversity* is a best practice that assumes similar products from the same manufacturer are often vulnerable to the emerging exploits in a similar manner, so an attacker could take advantage of this scenario and make it through multiple layers of defenses more effectively and efficiently. With vendor diversity, you would not then use the same vendor for, say, antivirus and host-based firewalls. Obviously, there are disadvantages to this practice as well, including the previously mentioned standardization that may cause your administrators to spend more time keeping products updated. However, having a few different products installed increases the likelihood that an attack missed by one solution will be caught by another.

Virus Signature Files

Antivirus software companies update their software regularly to add code that protects against new virus and spyware threats that are created every day. Having to update the entire software package on every user's computer in a company would be extremely expensive and impractical. Antivirus software companies use a virus pattern or signature file to patch users' systems conveniently and quickly. Each computer virus contains or creates a specific binary code that can be used as a unique identifier. From these binary signatures produced by the virus, the antivirus engineers create a signature file that can be used to identify the viruses when the antivirus scan engine program is used. These signature files can contain thousands of known virus types. They can even include special algorithms for detecting common virus-like behavior that can indicate a new virus. When a virus is identified, the antivirus software can use that information to quarantine the file or attempt to remove the virus from the file. To make use of these signature files, you must be diligent in regularly updating the system with the latest virus definition file. This usually involves connecting to the antivirus vendor's website and downloading and installing the latest signature file. Some antivirus programs can be set up to automate this process, checking for a new signature file on a schedule and automatically updating the file without user intervention. When you first install an antivirus program, you should immediately check for updated signatures to make sure you are scanning with the most recent signature files.

Anti-spam Software

One of the most annoying e-mail problems, *spam,* is a deliberate attempt by an advertiser or business to mass e-mail many users with unsolicited advertisements. Any time you enter your e-mail address on a public website or a newsgroup, you open yourself to the possibility of having your e-mail address added to spam mailing lists. These mailing lists are shared among Internet spam advertisers, and sometimes you can receive multiple junk e-mails every day. This annoys not only users but also network administrators because of the amount of space and bandwidth these mass mailings can consume. Many Internet service providers (ISPs) and corporate networks use anti-spam mail filters that block incoming spam e-mail from reaching users' inboxes. Spam has evolved from the early years of simple text adverts to full HTML messages with clickable links, images, and even spam messages hidden in attached images and document files. The links in spam messages are often redirected to malicious sites containing spyware, malware, and phishing activities.

Travel Assistance

For detailed information on anti-spam solutions that reside between your e-mail server and your e-mail client host, see Chapter 8.

Anti-spam software is widely available for host systems. Most e-mail clients now include spam-blocking applications that filter e-mail as it is downloaded from the mail server. Utilizing spam training identification, mail clients can automatically detect spam messages and move them to a special junk or spam e-mail folder. This keeps the spam and junk mail distinct from regular e-mail messages, which are passed directly to the mail client inbox. These types of spam blockers are normally not as efficient as dedicated anti-spam devices at the network border; however, they do provide an additional layer of protection for any spam messages that happen to make it to the client from the server. Users can typically add friends and co-workers to a trusted list that will bypass the spam scanner to ensure that these e-mails are never blocked.

Host-Based Firewalls

Most organizations have firewall servers or appliances that protect the perimeters of their network from Internet attacks and hide the details of the internal network. Computer users who connect directly to an Internet connection rarely have any type of hardware-based firewall. Software-based firewall applications, however, have become an absolute necessity for a user connecting directly to the Internet from home or work using a cable modem, digital subscriber line (DSL), or dial-up method. A software firewall application performs several critical functions to protect a user's host computer:

- **Blocks incoming network connections**   The primary purpose of the personal firewall is to block incoming network connections from the Internet. It can hide your system from port-scanning attacks whereby malicious hackers probe network-connected computers for open network ports and vulnerabilities. The firewall software effectively makes your computer invisible to those on the Internet, and it will not reply to any network probes or diagnostic utilities such as ping or traceroute. Worms and other malware threats that are spread through the Internet will be stopped in their tracks by the firewall software because they will not be able to see your system to connect to it.

- **Watches for suspicious outbound activity** A personal firewall application monitors outbound activity and allows the user complete control over what applications are allowed or blocked access to the Internet. For example, when your antivirus software periodically retrieves the latest virus signature file from an Internet site, your personal firewall will alert you that the application is trying to access the Internet. In this case, the activity is acceptable, and you can allow the software to pass through the firewall and to do so automatically on subsequent accesses so you will not receive an alert each time. This type of protection is extremely important to protect against Trojan horse and spyware applications that may be running on your computer and sending private information back to a malicious user. The personal firewall will detect the suspicious outbound activity and alert you. You can block the application if you do not recognize it and then attempt to remove it with your antivirus or antispyware software.

- **Provides ability to block/allow programs** All applications that potentially try to communicate out to the Internet can have their access controlled by the personal firewall. The personal firewall allows you to control which applications can send data to the Internet and which cannot. Some applications need to communicate with other servers to work properly, and care must be taken not to block critical system or application services. In addition, trusted applications can occasionally visit an Internet site to check for new updates to the software, and this can be considered acceptable activity. Other applications, however, may be secretly sending information out to the Internet, such as personal identification information or data about your activities on your computer, such as lists of websites you have visited.

- **Warns of unpatched software and outdated antivirus files** Many personal firewalls can scan your computer to make sure that your OS and application software are running the latest versions, and they will alert you if your software seems to be out of date. Most personal firewalls will alert you if your antivirus signature files are out of date and will prompt you to run the updated software to get the latest files.

- **Provides web browser security** Personal firewall software can also strengthen the security and privacy of your web browsing sessions. The software can block pop-up and banner ads to prevent you from accessing known phishing or spyware sites and to ensure that your web browsing cookies and web cache are not causing security and privacy issues. Many firewalls will also block websites that run scripting, which is a primary source for browser exploits and security risks. However, scripting and cookies are often necessary for certain websites such as online banking, and it will be necessary to adjust your firewall settings as appropriate to protect your web browsing sessions without impacting functionality.

- **Provides e-mail security**   Some personal firewalls monitor your inbound and outbound e-mail and can quarantine suspicious attachments to help prevent the spread of viruses, worms, and Trojan horse software. In some cases, if a worm infects you and your e-mail application is attempting to mail the worm to everyone in your address book, the personal firewall can detect this activity and block outbound mail from being sent out from your computer and prevent you from accidentally infecting other computers.

Web Browser Security

Because web browsers are the most widely used Internet applications, security is of the utmost importance. Web browser vulnerabilities and misuse can open a computer system to a vast array of security risks and threats, including viruses, worms, malware, spyware, and identity theft.

Security Modes and Trusted Sites   Many popular web browsers such as Internet Explorer, Firefox, and Safari come with enhanced security settings that allow users to run their web browser in a specific security mode—for example, as high, medium, or low. Each security mode offers a level of security that is contrasted with ease of use. For example, high-security modes typically disable many website features that cause security concerns such as scripting, ActiveX and JavaScript controls, and installation of third-party software and other potentially malicious software. Unfortunately, many legitimate websites use these technologies, and users can be frustrated with the number of warnings that occur when accessing these websites. Many popular websites also require scripting and pop-up windows and will not work properly if they are disabled. Lower-security modes tend to allow certain levels of scripting, while disabling the most obvious website security risks. Administrators can use security policies to force the use of a security mode that offers the highest security possible for all users. It is much safer to start with a strong security mode and to add exceptions to that mode rather than start with a weak security mode.

> **Exam Tip**
>
> Administrators must lock down operating systems and applications with a strong security mode and then add exceptions to that mode rather than starting with a weak security mode and strengthening as they go.

Users can add lists of trusted sites to ensure that these legitimate sites bypass any high-security controls. For example, a user may add an online banking website to the list of trusted sites to allow cookies, scripting, and pop-up windows to be used, while blocking all other websites with these functions.

Pop-up Blockers Several popular add-ons and extensions to web browsers allow certain types of *pop-up advertising* to be blocked before it appears on the user's monitor. These pop-up ads, typically generated by JavaScript or some other type of web scripting language, can be a nuisance when web browsing, as the ad will open a new browser window in front of the one you are currently viewing. The ad will link to another site for advertising purposes and will direct you to a new website if clicked. In many cases, closing the pop-up ad may cause another ad to pop up in its place. The website may also open several pop-up windows, and often it may be difficult to close them without having to shut down and restart the web browser. Pop-up ads can be a security issue if they link back to spyware and malware sites or download malicious scripts and applications to the browser.

Many pop-up ads contain a link or control to close the window, but the control is a link to another website or a control to download malicious software. For the user, it is sometimes difficult to know how to close the pop-up ad properly to prevent others from appearing. Most modern web browsers contain some type of pop-up ad-blocking capabilities, ensuring that when you visit a website containing pop-up ads, the primary website will appear, but all pop-up ads will be blocked and will not appear on your monitor. Some third-party ad-blocking software goes further by blocking banners ads within the primary website itself.

In some cases, pop-up windows are used for legitimate purposes, such as help windows with additional information or the installation of legitimate software. Most web browsers give you control on whether to block or allow pop-up ads and windows, and you can allow certain trusted sites to display pop-ups if you are aware of their content.

Cookies *Cookies* are small text files that are saved on your computer to store data for a specific website you have visited. Cookies can contain all types of data specific to that website, such as information to track unique visitors to the website, login information for the user, and information on other websites you have visited. Some cookies are cleared after your session on a specific website ends, other cookies expire over a certain period or time, and still other cookies do not expire at all but stay on your system until you delete them.

Due to the often-sensitive information they contain, cookies can frequently be a security and privacy risk in the event a malicious user accesses a cookie with your credentials for a specific website. Many web users also have privacy concerns with website cookies that track previous websites they have visited.

Most web browsers have a configuration option that lets you examine each cookie on your system. You can keep or delete cookies, or clear all the current cookies off your system. Cookies can also be expired after a certain amount of time has passed. When you start web surfing again, new cookies will appear in your cookie directory. You also have the option of blocking third-party cookies, which are typically cookies from advertising sites not related to the current site you are browsing. Blocking third-party cookies can greatly reduce the chance of your private web browsing history from being leaked to third-party sites.

Travel Advisory

To protect your privacy even more and to avoid sending demographic information to websites, most web browsers allow you to disable cookies and to delete any existing ones upon exiting the program. Unfortunately, many websites require cookies to be enabled to function properly.

Private Web Browsing Data   As you use your web browser, it collects data on the websites you visit, the site addresses, and any downloads you make from the website; caches certain types of content such as frequently loaded images; and stores cookies with personal identifying data for specific websites. Most of this data is helpful to store—for example, your browsing history will contain all the sites you have visited, and you may need to access the history to remember a specific website if you want to return there. Cookies also remember information about a specific website, such as login credentials, and fill that information in for you the next time you visit that website. Privacy concerns for your personally identifiable information and web surfing habits will increase as this data collects over time, so it's important to clear this data periodically. All web browsers offer some type of functionality to clear the information manually or automatically after a certain period. Most web browsers also offer anti-phishing protection to prevent your personal data from being revealed to phishing fraud sites. Some web browsers like Firefox also offer a "private" browsing mode that does not save any browse history or cache any data or images while you are web browsing.

Host-Based Intrusion Detection System

A *host-based intrusion detection system (HIDS)* monitors a specific host for suspicious behavior that could indicate someone is trying to break into the system. An HIDS monitors inbound and outbound network activity, networking service ports, system log files, and timestamps and content of data and configuration files to ensure they have not been changed. The host-based system can only monitor the system on which it is installed and is typically used for critical server systems rather than user workstations. A host-based system can detect attacks that occur from a malicious user who is physically accessing the system console. The unauthorized user may be trying to access an administrator account or trying to copy files to or from the system, for example. The intrusion detection system can also alert the administrator if someone has tried to log in to an account unsuccessfully too many times.

An HIDS using active methods of detection can take immediate steps to halt an intrusion. This is the preferable method, because it prevents the suspicious activity from continuing. Passive methods merely log the incident or alert the administrator, who might not see the message for many hours before she can act. If the intrusion is detected as originating at the system console, the system can shut down and disable that user account or automatically log out the user. Locking accounts is a form of detection used by most network operating systems that disable accounts if a predefined number of unsuccessful logins occurs. The disadvantage of active detection is the case of a false-positive detection, in which the system automatically shuts down services when no attack is occurring; this can cause unnecessary and often costly downtime. Passive detection methods do not take active steps to prevent an intrusion from continuing if it is detected. Passive methods typically include logging events to a system log that can be viewed by an administrator later, or if configured to do so, to forward the log entries through e-mail, instant messaging, or a text message. This enables the administrator to be notified as the intrusion is happening and gives the administrator a chance to catch the unauthorized user in the act and to prevent damage or data theft. If the administrator is not immediately notified, they must be sure to audit system log files regularly for critical warnings and errors that indicate suspicious activity.

Exam Tip
Remember that active intrusion detection takes steps to mitigate an intrusion, whereas a passive system typically logs the event or generates alarms.

Live Media

In the event of a crisis, *live media* can be a great way to roll back to a trusted configuration to begin recovering from any damage. Live media allows an administrator or first responder to boot directly from trusted media, commonly a CD or flash drive, in lieu of booting from the hard drive. This supplies nonpersistence, meaning that anything malicious or unauthorized currently residing on the main drive can likely be overcome. Creating live media also allows for a master image to be stored in multiple areas both onsite and offsite, allowing an almost automated course of action as needed. Generally, one goes into the BIOS of the system and changes the boot order to boot from the desired media that has a known good operating system and required drivers. On the other hand, live media can also be used to bypass secure operating systems and configurations for nefarious purposes if users use them instead of their required, secure operating system that would have been otherwise loaded. Take note that this is more difficult on UEFI systems and may not be possible if they are sufficiently locked down.

Virtualization

Virtualization has several situations that should be considered when host-based scenarios are discussed. Virtual machines (VMs) can take snapshots that allow the administrators to "roll back" to a point in time, perhaps before data loss or the introduction of malware into the enterprise. Virtualization allows elasticity, where resources can be divided ad hoc upon demand, with minimum—or no—downtime. This also provides a near-automated course of action as required, with the added benefits of being highly scalable and allowing resources to be allocated in a distributed manner. Virtual machines also allow so-called *sandboxing*, where the underlying machine layer supposedly is unharmed in the event of a malware outbreak or other security breach. Penetration tests that encompass virtualization are a good idea in an enterprise where virtualization is present.

Hypervisors

The hypervisor is an application that creates and runs virtual machines. There are two types of hypervisors: Type 1 and Type 2. A Type 1 hypervisor is essentially a bare-bones operating system that runs the host machine and serves to provide the single functionality of managing the virtual machines installed on it. These types of hypervisors are usually called *bare-metal* (or sometimes *native*) hypervisors, simply because they provide a very limited functionality, and exist to load the physical machine and handle resource access from the virtual machines. For the most part, Type 1 hypervisors are usually installed and then run in "headless" mode, meaning that they don't require a user to be located at the console, but are generally managed remotely through client software on a workstation. For larger environments, Type 1 hypervisors are normally used, and typically use powerful physical hardware.

A Type 2 hypervisor is an application that runs on top of a more conventional operating system. Popular Type 2 hypervisors include VMware and Oracle VirtualBox software. Type 2 hypervisors can create and manage a limited number of virtual machines, and are often used in small environments to create and test different aspects of virtualization, including applications that would not run natively on the host OS.

Virtualization Risks

Of course, even with beneficial technologies like virtualization, there are risks inherent to them. Virtualization is the solution to many problems, such as scalability, hardware production, and even security in some respects, but there are also risks that go with it. One of the risks that virtualization incurs is single points of failure for host machines, simply because if the host machine becomes unavailable, loses connectivity, or encounters a serious hardware error, all the virtual machines that reside on it are also lost. Another risk is that because there may be multiple virtual machines running on a host, some of which may have several different services or even levels of security controls running on them, this adds to the attack surface of the host, especially if the numbers have grown out of hand (known as *VM sprawl*), making their maintenance increasingly difficult. The different services that the virtual machines run communicate with the outside world and the network, so they represent different attack vectors as well. These represent a threat not only to each individual virtual machine, but also overall to the host. Finally, there are attacks, known as *VM escapes,* that attempt to "break out" of the VM environment and attack the hypervisor, or even the host operating system.

Travel Assistance
Virtualization is also discussed within Chapter 8.

Understand Mobile Security Concepts and Technologies

Mobile devices are everywhere! Consider that smartphones, tablet devices, laptop computers, e-readers, and even car stereos now contain the computing power of many traditional desktop machines only a few years ago; the proliferation of mobile devices has far exceeded the adoption of those desktop machines. The concern with mobile devices, however, is their care and maintenance from a security perspective. Have you considered patching your car recently?

Mobile Device Security

Mobile computing devices include laptops, as well as smartphones, tablets, netbooks, and other types of wireless devices. Security concerns for mobile devices derive from the nature of their portability, which makes them susceptible to theft, vandalism, and unauthorized access to data. The following areas describe additional security precautions to consider with mobile devices.

Securing Your Connection

As we've discussed throughout this book, connectivity allows you to transfer information from one point to another using more conventional means (such as cellular or Wi-Fi networks) to the more innovative or rare (ANT or infrared). Each of these has its own nuances that must be considered when you're looking to apply security controls, but there are often commonalities, such as minimizing your attack surface by disabling unneeded capabilities and keeping your devices patched.

Cellular Simple cellular service, while often considered more secure than using strange Wi-Fi hotspots, is still vulnerable to eavesdropping by several parties, not least of which is the cellular provider itself. When using a cellular device, it's a smart idea to disable any geolocation services that could allow you to be tracked and turn off other communications methods that might be in discovery mode (such as Wi-Fi, Bluetooth, and NFC) unless needed at that moment.

SATCOM Satellite communications (SATCOM) are the backbone of some truly critical systems, both military and non-military, including Air Traffic Control. If a hacker can gain access to a device that can communicate with one of the many satellites orbiting the earth, he or she can often monitor the traffic, or even worse, transmit false traffic, or deny it completely. There is growing concern that if you are using a SATCOM device, you should closely track patch availability, patch as quickly as possible, and look to build redundant, non-SATCOM capabilities if possible.

Wi-Fi When possible, use the highest level of encryption available to you, such as WPA2. Do not connect to SSIDs that you are unfamiliar with, such as free airport or coffee shop access points. Use a VPN whenever possible, even on mobile devices.

Bluetooth Without proper authentication, an unauthorized user can connect to unprotected Bluetooth devices and access any data stored on the device. If you choose to use Bluetooth, see if your device allows discovery mode to be disabled when not required.

NFC While the range of Near Field Communication (NFC) is limited to the immediate proximity of the devices, the standard itself is essentially an emanation and is quite vulnerable to eavesdropping and man-in-the-middle attacks by anyone within that same vicinity. Unless required, do not enable NFC, and if you do choose to use it as a connection method, disable it when not in use.

Travel Assistance

Securing wireless networks, including the use of Wi-Fi, Bluetooth, and NFC, is covered in more depth within Chapter 10.

Deployment Models

An organization must determine if or how personal mobile devices will be used within its facilities and on its network, what level of control the organization seeks over the devices, and what rights to content and privacy the employee has. This should be expressed in a formal policy that is distributed to and signed by all employees. The following sections describe a variety of deployment model options that can be used, varying in levels of organizational control.

BYOD

Once ownership of mobile devices became the norm, people began carrying both personal and corporate mobile devices, which is unwieldy. The *bring your own device (BYOD)* deployment model allows users to join their personal device to the corporate network and use it for official purposes. This creates many difficult scenarios, however, revolving around ownership of content, patching and antivirus, and loss or theft of the device.

CYOD

Another option is *CYOD*, or *choose your own device*. In this deployment model, companies have a list of approved devices that they will supply a user, and the user chooses the one that is best for his or her needs. Although this does allow some flexibility for the user, the company benefits from much more standardization and control than with the BYOD model.

COPE

An alternative for organizations that are wary of allowing users to bring their own devices is the *COPE* model, or *company owned, personally enabled*. This means that the company purchases the device but allows the user to use it both as a personal and a corporate device. This loosens the restrictions somewhat on what can be installed and what content can be resident on a device, but gives to the company greater standardization and more control than the BYOD model.

Corporate-Owned

Of course, there is the good old *corporate-owned* model, which means that the company chooses the model and supplies it to the user, with no ability to customize. Although this might not be the most flexible for the user, it does provide the company with the highest levels of control.

VDI

Finally, one solution you should also be aware of is the *Virtual Desktop Infrastructure (VDI)*, which allows legacy applications to be run on mobile devices, like how a virtual machine runs on a more traditional workstation.

Deployment Concerns

With the proliferation of mobile devices within the workforce, more organizations have begun allowing employees to use their own devices (such as mobile phones and tablets) for work purposes, requiring them to access the corporate information using their personally owned devices. Although this may seem to be logical (employees already have the device, requiring less up-front cost for equipment), several practical considerations should be addressed. Regardless of the deployment model in the organization, there are challenges that must be dealt with.

Ownership

- **Data ownership**   As discussed earlier, BYOD entails the employee using his or her own device to perform work. However, who owns the data on the device? Does the organization have policies supporting this?

- **Support ownership**   Who is responsible for performing technical support on an employee-owned device? Should the IT staff be responsible for supporting any device configuration?

- **Carrier unlocking**   Smartphones often are locked to a particular carrier, and can only be used on the carrier unless they are purchased specially or the contract has expired. Carrier unlocking outside of these parameters can often incur additional costs. Furthermore, all phones likely will not work on all carriers, so consider this when making choices about a carrier change.

Security Management

- **Patches and antivirus**   Patches, antivirus, and other security-related solutions are almost universally accepted on company-owned devices. However, when the device is employee owned, will the user accept this software being loaded on his or her device? Is there a policy in place to require these, and how will it be enforced?

- **Acceptable use policies and adherence**   Acceptable use policies (AUP) are designed to list the things that are not allowed on company devices, or traffic that is not allowed to traverse the company infrastructure. This generally includes things like pornography, gaming, and stock trading. However, can you force a user to not conduct these activities on a device they own?

- **On-board camera/video**   Many devices now have embedded cameras and video recording devices. Within high-security situations, these are often unacceptable. Even within lower-security workplaces, you may be uncomfortable with employees having the ability to record activities (think of a meeting discussing HR actions, for example).

- **On-boarding/off-boarding**   If a BYOD policy is implemented, there will need to be procedures for adding new devices to the infrastructure.

However, there should also be procedures for removing devices when employees leave. Just as you should remove user accounts across the enterprise, you should also have a plan to remove company accounts and data from employee-owned devices.

- **Architecture/infrastructure considerations**   These concerns have implications for your IT staff and potentially your architecture as well. Can your staff be expected to support a wide variety of devices? What software solutions will you implement on devices, and are they compatible with multiple mobile OSs? Will you need more or newer infrastructure to support the load?

- **Device loss or theft**   If a device used in a BYOD scenario is lost or stolen, who is it reported to in addition to the corporate security office? The police? The vendor's or user's insurance company? And who pays the replacement cost for the device? Some personal insurance policies and device warranties do not cover a personal device that is also used for work purposes. In addition, in the interests of protecting corporate data, can the device be remotely wiped? If the user has not backed up his or her personal data, it will be wiped as well. Is this acceptable to the user?

Legal

- **Privacy issues**   Employees may have concerns that their private data is not so private when their devices are connected to the company network. What will be the policies controlling access to this data, and what are the procedures in place for dealing with situations when private data is compromised?

- **Legal concerns**   As discussed previously, the device may be employee owned, but the company data should belong to the company, no matter where it resides. However, this issue needs to be intricately examined by the legal staff and codified clearly in a manner that strengthens the company's position in the event of a lawsuit or other legal action.

- **Forensic examinations**   Forensic analysis is often relied upon to uncover unapproved or illegal behaviors, even those that occurred some time ago and have been (mostly) erased. Much like more traditional computing systems, mobile devices can be a treasure trove of information regarding user activities, particularly for user movement (GPS) and contacts (text and e-mail messages); however, the tricky part can be distinguishing employee data from company data. Further, forensic analysis can uncover activities that, while unapproved on company time, are legal and legitimate during personal hours. Again, policies should be in place considering these situations and how they will be handled.

Protection from Theft

A mobile phone lying on a desk can be tucked into a coat pocket in seconds, but unattended laptops can disappear just as quickly off a user's desk, even during office hours. Mobile devices should never be left unattended, and small items such as smartphones and tablets should be safely secured in a pocket, purse, or belt holster. Larger items, such as laptops, can be secured to a desk or workstation using a special lockable cable.

Password/Screen Lock/Lockout

If a mobile device is stolen, a simple authentication scheme can deter the unauthorized user from accessing any sensitive information on the device. The thief may simply want the hardware rather than the data that resides within, but any device that contains confidential information can be stolen for its valuable content, such as company data or personal identity information. A simple screen lock password can block access to the device until the password is properly entered. On laptops, you can enable a BIOS password that is required at boot time before the operating system loads to prevent anyone from starting up the laptop unless the password is entered. Further, a lockout will disable the device after a certain number of attempts. For example, a mobile phone could be wiped remotely after five attempts; in the event of a lost or stolen phone, this could save the organization from any number of issues.

Biometrics

Biometric controls on a mobile device often include physical features such as fingerprints. Combined with other authentication factors such as a PIN or password, biometric elements can provide a very secure authentication mechanism.

Travel Assistance
Biometrics are discussed further within Chapter 7.

GPS Tracking

Many mobile devices, primarily phones, contain global positioning system (GPS) chips so that they can be tracked by and use the services of GPS satellites. If your device is ever lost or stolen, you can track the location of the device via its GPS coordinates and attempt to recover it. Understand that GPS functionality also allows pictures and other objects to be "geo-tagged," so a user's whereabouts can be tracked. Although this might be appealing for personal social media, geo-tagging has inherent privacy concerns, especially when those official mobile communications should be sensitive and private.

Remote Wipe

If your device is lost or stolen, an unauthorized person may be able to access your data if there are no authentication or encryption mechanisms in use. As a protection against such unauthorized access, many mobile devices can remotely delete their contents. Your mobile device can be tracked by its hardware address, and you can use a management application or a web browser application to initiate a remote wipe of the device so that all your data is deleted. You may have lost the hardware, but your private data is protected by removing it from the device.

Full Device Encryption

Beyond authentication, devices can be protected using encryption. When the contents of a mobile device are encrypted, the corresponding encryption key is required before any user can read any data. If the user does not have the key, no access is granted. This is useful for password files that users sometimes keep on their smartphones flash memory cards, and other mobile devices. Many OSs now come with encrypted file systems, such as BitLocker for Windows and FileVault for macOS. Users can selectively encrypt partitions or entire hard drives that require a password key for access. The files are encrypted and decrypted "on the fly" as the authorized user accesses them. The drive encryption typically employs Advanced Encryption Standard (AES) 128- or 256-bit encryption technology. This encryption slows down performance but provides excellent security for laptops and prevents an unauthorized user from accessing any contents of the hard drive.

Voice Encryption

Voice communications over mobile phones can be intercepted and captured just like any other network communication. For high-security environments and for personal confidentiality, you can encrypt voice communications between users. Software encryption programs are available that run on your mobile device and, when activated, encrypt the voice communication between two users. The other user requires the same software to decrypt and encrypt the communication.

Protection from Users

Although mobile devices are ripe targets for thieves and spies, perhaps the most worrisome group is the users themselves. Mobile devices will most often be used appropriately and for their intended purpose, but they present unique opportunities for malicious activities. The following areas should be considered to protect your company from intended (or unintended) employee bad behavior.

Mobile Camera Security

Almost everyone owns a personal and/or company mobile phone. Mobile phones are now used for more than telephone conversations and often offer a combination of features—such as a web browser, e-mail reader, music player, calendar, and camera. In high-security environments, mobile phones with cameras are often banned because they can be concealed and used to take high-resolution images that can be instantly transferred offsite via the cell phone network. In unprotected environments, it can be easy for an unauthorized user to connect a mobile phone or other type of mobile device to a computer and copy data to the device for later use. Mobile phones are considered vital communications devices, and it can be difficult to justify the temporary confiscation of a camera mobile phone. But in high-security environments, doing so protects the confidentiality and security of data.

Mobile Device Management

Mobile device management (MDM) requires an organization to develop an infrastructure that can account for all the different types of mobile devices used to process, store, transmit, and receive organizational data in the same way that more traditional devices do. MDM often includes software that manages applications on these mobile devices (called *mobile application management,* or *MAM*). MDM manages many of the same considerations you would have within a more traditional infrastructure, such as patch management, access control, antivirus, and authentication, along with the more mobile-specific requirements such as context-aware authentication and remote wipe in the event of loss or theft.

Organizations that distribute mobile devices to their users may choose to control the applications that are installed or executed, and the content that can be present or loaded on the device. For example, you could choose to remove the games, instant messaging features, or the ability to stream videos while connected to the corporate network. Another control that should be considered is blocking third-party application stores. Be mindful of the ability of users to potentially "root" or "jailbreak" their devices; this process uses mobile device software exploits to allow third-party applications to be loaded, as well as features that aren't approved to be used. Similarly, applications and custom firmware can be sideloaded, using external media.

Many companies, particularly those operating in sensitive environments, choose to also disable unused features or those that could present security concerns. These might include Bluetooth, Wi-Fi, cameras, voice or video recording, Short Message Service (SMS) or Multimedia Message Service (MMS) use (often known as *texting*), over-the-air (OTA) updates, use of external media or devices (using technologies such as USB on-the-go), the ability to connect to wireless ad hoc networks, tethering (use of the data plan to create a wireless access point), and the use of NFC payment methods, such as Apple Pay. Each of these can create its own security concerns and potentially compromise both the company and personal data resident on the mobile device.

After a policy has been created, the IT staff should implement that policy, whether it involves application control, disabling features, or both, using a group policy for mobile devices. Some mobile OSs are better suited for this; it is worth investigating what the implications will be and then determine the implementation and maintenance costs for a mobile rollout.

Asset Control

You'd never dream of allowing someone to casually walk out of your building with a desktop PC unless authorized. In fact, your organization might implement regular scans to determine equipment inventory and location.

Mobile devices require the same consideration, with the added challenge that they're often meant to walk out of the building. It's still a good idea to know who has what and where it is. You might implement inventory control through those same regular scans, as well as use stickers that have the organization name, a phone number to contact if lost, and a tracking number. You might also implement measures to turn on the GPS onboard the device for tracking, or *geo-location*. This type of asset tracking allows for potential recovery if lost, as well as device access control. Perhaps you don't want any mobile devices within sensitive areas of your building, like executive conference rooms or secure laboratories. In this case, you could use the GPS to "geo-fence" the area, and implement access control measures that track where devices are located within the facility, alerting you when mobile devices enter unapproved areas. Another scenario might be that users are given cellular phones or tablets, but are not allowed to plug them in via USB. There should be policies limiting this behavior, and the security solutions on the network should be configured to support those policies.

Push Notification Technologies

Push notifications are small messages sent to a device from a central server, often as alerts or notices. Notifications require that the device have a network connection; while push has been used for some time to deliver personal alerts such as news and sports scores, MDM now uses push notifications to perform a wide variety of management functions, including changes in policies or configurations. Notifications can also force applications to schedule an update at a given time or when reconnected to the corporate infrastructure.

Push notifications aren't the only way to send control messages and management commands to devices; the Short Message Service (SMS) that is typically used over cellular services to send text messages can also be used for many of the same purposes. Because SMS doesn't require as robust of data services, it can be used to send messages to the device if the infrastructure can't easily communicate with it, such as when there is a weak cellular connection.

Storage

Mobile devices now have quite a bit of storage space; in fact, today's cellular phones have as much (or more) storage available for use as desktop computers did less than ten years ago. Mobile devices also can function as removable storage devices, generally by plugging in through a USB interface. However, this also allows sensitive information to be offloaded to the device easily, either for malicious or just careless purposes. A good data loss prevention (DLP) solution would look for mobile devices that are connected and monitor (or block) any data transfer.

Mobile devices, like more traditional computer systems, can also support storage segmentation. This allows more performance-intensive applications to be executed in a segment that increases the performance of that application. Because mobile devices are somewhat less powerful than desktop or laptop computing systems, this can improve performance noticeably.

Data Containerization

Data containerization, often referred to as *mobile sandboxing*, creates containers within a mobile device that separate different types of data from each another, such as corporate and personal data. This is often used in BYOD implementations and allows the different types of data to be managed according to the organization's policy. For example, containers can be created that allow corporate data to be encrypted and only accessible by certain applications, and to disable the ability to copy and paste between personal and corporate applications. Data containerization also allows a remote administrator selectively to remove corporate data from the mobile device, in the case of a data leak other negative event, while not touching personal data.

CHECKPOINT

✔**Objective 11.01: Analyze and Differentiate Among Types of Malware** Slow responsiveness and high network activity can indicate malware activity on a system. Keep antivirus software up to date to detect new types of viruses and spyware. Don't connect malware-infected host systems to a network until they are cleaned.

✔**Objective 11.02: Carry Out Appropriate Procedures to Establish Host Security** Use antivirus software to protect yourself against a wide variety of malware programs. Host-based firewalls can monitor the inbound and outbound network activity of your system and notify you of abnormal behavior. They can also provide the ability to block or allow access. Use passwords and encryption to protect the data of mobile devices. Use security baselines and policies to establish a strong, secure foundation for your OS, applications, and web browsers for all your systems, including mobile devices.

✔**Objective 11.03: Understand Mobile Security Concepts and Technologies** Mobile devices present both opportunities and challenges to organizations. Strong policies should be implemented that consider measures such as full device encryption, screen locks and device lockout, use of cameras and video, and remote wiping. Understand the differences between the various deployment models. If your company chooses to allow personal devices to connect to the corporate network, understand that there are issues with data and support ownership, patch and antivirus management, and acceptable use within the network. Also, be aware that there are many legal and privacy concerns that are inherent with personal and company data residing on employee-owned devices.

REVIEW QUESTIONS

1. You suspect that your server has been compromised because it has been running slowly and is unresponsive. Using a network analyzer, you also notice that large amounts of network data are being sent out from the server. Which of the following is the most likely cause?

    A. The server has a rootkit installed.

    B. The server requires an operating system update.

    C. The server is infected with spyware.

    D. The server is part of a botnet.

2. As part of your security baselining and operating system hardening, you want to make sure you protect yourself from vulnerabilities in your operating system software. Which of the following tasks should you perform?

    A. Update antivirus signature files.

    B. Install any patches or OS updates.

    C. Use an encrypted file system.

    D. Use a host-based intrusion detection system.

3. On a mobile device, _____ allows more performance-intensive applications to execute within their own segment to improve performance.

4. A user has brought a virus-infected laptop into the facility. It contains no antivirus protection software and hasn't been hooked up to the network yet. What's the best way to fix the laptop?

    A. Get the laptop on the network and download antivirus software from a server.

    B. Boot the laptop with an antivirus boot CD.

    C. Get the laptop on the network and download antivirus software from the Internet.

    D. Connect the laptop to another computer and clean it up from there.

5. You are creating a standard security baseline for all users who use company mobile phones. Which of the following is the most effective security measure to protect against unauthorized access to the mobile device?

    A. Enforce the use of a screen lock password.

    B. Enable the GPS chip.

    C. Install personal firewall software.

    D. Automatically perform a daily remote wipe.

6. Your network has had a history of problems with users downloading software from the Internet that contains Trojan horse software with back-door access. A _____ will best detect and prevent this activity.

7. A security patch for your OS was released about a week after you applied the latest operating system service pack. What should you do?

    A. Wait until the release of the next full service pack.

    B. Download the patch only if you experience problems with the OS.

    C. Do nothing—the security patch was probably included with the service pack.

    D. Download and install the security patch.

8. Your application firewall is indicating that some type of HTTP worm is trying to infect one of your database servers, which also seems to be running an HTTP web server on port 80. This server does not need any type of web services. What should be done?

    A. Install antivirus software.

    B. Change the web server to use a different port.

    C. Disable the web server.

    D. Update your firewall software to the latest version.

9. To protect the confidentiality of users' web browsing history and website credentials, which of the following security baseline policies should you enable for all users' web browsers?

    A. Block third-party cookies.

    B. Periodically delete the browser cache.

    C. Enforce SSL.

    D. Disable JavaScript.

10. You have recently installed antivirus software on several client workstations and performed a full scan of the systems. One of the systems was infected with a virus less than an hour after the installation of the software. Which of the following is the most likely issue?

    A. The virus was preexisting on the system.

    B. Antivirus signatures need to be updated.

    C. The virus could only be blocked by a pop-up blocker.

    D. Operating system software was out of date.

11. There is an active shooter incident within your company, and your CEO has directed you to push a message out to all corporate mobile devices to account for the safety of all personnel by their "checking in." What is the *best* option to be sure that even personnel with weak cellular connections receive the message?

    A. MMS

    B. SMS

    C. Push notification

    D. E-mail

REVIEW ANSWERS

1. **D** If your system has been infected with a worm or virus and has become part of a botnet, at certain time, it may take part in distributed denial-of-service attacks on another system on the Internet and may exhibit slow responsiveness and a large amount of network data being sent out of the system.

2. **B** The most recent software updates and patches for your operating system will contain the latest bug and exploit fixes. This prevents known bugs and weakness in the operating system from being exploited.

3. **storage segmentation** Storage segmentation allows more performance-intensive applications to be executed in a segment that increases the performance of those applications. Because mobile devices are somewhat less powerful than desktop or laptop computing systems, this can improve performance noticeably.

4. **B** If a computer is infected with a virus, do not connect it to a network, or you run the risk of the virus infecting other computers and servers. Use an antivirus program on a boot CD to clean the virus off the laptop before connecting it to the network.

5. **A** To prevent unauthorized access to the device in the event it is lost or stolen, you can enable a screen lock password. The user will not be able to access the device until he enters the password.

6. **host-based firewall** Host-based firewalls can block incoming network connections and watch for suspicious outbound activity, helping to protect against Trojan horse malware attempting to allow back-door access.

7. **D** Even though you just installed the latest service pack, a security vulnerability might have recently been discovered, requiring that you install a new security patch. You will not be protected from the vulnerability if you do not install the security patch, and it might be too dangerous to wait for it to be included in the next service pack.

8. **C** Any application or service that is not needed by the server should be disabled or uninstalled. Leaving services enabled, such as a web server, could make the server vulnerable to web server attacks, including HTTP-based worms.

9. **A** Third-party cookies are typically from advertising sites not related to the specific site you are browsing. By blocking these cookies, you will protect any identifying information in your web browsing history from being leaked to third-party companies.

10. **B** Your antivirus software is installed with a default database of virus signatures. It may be several months out of date, and it is a best practice to immediately run the signature file update to make sure you are running with the latest signatures. Otherwise, the antivirus software may miss detecting a newly identified virus.

11. **B** Although push notifications work well with a strong, steady connection to either a cellular or Wi-Fi network, SMS is more likely to get the message out to users who might have a weak signal.

Securing Applications and Data

	NEWBIE	SOME EXPERIENCE	EXPERT
ETA	3.5 hours	2.5 hours	1.5 hour

As part of a layered security model, your network perimeter is the first layer of defense for preventing network attacks and unauthorized intrusion. If a hacker were to penetrate the network perimeter, the next layer of defense is the security for your host systems that provides protection against attacks and intrusions directed at specific host servers and clients in your network.

Application security is another layer of defense that provides protection for the applications that run on your hosts. These include Internet servers such as web, e-mail, File Transfer Protocol (FTP), and database servers. Internet web servers are the most common types of servers that come under attack, and extra care must be taken when you're deploying web applications because their public nature provides the opportunity for hackers to take advantage of vulnerabilities unique to web services, such as buffer overflows, input validation, cross-site scripting, and command insertion. A hacker can send malformed input to a web application, causing it to crash, provide unauthorized access, or result in data theft and loss. Clients who connect to malicious websites from their web browser can have their login credentials and session information stolen, thus allowing a hacker unauthorized access to perform actions with the credentials of the target client.

Application security also requires careful consideration of how the application was designed and developed. Secure coding concepts must be closely adhered to. This ensures that when the application is created and deployed, it uses a secure baseline to prevent the most common types of vulnerabilities.

The final layer of security protection is for the actual data on your host systems. Stored data must be secured from unauthorized access, theft, loss, and manipulation.

This chapter explores various security threats and risks for applications and describes secure coding concepts and application hardening. Protection for stored data is also discussed, including data loss prevention, encryption techniques, and security concerns for removable media.

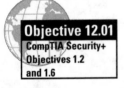

Objective 12.01
CompTIA Security+
Objectives 1.2
and 1.6

Analyze and Differentiate Among Types of Attacks and Vulnerabilities

Due to the wide variety of operating systems, programming languages, and application platforms, the chances of encountering security vulnerabilities are greatly increased due to the interaction of these different levels of software that host and provide application services. For example, a hacker may be able to insert operating system commands into a web application query input form that are run as if the hacker were the administrative user. Attacks on database servers and data queries can result in a hacker obtaining unauthorized access to confidential data stored by the database if the application is not secure and the stored data not encrypted.

Server administrators must be aware of the various types of application vulnerabilities that can exist within different types of Internet servers, such as web, e-mail, and database servers, as well as know how to mitigate them and prevent the vulnerabilities from being exploited.

Web Application Vulnerabilities

Internet web servers accept Hypertext Transfer Protocol (HTTP) requests from client web browsers, and they send back responses and the requested information to the clients. Web servers are the most common forms of servers on the Internet, and as a result, they are the most often attacked. An attack can occur in a variety of ways. Some attacks disrupt users from accessing the information on a website. Other attacks spread worms and viruses over the Internet. Some attacks vandalize websites and deface information on web pages or replace it with false information. Most of these attacks take advantage of security vulnerabilities in the web server. The following sections outline some of the more prevalent web application security vulnerabilities.

JavaScript

JavaScript is a scripting language created by Netscape, but it is unrelated to the Java programming language. JavaScript's code is not compiled; instead, it is *interpreted* by the web browser. JavaScript can interact with Hypertext Markup Language (HTML) source code, enabling web authors to create websites with dynamic content.

Since the introduction of JavaScript, the language has been plagued with security issues. The problems originate from the nature of JavaScript, which allows executable content to be embedded into web pages. These vulnerabilities include the ability for hackers to read files on a user's hard drive and to monitor and intercept a user's web activities. Security precautions are required to prevent malicious code from entering, executing, and retrieving data from the underlying system.

The insecurities of web browsers that implement JavaScript, rather than the JavaScript language itself, are the source of the vulnerabilities. Most security problems discovered in JavaScript implementations require the installation of software patches from the web browser vendor. JavaScript can also be disabled on your web browser. Check the browser's options to disable or enable the use of JavaScript for websites accessed by users.

ActiveX

ActiveX is a technology designed by Microsoft to create reusable components across Windows and web applications. This includes increasing the functionality of Internet applications. ActiveX components can be downloaded to the computer through the web browser. ActiveX functions are controlled by the users themselves. This requires the need for greater security controls because a malicious ActiveX component can be downloaded that could compromise the security of your system. Users must be careful when configuring their web browsers to control ActiveX programs.

> **Exam Tip**
>
> Know that ActiveX controls run with the same permissions as those used by the user currently logged in.

For web browsing security, ActiveX uses a form of authentication control based on security levels. The user's web browser can be configured to set a certain security level at which ActiveX controls can operate. The lowest level allows all ActiveX components to be downloaded automatically. Increased levels provide warning dialog boxes to alert the user of an ActiveX element and enable the user to download it or not. ActiveX relies on digital certificates and trusting certificate authorities to authenticate the origin of ActiveX controls. You should never download ActiveX controls that are unsigned because they will not have an identified and authenticated origin and are most likely malicious in nature.

Make sure your web browser is running the latest version so that the most recent security controls are in place and any previous security vulnerabilities are removed.

> **Travel Advisory**
>
> Many people, in the interest of higher security, disable some of the advanced web browser functions, such as downloading ActiveX components. Unfortunately, many websites require these to perform even the most basic functions, and if you disable these functions, you might be unable to access the site. Therefore, try to maintain a balance between convenience and security.

Buffer Overflows

Buffer overflow is a programming term used to describe when input data exceeds the limits recognized by a program. For example, a program might be expecting only a certain number of characters in an input dialog box. If the number of characters exceeds this limit, the added information might also be processed.

This extra code could be malicious in nature and cause the program or even the entire system to crash. Buffer overflow attacks typically result in command shell access in which the attacker has administrative privileges.

> **Travel Advisory**
>
> Several denial-of-service (DoS) attacks are in the form of buffer overflows.

The buffer overflow vulnerability is a common security concern for web servers and web browsers. A malicious web server set up by a hacker can crash the systems of the users connecting to that website by sending various HTTP buffer overflow data streams to the client. Similarly, a malicious hacker using a simple web browser can send certain HTTP data to a web server that overflows its software buffers and crashes the website.

Buffer overflows are caused primarily by poor input validation that allows illegal data to be entered into the application, which causes processing limits to be exceeded. Buffer overflows have long been a thorn in the side of companies that create web server and web browser software. These vulnerabilities are easy to exploit and can significantly affect the performance of a system or cause it to crash.

An *integer overflow* is like a buffer overflow in that it simply cannot be handled within its allotted space; however, it is the result of a mathematical operation that creates a numeric value that is too large (or sometimes too small). When it's successful, the outcome is like a buffer overflow. This can often be handled by converting the numeric value to a nonnumeric value when the value cannot be handled otherwise.

Resource Exhaustion

Resource exhaustion attacks take advantage of the limited resources that most modern computer systems have available for software applications. Resource exhaustion essentially creates a denial-of-service condition, because the resources that are needed to execute actions associated with an application are entirely exhausted (hence the name), leading to either an error, performance slowdown, or a denial of service. This can occur through a *memory leak*, where a software application incorrectly manages its memory resources and does not sufficiently release the memory used when it is no longer needed, or due to malicious network traffic that purposefully causes resource exhaustion.

Privilege Escalation

Many software applications contain bugs that create security vulnerabilities. In a privilege escalation scenario, an unauthorized user exploits these bugs within the software to gain more privileged access to a computer system to bypass the application and perform commands with escalated privileged access.

Vulnerabilities that typically lead to privilege escalation scenarios are most often found in website code, where scripting and other types of running programs can potentially reveal exploits for malicious users to take control of a system. These are often buffer overflow attacks, in which conditions and boundaries are not properly set on user-entered fields in an application or website and allow malicious users to crash the program or allow highly privileged command execution.

Protection against privilege escalation requires that programmers use input validation and test their code for bugs and exploits before releasing the software. If a documented exploit is found after the software is released, it is critical that a patch be quickly made available to fix the bug to prevent proof-of-concept exploits from turning into real security threats. Systems administrators must be diligent in ensuring that any software they run is using the latest patch level to guarantee that all known bug fixes are currently deployed.

> ### Local Lingo
>
> **proof-of-concept exploit**   A situation when a potential threat due to a vulnerability in an application or operating system has become known to the public, enabling malicious hackers to create code to exploit the vulnerability.

Hijacking

Cookies are a necessary part of most website application interaction, but they also represent a wide variety of security issues. Cookies contain session data for each website you visit that uses cookies. The data is usually composed of innocuous items, such as site preferences, that are reloaded when you revisit a site, but often the cookies also contain session data, including some authentication and web form information, along with referral information on websites you have already visited. *Locally shared objects (LSOs)*, often referred to as *Flash cookies*, operate in much the same manner, storing data collected from various websites.

Cookies are easily abused by malicious actors. Cookies are sent in clear text and can be easily captured by an unauthorized user using a network packet sniffer. An unsuspecting user might also click a web link that downloads a malicious script that collects data on the user's web browser cookies and transmits it back to the hacker's website.

Session hijacking can occur when a user's cookie for a website, which can contain session authentication credentials for a remote server, is hijacked by another user, who then uses that cookie to gain unauthorized access. The cookie might be transferred from the user's computer to that of the attacker, or it can be captured via a packet sniffer and a man-in-the-middle network attack.

To protect against session hijacking, web applications should regenerate session keys and IDs after a successful login so that a secondary attempt to use the same session credentials from a hijacked cookie will not work. Applications can also check other aspects of a session, such as the IP address, so if the address is different from the original cookie, a new session must be created and authenticated. High-security applications such as web banking can use Secure Sockets Layer (SSL) to encrypt sessions, including the transfer of information in user cookies.

Clickjacking occurs with multiple layers on a page, often transparent, that trick the user into clicking a link embedded within the page that redirects to malicious site, rather than the link that the user intended to click. This is also often referred to as a *user interface (UI) redress attack*.

HTML Attachments

File attachments received from e-mail messages, instant messaging (IM) messages, and download sites can often contain .htm and .html documents. These document types are the default files for web browsers. These HTML attachments, if opened, can automatically open your web browser and immediately connect to a malicious website. When you are connected to the malicious website, it may transfer files such as malware and Trojan horse software to your computer. Many e-mail readers automatically open HTML attachments, which can contain malicious dynamic content and automatically load other web data, images, or even hidden code that executes on the client.

If you receive an HTML attachment, make sure it is from a trusted source. Before opening it in a web browser, you should open the HTML file in a text editor to view its contents and check for any abnormal code. Most e-mail clients have security settings that prevent the loading of images in HTML messages unless you explicitly allow them. You can add known sites to a trusted sites list, which configures the e-mail client to automatically display images because you know they come from a trusted source.

Malicious Add-Ons

Most web browsers enable all the functionality of *add-ons,* which are installable modules that provide useful functionality to a user's web-browsing experience. These add-ons can be anything from decorative themes, to real-time alerts for weather and stocks, to web utilities. There is the possibility that these add-ons, if not from a trusted source, can contain malicious code that can do anything from installing a Trojan horse program that allows remote access to a user's computer, to stealing confidential personal information.

Make sure when you install add-ons to your web browser that they originate from a trusted source, such as the web browser's official site. As developers upload their add-ons for public use, they are analyzed and scanned for evidence of malicious code. If you download an add-on from an untrusted source, you have no verification that the code has been tested. Personal firewalls can also alert you to abnormal network connection behavior after you have installed an add-on.

CGI Scripts

Common Gateway Interface (CGI) scripts are programs designed to accept and return data that conforms to the CGI specification. CGI programs are typically written in scripting languages such as Perl and are the most common way for web servers to interact dynamically with users. Web pages that contain forms typically use a CGI program to process the form's data once it's submitted.

Each time a CGI script is executed, a new process is started. For some websites, multiple CGI requests can noticeably slow down the server. CGI scripts also are vulnerable to programming bugs, so they should be written with the same care and attention as any software application. Poorly programmed CGI scripts can intentionally or unintentionally provide information about the host system that can aid malicious hackers in accessing the web server. Scripts that utilize user input from web forms can be used against the client machine. For example, on a server system, a subverted CGI script can be used to run malicious code as a privileged user and provide unauthorized access to any part of the system, including sensitive user data as well as logins and passwords. Another concern of CGI scripting is the ability of the user to input data that can be used to attack the web server through buffer overflows and malformed requests.

Cross-Site Scripting

Cross-site scripting (XSS) is a type of website application vulnerability that allows malicious users to inject malicious code into dynamic websites that rely on user input. An example of this would be a search engine website or user message forum that utilizes user input. The malicious user can input a script or series of commands, such as JavaScript, within a legitimate input request that can provide the attacker with additional administrative access to hack user accounts and embed malicious code within cookies and other website code that can be downloaded by end users. An unsuspecting user can click a link that downloads a malicious script that collects data on the user's web browser cookies and transmits it back to the website.

Cross-Site Request Forgery (XSRF)

Cross-site request forgery (XSRF or CSRF) is a type of attack that relies on the ability to use a user's current web browsing state, including session cookie data and login identity credentials, and trick that user into navigating to a website that contains malicious code. At that point, the hacker's code can use the session information to make unauthorized requests as the target user, change the user's account information, or steal his credentials. XSRF vulnerabilities have been found on many major websites, including high-security banking sites.

Header Manipulation

Header manipulation is a type of web application vulnerability where invalid or malicious data is inserted into HTTP headers. HTTP request and response messages have headers that include various HTTP commands, directives, site referral information, and address data. This data is simple text that can be modified by a malicious user. By manipulating this header information, a hacker can then perform a variety of attacks such as cross-site scripting, session and web page hijacking, and cookie modification.

In general, most web applications process server-side headers, which are generally safe and cannot be manipulated, while ignoring client-side headers in HTTP requests because of the security concern that they are easily manipulated.

Injection

Extensible Markup Language (XML) is like HTML in that it is a markup language that uses tags to define data. XML differs from HTML in that whereas HTML is designed to process and display data, XML is used to structure, store, and transport data. In fact, XML carries no data at all, but is designed to structure it. XML is used in a wide variety of web applications.

XML injection attacks can modify how an XML application processes data. By injecting XML content into the XML application, the attacker causes the application to process data according to the malicious injected XML code. Web applications that process XML documents require input and document schema validation to prevent XML injection attacks from occurring.

DLL injections exploit Dynamic Link Libraries (DLLs) by inserting code into a DLL and then having the original process to load and then execute the code within the DLL. DLLs were designed to be loaded when required at runtime, making them uniquely qualified for this attack. Injections insert code into a running process, forcing another program to behave in a manner that the original program was not intended to do.

Sometimes, web applications without proper input validation can allow operating system–level commands to be inserted into uniform resource locators (URLs) or input forms that are executed on the server. This can allow an unauthorized user to perform commands on the server with escalated privileges or to gain access to sensitive data without authentication or authorization. Each type of *command injection* attack is specific to an operating system, such as Unix or Windows, or the programming language of the web application.

For example, a malicious user might be able to specify a URL with an escape character (such as ?), where he can type additional commands that are executed after the main URL. Unix systems can also make use of the pipe (|) command to allow additional commands to be run as part of the primary command execution.

You can prevent command injection by implementing input validation techniques that allow the user to input only limited data in web application fields and that filter out escape characters like the pipe character that a user might input to try to enter additional commands. Additional hardening techniques can be used to disable advanced functions in web applications that provide deep-level system access.

Directory Traversal

Directory traversal is a type of access vulnerability where a hacker can get unauthorized access to files on a web server other than the public files that are served on the website. For example, a hacker might be able to learn the directory URL structure of a site by studying the naming conventions of the links. The hacker can input a manual URL to try to guess the link of a specific file or can actually navigate the website directory tree through the URL, via ../ on a Unix system or ..\ on a Windows system, to go to the parent directory. If permissions are not properly set on the directory tree, the hacker might be able to read and copy important system files, including user login and password databases, such as / etc/passwd on Unix systems.

You can prevent directory traversal attacks by ensuring that input validation on all website input forms prevents changing directories, setting permissions on directories to prevent viewing their contents, preventing debugging information (such as error messages with full URL paths) from being displayed, and using back-end databases to store any information that needs to be viewed on a website so that any important data files are not stored on the web server.

Arbitrary Code Execution

Arbitrary code execution (sometimes referred to as *remote code execution*) describes the situation where an intruder can execute a command at will, whenever and wherever, thanks to a vulnerability on your system, usually in an application. This type of attack has been possible within any number of applications, from operating systems to programming frameworks, and even video games.

Arbitrary code execution is considered one of the most serious types of attacks because once an attacker has gained control of a process, he can potentially use this to gain access to (and potentially full control of) the entire system.

Zero-Day Attacks

A *zero-day attack* is a type of threat that has rarely or never been encountered, such as an attack technique that takes advantage of previously unknown weaknesses and vulnerabilities in an application or operating system software. Because the attack is brand new, no existing defense has been created to detect it.

Zero-day attacks are very difficult to defend against, but in most cases, OS and software application vendors are very responsive in patching their software in the event a new vulnerability is discovered. You must always make sure your software is running the latest version with all security patches available installed.

You can also use specialized security software such as an intrusion detection system to detect anomalous events that could indicate a zero-day exploit.

Race Conditions

Some software is designed to be executed as a series of steps: Step A is required to be performed before Step B, which is in turn required to occur before Step C, and so on. A race condition happens when the system is dependent on the steps to be performed in an appropriate order, and the steps are subsequently then executed out of order, creating a crash or other negative situation that can be exploited by an attacker. Race conditions can be used to cause a null-pointer dereference, where a pointer inside the code with a value of NULL is used rather than the valid pointer. This generally results in a crash unless handled properly.

Internet Server Vulnerabilities

Beyond web services, additional services such as file transfer, e-mail, domain and address translation, and database transactions are provided by other types of Internet-based servers. The nature of the Internet means that these servers are wide open to abuse from external users. Although network firewalls provide excellent protection against most types of attacks on your public-facing Internet servers, each type of server has its own way of providing information and services and could contain many security vulnerabilities that might allow it to be compromised by unauthorized users. The following sections outline popular Internet servers and identify their unique security vulnerabilities.

Exam Tip

Be aware of the different types of security vulnerabilities inherent with each type of Internet server and know how to prevent servers of that type from being exploited.

FTP Servers

FTP servers are used to transfer files from one system to another across the Internet. A server hosting the files will be running an FTP server service that awaits file transfer requests originating from clients using FTP client software. Many FTP server sites on the Internet are public in nature and allow anonymous users to log in and download or upload files to and from their server. Other companies use authenticated FTP servers to enable clients to download engineering or technical support files. To access the server, the client needs to authenticate using a login and password. Basic types of FTP communications are not encrypted, so any login and password information is sent over the network in clear text and can be easily intercepted by a malicious hacker. Secure FTP (SFTP) software uses encrypted communications to prevent interception by unauthorized users.

Exam Tip

Remember that basic FTP communications, including login and password authentication, are transmitted in clear text. SFTP should be used to encrypt the session utilizing Secure Shell (SSH).

FTP servers are a widely used resource on the Internet and one of the most popular targets for hacking attempts and abuse. FTP server software can be vulnerable to attacks because of inherent bugs in its programming. Software bugs in FTP programs allow unauthorized individuals to gain administrative access to the machine on which the FTP service resides. The malicious hacker can then use that machine as a starting point for other activities, such as performing DoS attacks or hacking attempts on other machines. Because of bugs, any FTP server software you use should be the latest version, with the most recent security patches installed.

Another problem with FTP servers is they are usually installed by default with an anonymous account. This account enables users to access the FTP server without having to authenticate. If the FTP server is a private server containing confidential data that should be accessed only by authorized users, this anonymous account and any anonymous access should be disabled.

DNS Servers

Domain Name System (DNS) servers provide a way to translate Internet domain names into IP addresses. For example, the website *www.server.net* can be translated to an IP address of *192.168.1.12*. This allows network applications and services to refer to Internet domains by their fully qualified domain name (FQDN) rather than their IP address, which can be difficult to remember and can often change. If a company changes its system's IP address, it can simply update the DNS tables to reflect this. External users will not see a difference because they will still be connecting to it by name.

DNS servers perform an extremely valuable function on the Internet, and wide-scale communication interruptions can occur if a network DNS server is disabled. Most client machines use DNS each time they try to connect to a network host. The client's DNS server is configured using its network settings, which can be set manually or automatically through services such as Dynamic Host Configuration Protocol (DHCP). Each time a client tries to access a host, such as a website, the local DNS server is queried for the IP address of the domain name. The DNS server translates the name into an IP address, which the client uses to initiate its connection.

DNS servers can suffer from DoS and malformed request attacks. In a DoS attack, the DNS server is inundated with DNS or ping requests. The load becomes so much that the DNS server cannot respond to legitimate DNS queries. DNS queries to servers can also be manipulated to include malformed input that could crash the server.

DNS servers are also susceptible to *cache poisoning,* where false DNS records are planted using spoofed addresses that result in your name server providing the IP address of a hacker's website instead of the intended destination.

DNS servers use zone transfers, which send DNS information to other name servers. An attacker could perform an unauthorized zone transfer that allows her to list the contents of the DNS records, which can reveal the addresses of critical servers and networking equipment. These zone transfers should be restricted to only allow transfers from designated and trusted DNS servers under your control.

To provide a strong base level of security for your DNS server, make sure that you are running the latest version of your DNS software with the most recent security patches installed. Software vulnerabilities are quickly identified and patched by DNS software vendors, and this will prevent attacks on any known exploits within your DNS software.

DHCP Servers

A *DHCP server* is used to allocate IP addresses and other network information on a network automatically, such as DNS and Windows Internet Naming Service (WINS) information, to clients as they access the network. DHCP servers can be configured instead of having to configure each client on the network manually with specific information. This greatly reduces administrative overhead because, with static manual addressing, if something changes on the network, such as the address of a DNS server, you have to change the information manually on every client.

The main vulnerability with DHCP servers is the lack of an authentication mechanism to allow or disallow clients. Any client system that accesses the network and is configured for DHCP is allocated network information so that it can communicate with the network. This means any unauthorized user can plug his system into a network and be automatically configured for access. A malicious user can also attack a DHCP server using DoS methods to overload it or by trying to use up all the available IP addresses in the DHCP address pool. Then, no new clients can be assigned an address to communicate with the network.

Local Lingo

DHCP address pool   A range of IP addresses set aside by the DHCP server to assign to new clients as they access the network.

As a countermeasure to some attacks, DHCP servers can be configured to communicate only with clients with specific Media Access Control (MAC) addresses. The list of MAC addresses should contain only computers and devices on your internal network. This way, when a DHCP server sees a configuration request from an unknown host, it will ignore the request. You should also keep the DHCP server up to date with service packs and security hotfixes.

Another security concern is the ability for an unauthorized user to set up a rogue DHCP server on the network. If the server manages to answer a client's request for configuration information before the real DHCP server does so, the client might be configured with bogus information that could cause the user's communications to be redirected to other servers under the control of the attacker. The only way to prevent this type of scenario is to scan your network regularly for rogue servers running these services and to control physical access to the facility.

Database Servers

Database servers typically contain relational data used as a back-end repository of information for front-end applications and web services. The most popular forms of database software are Oracle, Microsoft SQL, and MySQL.

The front-end application that accesses the database usually sends commands as a set of procedures for the database to run on the data so that it can return the required results. A malicious user can insert her own code into these procedures to run some query on the database that can reveal or damage confidential data. This is called a *SQL injection* attack and is like buffer overflow and invalid data types of attacks that can be performed from a web browser by passing certain parameters of input that transcend the boundaries of the software's thresholds. If the database software or query function is not configured or programmed correctly, the parameters could bypass built-in security to reveal confidential data or destroy thousands of data records. Normalization is important when managing complex infrastructures filled with a variety of applications and databases. Data must be normalized, or altered to follow a standard naming convention, in order to best support query and retrieval functions. By keeping your database and application software current and properly validating input, these security vulnerabilities can be avoided.

> **Exam Tip**
>
> SQL injection attacks harm database servers by inserting SQL commands into input fields of the application that provides the front end to the database. The commands are then run against the database, providing the unauthorized user with escalated privileges to harm the data stored there.

To protect data privacy and integrity, the use of authentication and access permissions should be configured for a database server. This creates a layered security model that first authenticates the user before she can use the database and then restricts the user's access using permissions and access control lists (ACLs). For example, for certain types of data, you might want most users to have read-only access. Other users who need more access can be granted permission to add, delete, and modify records.

LDAP and Directory Services

Directory services are a repository of information regarding the users and resources of a network. Directory services software applications and protocols are often left open and unprotected because the information they contain sometimes isn't considered important, compared to file server or database server information. Depending on the level of information they provide, however, directory services can be an excellent resource for unauthorized users and attackers to gain knowledge of the workings of the network and the resources and user accounts they contain.

A simple Lightweight Directory Access Protocol (LDAP) service that contains user names, e-mail addresses, phone numbers, and locations can be a resource for an unauthorized user or malicious hacker looking for an accounting user or an engineering user if he is performing corporate espionage. Other types of directory services, such as Microsoft Active Directory, can contain more critical network and user information, such as network addresses, user account logins and passwords, and access information for servers.

At the bare minimum, users who query directory services should be authenticated via a login ID and password. This will at least prevent casual unauthorized users from accessing the data on the network's directory services through queries. This is especially important for protecting more critical network-wide directory services, such as Microsoft Active Directory. Only the administrators of the network should have access to read and change the highest levels of the directory hierarchy, whereas common users should be allowed only to look up basic information, such as the e-mail address of another user. To increase security, directory services should be used in conjunction with secured, encrypted communications protocols, such as Transport Layer Security (TLS).

Applications that perform lookups to LDAP directories are also susceptible to injection attacks. *LDAP injection,* which is like a SQL injection attack, inserts code into user-based input that is utilized in a query to an LDAP server. If the application does not properly validate user input, commands can be inserted into the LDAP queries to perform malicious actions against the LDAP directory, including unauthorized queries and data modification.

E-mail Servers

E-mail servers store incoming mail for users and are responsible for sending outbound mail from local users to their destination. Most e-mail servers are configured to protect user inboxes by requiring users to authenticate to the account. If the user login or password is not valid, the user won't be able to access the contents of the inbox.

Post Office Protocol version 3 (POP3) is an Internet protocol that provides a way for users to retrieve mail from their inboxes using a POP-enabled e-mail client. The e-mail messages are stored on the server until the user connects to it and downloads messages to the e-mail client. Most POP accounts are set to delete the messages from the server after they've been retrieved.

The *Internet Message Access Protocol (IMAP)* is like POP in that it's used to provide a mechanism for receiving messages from a user's inbox. IMAP has more functionality than POP, however, because it gives users more control over what messages they download and how these messages are stored online.

Both basic POP3 and IMAP send credentials in clear text when authenticating. To protect the transfer of credentials from packet sniffers, you should use Secure POP or Secure IMAP services, which utilize SSL to encrypt the login and passwords.

Exam Tip

POP uses TCP port 110, and IMAP uses TCP port 143. Secure POP uses TCP port 995, and Secure IMAP uses TCP port 993.

The *Simple Mail Transport Protocol (SMTP)* is the e-mail message-exchange standard of the Internet. Whereas POP and IMAP are the Internet protocols used to read e-mail, SMTP is the Internet protocol for delivering e-mail. SMTP is used to navigate an e-mail to its destination server. Mail servers that run SMTP have a relay agent that sends a message from one mail server to another. Because mail servers, as per their function, need to accept and send data through an organization's routers and firewalls, this relay agent can be abused by unauthorized users who relay mail through the server. These e-mails are usually from spammers sending out unsolicited messages while hiding the original sending location of the e-mails through spoofed addresses. The need for e-mail server security becomes even more important when these users send malicious e-mails with attachments that contain viruses, malware, and phishing attempts.

To protect the mail server from this type of abuse, the SMTP relay agent should be configured to send only mail originating from its own network domain. SMTP authentication should also be enabled to allow only authenticated clients to relay through the SMTP server to send mail.

Exam Tip

SMTP uses TCP port 25 for communication, although many Internet service providers (ISPs) have started to use alternative ports to prevent connections from spammers' relays. It is a security best practice to disable SMTP relay on your SMTP server.

General Considerations

You should keep in mind several other general vulnerabilities—many of which we have discussed in previous chapters:

- Ensuring that embedded software is fully cataloged and accounted for
- Supply chain risk associated with third-party software and SDKs
- Driver manipulation (known as shimming or refactoring) that wraps older drivers to allow compatibility with newer software and hardware
- System sprawl and undocumented assets
- Architecture and design weaknesses
- Improperly configured accounts
- Certificate and key management
- Untrained users
- Lack of vendor support when software/hardware reaches end-of-life

Business processes also need to be accounted for. For example, consider the scenario where no change management processes are in place (we'll talk about change management in detail later in this chapter). Without proper change management, developers might be writing on top of each other's coding changes because no one is providing oversight. This business process scenario could easily be improved by implementing a change management processes that includes a form of version control for software development.

| Objective 12.02 |
| CompTIA Security+ |
| Objectives 3.4 |
| and 3.6 |

Explain the Importance of Application Security

With a wide variety of attack vectors, applications are extremely vulnerable to security issues. Poor input validation, weak error and exception handling, and misconfiguration can create vulnerabilities in your applications that can lead to crashes, unauthorized access, and loss of data. Application security begins in the design and development phase to create a secure architecture, whereas application hardening, configuration baselines, and software update maintenance provide continued security when the application is deployed and in use. The following sections describe important concepts and best practices for application security.

Development Life-Cycle Models

Software development methodologies generally divide the software development process into a series of phases to allow the process to be managed much of the same way as traditional projects. Taken together, these phases are known as the *software development life cycle (SDLC)*. The Waterfall and Agile development methods are two of the most popular SDLC methodologies.

Waterfall Method

The Waterfall method, named after the fact that its steps flow steadily downstream (much like a waterfall, if you can visualize it), is based on a more traditional project management model in which, software development proceeds through the phases of conception, initiation, analysis, design, construction, testing, production and implementation, and maintenance. The Waterfall method is not iterative, and when used, organizations do not move to the next phase until the current phase is assessed to be complete.

Agile Method

The Agile software development methodology, as introduced by the Agile Manifesto, is iterative in nature and utilizes teams to deliver earlier and continuously improve more rapidly (hence the name Agile) than the Waterfall development method. The Agile Manifesto states that the software development methodology is based around the values of individuals' interaction being more valuable than tools and processes; working software as more important than comprehensive documentation; customer collaboration being more valued than contract negotiation; and the ability to respond to change as being more important than following a specific plan. Comparing these values to the Waterfall methodology, you can see why this methodology might be valued in some organizational constructs but seen as riskier within others.

Secure Coding Concepts

Developers must build their applications from a secure base and use secure coding concepts to make sure that when an application is deployed, it does not contain security issues and is designed to be resistant to application errors and crashes that can create a condition of vulnerability within the application and potentially expose sensitive data or allow the system to be exploited. The following sections describe some basic secure development concepts that should be applied when creating software.

Secure Development Operations

Development operations (often shortened to *DevOps*) brings together the project and product managers, software developers, and the operations group to better facilitate rapid but secure software development, testing, deployment, and change management through a combination of automation, continuous integration, and secure baselines. As more organizations utilize more rapid software development methodologies, such as the Agile method discussed previously, DevOps became more important to securely but swiftly release software into production.

Emerging tools available to DevOps personnel include immutable infrastructure and infrastructure as code. *Immutable infrastructure,* although not completely standardized as a definition, means the infrastructure can never be changed once instantiated. If a change needs to be made, it must be replaced fully with another instance of the infrastructure that is fully tested and secure. Think about it this way: as software changes are made, the software and its infrastructure are tested and are ready to be deployed and made immutable (or unable to change). The infrastructure is deployed as a single set, and the old iteration is removed and its resources freed for use. This provides both performance and security benefits.

Software applications cannot be considered only in a bubble; you must also consider the surrounding infrastructure that supports them, often called a *data center.* DevOps personnel are required to consider these aspects and provision (appropriately prepare) and de-provision (appropriately release or redirect resources) data center assets to support software and user requirements. Whereas this is often done through the configuration of servers, network hardware, and software residing on subsequent software, *infrastructure as code* manages and provisions data centers through machine-readable files rather than the physical hardware. The physical equipment is generally a "bare-metal server" with virtual machines and configurations that all come together to be considered the "infrastructure." Infrastructure as code allows DevOps personnel to be much more automated and agile to spin up or shut down resources as needed.

Change Management

Version control and change management are critical because they keep developers from stepping all over themselves and deploying outdated or insecure code into the production environment. They also keep multiple developers from overriding changes that might be written by other developers. Change management also ensures that all the stakeholders associated with a software change, from the developers to the security management, are thoroughly in understanding of what changes need to be made, when they will be made, and any second- or third-order effects that might be associated with these changes. Ineffective or missing version control and change management procedures will end up putting your systems at risk—either of wasted time and effort, or more seriously, of an attack associated with improperly vetted software.

Input Validation

Input validation refers to the process of coding applications to accept only certain valid input for user-entered fields. For example, many websites allow users to fill in a web form with their name, address, comments, and other information. If proper input validation code has not been included in these types of web forms, in certain cases a malicious user can enter invalid input into a field that may cause the application to crash, corrupt data, or provide the user with additional unauthorized system access. Invalid input often leads to buffer overflow types of errors that can be easily exploited. Encoding proper input validation within an application reduces the risk of a user inadvertently or intentionally entering input that can crash the system or cause some other type of security concern.

Escaping

Another concept related to input validation is *escaping*. Without proper validation, hackers can input actual commands into input fields that are then run by the operating system. Escaping recognizes specific types of command characters and parses them as simple data rather than executing the text as a command.

Code Testing and Verification

Dynamic code analysis is conducted by executing software on a real or virtual processor, with inputs that allows the tester to determine how the software will behave in a potentially negative environment, looking for a race conditions, incorrectly handled exceptions, resource and memory release issues, and potential attack vectors. *Fuzzing* is a dynamic technique that can help test input validation and error/exception handling by entering random, unexpected data into application fields to see how the software program reacts. Many application vulnerabilities originate from input validation issues, buffer overflows, and error handling, and fuzzing helps make sure that the software does not crash, lose or manipulate data, or provide unauthorized access based on input validation defects. It is also possible to perform a dynamic verification of code at runtime by executing the software and extracting information to determine if it is operating in a secure state and within its modeled specifications.

Static analysis, conversely, allows analysis of code that is performed without executing the program, often using an automated tool, as many programs have become so large that having someone (or group of people) simply look through the code is not enough.

Stress testing checks the ability of a piece of software to undergo large amounts of stress, or extremely heavy operating loads. Stress testing puts the software beyond its normal or best-scenario operating environments, and determines what the behavior would be in a real-world, heavy-load situation. Stress testing is critical for software and supporting infrastructure where resiliency, reliability, and error handling might mean the difference between life and death, such as in industrial control systems or weapons platforms—though large retail outlets also find it important to use stress testing to understand how the holiday rush might affect their systems.

Error and Exception Handling

Developers must be careful when coding applications to determine how the software program should react to error conditions and exceptions. In many cases, an unexpected error condition can reveal security vulnerabilities that can be exploited. For example, a software program may crash and drop to a command line that can be used by a hacker, or error messages may indicate full file and directory paths that the hacker can use as knowledge to further penetrate the system.

Error and exception handling is largely determined by the operating system and the programming language environment in use because they can offer varying levels of tools to deal with software exceptions. Generally, developers must make sure that a program should still be able to retain its state and continue to function in the event of an error condition. The program should be able to roll back to its previous state without interrupting the flow of the application.

Error messages must be informative to the user, but system details should never be revealed unless the software is running in a special debugging mode only available to the developers, where verbose error logging will help them trace a problem to fix a programming issue.

Transitive Access

Transitive access occurs when you have access permissions or systems of trust between different components of a software application that allow users to pass through unexpectedly and without proper authorization to access another software component.

For example, consider an application or operating system that establishes a trust relationship between two software components, A and B, that allows full access for data passing between these components. Another separate trust relationship is set up between components B and C that allows similar full access between those two components. If there is no explicit nontransitive access specified, any user who is authenticated and authorized for component A is allowed access through component B, and then by the separate trust relationship, unauthorized access to component C.

You must be careful when coding software that no software components allow pass-through transitive access by ensuring that trusts between components are nontransitive and require explicit authorization before access is granted.

Server-Side vs. Client-Side Validation

As you know by now, validation is a strong mitigation strategy to prevent many attacks. The two main ways to conduct this are client-side validation and server-side validation, and they both have pros and cons.

For example, client-side validation can respond back to the user more quickly because the feedback can be generated almost instantaneously; if a user inputs numeric digits in a nonnumeric field, for instance, he can receive instant feedback rather than waiting for the server to respond. This type of validation requires fewer server resources for processing and is generally considered faster.

Server-side validation is more widely compatible; what if the user doesn't have the software installed that you require? A server-based implementation is more software agnostic. It also is generally considered more secure because the server doesn't show its code to the client.

Before implementing a validation technique (and it's incredibly important that you do), consider these benefits and drawbacks, and make the appropriate choice for your situation.

Cross-Site Scripting

Cross-site scripting can be prevented via careful web programming and strong input validation that does not permit additional code to be included in dynamic input and is effectively ignored by the application. To prevent command insertion, any special characters that could be interpreted as a command should be "escaped" as harmless data strings.

Cross-Site Request Forgery

To prevent cross-site request forgery attacks, a web application must verify that a request came from an authorized user, not just the browser of an authorized user. Web applications can require a second identifying value saved in a cookie that is compared with every request to the website. This ensures that the request is coming not only from the same user and browser, but also the same authenticated session. A hacker who manages to get a user to go to his malicious website and steals her session cookie still requires the temporary session request value to take any action as the target user.

Code Reuse and Third-Party Libraries

Code reuse is the use of existing source code for new purposes, either for a new program or a new environment. Although this obviously can have some cost- and time-saving benefits through a lack of duplication of effort, there are negative aspects to be considered. Reuse of code that contains weak cipher suites and implementations, often incorporated to better integrate with legacy software, can introduce inherent weaknesses into your new project. Similarly, third-party libraries and software development kits (SDKs) may not have had adequate quality or security vetting and can also introduce unknown weaknesses. One way to mitigate this is by looking for signed code where possible; *code signing* allows a certificate to be used to digitally sign executables and scripts to confirm that the software was developed by the appropriate author and has not been manipulated in any way, thus providing integrity and a measure of authenticity.

In a similar manner, *stored procedures* are saved subroutines that can be used within applications accessing databases, saving time and memory by combining the execution of several statements into one stored procedure and allowing applications to call that procedure rather than have those statements being coded duplicatively, thus further allowing for consolidation and centralization of that procedure. Although this can provide security benefits through the central management and less sprawling code, you need to be diligent in reviewing any stored procedures to ensure you're clear on what they are executing.

Secure Deployment

It's important to understand the different environments that are involved in securely staging and deploying software applications, most commonly in the following steps (with their common shortened names in parentheses):

- Development (DEV)
- Test (TEST)
- Staging (STAGING)
- Production (PROD)

The development environment is where, as the name might suggest, your software is developed. This is often done in a *sandbox,* meaning far away from the production systems and data, to minimize any impact from spillover that harms other code and processes resident on the system. The testing environment is where the software will be tested, either in a static or dynamic manner (or a combination of the two), often using a subset of production data to best mirror the live environment. The staging environment occurs prior to the production environment and allows the code to be subjected to final testing, in as close to a duplicate live environment as possible, before being moved into production. Production is the final, live environment that users are interacting with to get the work done. Because this is the most critical environment to keep resilient, it is important to baseline and monitor the integrity of the production environment after every code deployment. Deploying through these steps properly will ensure that your code is thoroughly tested and securely integrated into the environment in a way that does not introduce risk to your missions.

NoSQL vs. SQL Databases

Structured Query Language (SQL) databases are one type of what the industry considers "relational" databases, meaning that the data contained within them is structured in a format—in this case, rows and columns. The term *relational* refers to the inherent relationship between the rows and columns. Queries using the SQL language can be made within this format that allow manipulation and presentation of the data.

NoSQL databases use more flexible data structures than relational databases and are often used within cloud solutions or other scenarios requiring a database solution that can fit a need, such as increased performance. Because NoSQL databases are generally designed to store and present a certain type of data (for example, images or documents), they are very good at completing that task effectively and efficiently. However, one thing that most NoSQL implementations are not known for is security; in fact, the NoSQL community does not generally see security as a concern, choosing to focus on other areas of performance, such as speed. NoSQL implementations generally look to the other layers, such as the user-facing application, for their security.

If security is a major concern within your organization, a SQL database would likely be a better fit. Most relational databases have an inherent amount of security built in, such as access control to the individual elements based on usernames and passwords, as well as extensive logging capabilities. Relational databases are also more likely to provide regular patching cycles. If performance is more pressing, you could look at implementing a NoSQL solution and seek ways to offset the security concerns, such as increasing security within the application querying the database.

Application Hardening

Application software, just like any other software, such as a host operating system or device firmware, is vulnerable to security issues originating from existing bugs, out-of-date software, and misconfiguration.

For all the applications and services used in your environment, you must use application-hardening techniques to prevent application vulnerabilities from being exploited. By using a secure baseline of application configuration, hardening techniques, and patch management, you ensure that your application software is at a default level of high security that lessens the probability of issues originating from the application software.

Application Configuration Baseline

Depending on the type of application, the configuration can be very simple or very complex. What is most important is that the actual configuration of your application is, by default, set to a secure baseline. Only the most basic default options should be enabled on an application to provide most users with the functionality they require, and the baseline configuration should be closely checked for misconfigurations and weak configurations. Enabling additional options and services means the additional possibility of security issues. If they are not required, additional options and services should be disabled. For example, for word processing and spreadsheet applications, you may have a company-wide security baseline that prevents the running of external macros within these applications. This prevents users from being infected by macro viruses in documents they receive from external sources. To still allow macro functionality from trusted sources, you can enable access only for macros that were created internal to your organization.

Applications should also have proper authentication and authorization configured so that users are only allowed to use the services they require from the applications and do not have access to any other additional functionality. For example, another company-wide application is the web browser. For maximum security, you can install the web browser application with heightened security settings that cannot be modified by users. This ensures that when users browse the Web, they have a default application configuration that prevents connections to untrusted sites that could contain malware. Users will not have proper authorization to make any changes to the web browser configuration.

Application Patch Management

Application software can contain a variety of bugs and security vulnerabilities that can be exploited by malicious users. For internal application software, such as word processing, spreadsheets, and custom-built applications, bugs are usually annoying at most and might not provide real security threats. The usual effect of software bugs is simply interruption or corruption of services, which affect performance, productivity, and data integrity. Software applications specifically made for the Internet, however, can provide more than simple annoyances, because security vulnerabilities created in the software can allow an unauthorized user to access your internal network through the faulty application or service.

To protect yourself from inherent bug or security vulnerabilities, you should upgrade all application software to the latest version, and the latest service packs and security patches should be installed. In the most recent version of the software, known problems have been corrected. This does not, however, protect you from any problems that might have arisen since the most recent version was distributed. Continuing product research and testing, and the proliferation of compromised security incidents, might require the software vendor to release an interim update or patch (typically called a *security patch* or *hotfix*) for the affected program.

Vendor websites should be checked regularly for software updates for any applications running on your systems. Many vendors can automatically notify you through e-mail updates if you registered the software for technical support, or the software itself could contain a procedure that checks for the latest version of its components automatically.

Objective 12.03 Explain the Importance of Data Security

CompTIA Security+ Objectives 3.3, 3.7, and 5.8

Beyond network, host, and application security, data security is your last line of defense in your security infrastructure. Stored data must be secured from unauthorized access, theft, loss, and manipulation. Data exists in one of three states: at rest, in transit, or in use. *Data at rest* means that the data is resident on storage media and is currently not in a state of use. *Data in transit* is data that is currently being transferred, either within internal segments of a network or between networks. *Data in use* resides within a network or a system and is currently in an actively used state within one segment of a network; for example, data present in swap space or in active memory is considered data in use. Organizational policies regarding how data in these states will be stored, processed, and disposed of provide employees with guidance on how to conduct these activities.

Travel Assistance

There's more information on data policies in Chapter 2.

The following sections describe additional security issues and solutions supporting data security.

Data Loss Prevention

Most security concerns are centered on preventing inbound threats such as network attacks, malware, and viruses from entering your organization's network. For organizations that operate in a 24/7 digital world where there is a constant flow of data being passed in and out of their networks via e-mail, instant messaging, web, and other communications channels, the concept of *outbound* security has quickly become of equal importance.

Data loss prevention (DLP) is the concept of using security and content control features to prevent confidential, private data from leaving your organization's networks. DLP has become so important that certain types of organizations, including financial and medical companies, must adhere to strict guidelines and regulations regarding the storage and communication of private data. For example, banks and other financial companies must ensure that a customer's banking and credit card info are secure and never transmitted without being encrypted. Hospitals, doctors' offices, and other health-related organizations must ensure patient confidentiality regarding personal health records.

DLP requires that organizations create compliance policies that detail which users can send certain types of documents and data outside of their networks and the types of actions that should be applied to outbound messages that violate a policy. From a technical perspective, DLP techniques use deep content scanning (such as with a content filter network device) on outbound network traffic to act on messages or requests, depending on various criteria about their content. For example, a company can create content rules that automatically encrypt any outbound e-mail messages that contain patterns of credit card numbers or Social Security numbers. A high-security organization may block document attachments to e-mails, or even HTTP or FTP uploads of documents marked as "confidential" or "secret," to prevent them from leaving the network. DLP requires the ability to scan multiple network protocols and services (e-mail, web, IM, and so on) to ensure that there is no way that sensitive data can leave the network.

DLP becomes even more difficult when dealing with cloud computing, where data can be stored and transmitted within a distributed service cloud across public networks. Once the data is transmitted in the cloud ensuring confidentiality is much more challenging. Your DLP policies must ensure that specific confidential data is not transmitted out of your organization into the cloud.

Data Encryption

For data confidentiality, the ability to render data unreadable through encryption is a key component of data loss prevention. Most security resources are dedicated to protecting the confidentiality of data while in transit over a network using secure cipher suites and implementations. Of equal importance is the protection of data while it is stored on server hard disks, mobile devices, and USB flash drives. The following sections describe how data is encrypted using both hardware and software technologies to protect the confidentiality of stored data.

Travel Assistance

For details on cryptographic techniques for encryption, see Chapter 4.

Trusted Platform Module

A *trusted platform module (TPM)* is a special hardware chip that is typically installed within a computer system or device, such as on the system motherboard of a computer desktop or laptop. This module provides authentication by storing security mechanisms such as passwords, certificates, and encryption keys that are specific to that system hardware. The chip itself contains a built-in RSA (Rivest, Shamir, and Adleman) key that is used for encryption and authentication. In the past, hardware-based passwords on desktops and laptops were typically stored in clear text and, therefore, vulnerable to unauthorized access. With the advent of TPM, any system passwords are now stored and encrypted on the TPM chip. The TPM provides greater security benefits over software-based solutions because it runs in a closed hardware subsystem that mitigates external threats. TPM-based systems are compatible with most popular operating systems.

Laptops are especially prone to physical theft because of their portability, and if the hard drive contents are not encrypted, an unauthorized user can easily access these files. The TPM allows the contents of the hard drive to be encrypted; the user simply generates a key that is stored on the TPM chip. When the user needs to access the hard drive, she uses operating system software, such as Windows, to send the key to the TPM chip for authentication. This prevents an unauthorized user from accessing the hard drive contents of equipment.

Hardware Security Module

A *hardware security module (HSM)* is a specialized hardware appliance used to provide onboard cryptographic functions and processing. This physical hardware device can be a stand-alone device attached to a network or connected directly to a server as a plug-in card. HSMs are primarily used to host integrated cryptographic functions, such as a Public Key Infrastructure server for encryption, decryption, and secure key generation and management, but they can also be used to provide onboard secure storage of encrypted data. With their processing speed and security, HSMs are often used for banking applications (such as ATMs) that require scalable, performance-based solutions for critical key management and security.

Full Disk Encryption

With *full disk encryption,* the entire contents of a computer system's hard drive are encrypted, typically by encrypting the disk volume that contains all the operating system data; this does not include the booting instructions located in a boot volume or master boot record (MBR). By encrypting all files, including temporary and swap space files, you ensure that no unauthorized user can access this data if the system is compromised or stolen.

Many operating systems come with their own proprietary whole-disk encryption mechanisms that encrypt and decrypt data on the fly as the user is operating the computer. You can encrypt a system's operating system volume on the hard drive and provide authentication for the boot process (which cannot be encrypted). It is critical that disk encryption systems use some form of authentication for the boot process, such as a locked-down mini operating system or a TPM mechanism whose only function is to authenticate the user before booting the system. Otherwise, an unauthorized user can still boot the system and access user files as if he were the original user. To authenticate the user, a combination of passwords, passphrases, personal identification numbers (PINs), or hardware tokens can be used before allowing access to the encrypted disk volumes.

Database Encryption

Company databases can consist of millions of records and terabytes of data. Data is the heart of a company, and if this data is damaged, lost, or stolen, it could mean the end of that company. Although most security resources are spent on encryption of data in transit, you must also consider the confidentiality of data in storage.

Databases can be encrypted so that even if an attacker were able to gain unauthorized access to a database, she would not be able to read the data without the encryption key. You can encrypt the entire database itself or the actual physical database files (which also protects backups of the database). For more granularity, you can even encrypt individual cells/records in the database that are decrypted as authorized by the user.

As with other encryption methods, key management and authentication can create security issues, and it is a best practice that the encrypted key never be stored with the encrypted data. Encryption keys should be stored and managed by external devices such as an HSM.

Individual File Encryption

Data encryption can also be taken to a very granular level where only individual files and folders are encrypted by the file system itself, rather than the contents of entire partitions or a whole disk. This type of encryption has the benefit that each encrypted file or folder will have a different encryption key. This approach provides more strict access control; however, it requires efficient key management to properly oversee different keys with different user authorizations.

Removable Media and Mobile Devices

The ability to transfer information easily from one computer device to another has been made easier with removable media and mobile devices. Technologies such as removable hard drives, USB keys, and flash memory in mobile devices give users flexibility in moving data from one system to another.

Removable media can contain critical and confidential data that must be protected from unauthorized access and physical damage or destruction. The portable nature of many types of computer media means more opportunities for an unauthorized user to obtain or damage the information they contain. Security must be a priority to protect the confidentially and integrity of data, especially when this information is being physically moved from one place to another. This involves the use of encryption and authentication to secure access to the data, as well as physical and environmental protection of the removable media itself.

While the data is protected by encryption, there are security concerns with the methods used to access and decrypt data. A user must authenticate using a password, passphrase, or some other identifier before he can decrypt the contents of the device. If the authentication process is weak, the strong encryption techniques can be easily subverted. More advanced USB flash drives can store the actual encryption key on a separate controller part of the USB device that is protected from the main flash drive where the data is encrypted.

Data Destruction and Media Sanitization

There are several basic types of data destruction and media sanitization techniques. According to NIST Special Publication 800-88, media that will be reused and will be leaving an organization's control should be purged, meaning the data cannot be recovered. If the media will be reused and will not be leaving an organization's control, then clearing through a simple overwrite is a sufficient method of sanitization. Finally, if the media will not be reused at all, then destruction is the method for media sanitization. The following options can be used to either destroy data and associated media completely or render it safe for reuse:

- **Burning**   Tossing whatever media you wish to destroy into an incinerator that will burn it beyond recovery.
- **Shredding**   Commonly used with paper or optical media to shred the item again beyond recovery, generally in strips or further into small, confetti-style pieces; it is important when employing the shredding technique that your chosen shred solution creates such small pieces they cannot be pieced back together.
- **Pulverizing**   Much like shredding, but reduces the media to dust.
- **Pulping**   Water and special chemicals are mixed with the paper to remove any ink; the paper can then be recycled.
- **Degaussing**   Involves running a strong magnet over magnetic storage (such as a non-solid-state hard drive) to erase the contents and restore it to a blank and generally unusable state.
- **Wiping**   The use of a program to conduct "passes" of random or non-random data, overwriting a file or an entire drive. This is generally done in one or more passes, with the larger number of passes taking more time, but considered more secure.

Travel Assistance
More details on the policies associated with data handling and destruction are in Chapter 2.

Cloud Storage

Cloud storage is such an amazing concept—the ability to seamlessly store files in a remote infrastructure where they are kept safe and secure, ready to be retrieved when you need them. Some implementations even keep files locally and sync them remotely as soon as you connect to the Internet. It's a great solution for writers, students, and people who simply want the peace of mind that a current backup of their data being stored in an offsite location brings. However, cloud servers have the same inherent security concerns that other servers have. Hackers can download sensitive data for exploitation. Fire and flood can cause availability issues. How can a user balance these concerns with the clear benefits cloud storage brings?

Understanding how a cloud solution brings potential pros and cons versus an on-premises or a hosted solution is important to address this balance.

A cloud storage solution might employ a few mechanisms designed to provide defense-in-depth. For example, a provider might require multifactor authentication that includes a username/password combination along with a *time-based one-time password (TOTP)* token to access the data. The provider might also encrypt data that has been classified as particularly sensitive by the data owner. Utilizing a *cloud access security broker (CASB)*, which acts as an intermediary between the user of the cloud service and the cloud provider and enforces the enterprise security policy, can also ensure that the appropriate levels of visibility and security are met.

To address availability concerns, cloud providers can take a page out of the high-availability handbook and implement redundancy and well-established (and tested) policies and procedures in the event of a disaster or disruption. Cloud storage also often resides within large server facilities that generate immense amounts of heat; to keep the systems properly cooled, effective heat dissipation and cooling solutions should be considered.

Travel Assistance
More details on cloud computing are in Chapter 8.

Storage Area Networks

Storage area networks (SANs) are, funny enough, networks devoted to storage, and are often useful during disaster recovery situations. They generally allow attached devices to appear as local drives within the operating system environment. This differs from network-attached storage (NAS) in that an NAS is presented to a client system like a file server, whereas SAN disks are available in a manner like a local disk.

SAN storage security often implements the concept of *zones*, which allows segmentation of data by classifications and restriction of that data by device. For example, sensitive HR data can be restricted to access only by devices within the HR department.

The SAN should also provide data security while at rest and in transit. Data at rest will often require encryption while residing on the SAN. Communication between devices should be encrypted also to protect data while in transit.

Handling Big Data

Big data is simply that: *big*. The thought is generally to collect everything—logs, files, even data thought to be previously frivolous—and perform analysis on it to determine trends and make decisions. The low cost of storage now allows much more data to be collected and stored; even data that now seems pointless to retain might be saved in the event future tools can squeeze value out of it.

However, consider for a moment the implications of collecting and storing this much data. Imagine, if you will, a box of black dots. If you start pulling dots out of the box, you can connect them. Now, if those dots are data, such as phone numbers, IP addresses, and physical locations, you could potentially gain a robust picture of a situation through their analysis.

This is both positive and negative. Security administrators can store much more data and use analytical tools to spot anomalies within operations. However, malicious intruders can use those same "dots" for business intelligence, identity theft, or just general threats to privacy.

CHECKPOINT

✔**Objective 12.01: Analyze and Differentiate Among Types of Attacks and Vulnerabilities**   Popular web application attacks include cross-site scripting, cross-site request forgery, buffer overflows, poor input validation, scripting, directory traversal, and command injection. Disable anonymous accounts for FTP, and use SFTP or other secure alternatives. Use Secure DNS servers to prevent cache poisoning and unauthorized zone transfers. Database servers need to be secured from SQL injection attacks that result from SQL commands being run in input queries. LDAP is vulnerable to similar injection attacks from command insertion. Disable SMTP relay on e-mail servers to prevent spammers relaying mail through your server.

✔**Objective 12.02: Explain the Importance of Application Security**   Applications must be designed and developed with security in place. Use input validation to make sure hackers cannot insert malformed input or command requests in application input forms. Escape out special characters and command characters so that they are processed as data, not actual commands. Software should be developed to combat resource exhaustion and memory leaks. Use fuzzing to test input validation by entering random, unexpected characters into application input forms. Don't display filename and directory paths in error messages. Make sure your application handles exceptions without crashing or providing unauthorized access. Make sure applications have secure configuration baselines and that all software is up to date with all security patches installed.

✔**Objective 12.03: Explain the Importance of Data Security** Use data loss prevention concepts such as outbound content filtering and encryption to prevent confidential data loss and interception. Use TPMs for secure storage of encryption keys and certificates for hardware platforms. HSMs are used for high-end security applications that require secure key generation and management on a separate hardware appliance. Whole-disk encryption encrypts an entire disk or volume while providing authenticated access for the boot partition of the disk. Database encryption can secure data in storage on a database server. You can encrypt the physical database files, or you can encrypt data cells/records within those files for granular protection that includes user authorization for accessing specific encrypted data. Understand how to securely destroy data and media. NoSQL databases, as opposed to relational databases, are built for speed and are generally less concerned with security. SAN data should be protected while on the SAN and in transit. Big data collects a wealth of data that can be used for security analytics and many other applications, but generates many privacy and security concerns.

REVIEW QUESTIONS

1. Your e-mail server has been listed on a spam blacklist because a large amount of spam is being relayed through it. Which of the following actions should you take?

   A. Enable SMTP relay.

   B. Use an anti-spam filter.

   C. Disable SMTP relay.

   D. Use SMTP relay authentication.

2. A _____ database is known for performance and may require increased security within the application.

3. While testing exception handling with a web application, you encounter an error that displays a full URL path to critical data files for the application. Which one of the following types of vulnerabilities would this application be susceptible to?

   A. Buffer overflow

   B. Session hijacking

   C. Cross-site scripting

   D. Directory traversal

4. Your web application currently checks authentication credentials from a user's web browser cookies before allowing a transaction to take place. However, you have had several complaints of identity theft and unauthorized purchases from users of your site. Which of the following is the mostly likely cause?

   A. Cross-site scripting

   B. Session hijacking

   C. Header manipulation

   D. Lack of encryption

5. To protect your users while web surfing, you create a web browser configuration baseline that will be applied to all of your users in your organization. Which of the following components should you block by default?

   A. Unsigned ActiveX controls

   B. JavaScript

   C. Search engines

   D. Web browsing history

6. As part of your application-hardening process, which of the following activities helps to prevent existing vulnerabilities in applications from being exploited?

   A. Exception handling

   B. Fuzzing

   C. Updating to the latest software version or patch

   D. Escaping

7. An executive is traveling with his laptop computer to a conference. The contents of his laptop contain very confidential product information, including development specifications and product road maps. Which of the following techniques can be implemented to protect the confidentiality of the data on the laptop?

   A. Make sure all software is up to date.

   B. Password-protect the laptop BIOS.

   C. Move the confidential documents to a USB key.

   D. Encrypt the hard drive using a TPM.

8. You have had several instances of product development plans for your company being leaked to other rival companies. Which data loss prevention technique can you use to prevent these documents from leaving your organization's networks?

   A. Use Secure FTP for file transfers.

   B. Block access to file-sharing websites.

   C. Use a content filter to block development documents from being sent outbound.

   D. Use a network firewall to block outbound connections to rival companies.

9. _____ can help protect against the insertion of database commands into your web application input fields.

10. During testing of a web application, you discover that due to poor input validation, you can easily crash the server by entering values in the input forms much greater than the system can handle. What type of vulnerability is this?

    A. Session hijacking

    B. Buffer overflow

    C. Privilege escalation

    D. XML injection

REVIEW ANSWERS

1. **D** By using authenticated SMTP relay, you allow only authorized mail servers and clients to connect to your e-mail server to send and relay messages.

2. **NoSQL** NoSQL databases are often designed for increased performance and leave the security concerns to other parts of the process, such as the application layer.

3. **D** Directory traversal is a vulnerability that allows an attacker who knows the details of an application server's directory tree to manually traverse the directory using input commands in the URL location bar or input forms in the application. Error messages should never display the full paths of files to prevent hackers from discovering the directory structure.

4. **B** Session hijacking occurs when a malicious hacker is able to access your session cookie and then use the session information to make unauthorized requests as the target user.

5. **A** Although ActiveX controls are required for many websites to run correctly, you should never allow users to download unsigned ActiveX controls. If ActiveX controls are not properly signed and authenticated, they are most likely malicious.

6. **C** Application vendors will release updated software versions of their product or provide a security patch to resolve any security vulnerabilities in previous versions of the software. It is a best practice to always keep your application software up to date.

7. **D** A trusted platform module (TPM) allows the contents of the hard drive to be encrypted with encryption keys that are stored on the TPM chip, which can only be accessed by the end user. This prevents an unauthorized user from accessing the hard drive contents of equipment.

8. **C** Using a content filter on your outbound traffic, you can detect and block development documents that are being sent outbound via e-mail attachments, IM file transfers, FTP, and web uploads.

9. **Input validation** SQL injection, for example, takes advantage of poor input validation to send database commands from a web form directly to the back-end database. Proper validation will help stop this and other attacks utilizing this vector.

10. **B** Buffer overflows are caused primarily by poor input validation that allows illegal data to be entered into the application, causing processing limits to be exceeded.

Threats and Vulnerabilities

Monitoring for Security Threats

ITINERARY

o **Objective 13.01**   Analyze, Interpret, and Troubleshoot Different Types
of Mitigation and Deterrent Techniques

	NEWBIE	SOME EXPERIENCE	EXPERT
ETA	3 hours	2 hours	1 hour

With massive amounts of access control, network, and system information being collected every minute, every hour, and every day, administrators can find it difficult to stay abreast of current issues and find time to examine and analyze monitoring and logging information for anomalies that indicate possible security problems.

Small issues can quickly escalate into serious breaches and attacks against your systems. A denial-of-service (DoS) attack on an Internet web server might be noticed immediately on the network, but other security issues are not so easy to detect, such as unauthorized access of files, users with improperly assigned rights and permissions, unauthorized access to a locked area, and Trojan horse programs installed and running silently on a workstation.

To aid administrators, a variety of monitoring, logging, auditing, and reporting tools are available that can quickly identify possible security issues and notify them through alerts and notifications. These monitoring utilities must be configured and customized specifically for your environment to be able to detect behavior that is not consistent with your regular activities; to be most effective, you must be able to interpret their outputs to inform decisions, and be able to troubleshoot issues as they arise.

This chapter describes the various monitoring, logging, and auditing procedures, as well as monitoring methodologies and tools that aid administrators in monitoring a network and systems for security-related issues.

Objective 13.01
CompTIA Security+
Objectives 2.3, 3.5,
3.8, and 4.4

Analyze, Interpret, and Troubleshoot Different Types of Mitigation and Deterrent Techniques

Several security tools are available to administrators to detect suspicious behaviors that have passed the thresholds for normal system and network operation. From specialized network monitors and intrusion detection systems (IDSs), to general utilities such as system and performance monitors and logging applications, these tools must be customized by the administrators, who must also employ proper procedures and methodologies to maximize their benefits. The following sections describe best practices for security monitoring and provide an overview of the tools and methodologies for efficient detection of security issues.

Security Posture

Your security posture is your organization's overall philosophy toward monitoring for security threats and anomalies. The following are the three main concepts that should be implemented in your overall security posture:

- **Initial baseline configuration**   With any type of monitoring or measurement over time, you must initially start with a baseline of current activity and then measure this against future activity. The initial baseline provides you with a level of activity that is considered "normal" for your environment. When you have your baseline, and continue to monitor further activity, any anomalies that go beyond your measured baseline thresholds will be easily apparent. This is done through file integrity monitoring, which alerts administrators on baseline deviations, allowing them to determine if the issue is malicious or a result of a misconfiguration. Several leading security compliance regulations and standards, such as the Sarbanes–Oxley Act (SOX) and the Health Insurance Portability and Accountability Act (HIPAA), require file integrity monitoring.

- **Continuous security monitoring**   Security monitoring is a continuous process that requires constant vigilance. Whether it is watching security cameras, sorting through event logs, using network monitors, or reading and reacting to alarm notifications, security monitoring is a 24/7 operation that never ceases. Even though you may have automated security monitoring and notification methods in place, an administrator must still be aware of the result of that monitoring; be ready to react to security alerts, alarms, and notifications; and study reports of activity trends over periods of time.

- **Remediation**   The remediation aspect of security monitoring is being able to take swift action against immediate security events. This requires that you have recorded your initial baselines, have properly configured your monitoring and alert systems, and have set procedures in place to deal with immediate security issues. This can be handled by manual procedures, or through automated courses of action that are triggered after events occur. In either event, it is critical that you have defined the thresholds that constitute an event and what the appropriate response will be. You must also be able to deal with issues that grow more apparent over time by studying trends in your security reports; this is often a good way to make user training more effective also. Remediation requires the resolution of an issue, using proactive prevention methods to prevent the issue from happening again or mitigate it when it recurs, and adjustment of your monitoring and alert procedures to more quickly and accurately detect the event in the future.

Detecting Security-Related Anomalies

Several monitoring tools can help administrators collect data on system and network performance and usage and compare these statistics against measured baselines of typical system and network behavior. By analyzing performance trends over time, administrators can discover anomalies in the behavior of the system that differ greatly from the performance baselines; such anomalies can indicate a security issue such as a network attack or virus/worm infections. The following sections describe some of the common concepts and security tools for monitoring your systems and networks for security-related issues.

System and Performance Monitoring

System and performance monitors examine how much central processing unit (CPU), memory, disk input and output, and network bandwidth are being consumed at any time or during a specified period. Administrators can examine the resulting data for trends that might indicate anomalous behavior.

For example, if a web server is infected with a virus or worm, it can be unresponsive to client requests or fail to respond in a timely manner. Several unrecognized processes might be running on the system and taking up most of the CPU processing time (with levels of 90 percent or more), memory usage might be unusually high, and network usage may have jumped as the worm tries to replicate itself to other servers. In other cases, excessive network usage (especially a large amount of network connections from external systems) often indicates a DoS attempt.

Exam Tip

Recognize what types of performance behaviors can indicate security issues when using system and performance monitors. High processor usage and network usage could indicate potential DoS attacks or virus and worm activity.

You can establish *performance baselines* and then track performance data to look for thresholds that surpass the baselines. This information allows you to recognize anomalous system behaviors and perform a closer examination to discover the source of the anomalies that affect system performance, such as misconfigured devices. To establish a good performance baseline, you must measure your system activity for 24 hours a day for at least seven days. Data will be collected during working hours, nonworking hours, and weekends to provide an accurate view of your system performance at different times of the day and days of the week. Simply sampling performance data for a few hours during the day will not provide an adequate overview of system performance trends.

Likewise, measuring performance for only a few days during the week will not produce a sufficient baseline for activity during off-work hours and weekends.

The performance baseline should indicate that most primary activity occurs during normal working hours, with lighter activity during nonworking hours. Occasional spikes in activity in off-hours can also indicate normal behavior; system backup or archiving processes, for example, will increase CPU, memory, disk, and network activity during the times the processes are taking place. Your baseline will include this information as well so that you can anticipate that performance spike. Performance spikes that you cannot account for can indicate unauthorized activities or other security-related issues.

After you have recorded a system baseline, many performance monitors allow you to set alarm thresholds for parts of the system. For example, the system can notify you when CPU or memory usage exceeds a specific threshold (such as 90 percent).

Take care when setting thresholds, however, to be sure that you don't receive alarm notifications for slightly above-average behaviors or for very short spikes in activity. For example, you might set your performance monitor to send an alert when CPU usage exceeds 90 percent for at least 30 minutes; this ensures that each momentary processing spike will not generate an alert and that prolonged usage at a high rate will generate a notification.

Protocol Analyzers

A *protocol analyzer* is a device or application that can intercept, log, and analyze network traffic. Each individual network packet can be examined to decode its header information (which contains the packet's origin and destination) and its contents. Figure 13.1 shows a typical protocol analyzer display from a popular program called Wireshark, which shows each inbound and outbound network packet and the exact details of each packet's contents.

Travel Assistance

More information on Wireshark can be found at www.wireshark.org.

Protocol analyzers are not used continually to monitor every packet that passes through the network. Because of the huge amounts of data flowing across a network, this would be an impossible task. Instead, they are used to troubleshoot specific network segments or traffic to and from a specific host on the network. Administrators can use an analyzer to track specific network protocols as they send out queries and receive responses; this helps narrow

FIGURE 13.1 The Wireshark protocol analyzer

down sources of communications issues. They are also useful for helping spot any unencrypted, or cleartext, credentials that might be passed.

In terms of monitoring for security issues, protocol analyzers are very useful for viewing the source, destination, and content of specific network packets. For example, a network administrator might suspect that a specific workstation on the network is infected with a Trojan horse program that is exfiltrating data from the workstation to an attacker's computer over the Internet. By using the protocol analyzer, the administrator can watch every single network packet that leaves the workstation and narrow down the search using the ports specifically used by Trojan horse programs. Examining the workstation will show communications to and from these ports to a specific external IP address on the network. At this point, the administrator can confirm the type of Trojan horse program being used and attempt to clean it off the infected workstation. The external IP address to which the Trojan horse program is communicating can also be blocked at the firewall to prevent any future occurrences of data being transmitted to that address.

Protocol analyzers and similar network monitoring tools can also be used to track general trends in networking bandwidth. For example, suppose you hear complaints from users that a specific web server is too slow to respond. By enabling the protocol analyzer to analyze network packets going to and from the web server, you discover massive amounts of network traffic originating externally from the network. By analyzing the network packets, you discover ping messages from multiple IP addresses. This indicates that your web server could be suffering from a distributed denial-of-service (DDoS) attack in which multiple computers on the Internet are sending a flood of ping requests to the web server to slow it down or crash it. You can then take steps to mitigate the attack, such as disabling the ping service on the web server.

Network Monitor

Network monitoring applications allow administrators to take a real-time view of current network activity on the entire network. Network monitors display a map of the network and indicate bandwidth usage and network trends, like how a traffic congestion map would depict a major expressway. Network monitors are usually located in full view of administrators so that they can constantly monitor the health of the network with a quick glance, as well as provide asset management through alerts when new assets have been joined, reducing asset sprawl and unauthorized device use.

Administrators can be alerted if a specific section of the network has lost connectivity due to a failed switch or network cable. The display will indicate that section of the network in a warning color (such as red) that can be noticed immediately by the monitoring administrator. Alerts can also be sent via e-mail, text message, and pager to notify administrators of critical network errors.

Beyond general network troubleshooting issues, network monitors can be a valuable resource for alerting administrators to network problems that result from security-related issues. For example, if one of the organization's Internet web servers is experiencing a DoS attack, the network monitor will indicate severe congestion on the network between the primary router/firewall and the web server. In many cases, the network monitor can show the web server as completely unavailable, as it cannot respond to the diagnostic queries from the monitor due to the attack. Network monitors can also be configured to alert if new access points are set up that might indicate unapproved wireless connectivity.

Abnormal network activity can also be detected by the monitor on specific hosts on the network that could be infected with a worm, virus, or Trojan horse program that is trying to replicate itself to other systems on the network. This allows the administrators to pinpoint the source of the anomalous network activity quickly and take immediate steps to shut down the server or workstation and run diagnostics and antivirus scans to try to clean the infected host.

Intrusion Detection and Intrusion Prevention Systems

An *intrusion detection system (IDS)* can monitor networks, host systems, and physical locations for suspicious behavior that can indicate a malicious hacker or insider threat is trying to break in to or damage a network or host system, or gain unauthorized physical access to an organization's building. The detection system can immediately notify an administrator or security guard of an intrusion through methods such as an e-mail, pager, and audible and visible alarms.

An *intrusion prevention system (IPS)* takes active steps to repair an intrusion situation, such as to disconnect suspicious network connections or turn off network services on a host that is under attack. A user who triggers an intrusion detection system while physically entering a facility without authorization could find himself trapped between two automatically locked doors, such as in a man-trap.

Detection systems do just what the name implies: they detect a security intrusion and alert you to that intrusion. The disadvantage of security systems that merely detect security issues is that by the time you can react to the detection, the hacking attempt may have already performed its intended damage, or the perpetrator may have already stolen equipment and left the premises in the case of a physical intrusion.

The advantage of prevention systems is that they take active steps to mitigate the intrusion before it causes damage or loss. Consider the case of a security camera and a security guard. If your physical security involves only cameras and recorded video, an unauthorized person may break into a facility, triggering alarms and surveillance recordings, but he is still able to perform whatever malicious act was his intent. If the video monitoring and alarm system is not checked until the next day, the intruder is long gone and his intended security transgression has already been completed.

A physical security guard who, in conjunction with alarms and video surveillance, can patrol an organization's building would be able to confront, scare off, or apprehend the unauthorized intruder before he could do damage to your premises or its assets.

The advantages and disadvantages with detection versus prevention are also affected by budget concerns. Generally, any type of active prevention system will cost much more than a detection system. It will cost you much more money to hire a physical security guard to patrol and monitor your premises than it would to install camera surveillance equipment. As part of your risk analysis, you must decide whether the assets and data you are protecting are worth the extended money required to use prevention systems in your organization.

Travel Assistance

Network intrusion detection systems (NIDSs) and network intrusion prevention systems (NIPSs) are discussed in more detail in Chapter 8. Host intrusion detection systems are discussed in Chapter 11.

Bypass of Security Equipment

As part of your security monitoring procedures, some thought and preparation must also be put into resolutions for situations where your monitoring and detection equipment is bypassed, whether through manual bypassing of controls, loss of power, system failure, or some other sudden and unexpected event. For example, during a power outage, a physical intruder would be able to bypass security lighting, camera surveillance, and possibly even electronic access control equipment. An intruder could cut phone, network, power, and video cables to prevent the operation of detection systems. Many security systems use phone or network lines to send alerts to central monitoring stations. If these lines are cut, the security system may not register any activity at all. Many systems use wireless network as a failback in the event physical communications lines are cut. The following concepts describe different ways for security systems to react to these extraordinary events that can bypass their functionality.

Fail Secure   The security system reacts to a failure in the most secure way possible. In a *fail-secure* scenario, the security system will lock down entirely, or even disable functions to prevent usage or entry. For example, in the event of a power outage, a door that is operated through an electronic key reader will remain locked until the power is restored. This ensures that the door cannot be opened if the power is shut down or the electronic reader suffers a malfunction. In the situation of a network server that reboots due to a crash or malfunction, it may only reboot to a nonprivileged state that requires administrative intervention before it is brought back to its full functionality. This prevents hackers from bypassing security controls due to system malfunction or failure and gaining command-line access to the system. Where possible, most security aspects of an application or security system should default to a fail-secure mode. This makes sure that security is not compromised during exceptional events or system failures.

Fail Open   In a system using *fail-open* (or *fail-safe*) security, the system will default to a nonsecure and permissive state. In the previous example of the door with the electronic key reader, if power is lost or the key reader malfunctions, the door will be unlocked for the duration of the outage. Depending on the facility, this may be the proper method to implement for employee safety in the event of a disaster such as a fire. The employees in that area of the building would not be able to escape if the door automatically locked in fail-secure mode. In the example of a network device in a facility that requires connectivity always, it may be a better policy to allow network traffic to flow through unprotected than to shut down the system entirely because of a failure. The monetary damage that could be caused by blocking all communications is considered worth the risk of allowing network traffic through without network security.

Monitoring Logs

Each aspect of a computer system or device, whether it is the operating system, an application, or a system service, generates log files. Log files are used to track informational notifications, warnings, and critical errors within each of these critical system components and services. These logs contain information vital to the system's health and security, and they must be analyzed by the security administrator on a regular basis to monitor for behaviors and anomalies that are inconsistent with regular system operation.

The following sections describe some of the most important log files to examine on a system or network and cover how to analyze their contents properly to identify security threats.

System Logs

System logs record information such as warnings, notifications, and critical error messages on a variety of system processes, such as kernel processes, application processes, memory and disk warnings (such as low disk space), and just about any service running as part of the core operating system. Many types of services and applications have their own logs outside the primary system log, but most of the critical information about the primary operating system is stored in the system log.

Although security issues are more likely to be discovered using an external log analyzer and IDS/IPS that can automatically detect anomalies, smaller organizations without an expensive security infrastructure can rely on manual examination of the system logs for any security issues.

In many cases, the log files are not in a format that is easily readable by the administrators, and an external log viewer is required. Due to the great amount of information that is stored in the system log, administrators must be able to parse and search the log files for pertinent information. For example, if you know the name of a specific process for troubleshooting, you can load the log file into a log analyzer program and search the file using the name of the process, such as *smtp,* to display only log entries specific to the Simple Mail

Transfer Protocol (SMTP) e-mail server process. From here, you can analyze each mail server connection and response and more easily troubleshoot the issue you are experiencing.

It is also important that you configure the system logs to record and display only the information you need; many logging subsystems can be configured to show only warning or critical error messages, while not logging each minor occurrence on the system. This will make logs easier to search and analyze, as well as decrease the amount of resources (especially disk space) required to process and store the logs. However, certain logs, such as access logs, should display all information for tracking all system logins and logouts.

Performance Logs

Performance monitors examine how much CPU, memory, disk input and output, and network bandwidth are being consumed at any time or over a specified period. From this information, administrators can examine the *performance log* data for trends indicating anomalous behaviors. The log tracks performance trends against a baseline of normal behavior. Several system characteristics can be tracked (such as CPU, memory, disk usage, network usage, and so on) and compared to the baseline over time. Figure 13.2 shows an example of the Windows Performance Monitor screen that is monitoring CPU, memory, and disk usage.

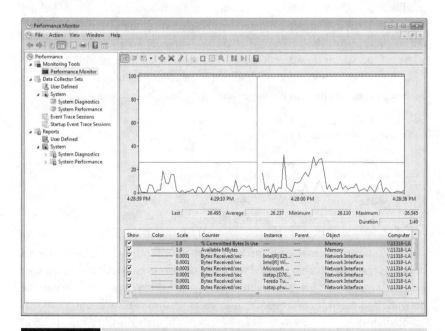

FIGURE 13.2 Windows Performance Monitor

Performance logs provide data spanning minutes, hours, days, and weeks, and performance trends can be mapped based on this data to indicate any anomalous trends or spikes in behavior. For example, an administrator might notice from the performance log data that CPU usage spikes for a few hours starting at midnight until 2:00 A.M. However, this is the time that the server runs its daily backup routines, so the CPU spike appears in the performance report every day at that time. This is a baseline behavior for this system. CPU spikes that occur for large periods of time at other times of the day, especially during nonworking hours, could indicate that the server is under attack or that a Trojan horse program is sending out data at specific times.

Access Logs

Access logs provide information on user logins and logouts from specific servers and network resources. Access logs are a valuable audit tool because they provide information on when a specific user has logged in or out of the network, and can be used to pinpoint not only malicious behaviors, but authentication issues. If security anomalies occur during a certain time, you might be able to narrow down what users were logged in at the time of the incident.

Access logs also record failed attempts at logging in, and patterns of behavior can be detected by checking the access logs for numerous attempts at trying to access an account. For example, suppose the access logs show that someone has tried to access the administrator account over the network during nonworking hours. After several attempts at guessing the password, the account was locked out to prevent further brute-force attempts. The access logs will show the IP address from which the attempted logins originated, and the administrator can determine whose workstation is the source of the attempted unauthorized access.

A typical access log can display information like the following:

```
08:33 Login: admin 192.168.1.110 Success
08:52 Logout: admin 192.168.1.110
10:45 Login: admin 192.168.1.110 Success
11:50 Logout: admin 192.168.1.110
15:20 Login: admin 192.168.1.110 Success
17:10 Logout: admin 192.168.1.110
23:11 Login: admin 192.168.1.99 Failure
23:57 Login: admin 192.168.1.99 Failure
23:59 Login: admin 192.168.1.99 Failure
```

This indicates normal login and logout behavior for the admin user from his or her workstation during normal work hours. However, starting at 11:11 P.M., a user attempted to log in as the admin user from a different workstation on the network and failed three times. In most cases, if automatic account lockout is enabled, the admin user account can be locked out after the third unsuccessful attempt, depending on the configuration.

DNS Logs

DNS logs typically contain information on Domain Name Service (DNS) queries to the server, including the source IP address of the request and the domain name of the destination IP address that the DNS server will return in the response. DNS logs can also contain error messages and notifications for regular processes, such as failed zone transfers that occur when the DNS server cannot update zone information to another system.

This information can help administrators track the source of possible DNS poisoning attempts, in which the DNS tables of IP addresses and hostnames are compromised by replacing the IP address of a host with another IP address that resolves to an attacker's system. If authentication measures are in place to protect against DNS poisoning attacks, you might see several failed attempts to update the zone information on your DNS server in the DNS logs. These logs can help you track down the IP address of the attacker's server, which will be indicated in the DNS queries.

In a DoS attack, DNS logs will indicate that a specific host is sending large amounts of queries to your DNS server. If you determine the IP address source of the queries, you can take steps to block that address from connecting to your DNS server.

Travel Advisory

Typically, DNS logging is enabled only while you're trying to troubleshoot an issue. If the DNS server is logging every single query from clients, the massive amounts of DNS lookup queries that can occur in a large organization can cause performance issues.

Firewall Logs

Because all inbound and outbound network traffic passes through the network firewall, the firewall logs are a critical resource when you're examining network trends and analyzing for anomalous behavior. A firewall is the first line of defense at the network's perimeter, and network attacks are often first detected and discovered in the *firewall logs*. For example, when new worms infect Internet servers and then try to spread to other Internet servers, the connections must pass through an organization's firewall. The network administrator who monitors the firewall is the first to notice and report these worm outbreaks. The administrator will notice hundreds of denied connections to servers on the network, as the firewall is blocking these connections from entering. DoS attacks are also detected in a similar manner.

The most common types of anomalous network behaviors that can be detected at the firewall are port scans. Hackers often use port-scanning software to scan a specific network address to probe for open ports, or to perform a scan of all IP addresses on the network to see which systems respond. Hackers can then use this information to target systems they know are alive on the network and to listen for requests on specific ports. Firewalls (if they are implemented properly) will protect the details of the internal network and will not allow port and IP scanners to glean any information from the network.

Firewall logs can be scanned for patterns of port-scanning behaviors, such as a single network address trying to connect to consecutive port numbers on the same system from port 1 to 65525, or an IP range scan in which a single network address is scanning banks of IP addresses such as 192.168.1.1 to 192.168.255.255. For example, the following log trace shows behavior of a port scan from a specific IP address:

```
Source: 172.16.1.12 Destination: 192.168.1.128 TCP Port 21
Source: 172.16.1.12 Destination: 192.168.1.128 TCP Port 22
Source: 172.16.1.12 Destination: 192.168.1.128 TCP Port 23
Source: 172.16.1.12 Destination: 192.168.1.128 TCP Port 24
Source: 172.16.1.12 Destination: 192.168.1.128 TCP Port 25
Source: 172.16.1.12 Destination: 192.168.1.128 TCP Port 26
Source: 172.16.1.12 Destination: 192.168.1.128 TCP Port 27
```

The port scan will continue until it reaches port 65525 to find open ports that can be accessed and potentially attacked.

Exam Tip	
Recognize different types of attacks based on the details of firewall log messages.	

Firewall logs (including personal software firewalls) are also an important tool for exposing Trojan horses or other types of malicious software installed on client computers that are trying to communicate through the firewall back to the hacker's computer. An administrator can see the source and destination IP addresses of the request and identify which computers might be infected on the network and then take immediate steps to clean the Trojan horse program.

Antivirus Logs

Antivirus logs are generated by antivirus software running on server and client systems. They contain important information on the number and types of viruses that have been detected, quarantined, or cleaned on the system, and they provide diagnostic information on the antivirus signature updates.

In many cases, client logs can be coalesced on the central antivirus server for more efficient log monitoring and auditing.

Administrators can analyze antivirus logs to gather information about computers on the network that have been attacked by viruses, computer files that have been quarantined or cleaned, or, more important, computer files that are infected and cannot be cleaned. This information can alert the administrators to clients on the network that are continually infected or attacked, which can indicate that a user's antivirus program is not working properly or the user is involved in risky Internet behaviors, such as unauthorized downloading of files or receiving viruses via infected removable media, participating in instant message chat sessions, or accessing unauthorized websites.

Antivirus programs use *signature files,* which are databases of patterns of known viruses that are continually updated and downloaded by antivirus programs at scheduled intervals. If this update process breaks down and the antivirus program cannot communicate with the antivirus signature file server (after being blocked by a firewall or if the signature server is unavailable, for example), your system will not be protected from the newest virus threats. By regularly analyzing the antivirus logs, administrators can ensure that they are regularly updating their signature files and that no communications issues exist between the antivirus program and the signature update server. If the update fails at each scheduled interval, an administrator can troubleshoot the network path to determine what is blocking the updates from being downloaded.

Security Logging Applications

Because a specific system or network device can contain log files for a variety of operating system processes, system services, and application programs, several different log files might need to be analyzed by the security administrator. Many of these logs are extremely large and can generate megabytes of data within a single day of operation. It would be very difficult for the administrator to be proactive and manually monitor and analyze each of these logs every single day.

For Unix-based systems, the *syslog* (system logger) functionality allows all systems on a network to forward their logs to a central syslog server. The syslog server stores these log entries in one large log file. The administrator can perform simple text and pattern searches on this log to pinpoint specific information required from all the server logs on the network.

Windows-based systems rely on the Event Viewer (shown in Figure 13.3), an application that provides a centralized location to view application, system, and security logs. Log entries are typically divided into different categories such as Error, Warning, and Information that allow the administrator to sort and scan the logs for critical errors and warnings, while ignoring more informational log

FIGURE 13.3   Windows Event Viewer

entries. Security logs typically contain entries indicating "Success" or "Failure," such as when a user accesses a specific file or directory.

Reports and Trend Monitoring

Most security monitoring applications can coalesce information from several log sources into one database that can be easily searched and analyzed using the logging application, and they can generate reports on log entries for specific services or overall trends in the logging data. This is much easier and more efficient than scanning through individual log files. Reports can scan the most important information for you to know and display them in an easy-to-read format with graphs and charts.

Important reporting information to generate includes the following items:

- **Antivirus and malware reports**   Show how many inbound viruses and malware programs were blocked, and can also show how many virus- or malware-infected messages were sent outbound from systems internal to your network.

- **Firewall reports**   Analyze trends in the total amount of network activity inbound and outbound. These reports can also highlight the top types of attacks that were blocked by the firewall.

- **Anti-spam and mail content filtering** Reports on the number of spam messages that were blocked by your anti-spam filter and any specific content blocked inbound or outbound from deep content scanning of e-mail messages and their attachments.

- **System reports** Indicate the amount of disk space used, CPU, memory, network usage, and other hardware-related trends. These reports are important for capacity planning and identifying servers that need to be upgraded, or identifying where additional servers are required.

Reports should be created, at minimum, on a weekly basis. By comparing reports on a week-to-week basis, you are more likely to spot short-term spikes and anomalous behavior that can indicate a security issue, while other trends, such as network usage, can be monitored longer term for capacity planning. For the executive level, you can create monthly and yearly reports to analyze overall trends that have a longer-term impact on your systems for capacity planning and expansion. This should help inform your training plans and allow you to spot personnel issues that could be affecting your security posture.

Alarms and Notifications

Most security logging applications and monitors can scan current activity and the system log files and generate alarms and notifications of specific critical errors to the administrators. Alarms and notifications can be sent in a variety of ways, including an onscreen alert (from your monitoring application or personal computer), e-mail message, page, and text messaging.

Alarms should be triggered by any monitoring function that exceeds a threshold. For example, you want to receive an immediate alarm notification if one of your hard drives is running out of space, or if your network intrusion detection system has detected a critical security intrusion. You must be careful to fine-tune your thresholds so that you are not receiving too many alarms for issues that are noncritical. If you receive too many, you will eventually stop paying attention to them and critical alarms may go ignored. Alarm notifications need to be flexible to allow you to fine-tune the results of your monitoring applications to view and report only on serious or critical errors. Informational data, such as general notifications or low-level warnings, are usually ignored.

System Auditing

No matter how many security procedures you have in place, an active community of hackers and crackers will invent new ways to circumvent them. Fully effective security policies and procedures must be audited on a regular basis to test and assess their efficiency. *Auditing* also ensures that both users and network administrators are conforming to security procedures. Auditing can be general in nature, where logs of the most common activities are analyzed for any suspicious behavior. More advanced and detailed techniques can involve proactive monitoring of as many systems as possible, even down to the desktop level. Auditing is, ultimately, a way of ensuring accountability and preventing small problems from escalating into large security breaches.

System Baselines

The goal of any type of auditing is to create a baseline of current activity and then measure future activity against this baseline for changes from preexisting thresholds. Creating a security baseline involves analyzing user activity, such as physical entrance and exit from the facility, recording logins to systems, and recording file and application access. The amount of information that can be collected is daunting, and the security administrator must balance the time needed to analyze all this activity versus the security risk levels it represents.

Auditing Event Logs

When monitoring the event log files on your system, you must check for the most common types of security-related events and then compare them with your baseline to discover any anomalies that require investigation.

Information recorded from user activity can be organized into the following specific event areas.

System-Level Events   *System-level events* are events specific to a certain system or a network of systems, including the following:

- **Login and logout times**   The logs of users that entered and exited a system can be helpful in determining which user was accessing the system at the time a security event occurred.
- **Login attempts**   If a user seems to be trying to access an account too many times with the wrong password, this could indicate someone is trying to hack into that account. Many network operating systems can limit the login attempts by disabling the account if too many unsuccessful logins occur.
- **Password and account changes**   By analyzing account and password changes, you can monitor whether a user has suddenly gained privileges she never had before and that weren't entered by the network administrator.

Privileged-User Events *Privileged-user events* include events performed only by users with elevated privileges, such as the following:

- **Account creation** Knowing when an account was created can help you identify unauthorized accounts, such as those created by malicious intruders looking to gain persistent access to a system.
- **Assignment of rights, privileges, and permissions** That same intruder might be looking to gain elevated privileges within his new account. Perhaps he is looking to use his privileges to move laterally within your network. Understanding who has privileged access (and why) and reviewing this frequently will help sort out the accounts that need that level of access and those that don't. You should also be sure that an account with privileged access is not shared across multiple users.
- **Disabling accounts** Accounts should be disabled after a certain number of days without use or when a user has gone into a status where she temporarily doesn't need access (such as long-term leave).
- **Deleting accounts** Users who have left the organization for any reason, or accounts that have been disabled due to non-use, should be deleted within a set period of time to ensure that they can't be used— either by that user who might be attempting to gain unauthorized access, or a hacker who is looking to hide his activities using a legitimate account.
- **Changes to critical files and logs** Losing files that have been determined to be particularly important, such as executables and dynamic-link libraries (DLLs), as well as security logs, could be devastating. Logging any changes to those files and then alerting administrators is a good idea.

Application-Level Events These events happen at the *application level* (for example, when a user is using an application to view or manipulate data). The amount of information that can be collected with this type of monitoring can be overwhelming, so only certain key elements should be recorded:

- **File access** The application logs can record which files were accessed and what times certain files were modified from their original form. Monitoring critical system files for this type of activity is especially important.
- **Error messages** By recording error messages that occur during the use of an application, you can analyze whether the user is intentionally trying to use the application in a manner for which it wasn't designed.

- **Security violations**   Any attempts at using an application to compromise access permissions should be recorded. Repeated security violations of the same resource can indicate improper behaviors.

> ### Exam Tip
>
> Know what types of networking and system activities beyond everyday use can be considered suspicious.

User-Level Events   *User-level events* can be recorded to monitor activities performed by users. Like application-level events, a large list of activities can be recorded. The following are the most common user-level events that should be recorded:

- **Use of resources**   The administrator can record what resources a user accessed during a login session, such as files, servers, printers, and any other network services. This will help indicate whether users are accessing information to which they should not have access or information that is inappropriate to their job and security level.
- **Commands and keystrokes**   At a granular level, the keystrokes and commands used by a user while logged in can be recorded and analyzed for unusual activity. This sort of logging can be the most time consuming to analyze.
- **Security violations**   Each time a user attempts to access a resource for which he doesn't have the necessary privileges, an entry can be written to a log. Too many attempts at inappropriately accessing resources can indicate attempted unauthorized activity.

User Access Rights Review

Beyond monitoring and auditing system log information for security breaches and anomalous behavior, security administrators must also regularly review the access rights and permissions granted to users on the network. Evidence of a user having inappropriate access privileges can be gleaned from an audit log that identifies specific files being accessed by a user who should not be granted access. Realistically, many users can have access permissions they don't require. Analyzing user security rights and policies on a regular basis is critical to ensuring that existing security holes in user policies can be repaired before a user accesses or damages data to which she should not be allowed access. This is also important to prevent the installation of unauthorized software applications or violations of software licensing (that could cause expensive fines or legal issues) due to elevated privileges.

Group policies are often the most common source of users gaining inappropriate rights and privileges within Microsoft Windows–based architectures. Network administrators who lack knowledge about how to use these policies can assign inappropriate access rights to several users in a group. A specific user typically has access only to the files in her own private home directory. When group permissions and policies are applied to that user, she gains the additional rights allocated to the group. A user can belong to several groups, each with its own set of security rights. For example, suppose a user was transferred from one department to another (such as from sales to marketing). When analyzing that user's security rights, an administrator realizes that she still has access rights to the sales department's files in addition to those granted to the marketing department. The administrator can remove the user from the sales group to remove her access rights to sales directories and files.

Group policy management software systems can aid the administrator in managing an organization's group policies to ensure that policies such as group policies, domain policies, and individual user policies do not give a user inappropriate access rights. Group policy management software can accurately determine the final policy applied to a user, which helps the administrator determine what access rights a user has when all policies are applied.

Reviewing Audit Information

Simply recording and collecting information isn't helpful unless the information is reviewed and analyzed. The auditing information can be viewed manually or forwarded by an automatic system, but you must construct meaningful information from the data before it can be useful.

Reviewing all this information can be a daunting task, but many tools and reporting applications can translate the raw data into something coherent and useful. To maximize the efficiency of your reporting procedure, only data perceived as beyond normal operating thresholds should be included. For example, unless a specific incident occurs, you'd have no need to analyze logs of which users logged in and out during normal working hours. Instead, you might choose to look for suspicious activity by viewing only those users who logged in after normal working hours.

Auditing the Administrators

In most corporate environments, the network administrators analyze and audit network activity. In high-security environments, an independent auditor can be asked to analyze the log information. The network administrators have full access to all systems in the company, and their activities must also be recorded and monitored along with that of regular users. High-level functions, such as user account creation, modification, and deletion, as well as changes to system configuration files, should be monitored and analyzed on a regular basis by another security professional. Don't let the fox always guard the henhouse without making sure that someone is keeping an eye on the fox.

Storage and Retention Policies

Security administrators have the task of regularly examining logging and audit data such as system and network intrusion logs. In most cases, this information is collected in an automated fashion and saved to a specific location to be retrieved and analyzed by the administrators. Data storage and retention policies that are applied to typical company information such as user data files and e-mail messages should also apply to logging information. This policy ensures that log data can be stored and retained for enough time so that it can be analyzed properly and preserved as legally required for evidence in investigations of security incidents. Be careful to ensure that you have considered the following within your policies:

- **Log rotation** Log rotation allows a log to fill to a specified size and then be renamed and moved to a safe location. This is often done through an automated process like cron within Unix operating systems. For example, security_log might be renamed to security_log1, compressed, and moved to a central log repository that is only accessible by administrators.

- **Overwriting logs** Logging is great… until you realize that you've had an intrusion and your logs were overwritten before you discovered the incident. Be aware of when your logs could be overwritten (generally, there is a time or size limit) and incorporate that into your policy. You might choose to rotate the log off rather than allow it to be lost.

- **Log reviews** Logs are a great resource if you need to do a deep dive after a device failure or other event. However, you should implement some sort of a review even when you don't know that anything has gone wrong. You might discover behaviors that require more investigation, or you might find out that you're not logging the proper events. Log reviews should take place on a periodic basis and themselves be logged.

Hardening the System

System hardening is the process of applying comprehensive measures, including key configuration changes and protection of applications, management interfaces, and passwords. We've already discussed many of these in depth within the previous chapters; bringing these security layers together creates a more holistic protection strategy. A few recommendations are provided in the following sections.

Disable Unnecessary Services

Have you ever started the Task Manager function within Microsoft Windows and viewed how many services are running, even when you really don't seem to be doing much on the system? Most modern operating systems run many unnecessary services, from allowing use of legacy network protocols to using shiny new graphical themes. Each of these services can expose vulnerabilities to an eager intruder. It is worth your time to research the unnecessary services running on your operating system of choice and disable them.

Travel Assistance

Disabling services is also discussed in Chapter 9.

Protect Management Interfaces and Applications

What are the tools, interfaces, and applications that administrators use to do their daily work and what might happen if a malicious intruder gained access to these tools? Network administrators, for example, might use the firewall interface to manage the access control lists allowing (or blocking) traffic to and from the network. If these lists are compromised, it could allow a malicious intruder not only free access to the network, but also the ability to readily cover his tracks and remain undetected. Don't give hackers access to the "keys to the kingdom"—protecting these management tools and interfaces is crucial.

Utilize Password Protection

Even in the advent of multifactor authentication and biometric solutions, passwords are still the most common method of system authentication. It's critical that these be protected from intruders. One method of password protection is to use password management tools. These applications generate unique passwords and then organize them; they can then be accessed with a master password.

The easiest way to protect user passwords, however, is to simply enforce a strong password policy. The stronger the password, the less likely that it's worth the time and computing power to crack it.

Travel Assistance

More information on creating and managing secure passwords can be found in Chapter 6.

Disable Unnecessary Accounts

The more accounts that are allowed access to a system, the more likely it is that a hacker (or even a malicious insider) could use an account to perform unwanted activities. It's a great idea to audit and then disable accounts that aren't needed; these can be guest accounts or just users who have temporarily or permanently lost access through termination of employment or other changes. This provides a smaller attack surface to secure.

Travel Assistance
Account management is covered in depth in Chapter 6.

Improve Baseline Configurations

Application whitelisting works off the basic premise that certain programs or applications that are trusted are "good" while others are not trusted and should not be allowed to be loaded or executed. Good applications are "whitelisted." *Application blacklisting,* conversely, involves creating a list of applications that have been established to be malicious or untrustworthy and will therefore not be permitted access. Both are great approaches; however, application whitelisting is the better choice because you can control exactly which applications can run on a system. Blacklisting only allows you to specify a finite number of disallowed applications—where there are probably dozens (if not hundreds) more that you don't know about but wouldn't want to run on your hosts. Think of application whitelisting as a *default deny* type of rule (where anything that is not specifically allowed is denied by default), and blacklisting as a sort of *default allow* rule (anything not specifically denied can run). NIST SP 800–167, "Guide to Application Whitelisting," is a recommended place to start if you want to better understand these concepts and how to enable them within your organization.

Data Execution Prevention (DEP) debuted within Windows XP and Windows Server 2003 operating systems natively; it is a feature that attempts to protect your computer from malicious code by disallowing the ability to execute code from memory locations that are reserved for Windows and other programs that are known to be good. If an application does attempt to run code from one of these locations, a memory violation occurs and the process is terminated. If this occurs, an administrator should look to determine what the offending application is; it could be a truly malicious situation, or an internal application that has not been coded properly. Be mindful that applications using dynamic code generation often have issues with DEP-enabled systems.

Ensure Systems Are Up to Date

It's not unusual for issues to arise occasionally with operating systems, where bugs are discovered, functionality needs to be improved, or newly discovered vulnerabilities must be addressed. Operating system vendors release patches and security updates to address these issues. For the most part, modern operating systems are configured to seek out and download patches from their manufactures automatically, although in some cases this must be done manually. In a corporate environment, a formalized patch management process should be in place that works closely with the change management process.

A new patch should be researched to discover what functionality it fixes or what security vulnerabilities it addresses. Administrators should then look at the hosts in their environment to see if the patch applies to any of them. If it is determined that the patch is needed, it should be installed on test systems first to see if it causes issues with security or functionality. If it does cause significant issues, the organization may have to determine whether it will accept the risk of breaking functionality or security by installing the new patch, or if it will accept the risk incurred by not installing the patch and correcting any problems or issues the patch is intended for. If there are no significant issues, then there should be a formal procedure or process for installing the patch on the systems within the environment. This may be done automatically through automated patch management software; unfortunately, manual intervention may be required by administrators, requiring the patch to be installed individually on hosts.

Implement User Training

As stated previously, administrators who are giving careful attention to data collection and analysis, and using the proper tools within systems and networks, will begin to spot trends that can indicate poor user training or malicious user behaviors. This information should be fed back into your user training program (all users, including administrators and senior leaders) to help users make better decisions. For example, if you see an uptick in spillages between classified and unclassified networks within a certain department, this is a great time to ensure that all the personnel in that department receive additional training on the dangers and penalties associated with this behavior.

Network Security

Tightening security through better personnel training, awareness, and policies is one challenge; another is properly configuring the devices that both support your daily activities and protect you from the outside world. This includes controlling the devices that can connect to the network, as well as the administrators who can manage the network devices. It also includes the various methods used to securely manage the network devices.

Limit and Filter MAC Addresses

The Media Access Control (MAC) address is a unique "calling card" identifying a specific network card. For wireless security, access points can hold a list of MAC addresses associated with the clients (computers, mobile devices, and so on) that can access the wireless network. If a client's MAC address isn't listed, the client isn't allowed to connect. In wired implementations, both virtual local area networks (VLANs) and 802.1X methods use MAC filtering. VLANs base membership on MAC addresses when wired clients are plugged into switches and can place the wired host in the correct VLAN, or even deny access to the network based on MAC (as can regular switch port security). MAC filtering, although better than nothing, isn't considered terribly secure and can be easily defeated through spoofing.

Travel Assistance
MAC addresses are discussed in more depth in Chapter 10.

802.1X

The *IEEE 802.1X* standard is a port-based authentication mechanism for devices connecting to wired or wireless networks. For wired networks, 802.1X is implemented on network devices such as switches to provide access control by authenticating connecting clients based on the user or system identity. You can then allow or block network connectivity and apply network access policies based on this authentication.

In wireless networks, a client automatically connects to the closest access point and then authenticates to the network by directly communicating with the network's native authentication.

Be sure to configure 802.1X properly so that unauthorized clients connecting to the network cannot perform ping requests. This can be handled through strong encryption within the architecture.

Travel Assistance
802.1X is also covered in Chapter 7.

Disable Unused Interfaces and Ports

Is your company using ColdFusion? No? Then why is the port associated with ColdFusion web server traffic (port 8500, by the way) open? It's a good idea to review the ports that are open on your systems, both internally and externally, and disable any that aren't necessary. Having fewer ports open means less concern for their unintended use. It's also a good idea to document the ports, protocols, and services that use them on the network for easy reference when reviewing open ports. This will help you easily find discrepancies.

Rogue Machine Detection

Imagine a large enterprise with hundreds, perhaps even thousands, of users and consider of the sheer number of desktops, laptops, mobile devices, and assorted peripherals in use. It must be a nightmare to be sure that no rogue devices are plugged into the network, correct? *Rogue machine detection* is a solution that generally involves a piece of software (called an *agent*) that runs on each client and reports to a central administration server on a constant basis. If an agent reports that a new piece of hardware has been connected and it is not recognized or approved, administrators are alerted to the machine. This helps ensure, for example, that users don't plug their personal mobile devices in (if that's against policy) or that sensitive machines will be connected to a less sensitive network. It also helps monitor for asset sprawl.

Other methods of preventing rogue machines and devices from entering the network include the use of restrictive VLANs, network access control devices, and certificate-based authentication for authorized devices.

Mitigating Threats in Alternative Environments

We've mainly discussed traditional computing environments in this book, including company mainframes and mobile devices. Although these are still the bread and butter of a security professional's knowledge base, it's important to consider emerging, alternative environments, such as the so-called Internet of Things (IoT) and wearable devices. Control redundancy is important for true defense-in-depth; think of how to apply the tools, techniques, and procedures you've learned about within these scenarios.

Computers are amazing things. Not only can you read a book (even this one!), surf the Web, and play a game on a computer, you can do so many other things... perhaps even operate a utility system. A *Supervisory Control and Data Acquisition (SCADA)* system is simply another type of network-enabled information system—albeit one that has huge threats of its own. These systems are used to control utilities, automated systems, and machinery of all sorts, usually using an IP-based network to do so. Often, these systems use older operating systems that are not patched as regularly as traditional computing systems. A key consideration within these types of systems is their Internet connectivity. A SCADA system should *never* be connected to the Internet; in fact, it's best that its internal connectivity even be limited through *network segmentation* to reduce the possibility of lateral movement within the network. Consider implementing manual updates, or updates that you push to the system after thorough testing procedures have been conducted.

Embedded systems are growing daily. These include gaming systems, printers, appliances, in-vehicle systems, medical devices, cameras, home automation, and HVAC (heating, ventilating, and air conditioning) controls that are network enabled, and sometimes Internet connected, for remote access. Imagine a network in your home that you could use to remotely manage all your devices in the house, including the alarm system, light timers, and even data on how much milk is in your refrigerator from barcode sensors on it. Embedded systems are enabled by emerging concepts such as System-on-a-Chip (SoC) that are exactly what they sound like: a single chip, or circuit, that contains all the major components of a computing system, including the microprocessor, memory, networking interfaces, power management, and more. Their shrinking size and growing speed are enabling embedded devices to be more powerful than ever before. Another breakthrough is the use of real-time operating systems (RTOSs) that enable better responsiveness and reduce the resource overhead by more efficiently managing applications.

The Internet of Things (IoT) continues to grow as items that range from unmanned aerial vehicles (UAVs), to personal assistants (like Apple's Siri), to wearable devices such as the Fitbit and Apple Watch become more intertwined with our daily lives. For example, you might listen to your morning Flash Briefing using an Amazon Echo, have the refrigerator remind you that you are running low on orange juice and need to stop by the store (or you could just use one of the growing number of online services that will ship that item to your doorstep), and have the reminders sent to your Apple Watch at a certain time or when you are within proximity to the store. Although this makes modern life more convenient in many ways, it also introduces privacy and security concerns. Think of how dangerous it could be for a potential home intruder to know exactly where you are, based on the data streaming constantly from your devices, especially if they are connected to social media. Be mindful of the data that is being processed and disseminated by these devices, any potential third-party application or social media linkages, and the privacy settings associated with those devices.

Have you ever seen an intrusion detection system for a refrigerator? Not likely, but as more Internet-connected devices become more prevalent, it will be more important to understand what devices you have that are network enabled, if they allow remote access, and how they are protected. Although it may seem ridiculous to have an IDS/IPS system for a refrigerator, these types of devices often are connected to other systems or networks and could be used as an entry point into a larger, more critical system (like your home alarm system). Strong passwords (when possible) are the key. Version control of the firmware, when possible, will allow you to monitor any changes to the programmable aspects of your embedded systems and debug in the case of fault or error. Any wireless communications between embedded systems must also be secured. Gaming systems also often have video and audio capabilities that should be monitored and disabled when appropriate.

CHECKPOINT

✔**Objective 13.01: Analyze, Interpret, and Troubleshoot Different Types of Mitigation and Deterrent Techniques** Anomalous behaviors can be detected by performing a baseline of normal system operation and then analyzing data that goes beyond the thresholds of the baseline. *Fail secure* means that you implement maximum security in the event of a failure or malfunction, while *fail open* or *fail safe* errs on the side of permissiveness during a failure scenario. Signature-based monitoring systems contain predefined signature databases of known attacks, but they are unable to detect the newest attacks that do not yet have signatures available. Behavior-based monitoring systems start from a baseline of normal system behavior and then learn from these system performance profiles to recognize behavioral anomalies that pass the thresholds of the normal system baseline. Rule-based security monitoring systems rely on an administrator to create rules and define the actions to take when those rules are transgressed. Configure your logs to display only the information you require to reduce resource usage and allow more efficient log searching. Performance logs can indicate security issues via behaviors that stray from the system baseline. Access and security logs provide an audit trail of who has logged in and out of the system. Consider nontraditional, alternative environments such as embedded and industrial systems when developing your security plan. Be sure to include methods to protect those unique systems.

REVIEW QUESTIONS

1. You are setting initial performance baselines for an important database server. Which of the following collected data is considered a good indication of a system performance baseline?

   A. Network bandwidth usage per hour for a 24-hour period

   B. CPU processing trends measured during typical working hours

   C. CPU, memory, and network usage data collected for an entire week

   D. Concurrent connections during the busiest server times

2. A signature-based monitoring system has failed to detect an attack on one of your web servers. Which of the following is the most likely cause?

   A. A firewall is misconfigured.

   B. Signature-based systems scan only outbound traffic.

   C. You did not properly implement an access rule for that type of attack.

   D. This is a new type of attack that has no signature available yet.

3. Which of the following types of scanning methodologies checks for anomalous behavior on a system that differs from its routine baseline performance?

   A. Behavioral-based

   B. Rule-based

   C. Signature-based

   D. Role-based

4. Your building's physical security is very critical, and you need to implement procedures to deal with security issues in the event of a malfunction with the security card access control system or a power outage. For maximum security, which of the following concepts should you use in your implementation?

   A. Surveillance video

   B. Fail-open security

   C. Security guards

   D. Fail-secure security

5. Due to downsizing, your department of IT administrators has been drastically reduced, and the time available to monitor your security applications and logs is at a minimum. Which of the following logging procedures would reduce the amount of time needed to examine and analyze several different logs?

   A. Disabling logging

   B. Logging only minor errors

   C. Logging only warning and critical errors

   D. Enabling verbose logging of all errors

6. You are auditing a performance log for your web server. Which of the following performance statistics may indicate a security issue?

   A. Disk space free at 70 percent

   B. Memory usage at 45 percent on average

   C. CPU usage at 99 percent 75 percent of the time

   D. Network bandwidth usage at 50 percent on average

7. During routine examination of the firewall logs, you notice that a specific host is attempting to connect to the same internal IP address starting at port 1 and continuing to port 65525. Which of the following issues could this be evidence of?

   A. A ping sweep of a server on your network

   B. Port scanning of a server on your network

   C. Normal behavior for network diagnostics

   D. DNS requests for name resolution

8. It has come to your attention that a confidential file was accessed without proper authorization. The _____ would allow you to find out which users were logged in during the time the issue occurred.

9. After a security audit, which of the following items would *not* be considered anomalous behavior?

   A. Several unsuccessful attempts to log in as the administrator

   B. A ping sweep on the firewall for the IP range 10.10.0.0 to 10.10.255.255

   C. Error messages in the system's log that indicate excessive disk usage

   D. A member of the sales group accessing the sales group's shared file directory

10. You are developing a security policy for a SCADA system. Which of the following should be the *first* consideration?

A. Extra firewalls

B. More IDS coverage within the network

C. Internet connectivity

D. Remote access

REVIEW ANSWERS

1. C To establish a performance baseline, you must measure your system activity for 24 hours per day for at least seven continuous days. This ensures that you have data for an entire week's worth of activity, including working hours, nonworking hours, and weekends. Simply sampling performance data for a few hours during the day will not provide a sufficient indication of performance trends.

2. D Signature-based systems are powerful and efficient because they rely on the collective knowledge of security vendors who analyze and collect information on Internet security threats and trends and can update their databases very quickly when new threats arise. However, they are unable to detect very new attacks that do not have signatures available yet.

3. A Behavior-based monitoring systems start from a baseline of normal system behavior and then learn from these system performance profiles to recognize behavioral anomalies that pass the thresholds of the normal baseline of the system.

4. D *Fail secure* means that you implement maximum security in the event of a failure or malfunction. In this example, making sure doors stay locked during an access card reader malfunction or power outage is an example of using fail-secure concepts.

5. C To reduce the number of minor and informational types of messages in the logs, administrators should configure their logging systems to log only warning and critical error messages. This reduces the amount of resources required to store logs and reduces the time required to analyze them because only the most important data is logged.

6. **C**   A system running with its CPU usage at 99 percent for a long time can indicate that some anomalous process (such as a virus, Trojan horse, or worm) is causing CPU processing to spike beyond the normal system operating baseline.

7. **B**   A host system that is scanning a server for any open ports using the entire port range indicates that a port-scanning program is being used to determine which services are running and which ports are open and available. A malicious hacker might be trying to find vulnerabilities and attack your system.

8. **Access log**   The access log is a valuable audit tool because it provides information about when a specific user has logged in to or out of the network. If security anomalies occur during a certain time, you might be able to narrow down which users were logged in at the time of the incident.

9. **D**   A member of a group accessing the shared files for the group to which she belongs does not constitute anomalous behavior; however, ping sweeps against the firewall, disk error messages in the system's log, and several attempts to access the administrator account are all security issues that should be carefully examined.

10. **C**   The first thing to consider for SCADA systems is their Internet connectivity. SCADA systems should *never* be connected to the Internet, and only rarely to other networked systems.

Vulnerability
Assessments

	NEWBIE	SOME EXPERIENCE	EXPERT
ETA	2.5 hours	1.5 hours	1 hour

The networks and systems in your organization are always under constant threat of attack from hackers, physical intruders, and malware. No matter how secure your network is, there will always be risks from known and unknown vulnerabilities that can be exploited.

A variety of tools are available to the network administrator and security professional to test networks and systems for vulnerabilities and weaknesses; unfortunately, these tools are also available to unethical hackers who use them to exploit specific vulnerabilities. By proactively monitoring your network for vulnerabilities and taking immediate steps to rectify them, you ensure that hackers using the same tools will not find vulnerabilities to exploit. You must routinely scan your network for vulnerabilities, whether they be unpatched operating systems and application software (such as web servers and database servers) or unused open ports and services that are actively listening for requests.

When coding your own software applications, you must also be wary of developing code that contains vulnerabilities, and right from the design stage place security as a top concern in your application architecture. As you develop your software code, you must stay within your secure design to prevent vulnerabilities from being introduced into your software.

Finally, to test your countermeasures and solutions for existing vulnerabilities, several methods are available to simulate attacks on your current systems to ensure that your security controls are properly implemented and cannot be bypassed.

This chapter describes how to conduct vulnerability and threat assessments, including an overview of vulnerability testing tools, such as port scanners, network mappers, and protocol analyzers, which can aid in identifying vulnerabilities in your network. As part of your prevention and mitigation techniques, the importance of penetration testing is also discussed, including how it differs from and complements vulnerability assessments.

Objective 14.01
CompTIA Security+
Objectives 1.5 and 5.3

Implement Assessment Tools and Techniques to Discover Security Threats and Vulnerabilities

As part of your overall vulnerability and threat assessment procedures, you must perform an assessment for each asset in your organization to ascertain the risks and potential impact to that asset. All possibilities, both physical and nonphysical, should be assessed. For example, confidential data can be stolen from a file server by someone physically stealing the system, or by a hacker accessing the data through network security vulnerabilities.

Identify the following when performing a vulnerability and threat assessment:

- **Vulnerability**   A *vulnerability* is a security weakness that could be compromised by a threat. An operating system (OS) might be vulnerable to network attacks, for example, because it was not updated with security patches. A file server could be vulnerable to viruses because no antivirus software is installed. Web servers and database servers might have vulnerabilities that allow cross-site scripting and SQL injection attacks. *Physical vulnerabilities* affect the physical protection of the asset. Physical assets, such as network servers, should be protected from natural disasters and physical theft by storing the equipment in special rooms with protective mechanisms to prevent these threats. *Nonphysical vulnerabilities* usually involve software or data. Software security vulnerabilities can be created because of improper software configuration, unpatched or buggy software, lack of antivirus protection, weak access and authentication controls, unused open network ports, and misconfigured or nonexistent network security devices.

- **Threat**   A *threat* is a negative event that creates the possibility of a vulnerability being compromised. A variety of threats can pose security risks, including the following:

  - **Natural disasters**   A natural disaster is a fire, flood, or other phenomenon that causes physical damage to company assets—usually the facilities and the equipment within them.

  - **Equipment malfunction**   Electronic equipment is vulnerable to normal wear and tear that can result in failed components—from a failed power supply fan to a failed hard drive.

  - **Employees**   Assets face both malicious and unintentioned threats from employees. The source of the threat could be human error, such as someone deleting a directory of files by mistake, or theft, vandalism, disgruntled employees, or corporate espionage.

  - **Intruders**   An unauthorized person can compromise the access controls of a facility to gain access and perform theft, vandalism, or sabotage.

  - **Malicious hackers**   Malicious hackers present a nonphysical threat that involves a hacker's ability to compromise network security to access or damage assets on a company's network.

- **Threat vector**   A *threat vector* describes the actual means by which a threat is realized. For example, a malicious hacker could use malware disguised as a legitimate e-mail attachment to implant a back-door tool onto a system. In this case, the e-mail attachment is the threat vector that the attacker used to enter the system.

- **Risk**   After threats and vulnerabilities have been identified, your next step is to assess the risk of a threat compromising a vulnerability—such as what can happen in a security breach. For example, a combination of the lack of antivirus software protection (a risk) and the introduction of a virus (a threat) would result in a virus-infected server, which could damage or delete sensitive data. Or an unused open network port could be a target for a denial-of-service (DoS) attack that renders the server unable to respond to legitimate network requests.

- **Impact**   A *risk assessment* reflects the worst possible scenario of a security failure and should be quantified with a financial value for both direct and indirect losses. A company should reflect on the amount of damage to reputation and financial security that would occur if a hacker were to launch a successful DoS attack on the company's web servers. A loss of service—even for a few hours—can severely damage a company; consider, for example, the case of a company that offers stock-trading services. On top of immediate costs for equipment or data loss, the potential loss of prolonged downtime must be factored into the equation. Hundreds of thousands of dollars of revenue can be lost while the site is unavailable to customers. Once the potential loss is calculated for each type of risk, the results can be used to create solutions and countermeasures that are cost efficient, depending on the risk situation.

- **Likelihood**   The final factor for the assessment is how likely it is that a vulnerability to a threat will occur. For example, the probability that a malicious hacker will attempt to attack the network is greater than the chances that a natural disaster will occur. Certain software vulnerabilities are more likely to be exploited than lesser known ones. By assessing the likelihood of the threat, you can allocate solutions for mitigation according to its impact and probability of occurrence.

Vulnerability Assessment Tools

As part of your vulnerability and threat assessment, you need to be able to examine your network and systems for existing vulnerabilities.

Vulnerability assessment and network-scanning programs are important tools for a network administrator who routinely runs preventive security scans on the network. These programs provide detailed information about which hosts on a network are running which services. They can also help identify servers that are running unnecessary network services that create security risks, such as a file server running File Transfer Protocol (FTP) or Hypertext Transfer Protocol (HTTP) services that could provide unauthorized access to data.

Common tools and techniques such as network mappers, port scanners, vulnerability scanners, protocol analyzers, honeypots, and password crackers are used by network administrators to identify and prevent such attacks. Unfortunately, these same tools are major weapons in the malicious hacker's arsenal. Attackers can use them to determine what systems are running on your network, what services and open ports they are running, what operating system and application software they are running, and what vulnerabilities can be exploited. Due to their simplicity, these tools are commonly used to probe and scan networks, even by amateur hackers who have no knowledge of networking protocols.

Banner Grabbing

Banner grabbing allows a hacker to learn more about a system by sending data, in many cases malformed, and then waiting for the system's response. If the system replies with a standard error message, that can be used to determine the operating system and potential applications running on the system, such as web server software. This information allows a potential attacker to better craft his attacks to the specific system. You wouldn't need to attempt Unix-specific attacks if you knew the system was running Microsoft Windows, or Apache attacks if the system used Internet Information Server (IIS). Banner grabbing can be performed with several tools, such as Telnet.

Network Mappers

A *network mapper* program scans a network and uses network IP packets to determine which hosts are available, what operating systems are running, and other types of information about a network host. Most network mappers use the ping utility to perform Internet Control Message Protocol (ICMP) sweeps of entire ranges of IP addresses, looking for hosts that respond. The response contains a lot of information about the host and its place on the network, such as whether it's behind a router or firewall on a subnetwork. Hackers who already know the address of a specific target can also use a network mapper to analyze the host for open ports, services, and OS specifics. This information offers a virtual map of the entire network for a malicious hacker, who can narrow his scope of attack to specific systems, or for the network administrator, who needs to find and correct weaknesses on a network.

One of the most popular tools used for network mapping is an open-source and publicly available utility called *Nmap*. It is used by hackers to scan and map networks and is used by administrators to audit their networks for security weaknesses. The Nmap command-line utility uses simple text commands with switch options to perform tasks. For example, to perform a ping sweep on a system with Nmap, you'd enter the following:

```
nmap -sP 192.168.1.128
```

```
Host 192.168.1.128 appears to be up.
MAC Address: 00:B1:63:3F:74:41 (Apple)
Nmap done: 1 IP address (1 host up) scanned in 0.600 seconds
```

To perform a scan to identify the OS of a system, you'd enter this:

```
nmap -O 192.168.1.128
```

```
MAC Address: 00:B1:63:3F:74:41 (Apple)
Device type: general purpose
Running: NetBSD 4.X
OS details: NetBSD 4.99.4 (x86)
Network Distance: 1 hop
```

Travel Assistance

The Nmap tool can be downloaded from www.nmap.org.

Port Scanners

After an attacker has determined what systems are on a network and identified IP addresses that respond with acknowledgments of a live system at those addresses, the next step is to discover what network services and open ports are running on the system. By using a *port scanner,* an attacker can determine which ports on the system are listening for requests (such as TCP port 80) and then can decide which service or vulnerability in the service can be exploited.

For example, if an attacker sees that Simple Mail Transfer Protocol (SMTP) port 25 is open and listening for requests, he knows that an e-mail server is operating and can launch more probes and tests to determine what mail server software is running and whether vulnerabilities can be exploited to relay spam through the server. The following example shows a listing of a port scan from the Nmap application:

```
nmap -sT 192.168.1.128
```

```
Interesting ports on 192.168.1.128: Not shown: 1709 closed ports
PORT STATE SERVICE 21/tcp open ftp 53/tcp open domain 554/tcp
open rtsp 10000/tcp open snet-sensor-mgmt
```

A standard set of ports, including 65,535 TCP ports and User Datagram Protocol (UDP) ports, are available for running network services on a computer system. The first 1024 ports are *well-known* ports, which means they make up the most common types of network ports, such as DNS (53), SMTP (25), HTTP (80), HTTPS (443), and FTP (21). Beyond these first 1024 ports are tens of thousands of port ranges that are used by third-party applications, services, and networking devices. Table 14.1 lists the most common well-known protocols and services and their corresponding TCP/IP ports.

Travel Advisory

Many of these services also listen on UDP ports as well as TCP. For example, the Domain Name System (DNS) uses TCP port 53 for zone transfers and UDP port 53 for DNS queries.

A port scanner will send probing network packets (sometimes called a *port sweep*) to each of the 65,535 ports (both TCP and UDP) and listen for a response. If the system port does not respond, the attacker knows it is either disabled or

TABLE 14-1	TCP/IP Services and Port Numbers
Service	**TCP/IP Port Number**
HTTP	80
FTP (Data)	20
FTP (Control)	21
DNS	53
DHCP	67
SMTP	25
SNMP	161
Telnet	23
POP3	110
IMAP	143
NTP	123
NNTP	119
SSH	22
LDAP	389

protected (behind a network firewall or proxy server, for example). When it does respond, this service is running on the target system, and the attacker can then use more focused tools to assault that port and service. For example, a SQL server may be listening on port TCP/UDP 1433. If a port scanner receives a response from this port, the attacker knows that this system is running a SQL server, and he can then direct his attacks against specific SQL vulnerabilities.

The following are different types of port-scanning methods that can be used to detect open ports on a system:

- **TCP scanning**   A TCP scan uses the TCP protocol and its commands to connect to a port and open a full TCP connection before breaking off the communication. For example, when scanning a system for Telnet port 23, the port scanner will fully connect to that port on the destination host. If no response is received, the port is deemed closed or protected by a firewall.

- **SYN scanning**   A SYN scan uses small basic IP packets to scan a host and does not open a full TCP connection to the destination host. The SYN scan will break off the communication before the handshake process is complete. This is often called *stealth* scanning and is less intrusive than a TCP scan, which opens a full connection to receive its information.

- **UDP scanning**   The UDP scan is not as effective as other scans, because UDP is a connectionless protocol. This scan gets its open-port information by detecting which ports are not returning acknowledgments to requests, because a UDP request will receive a "host unreachable" message via ICMP in response. If no response is received, the port is open and listening for requests. However, this method is not foolproof, because if the port is blocked by a firewall, the user/attacker will receive no response and might assume the port is open.

Port scanners are often built into popular network-mapping and vulnerability assessment tools such as Nmap because they provide the foundation for determining what services and open ports are on a system, which then leads to a specific vulnerability scan against those services and ports.

Vulnerability Scanners

When an attacker has ascertained which systems are available on the network, his next step is to probe these systems to see what vulnerabilities they might contain. At this point, he has an idea of what systems are alive and which network ports are open and listening for requests.

A *vulnerability scanner* is a software program specifically designed to scan a system via the network to determine what services the system is running and whether any unnecessary open network ports, unpatched operating systems and applications, or back doors can be exploited. Network administrators can use the same vulnerability scanner software to take preventive measures to close vulnerabilities that exist on their systems.

Travel Assistance

Nessus (available at www.teneble.com) is a popular commercial vulnerability scanner, available in both Linux and Unix versions, that scans systems for thousands of vulnerabilities and provides an exhaustive report about the vulnerabilities that exist on your system. Another popular tool, GFI LANguard (www.gfi.com), is a commercial software network security scanner for Windows systems. An open-source alternative is OpenVAS (www.openvas.org).

Vulnerability scanners can include a few scanning and security assessment capabilities, such as port scanning, network scanning and mapping, and OS and application server scanning. The vulnerability scanner contains a database of known OS weaknesses and application program vulnerabilities (such as web and database servers), and it scans the target system to determine whether any of the vulnerabilities listed in its database exist. For example, a database server and front-end web application can be scanned to determine whether they are vulnerable to specific database and web server attacks. By determining the OS of a system, such as Windows or Unix, and then using the database of known vulnerabilities and weaknesses for that OS, the attacker can target his attacks.

Protocol Analyzers

A *protocol analyzer* can intercept, record, and analyze network traffic. Network administrators use the analyzer to track specific network protocols as they send out queries and receive responses and to narrow down sources of communications issues; however, they are also used by hackers to intercept clear-text communications (such as user account and password information) that are transmitted over unsecured protocols. For example, HTTP web traffic is transmitted in clear text, and any information transmitted to a website in clear text, such as a login ID and password, is not encrypted and can be easily viewed by a hacker using a protocol analyzer. Confidential information can also be captured from sensitive e-mail messages passed over the network.

To protect against unauthorized sniffers, a network switch can keep network broadcast traffic isolated on its own network segment; hackers would need access to the specific network segment to get at the data stored there. In addition, any sensitive data should be transmitted over the network using secure protocols that encrypt their contents.

> ### Exam Tip
>
> To prevent network traffic from being intercepted by a protocol scanner, use secure protocols such as Hypertext Transfer Protocol over Secure Sockets Layer (HTTPS) instead of HTTP for web traffic, or Secure Shell (SSH) instead of Telnet for remote access.

Password Crackers

Password cracker programs (also referred to as *password auditing tools*) are used by hackers to attack a system's authentication structure (such as its password database) and attempt to retrieve passwords for user accounts. The programs are also used by security administrators to proactively audit their password database to look for weak passwords.

Password crackers use a variety of methods:

- **Dictionary attack**   This type of attack employs a list of dictionary words that are tried against the authentication database. Because users often use known dictionary words as passwords, this attack can succeed in cracking many passwords.
- **Brute-force attack**   This attack uses a calculated combination of characters to guess the password. The brute-force method will keep trying every single combination until it gets the password right.
- **Hybrid attack**   Many programs use a combination of dictionary and brute-force attacks to add numbers and special characters (such as the @ symbol for *a*) on to the dictionary words to crack more difficult passwords.

> ### Travel Advisory
>
> Examples of password-cracking programs include standbys such as John the Ripper and Cain & Abel, as well as newer, GPU-based options.

After the attacker cracks a specific password, she will be able to access that user account. The administrator account for a system is most commonly attacked because it has full access privileges.

Many older computer authentication schemes stored the passwords in clear text, making it easy for a hacker who can access the password database file to crack an account. Most modern operating systems, at the very least, provide some type of one-way hashing function to protect the password database. If the password database file is accessed by a hacker, it will be of no use because the contents are encrypted. However, many sophisticated password-cracking programs can analyze the database and attack weak encryption methods repeatedly to crack passwords over time. For example, the LANMAN hash used in older Windows-based systems to protect passwords was weak and could be cracked easily if the hacker could gain access to the password database.

Protecting against online password-cracking programs relies on a strong password policy, as discussed in previous chapters. Setting maximum login attempts will lock out an account if the password has been unsuccessfully entered a set number of times. It is important to discern here between online attacks versus offline: Online attacks (conducted against passwords as they reside on a live system) can be mitigated through lockouts and password policies resident on the affected system. Hackers conducting offline attacks generally move the file (or files) they wish to use to their own system, where they can run a password cracker or other tool against it without being locked out. The same mitigations for the online attack aren't effective here; strong passwords are the key to slowing down this type of attack, as well as the obvious solution: don't let the file leave your system!

Exam Tip

Know what constitutes a strong password to protect against offline attacks, such as dictionary attacks. Remember that a lockout countermeasure allows only a specific number of login attempts before the account locks to protect against online brute-force attacks. Understand the difference between offline and online attacks, and mitigating measures for each.

Protecting the password database is a primary concern. Although a maximum login attempt policy will prevent most online brute-force attempts from guessing a password, if a hacker manages to access the database itself, he can run a cracking program (perhaps using a precomputed table of hashes, such as a rainbow table) against it offline for many days and weeks to crack the passwords in the database. One method of protecting the password database other than using traditional security methods such as access permissions is called *salting*, which refers to adding a suffix of random characters (called a *salt*) to the password before it is encrypted. Each password has its own salt, which is different for every password in the database, even identical passwords. Salting makes it difficult for a hacker to use brute-force methods to crack the password database. The longer the salt added to the password, the less likely it is to be cracked. Early implementations used 12-bit salts; however, today 256-bit salts are recommended.

Unix-based systems also protect their hashed password databases by using a *shadow password database*. The normal password database (located in /etc/passwd) contains usernames, and the whole file itself is readable by users other than the root user. In password shadowing, the hashed passwords are stored in a file (/etc/shadow) that is not available to unprivileged users; hackers cannot access the shadow password database to take it offline and run cracking programs on it.

Honeypots and Honeynets

A *honeypot* is a device or server used to attract and lure attackers into trying to access it, thereby removing attention from actual critical systems. The name refers to using a pot of honey to attract bees, which in this case are malicious hackers. The honeypot server is usually situated in the network demilitarized zone (DMZ) and runs popular Internet services that are vulnerable to attack, such as web or FTP services. The server does not have many basic security features enabled, and it freely advertises open Internet ports that can be picked up by malicious hackers' port scanners, as shown in Figure 14.1.

A slight security danger exists if the honeypot isn't configured correctly. If an unauthorized user hacks into the server, she might be able to attack other systems on the DMZ. To prevent this scenario, some honeypot systems can emulate services instead of running them, or they are installed as a stand-alone server with no existing connection to other critical servers.

Travel Advisory

To ensure your honeypot system does not allow an intruder to attack other machines, use service emulation rather than running the full services, or isolate the honeypot on its own network segment.

| FIGURE 14.1 | A honeypot |

Honeypots can be used as decoy devices that attract attention away from real production servers, or they can be used by network administrators to learn the identity of malicious hackers through logging and auditing. By keeping accurate logs of the IP addresses being used by an attacker, the administrator might be able either to track down the source of the attack or to pass information to legal authorities. From a legal standpoint, however, doing this can be tricky, especially if the server advertises files for downloading or viewing, because this is considered entrapment and is illegal.

Honeypot systems are best suited for understanding the different types of attacks that can happen to your network. You can log when and what types of attacks are occurring in the system logs and then use that information to secure your network even further by including protection against attacks that were overlooked in the original security plan.

A *honeynet* is a large-scale network of several honeypot servers that more accurately resembles a target network. Several different network services run on the honeynet to attract more types of attacks while diverting these attacks from your production network. Virtualization services can also be used to emulate a honeynet network on a single system to provide enhanced security while using fewer hardware resources.

> ### Exam Tip
>
> *Honeypot* is the name given to a device or server used to attract and lure attackers into trying to access it, diverting their attention from actual critical systems. *Honeynet* is a network of honeypot servers that more accurately reflects a target network.

Other Command-Line Tools

A vulnerability assessment team can use many tools to best determine how secure (or insecure) a network or system is. The following are important for you to understand and are worth digging into as a professional in the field:

- **Netstat**   Displays any active TCP connections that are present. With parameters, it can display the ports where you are listening as well as the routing table, and it can be used to determine if there are problems in the network and if any traffic is present.
- **Nslookup**   Used to search the domain name system (DNS) to determine domain-name-to-IP mapping.
- **Traceroute/tracert**   Displays the route of packets between point A and point B, and it helps you understand where potential delays are arising.
- **Netcat**   A multifunctional utility that allows read/write access across the network from the command line and is the back end that "powers" a number of other tools.
- **Arp**   Used to view and make changes to the ARP cache.
- **Ipconfig (Windows) / ifconfig (Unix)**   Used to view the current configuration of IP interfaces; ifconfig permits the enabling and disabling of interfaces.
- **Tcpdump**   Used to view network packets and to output to a file.

OVAL

The *Open Vulnerability and Assessment Language (OVAL)* is a security standard that provides open access to security assessments using a special language to standardize system security configuration characteristics, current system analysis, and reporting. OVAL is not a vulnerability scanner, but it provides a language and templates that help administrators check their systems to determine whether vulnerabilities, such as unpatched software, exist.

OVAL uses Extensible Markup Language (XML) schemas as its framework, with three schemas geared toward specific parts of the security standard (system characteristics, current system definition, and reporting the assessment results). These XML files can be fed through an OVAL interpreter program that examines the system, compares it to public databases of known vulnerabilities, and generates the test results that indicate any open vulnerabilities on the system.

Local Lingo

XML   Extensible Markup Language is a markup-language specification that allows structured data to be shared across different computers and platforms. XML uses custom property tags to ensure data is stored and communicated properly, but does not define how the data is displayed, which is typically a function performed by HTML.

This information relies on repositories of publicly available security content that contain a collection of security definitions provided by the security community, which continually adds to the collection and drives OVAL development and evolution. This process provides a comprehensive testing and reporting standard supported by the security community that creates a baseline and checks for known vulnerabilities on computer systems.

Travel Assistance

More information about OVAL can be found at http://oval.mitre.org.

Application Code Assessments

The previous sections described tools and techniques to perform vulnerability assessments on existing network devices, servers, and applications. Another critical aspect of vulnerability assessment that occurs before an application even exists is that of the development cycle. While vulnerability testing is vital for the security of existing applications, you significantly lower the probability of existing vulnerabilities by assessing your application for security issues during its design, coding, and testing phases.

The following sections describe how to code applications from the ground up with a secure foundation and maintain the security baseline throughout the application's development.

Baseline Reporting   A *baseline* is a report of the planned and approved architecture, design, and default configuration of your software application. Created during the design stage of your software, the baseline report is compared to your actual development progress to make sure you are on track with your original plan.

The baseline report includes all networking services and ports to be used, data storage techniques, linked modules, default access permissions, authentication mechanisms, user accounts, and default configuration and security settings. The baseline should represent the most secure design and configuration for your application that must be adhered to when coding.

Use the baseline to keep your development coding on track to prevent any additional items that may cause security issues from creeping into your code, such as new services and network ports that are not required, or unnecessary administrative privilege access for certain application processes. The development process is never perfect, and additional requirements and features may appear during coding. Adjust your baseline if the services are required for the application and new attack surfaces appear, but continue to focus on security as your top baseline priority, and never add services that are unnecessary.

Determine Attack Surfaces   Using your baseline report, you can determine your current level of attack surfaces. An *attack surface* is an aspect of your software application that is vulnerable for an attacker to exploit. The most obvious examples of attack surfaces include network ports and running services. Other attack surfaces include input boxes, authentication and authorization methods, and insecure third-party libraries and programs.

For example, your web application may listen for requests on HTTP port 80, use basic clear-text authentication credentials, and store data in an unencrypted third-party database on the same server. That makes three attack surfaces that leave your application open to attack from a hacker who can exploit these vulnerabilities. In reviewing your design, you can decide to use HTTPS instead of HTTP for SSL encryption, switch to a secure authentication method such as Secure Lightweight Directory Access Protocol (LDAPS), and use a third-party database program that offers greater security for storing your web application's data, such as database encryption.

You must review your existing attack surfaces throughout the entire development cycle. From week to week, you may add functionality that creates a new attack surface that you did not think about during the architecture and design phase.

Attack surfaces cannot be eliminated entirely, or your application would not work at all, but they can be reduced to the bare minimum required for your application's features. From your baselines established at the beginning of the development process, you can determine the number of acceptable attack surfaces that are required and keep to that framework throughout the entire development cycle of the product.

Architecture   When designing an application, software architects and developers must create the architecture with security first and foremost in mind. Coding should be defensive in nature and not aggressive in the amount of permissiveness provided to end users. Much theoretical work, diligent experimentation, and testing are needed to deliver a framework for an application that provides strong security as its foundation.

Any attack vectors, such as running services and network ports, must be kept to a minimum, secure network protocols must be used for communication, and authentication must be built into the application to provide proper authorization for specific tasks and operations. The goal is to create an application that runs on a secure foundation, operates efficiently, and provides all the required features in a secure, authenticated environment.

Design Reviews   In a *design review*, the initial product design specification created by the software architects and developers is reviewed by several cross-functional areas, including other developers, quality assurance, and other technical groups, to evaluate the application design.

This provides a peer review of the original design and planned architecture to ensure that the software is built as per the feature specification and that it meets all secure design goals. The application must be coded with strong security in place by keeping the number of attack surfaces to a minimum.

Design reviews occur before coding of an application begins. When the basic architecture of an application is already functionally coded, it is very difficult to go back and rework it when a critical security issue is found in later stages of coding and testing. You may also break existing functionality when you try to rework your design. If specific design flaws are discovered during the review, the architect and developers can rework the design to resolve the flaw before any development begins.

Code Reviews   Just as a writer who is too familiar with her own written output requires an editor to review it, a developer requires a *code review*, which is a detailed, line-by-line review of his code by another developer. Code reviews are a necessary part of the development life cycle to prevent security issues arising from poor coding practices.

By allowing another developer to scan your code, you provide a fresh set of eyes to review your work from an objective viewpoint for any issues, whether performance, efficiency, or security related, and offer alternative solutions to provide a stronger, more secure code base.

While quality assurance teams can test the final compiled code to make sure it works according to the official design specifications and test cases, development code reviews provide an additional layer of design testing before the code is compiled to eliminate security and performance issues before the code reaches the testing stage.

Objective 14.02 Implement Penetration Tests When Appropriate

CompTIA Security+
Objective 1.4

The preceding sections discussed the use of vulnerability scanning to examine your network systems for unnecessary running services and open ports, unpatched operating system and application software, or any other types of network vulnerabilities that can be exploited by a hacker. Generally, vulnerability scanning comprises these characteristics:

- **Passively test security controls**   Vulnerability scanning is a passive test of your security controls and configuration using tools such as port scans, network mappers, and protocol analyzers. *Passive scanning* means that the system is not being actively attacked, but you are making a step-by-step examination of your system to look for vulnerabilities that can lead to an attack.

- **Identify vulnerabilities**   Vulnerability scanning is specifically used to identify certain vulnerabilities. A port scanner can instantly detect what unneeded running ports you have on your system. Operating system scans can identify if you are not running the latest patches and software. A vulnerability scan involves simple, fact-oriented information gathering and will not be able to tell you the result from a security standpoint of the exploitation of a vulnerability or flaw.

- **Identify lack of security controls**   Vulnerability assessments specifically identify areas with a lack of security controls. With its all-encompassing scope of scanning, vulnerability scanning examines all aspects of your system for issues, including the configuration of your operating system or application.

- **Identify common misconfigurations** Using vulnerability-scanning techniques, you can also identify specific areas of your system's configuration that require tightening to prevent security issues deriving from a poor default or user-defined configuration.

- **False positives** You likely will come across false positives while conducting a vulnerability assessment. These may be caused by tools alerting on the presence of vulnerabilities within software that doesn't exist on the system, or perhaps even wrongly flagging patches as out of date. It's worth looking at each result to be sure it is legitimate, especially if you plan to use the results to make enterprise-wide changes.

Penetration testing evaluates the security of a network or computer system by actively simulating an attack. Attacks are performed using the same types of tools and exploits that malicious hackers use to compromise system security. These tools can be used to test network and system resilience to a real attack scenario and test the effectiveness of existing security measures implemented after a vulnerability assessment. While a vulnerability scan can identify security risks and vulnerabilities, it cannot simulate the effect of real attacks.

Exam Tip

A vulnerability scan is used to identify specific weaknesses in current systems and networks, but it cannot simulate real attacks. Penetration testing is used to simulate an actual attack on a system and can be used to test your security countermeasure and resilience to an attack.

Penetration testing provides the following additional benefits beyond vulnerability scanning:

- **Verify a threat exists** Penetration testing can verify that a real threat exists if a specific identified vulnerability is exploited. The outcome of an exploit is never certain unless you take active steps to test the vulnerability and realize how deep a threat it represents.

- **Bypass security controls** You can use penetration testing to find out what occurs when specific security controls are bypassed. For example, a simple vulnerability scan on weak passwords in your authentication system will not be able to detect any issues in the event a hacker can disable or bypass the authentication system. Penetration testing uses real-time attack scenarios that can't always be addressed through vulnerability scanning alone.

- **Actively test security controls** Penetration testing actively tests security controls by simulating real attacks against the host system or application. This differs from the passive nature of vulnerability testing and can test the true depth of security controls, along with the level of weakness for specific vulnerabilities.

- **Exploit vulnerabilities** Vulnerability scanners can detect a potential security issue, but only penetration testing can reveal whether that vulnerability could result in a specific security threat. Through active penetration testing, the vulnerability can be exploited, and the result will determine how deep the vulnerability is. After initial exploitation, a penetration team can assess the ability to pivot to other systems and networks, escalate privileges, and maintain persistence in the same way an adversary would. This provides a more realistic picture of your vulnerability.

- **Credentialed versus noncredentialed** You can provide your testing team with credentials to gain ready access to the system, or you can take a more external approach and ask them to attempt to gain credentials, in much the same way as a threat actor would working from the outside. There are benefits to both: providing credentials may allow the team to do a more thorough job assessing your security posture, whereas not providing credentials could be a more realistic assessment.

- **Intrusive versus nonintrusive** You can specify (hopefully in advance and in writing!) how intrusive you want your testing to be. Do you want the test to really determine how a system would handle an attack in a legitimate incident scenario? That might end up halting regular business for a time, or even causing lingering issues that need time to resolved. This would be more intrusive, but also more realistic. Consider how honest you want to be, and weigh that against the potential drawbacks posed by active testing. Penetration tests are generally much more intrusive than vulnerability assessments.

One of the drawbacks to penetration testing is that it can disrupt a live production system. To lessen the effects of the simulated attack, you could perform penetration testing after regular work hours at a time when any disruption to the network will not affect many users. Because of the disruptions tests can cause, many network administrators are able to perform only vulnerability assessments on their networks and systems; they cannot go a step further and perform actual penetration testing.

> **Travel Advisory**
>
> Check with your company's security policies to determine whether you can perform penetration testing before you start such a process. Authorization is critical!

Penetration tests are often performed by outside vendors who are allowed access to the network by upper management—in some cases, without the network administrator's knowledge. This ensures the testing scenario is as close to a real unsuspected attack as possible, and it provides a detailed analysis of any weaknesses in network and system security that remain even after vulnerability assessments have been performed.

White, Black, and Gray Box Testing

When performing vulnerability and penetration testing, you can use any of several types of methods, each with its own advantages and disadvantages. What is important is that you use a variety of methods, from detailed internal testing of software code and internal processes to simulations of attacks from users who are completely unfamiliar with the inner workings of the system. By testing the software from different viewpoints and attack scopes, you can uncover vulnerabilities that might not have been apparent during other types of testing.

Do not confuse white, gray, and black box testing with white-, gray-, and black-hat hacking. The latter are terms used to describe the different intentions of various types of hackers. For example, white-hat hackers use their skills to—legally and within the confines of an agreement with the organization they're supporting—attack the security posture of a defined set of systems or a whole network infrastructure. Compare that to a black-hat hacker who attacks for glory, financial gain, or any number of other reasons. We generally associate these people with the "hacker" stereotype. Somewhere in the middle is the gray-hat hacker, who might have good intentions but still conducts illegal activities within his "testing."

White Box Testing

A *white box* test refers to the testing scenario where the user testing the system has prior knowledge of the system coding and design and is not testing the system from the perspective of an end user who would have no access to the internal details of an application.

White box testing is usually performed by quality assurance and system integration specialists who can test every aspect of the application, including deep levels of the application programming interface (API), network services, the underlying operating system, and manipulation of the input to the system for the full range of input validation.

This type of detailed testing is usually conducted with direction from development using detailed test plans and test cases for the code. The goal of white box testing is to deeply test the internal code of the system in terms of every functional operation the application can perform. Through this vigorous testing, the most obvious and critical of internal architectural errors can be discovered and resolved.

Black Box Testing

Black box testing is a method of security vulnerability and penetration testing that assumes the tester does not have any prior knowledge of the system she is trying to crack. The tester has no idea how the software was developed, what languages are used, or what network services are running.

Black box testing is an excellent way to test your system's security by simulating an attack. From the tester's perspective, she is seeing this system or application for the first time and therefore can be a very objective and unbiased evaluator. Without any prior knowledge of the underlying code or operating system, the tester can start off using the simplest penetration and vulnerability-seeking techniques and then proceed to more advanced methods to try and break the system.

Black box testing is a complementary testing method to white box testing and can often find bugs that the original developer could not find. However, because the tester has only limited access to the system and no access to back-end aspects of the software, a black box test is not a comprehensive full-system test and cannot be solely relied on for accurate vulnerability and penetration testing.

Travel Advisory

Be sure to clearly define what type of testing you plan to conduct, put it in writing, and get the proper signatures from management. Be sure to cover the scope, limitations, and possible repercussions of the testing. Getting a legal review isn't a bad idea either!

Gray Box Testing

Gray box testing is a hybrid method that includes aspects of both white box and black box testing. Gray box testing uses some prior knowledge of how the software application is designed, as in a white box test, but the testing is performed from the perspective of an end user, as in a black box test.

By combining the best of both methods, gray box testing can find security issues and bugs that may not have been discovered using one of the other primary testing methods.

Exam Tip

White, gray, and black box testing require varying levels of prior tester knowledge and access to the system. Understand the different but related concepts of white-, gray-, and black-hat hackers.

CHECKPOINT

✔**Objective 14.01: Implement Assessment Tools and Techniques to Discover Security Threats and Vulnerabilities** Vulnerability assessment tools can be used by network administrators to find and mitigate vulnerabilities, but malicious hackers have access to the same tools to find vulnerabilities to attack. Perform port scanning to determine what services and open ports are running on your systems, and then disable those that are not required. Protocol analyzers can capture and analyze individual network packets, including any clear-text data sent within them. Use vulnerability scanners to determine whether your operating system and application software are up to date with the latest updates and patches. Ensure that password databases are protected via limited access rights and encryption to prevent attacks from password-cracking programs. Use secure coding methods and perform early design reviews before coding starts to provide a secure foundation for a newly developed application.

✔**Objective 14.02: Implement Penetration Tests When Appropriate**
Penetration testing evaluates the security of a network or computer system by simulating an actual attack. Vulnerability testing and assessments are helpful in identifying existing vulnerabilities and weaknesses, but only penetration testing can determine the effectiveness of the countermeasures used by the network administrator to fix these vulnerabilities. They both have their strengths and weaknesses and should be used within their appropriate contexts. White box testing is a detailed test by users who are familiar with the system design and code. Black box testing simulates an attack from a user who is not familiar with the inner workings of a system. Gray box testing is a combination of white and black box testing.

REVIEW QUESTIONS

1. Which of the following aspects of vulnerability and threat assessment has a greater bearing on the allocation and budgeting for solutions and countermeasures?

   A. The likelihood and impact of the threat

   B. The risk of a threat compromising a vulnerability

   C. Whether the vulnerability is physical or nonphysical

   D. The nature of the threat

2. Which of the following is the most dangerous threat to a fault-redundant file server located on the network administrator's desk and fully secured with an antivirus program, strict authentication, and access controls?

   A. Equipment failure

   B. Virus

   C. Hacking

   D. Theft

3. You are designing a new web application service for your company. After an initial design review, several attack surfaces have been revealed that go well beyond the initial baseline proposed for the application, including unneeded network services that are enabled. What should you do?

   A. Rework the initial baseline.

   B. Perform a black box test.

   C. Reduce attack surfaces by removing unneeded services from the design.

   D. Reduce the attack surfaces during actual coding.

4. Match the following testing methods with their proper definitions:

The person testing the system has some prior knowledge of the system, but the test is performed as if he is an end user.	A. Black box testing
The person testing the system has prior knowledge of the system and is not testing from the perspective of an end user.	B. White box testing
The person testing the system tests from the perspective of an outside user who has no knowledge of the system.	C. Gray box testing

5. Your intrusion detection system has detected several attempts at brute-force password attacks against your authentication server. Which of the following would be the most effective countermeasure against future password attacks?

   A. Allowing dictionary words as passwords

   B. Minimum password lengths

   C. An account lockout policy

   D. Firewall rules

6. You have a legacy Unix server that you use for authentication for your development group. Which of the following security controls provides access-control protection for a Unix password database?

   A. Salting

   B. LANMAN hash

   C. Shadow password file

   D. Minimum password lengths

7. A port scanner has reported that your web server running with a supporting SQL database is listening and responding on TCP ports 80, 443, 21, and 1433. Fill in the blank: Port _____ is unnecessary and should be closed to prevent hacking attempts.

8. You are performing a vulnerability assessment for a web server. Which of the following web server characteristics would be detected as a risk by a vulnerability scanner?

   A. Operating system not updated to latest patch level

   B. HTTPS server listening on port 443

   C. Network packets being sent in clear text

   D. HTTP server listening on port 80

9. After a security audit and vulnerability assessment, several servers required software patches and unused open network ports needed to be disabled. Which of the following should be performed after these vulnerabilities are fixed to ensure that the countermeasures are secure against a real attack?

   A. Advertise the system's IP address publicly.

   B. Put systems back into live production.

   C. Perform additional port scanning.

   D. Perform penetration testing.

10. New management has decided to test the security of the existing network infrastructure implemented by the current network administrators. Which of the following should be performed to provide the most objective and useful test of your security controls?

    A. Hire a real hacker to attack the network.

    B. Perform third-party penetration testing.

    C. Perform penetration testing by the network administrators.

    D. Initiate an external denial-of-service attack.

REVIEW ANSWERS

1. **A** By assessing the likelihood and impact of a threat, you can allocate solutions for mitigation based on its impact and probability of occurrence. You will not spend money on countermeasures for a threat that is not likely to occur or has minimal impact.

2. **D** Because the file server isn't stored in a secure location, anyone walking by the area could steal it. All the other protections are for network-based threats.

3. **C** If you discover a few additional attack surfaces in your software design, you should review them and, if they are not required by the application, remove the services from your initial design. If you wait until the coding stage, it may be too late to undo work that could break other parts of your application.

4. The answers are as follows:

The person testing the system has some prior knowledge of the system, but the test is performed as if he is an end user.	C. Gray box testing
The person testing the system has prior knowledge of the system and is not testing from the perspective of an end user.	B. White box testing
The person testing the system tests from the perspective of an outside user who has no knowledge of the system.	A. Black box testing

5. **C** A brute-force attack tries multiple permutations of password characters to try to guess the password. By limiting the number of incorrect logins (such as three to five attempts), you have the system automatically lock out the account to prevent any further attempts at cracking the password.

6. **C** Unix-based systems protect their hashed password databases by using a shadow password file. In the shadow file, the hashed passwords are removed from the main password database and are stored in a location that is unavailable to unprivileged users.

7. **21** In this scenario, only port 21 is unnecessary and should be closed to prevent hacking attempts.

8. **A** A vulnerability scanner is designed to scan a system and determine what services that system is running and whether any unnecessary open network ports or unpatched operating systems and applications exist. In this case, HTTP listening on port 80 and HTTPS listening on port 443 are normal operating parameters for a web server. Unless you are using HTTPS, web network packets are always sent in clear text. The vulnerability scanner will detect that the system is not running the latest operating system patches and advise you to update the system.

9. **D** Penetration testing evaluates the security of a network or computer system by simulating an actual attack. This helps test a network's and system's resilience to a real attack as well as test the effectiveness of existing security measures implemented after vulnerability assessments.

10. **B** Penetration tests are often performed by third parties who are allowed access to the network by upper management—in some cases, without the network administrator's knowledge. This ensures the testing scenario is as close to a real unsuspected attack as possible and provides a detailed analysis of existing vulnerabilities.

Appendixes

Career Flight Path

The CompTIA Security+ certification is an international, vendor-neutral credential that validates a candidate's knowledge of industry-recognized security principles and best practices. CompTIA recommends that exam candidates have at least two years of experience in IT administration with an emphasis on security. CompTIA also suggests that candidates have day-to-day technical information security experience and a broad knowledge of security concerns and implementation.

CompTIA Security+ certifications are valid for three years from the date the candidate is certified. After three years, the certification must be renewed by passing the most current version of the exam, or by participating in CompTIA's Continuing Education Program, which allows individuals to keep their skills current and their certification up to date without retesting. For more information on the CompTIA Continuing Education Program, visit http://certification.comptia.org/stayCertified.aspx.

To achieve the CompTIA Security+ certification, candidates must pass one exam: Exam SY0-501.

The CompTIA Security+ exam is organized into six domain areas:

- **Threats, Attacks, and Vulnerabilities (21 percent)** Includes topics such as malware, network attacks, social engineering attacks, wireless attacks, application attacks, monitoring, vulnerability scanning, and penetration testing.
- **Technologies and Tools (22 percent)** Includes topics such as emerging technologies and leading security solutions for securing the network, data, and hosts, including mobile security, network security, host security, data security, and mitigating security risks in nontraditional environments.
- **Architecture and Design (15 percent)** Includes topics such as application security controls and techniques as well as secure administration and network design.

- **Identity and Access Management (16 percent)**   Includes topics such as authentication, authorization, access control, and security controls for account management.
- **Risk Management (14 percent)**   Includes topics such as risk management and mitigation, security training and procedures, incident response, physical security, environmental controls, business continuity, and disaster recovery.
- **Cryptography and PKI (12 percent)**   Includes topics such as general cryptography concepts, hashing, encryption algorithms and protocols, public key cryptography, Public Key Infrastructure (PKI), and certificate management.

CompTIA Security+ Exam Format

The CompTIA Security+ exam is a mix of multiple-choice and performance-based formats. Unlike multiple-choice questions, the performance-based questions require the exam candidate to perform a task or solve a problem in a simulated environment. According to CompTIA, "Each question is designed around real-world computer scenarios that will test a candidate's skills and knowledge. Depending on the nature of the exam and the exam question, the simulated environments may include different aspects of IT infrastructure, such as command prompts, Windows, or networking environments."

Exam Tip
Simulated performance-based questions are included in the "Review Questions" sections throughout this book and in the electronic practice exams that accompany it. Although these questions may not be in the same format as those you see on the actual exam, they are meant to simulate the task-oriented nature of the exam's performance-based questions.

CompTIA Security+ and Beyond

The CompTIA Security+ certification is an excellent credential that allows candidates to prove their knowledge of security concepts, tools, and procedures, as well as their ability to anticipate security risks and guard against them. The CompTIA Security+ credential is also a great stepping-stone for more advanced security certifications such as CompTIA Cybersecurity Analyst (CSA+), CompTIA Advanced Security Practitioner (CASP), and Certified Information

System Security Professional (CISSP). If you have at least five years of experience in information security, the CISSP certification is a logical next step for professionals who look to manage information security programs. If you have ten years of experience in IT administration, including at least five years of hands-on technical security experience, the CASP certification will certify your technical knowledge and the skills required to conceptualize, design, and engineer secure solutions across complex enterprise environments.

Getting the Latest Information on the CompTIA Security+ Exam

The CompTIA Security+ exam is a great place to start your IT security professional career. To learn the latest information about the CompTIA Security+ exam, please visit www.comptia.org.

About the CD-ROM

The CD-ROM included with this book comes complete with Total Tester customizable practice exam software with 200 practice exam questions and a secured PDF copy of the book.

System Requirements

The software requires Windows Vista or later and 30MB of hard disk space for full installation, in addition to a current or prior major release of Chrome, Firefox, Internet Explorer, or Safari. To run, the screen resolution must be set to 1024×768 or higher. The secured book PDF requires Adobe Acrobat, Adobe Reader, or Adobe Digital Editions to view.

Total Tester Premium Practice Exam Software

Total Tester provides you with a simulation of the CompTIA Security+ exam.

Exams can be taken in Practice Mode, Exam Mode, or Custom Mode. Practice Mode provides an assistance window with hints, references to the book, explanations of the correct and incorrect answers, and the option to check your answer as you take the test. Exam Mode provides a simulation of the actual exam. The number of questions, the types of questions, and the time allowed are intended to be an accurate representation of the exam environment. Custom Mode allows you to create custom exams from selected domains or chapters, and you can further customize the number of questions and time allowed.

To take a test, launch the program and select Security+ PP5 from the Installed Question Packs list. You can then select Practice Mode, Exam Mode, or Custom Mode. All exams provide an overall grade and a grade broken down by domain.

Installing and Running Total Tester Premium Practice Exam Software

From the main screen you may install the Total Tester by clicking the Total Tester Practice Exams button. This will begin the installation process and place an icon on your desktop and in your Start menu. To run Total Tester, navigate to Start | (All) Programs | Total Seminars, or double-click the icon on your desktop.

To uninstall the Total Tester software, go to Start | Control Panel | Programs And Features, and then select the Total Tester program. Select Remove, and Windows will completely uninstall the software.

Secured Book PDF

The entire contents of the book are provided in secured PDF format on the CD-ROM. This file is viewable on your computer and many portable devices.

- **To view the PDF on a computer**, Adobe Acrobat, Adobe Reader, or Adobe Digital Editions is required. A link to Adobe's website, where you can download and install Adobe Reader, has been included on the CD-ROM.

> ### Note
> For more information on Adobe Reader and to check for the most recent version of the software, visit Adobe's website at www.adobe.com and search for the free Adobe Reader or look for Adobe Reader on the product page. Adobe Digital Editions can also be downloaded from the Adobe website.

- **To view the book PDF on a portable device**, copy the PDF file to your computer from the CD-ROM and then copy the file to your portable device using a USB or other connection. Adobe offers a mobile version of Adobe Reader, the Adobe Reader mobile app, which currently supports iOS and Android. For customers using Adobe Digital Editions and an iPad, you may have to download and install a separate reader program on your device. The Adobe website has a list of recommended applications, and McGraw-Hill Education recommends the Bluefire Reader.

Technical Support

For questions regarding the Total Tester software or operation of the CD-ROM, visit **www.totalsem.com** or e-mail **support@totalsem.com**.

For questions regarding the secured book PDF, visit **http://mhp.softwareassist .com** or e-mail **techsolutions@mhedu.com**.

For questions regarding book content, e-mail **hep_customer-service@ mheducation.com**. For customers outside the United States, e-mail **international_cs@mheducation.com**.

Index